The Lord's Distant Vineyard

A HISTORY

OF THE OBLATES

AND THE

CATHOLIC COMMUNITY

IN BRITISH COLUMBIA

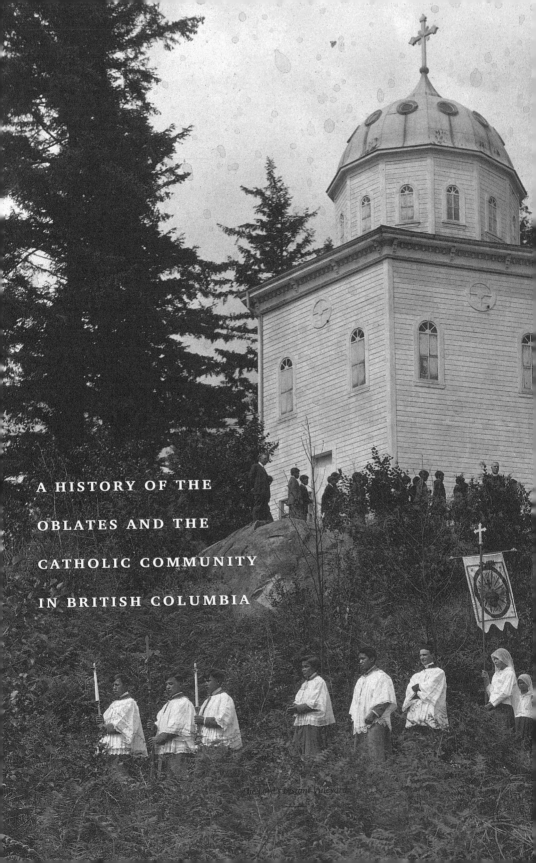

A HISTORY OF THE

OBLATES AND THE

CATHOLIC COMMUNITY

IN BRITISH COLUMBIA

The Lord's Distant Vineyard

THE LORD'S Distant Vineyard

Vincent J. McNally

 The University of Alberta Press
Western Canadian Publishers

First Published by
The University of Alberta Press
and Western Canadian Publishers

The University of Alberta Press
Ring House 2
Edmonton, Alberta, Canada T6G 2E2

Copyright © The University of Alberta Press 2000

ISBN 0-88864-346-2

Canadian Cataloguing in Publication Data

McNally, Vincent J. (Vincent Joseph), 1943–
  The Lord's distant vineyard

Copublished by: Western Canadian Publishers.
  ISBN 0-88864-346-2

  I. Oblates of Mary Immaculate—Missions—British Columbia—History.
  2. Indians of North America—Missions—British Columbia—History.
  3. Catholic Church—British Columbia—History. I. Title.
  BX3821.Z6B7 2000   266'.2711   C00-910802-5

Printed on acid-free paper. ∞
Printed and bound in Canada.
Printed by Hignell Book Printing Ltd., Winnipeg, Manitoba, Canada.

The University of Alberta Press gratefully acknowledges the support received for
its publishing program from The Canada Council for the Arts. In addition, we also
gratefully acknowledge the financial support of the Government of Canada through
the Book Publishing Industry Development Program for our publishing activities.

THE CANADA COUNCIL
FOR THE ARTS
SINCE 1957

LE CONSEIL DES ARTS
DU CANADA
DEPUIS 1957

In loving memory of my parents

Contents

Foreword

✠ REVEREND DOCTOR VINCENT J.
MᴄNᴀʟʟʏ's *The Lord's Distant Vineyard* is the fourth in a series of books
dealing with the activities of the Missionary Oblates of Mary Immaculate in
the western and northern regions of Canada. It is the first scholarly and comprehensive history of the Oblate presence in British Columbia. In addition to
analyzing the Oblate establishment in "far western Canada," the author has
placed it in the context of the history of the province and that of the Catholic
Church.

The author has also singled out the uniqueness of British Columbia, not
only in terms of its obvious geographical features, but more importantly in
terms of the social, economic and political development of the region and the
mentality of its population. In British Columbia the Oblates were able to
respond to local challenges with their customary pragmatism in the form of
Paul Durieu's "System" and Fergus O'Grady's Frontier Apostolate established
in the diocese of Prince George in 1956. British Columbia never possessed a
historical or constitutional tradition with respect to bilingualism and confessional education and this had a profound effect on the Oblate apostolate and

Church policy in that province. Increasingly in the twentieth century the Oblate apostolate in British Columbia became English, and while that undoubtedly accorded with the desires of the dominant anglophone community, it did not respond to the aspirations of the province's First Nations or those of European extraction. In the sphere of education the efforts of the Oblates and the Catholic Church to promote confessional schools found little support in a province that insisted on nondenominational schools.

By its comprehensive and analytical nature, Reverend Doctor McNally's study has transcended the bounds of traditional church history. His training as a professional historian has facilitated the preparation of a study that is both critical and objective, but it is as someone with years of pastoral experience and a professor of church history and patristic theology that he makes insightful comments on the relevance of the Catholic Church in the life of the average contemporary Canadian.

Raymond Huel
GENERAL EDITOR
WESTERN CANADIAN PUBLISHERS

Acknowledgements

✤ MANY PEOPLE, INSTITUTIONS AND ORGANIZATIONS have assisted me in my work. First and foremost are the Western Oblate History Project and Western Canadian Publishers, whose underwriting of my research and travel expenses made this book possible. In this regard I am indebted to its former and late director, Guy Lacombe, but especially to its present director and chief editor, Dr. Raymond Huel for his invaluable advice and encouragement. I am also grateful to the Social Sciences and Humanities Research Council of Canada for funding some of the earlier research.

Among other individuals, I am particularly obliged to Dr. Patricia Roy of the University of Victoria for her expert critiques as well as for her quiet reassurances that are so essential in such an undertaking. I also wish to express my very sincere gratitude to Sr. Margaret Cantwell, S.S.A, Sr. Edith Down, S.S.A., Dr. Jacqueline Gresko, Fr. James Hanrahan, C.S.B., and Ms. Margaret Whitehead for their general helpfulness and very useful guidance as well as for the important pioneering work they have done in the field.

In addition, I want to pay special tribute to the late Father Thomas Lascelles, OMI, with whom I was originally to share the responsibilities of completing this work, but whose premature death in 1994 made that impossible, yet who as an historian and archivist did so much to advance historical research in St. Paul's Province, and whose important contributions made my work so much easier.

Of all the archivists in the many private and public facilities who aided me in my research, Father Romuald Boucher, OMI, director of the Archives Deschâtelets in Ottawa deserves my greatest thanks, especially for his extraordinary grasp of Oblate history. I would also like to express my appreciation to the many Oblates I knew already and have met as a result of my study for their personal reflections on their lives as Oblates and their future hopes for their Congregation and the Catholic Church, and many of which I very much share.

In addition to the two discerning press reviewers, I am also very indebted to the editing work of Ms. Mary Mahoney-Robson of the University of Alberta Press. My thanks to Lara Minja of Lime Design Inc., who designed the text and cover. I am also most appreciative of the direct and indirect assistance and encouragement provided by many of my colleagues at Sacred Heart School of Theology.

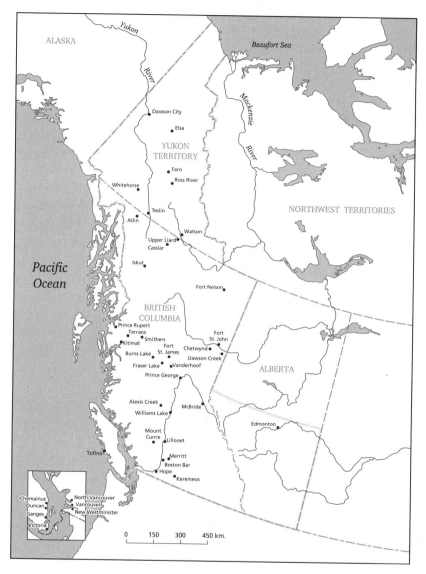

ALASKA

Yukon

River

Dawson City

Elsa

YUKON
TERRITORY

Faro

Ross River

Whitehorse

Mackenzie

River

Beaufort Sea

NORTHWEST TERRITORIES

Teslin

Atlin

Watson

Upper Liard
Cassiar

Iskut

Fort Nelson

*Pacific
Ocean*

BRITISH
COLUMBIA

Prince Rupert
Terrace
Smithers
Kitimat
Burns Lake
Fraser Lake

Fort
St. James

Vanderhoof

Fort
St. John

Chetwynd

Dawson Creek

ALBERTA

Prince George

Alexis Creek

Williams Lake

McBride

Edmonton

Mount
Currie

Lillooet

Tofino

Merritt
Boston Bar
Hope

Keremeos

Chemainus
Duncan
Ganges
Victoria

North Vancouver
Vancouver
New Westminister

| 0 | 150 | 300 | 450 km. |

St. Paul's Province, British Columbia

Preface

✤ THE LORD'S DISTANT VINEYARD IS
the first history of the Oblates and the Catholic Church to focus on the far
west, and to explore the Church's development in British Columbia.[1] Early
in this century, the Oblate, Adrien-Gabriel Morice published two works
dealing with the Oblates and the Catholic Church. However, Morice devoted
most of both volumes to events east of the Rocky Mountains, and only a
small percentage of his overall space was on the history of the Catholic
Church in British Columbia.[2] More importantly, both works are extremely
sketchy, largely narrative, denominational and apologetic, and are not good
examples of thorough, balanced and professionally critical historiography
that should always be the principal aim of sound history. It is my hope that
The Lord's Distant Vineyard fulfills that admittedly very difficult objective.

Church history provides an important means of understanding the
Christian people and their church, since, if it is willing to use the historical
critical method, it thereby reveals where Christians have been and gives
them some important clues about where they are going. The picture it
reveals, if it is striving to be critical as well as objective, does not always

please. Shadows are part of all people and the institutions that they create. Institutional shadows can be ignored or deliberately concealed, but the price is a heavy one, for ultimately such studied ignorance weakens and even kills the human spirit, which in turn fosters apathy and finally institutional irrelevance. In following such an argument, there are church historians who would insist that we must always avoid making "moral judgements" about what happened in the past. However, if being a church historian means avoiding "moral judgements" about the past, then, as a profession, it must surely relinquish its claim of having anything of much importance to teach to the present or future generations. However, having the courage to critically examine and accept the shadow can provide the human spirit with a new sense of unity, hope, and compassion and the possibility of individual and institutional reconciliation, reform and renewal.

Organized religion is in crisis, especially in the western world. Though the cradle of Christianity, western society has become essentially dechristianized; throughout the West, traditional beliefs in God, faith and especially in churches have become increasingly unimportant in the lives of most people. Certainly Canada is no exception, for there most view organized religion to be "irrelevant" to their lives because it "just doesn't work."[3] It is hoped that by examining the history of the Oblates and the Catholic Church, it may offer some insights into a better understanding of this situation. Perhaps we can all learn from our past and apply its lessons in assisting the churches to better cope with an increasingly globalized society that demands a very different role for Christianity. Ironically, it is the very one envisioned by Christianity's Founder: "that they may be one." It is a challenge to the Christian churches to become something that they have rarely been, that is counter-cultural forces that challenge society to be ever more just, compassionate, truthful and united because of, and not despite, their great diversity. However, before that can happen, the churches must practice what they preach and strive to remember and learn from their past sins of omission and commission. In addressing this issue, Pope John Paul II observed that "these sins of the past unfortunately still burden us," and thus "it is necessary to make amends for them," especially those sins of "intolerance and even the use of violence in service" to the gospel or the good news.[4]

"To proclaim the good news to the poor," the Oblate motto, in some ways begs the important question: who are the poor? In a real sense we are all poor, perhaps not in material things, but certainly in those things that truly count, such as love, justice and truth. We have much to learn from others, especially the "out groups" that we have all created. In the case of Canada, certainly the Native peoples are paramount in this regard. In their now well-known *Apology* of 1991, the Oblates seemed to realize their own spiritual poverty in their historic treatment of the Native people and their culture, and especially their spirituality that the Oblates tended to dismiss as largely irrelevant, if not evil.

In their *Apology*, the Oblates describe themselves and the Native people as members of "the same family." Thus, the Oblates note that "it is imperative that we come again to that deep trust and solidarity that constitutes families. We recognize that the road beyond past hurt may be long and steep, but we pledge ourselves anew to journey with the Native Peoples on that road."[5] It is a journey that all must be willing to take in order to learn and grow from the lessons that the past has to teach us.

The Oblates had an enormous impact upon the history of the Catholic Church in many parts of the world, including British Columbia. There, in fact, they still constitute either the overwhelming majority of the clergy (dioceses of Prince George and Whitehorse) or, with the exception of the diocese of Victoria, the dominant male religious community. However, as elsewhere, they did not exist in a vacuum, either in the Catholic Church or in the larger society. They are an important part of the region's history, but only a part. Therefore, while the Oblates have had a central place in the history of the church in far western Canada, it is not possible to examine them without also examining the role of others in that history, especially other members of the church as well as the larger society. Thus those who are not Oblate must also be given their voice if a history of the Oblates and the Catholic Church in British Columbia is to receive the justice it deserves.

Organized religion has never played a very important part in the history of British Columbia, especially when compared to most other regions of this enormous nation, particularly its eastern half. In reflecting upon this reality, the first Anglican bishop of British Columbia, the English born George Hills provided an underlying clue, if not an explanation. In 1881, Hills, who by then had lived for over 20 years in the region, predicted that the major social and culture influences in British Columbia were destined to be both "non-sectarian" and "non-Christian," due to the "constitutional religious apathy" that marked "the people of the whole Pacific slope." It is an "apathy" that, over the years, has been consistently confirmed by Statistics Canada.[6]

General histories of the region have also reinforced Hills's conclusion, and except for biographies of individual missionaries of various denominations, religious historiography in British Columbia has been more neglected than in any other region of Canada. The grounding breaking work *British Columbia: A History* (1958) by Margaret Ormsby almost totally ignores organized religion. More recent ones, such as Jean Barman's *The West Beyond the West* (1991), mention the topic, but only peripherally.[7] Consequently, except for passing references, few historians of British Columbia have ever considered the topic of local church history important enough to research in its own right, and none have undertaken a history of the Catholic Church there.

In trying to understand this lack of interest, it is important to remember that the Rocky Mountains are not only a natural barrier, but also a social, economic, political and, perhaps especially, a psychological one. People who cross them to settle in the far west have tended to leave behind many of those things that formerly defined them, including organized Christianity.[8] Therefore, accustomed to the liberal anticlericalism of Europe, the Oblates, like other committed Christians who came to British Columbia, often found it difficult to understand this general indifference towards organized religion among European settlers, for it was very rarely overtly hostile. Nevertheless, this attitude is a most important element in British Columbia's social and cultural landscape, as well as the other parts of the region, including the Yukon Territory and the states of Washington and Oregon. This attitude must be understood before embarking on any study of Catholicism west of the Rocky Mountains. Certainly, it was very different from the overt anticlericalism that the Olates experienced in France. Nevertheless, both the Oblates and anticlericalism were by-products of the French Revolution.

We have fed the heart on fantasies,

The heart's grown brutal from the fare.

W.B. YEATS,
"THE STARE'S NEST BY MY WINDOW,"
THE TOWER (1928).

Prologue

✤ THE French Revolution (1789–95) brought the Oblates into existence and that historic watershed still affects them today. But for that Revolution, the Oblate founder and nobleman, Eugene de Mazenod, now a canonised saint, would never have attempted that undertaking. For with the triumph of the bourgeoisie, the Revolution robbed him and his class of their ancient patrimony and it ultimately prompted Eugene to look to the Catholic priesthood not only as an essential avenue towards regaining a sense of balance and meaning in his own life, but also as a method of hopefully restoring the old order to its former prominence. Especially by rekindling "the fire of faith" among the poor of his native Provence, where, he admitted, it had "all but died out." For Mazenod the poor would become the vanguard in returning the French Catholic Church, and ultimately the monarchy, to its rightful, pre-Revolutionary position. Since in Eugene's eyes, only when the noble class had regained their "divinely ordained" place in both the church and state of France would France be France again.[1]

And so on 2 October 1815, Mazenod inaugurated *the Society of the Missionaries of Provence* in a former Carmelite monastery in Aix, and by the following January they had obtained diocesan approval. If, as he hoped, the urban poor were to form the major supporters of the church's renewal, then they must be educated to their new role. With Eugene as their elected superior, six secular or diocesan priests formed the first community that would eventually become the Oblates. Together they began preparation to carry out their dual mandate, namely, personal sanctification and the preaching of parish missions. Initially, they put the second into operation in September 1816 with a mission that was organized around the re-education of the poor, especially its youth, the obvious and future hope of the church. The following month, Eugene noted to a fellow nobleman and priest, Charles de Forbin-Jansen, that their little community was not only "very fervent," but, he wrote, there "are no better priests throughout the diocese" of Aix.[2]

Such an attitude soon created serious problems for the fledgling community, and the subsequent need to rescue it. For the "wicked" bourgeois clergy of Aix, as Eugene referred to them, resented the Society's missions that were being conducted without their permission and, in turn, were at least perceived as robbing them of their parishioners. In 1817, after official complaints, the government in Paris sided with the aggrieved pastors of Aix, and soon the Society was being ordered out of the diocese. Mazenod met this first crisis, and set a precedent that the Oblates would long follow. He had his priest-uncle and nobleman, Fortuné de Mazenod appointed as the next bishop of Marseilles, and thus created a safe haven for his Society.[3]

The crisis also revealed Mazenod's and the Society's spirituality and philosophy of life that were greatly influenced by an Augustinian theology of suffering, fatalism and original sin, that is dominated by a vengeful God and which in its extreme, viewed human free will as hopelessly destroyed and dependent on grace-alone for its salvation, or in a word Jansenism. For example, Eugene was convinced that his call to be a priest must be followed "under pain of damnation." Again, when the Society was expelled from the diocese of Aix, Mazenod's assistant and close confidant, Father François de Paule Henry Tempier, reflecting his own Jansenistic view of the hopelessly fallen state of human nature and free will, and thus the absolute need for a divine grace that could only come through much suffering, wrote: "Would that God would always treat us so!" But without doubt the most extraordinary expression of this type of spirituality was occasioned by

Eugene's uncle's insistence that he would only accept Marseilles on condition that his nephew and Tempier were willing to become his vicars general. This prompted the other members of the Society to come to the obvious conclusion that Mazenod had used them to gain high church preferment, for, in fact, he would succeed his uncle as bishop of Marseilles in 1837. In reaction, Eugene called for a general meeting at which, after stripping to the waist, he proceeded to inflict "a bloody flagellation upon himself in the midst of the tears and sobs of all his sons." Immediately Eugene's "spiritual sons" swore to him that they would never again challenge their "spiritual father" who, like a latter-day messiah, had saved them and his Society, and by the shedding of his own blood![4]

Another early Oblate hallmark was its championing of Gallican-ultramontanism and its accompanying Marian theology. Perhaps the most dramatic consequence of the Revolution for the French church was that it was robbed of its enormous wealth, which had comprised one-third of the lands of France. The Revolution ended the Church's financial independence, and the state assumed the direct funding of the Church. As the state became increasingly liberal and anticlerical during the nineteenth century, the French church became more reactionary. In turn, Rome became a ready defender and assumed an ever-increasing influence over church affairs in France. This was reflected in concordats between Rome and Paris, the first of which was signed in 1801. In exchange for continued state influence over important church appointments, especially bishops, the pope had the right to intervene in and even control the French church. For the Holy See, a major means of achieving this was by encouraging the founding of regular or religious clergy, instead of secular or diocesan clergy who were directly under the local bishop. These communities, with their head superiors increasingly residing in Rome, were thus as independent of local church authority as they were dependent upon the Vatican.[5]

For many centuries devotion to Mary or Marianism was central to Catholic piety. Mary had long been seen as a spiritual bridge between the Christian worshipper and an increasingly remote Jesus, which was influenced by the heresy of docetism that stressed only the divinity of Christ. Thus, taping into this ancient devotion, Rome saw to it that Marianism was strongly linked with the growth of nineteenth century papal absolutism or ultramontanism. The Holy See would be greatly strengthened by joining Marianism and the papacy as mutually supportive of each other; each would glorify the other. This development culminated in two major events that defined the modern papacy: the definition of the Immaculate Conception of Mary (1854) as revealed Roman Catholic doctrine and, at Vatican I (1869–70), the first acceptance by a church council of the doctrine of papal infallibility. Both dogmas were the work of a principal architect of the modern papacy, Pius IX, whose reign, the longest in papal history (1846–78), would confirm and greatly strengthen the previous progress of nineteenth century Marianism and ultramontanism. By making Marian devotions synonymous with papal absolutism by ever increasingly identifying with and encouraging them, Pius and his successors further strengthened the papacy's own power and control over universal church government.[6]

Mazenod could not have selected a better moment in which to seek papal approval of his Society. On Friday, 17 February 1826, only two months after Eugene had first approached the Holy See, it confirmed the Constitution and Rules of the new Congregation of the Oblates of Mary Immaculate. He had only selected the title while he was preparing his petition in Rome, however, given papal politics then and in the future, it was clearly one that would strengthen the position of the Oblates in Roman circles. Mazenod used the word "consecration" in describing his decision to adopt the Marian title both to describe and "consecrate" his new society. Reflecting his Augustinian-Jansenist theology, he concluded that his choice of Marian and thus papal patronage was also "a sign of predestination" for the Oblates in marking them for divinely ordained glory and success in their mission to renew the Roman Catholic Church.[7]

The preached mission was a major Oblate tool in evangelisation and one strongly supported by the papacy. Begun in the seventeenth century, and with Vincentian and Redemptorist roots, it stressed common techniques of preaching hell, fire and brimstone sermons that emphasised a strong theological dualism. Added to this were Masses, catechising, processions, religious theatricals, especially passion plays, the planting of crosses in public spaces, and the organizing of parish societies that were usually devoted to some practical objective such as temperance. In the nineteenth century, Marian devotions also became important both during and after a mission, as were papal indulgences, which forgave the temporal or purgatorial punishment for sins, and which were usually extended to all of the participants.[8]

Whatever the enticements, there were no guarantees of success. However, in 1823 in Taillard an Oblate mission not only apparently converted the mayor, doctor and justice of the peace, but for some time the entertainment at local wedding receptions was limited to "singing hymns." Admission of "wrong doing" by former revolutionaries was also welcomed, and at Barjols, Eugene happily reported that the "bourgeoisie all came forward and vied with one another in making amends" for their "revolutionary sins." As for their overall success or failure, the evidence would indicate that missions did little to restore a general public fervour for the Catholic faith, especially among the poor, one of their major objectives. And while French dioceses promoted them, and a few required them, in all cases, they were usually only held every eight to ten years. Although the Oblates and papacy insisted that the poor were a major concern, they ended up defending the social, political and economic status quo in France. In time the French church would become as strong a defender of bourgeois interests as personified in the industrial revolution and laisse-faire capitalism, as they had originally been of the landed wealth and privileges of the old aristocracy.[9]

Expansion outside of France was a decision the Oblates made quite early in their history. Until 1830, France remained the focal point of Oblate growth, and by Mazenod's death in 1861, there were two provinces and noviciates and over two hundred Oblates ministering there. However, between 1830 and 1861 the Oblates established foundations in Switzerland, England, Ireland, Scotland, Ceylon, Algeria, Natal and Canada.

Well before and until at least 1840 the Catholic Church in Lower Canada was not popular. Most Catholics in Quebec viewed the church as a major supporter of British interests there, and, as in Ireland, the church would not gain in popularity there until after 1840 when it began to identify itself with Quebec nationalism.[10] Thus the lack of vocations to the priesthood and religious life that accompanied this public indifference would not fully be reversed until the mid nineteenth century. In the meantime, bishops such as Ignace Bourget of Montreal had to look abroad for help. Consequently, in response to a plea from Bourget, in 1841 Mazenod sent the first Oblates to Canada.[11] Within thirty years, because of their numerical growth, the Oblates had become a major force in the Canadian Church, and, following Eugene's mode of protecting his Congregation from local ordinaries or bishops, especially secular or diocesan ones, by then there were Oblate ordinaries in Ottawa, St. Boniface and St. Albert. In fact, by 1871, the year British Columbia would enter Confederation with Canada, the Oblates had become the dominant clergy in the Catholic Church there.[12]

Part One
Beginnings in the Far West

"Now that I am the first bishop of

Vancouver Island, I do not know

in what terms to express my misery!"

BISHOP MODESTE DEMERS

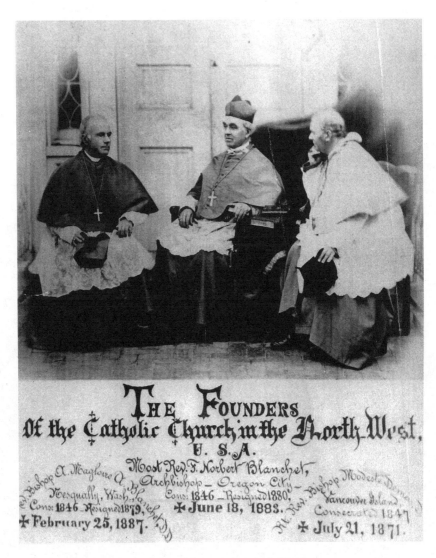

First Bishops of the Oregon Ecclesiastical Province
(l-r) Bishop Augustin Blanchet, Archbishop Norbert Blanchet,
Bishop Modeste Demers (AD)

I

The First Europeans

✤ WITH THEIR SIGHTING OF THE Queen Charlotte Islands in 1774, the Catholic Spanish became the first Europeans to reach what is now far-western Canada.[1] They were soon joined by Russians, British and finally Americans. Russia, content with her fur trade in Alaska, never seriously challenged Spain or Britain, but the fear of Russian intentions inspired the remaining challengers to assert and reassert their claims.

In the 1780s, Nootka Sound, an otherwise insignificant geographical point on the west coast of Vancouver Island, became the centre of an international dispute. Spain used the discoveries claimed by Quadra (1775) and Britain those by Cook (1778) to establish their right to the region. By 1787, English fur traders carrying Portuguese papers were using Nootka Sound as their headquarters. However, in 1789 Spain forcibly removed the English and formally took possession of this symbolic bit of real estate, but abandoned it in the same year due to major events in Europe.

By 1793 the French Revolution, which had begun in 1789, had become an overwhelming threat to the old order, demonstrated with the execution of the French monarch, Louis XVI. Such extraordinary events made former enemies allies, if not friends. For Spain, European politics outweighed colonial interests and convinced her to be content with her empire further south. However, before Spain physically abandoned its tiny settlement at Nootka in 1789, on June 24th an unrecorded Spanish priest celebrated there the first Catholic Mass in what would eventually become the far-western boundary of British North America.[2]

✤ The Hudson's Bay Company

WHILE BRITAIN WAS A CHRISTIAN NATION, as the home of both the industrial revolution and modern, laissez-faire capitalism, business interests held pride of place and the Hudson's Bay Company (HBC) was a marvellous reflection of that fact. Chartered by Charles II in 1670, it gained exclusive trading rights from the British government to the regions between the Great Lakes and the Pacific. To the Company trade meant profits from furs; for its shareholders, this was its sole purpose. The Company viewed organized religion, hopefully segregated from the rankling of denominationalism, as a cheap aid in maintaining discipline and morale among its employees in its trading territories.[3] It was in just such a new trading territory, or department (the name the Company gave to the large units formed when it subdivided its territories) that organized religion first officially appeared in what are now the states of Washington and Oregon and the province of British Columbia.

The Columbia Department, part of the enormous Oregon Territory, constituted the beginning of the Company's influence in the region. Since 1818 both the United States and Great Britain had agreed to joint occupancy of all land west of the Rocky Mountains between California and Alaska. As two governments meant no official government, for years HBC fur trading forts in the region represented and often effectively controlled the political, social and economic realities for many European Canadian and American settlers in much of this huge area.

In 1824, Dr. John McLoughlin, a Canadian with Scotch-Irish roots, and recognised officially as the Father of the state of Oregon, became the administrator or chief factor of the department with his headquarters at Fort Vancouver, at what is present-day Vancouver, Washington. Given the continued international status of the area, he was in effect the region's sole European ruler and Fort Vancouver was its "capital." The evidence indicates that he was an unusually agreeable and open-minded man. McLoughlin had very early on invited the Americans as well as his fellow Canadians to move into the area, though, to bolster the British claim to the territory north of the forty-fifth parallel, he insisted that the Canadians settle on land north of the Columbia River.[4]

✤ *The Coming of Organized Religion*

McLoughlin, who converted to Catholicism in 1842, like most HBC factors, viewed religion as an important vehicle for promoting western civilisation and especially western "morality," and as a vital element in the social control and development of a community. As an effective administrator, he had encouraged the French Canadians, who comprised the bulk of the employees or retirees of the Company and who were almost all Roman Catholics, and the American settlers, who were mostly Protestant, to worship and work together. In 1834, he was given the opportunity of enhancing this objective when he welcomed the arrival of several American Protestant missionaries, the first permanent Christian clergy in the region. By 1837 Protestant clergy from several American denominations had established missions in the area, and both the Canadians and Americans attended their churches. Most French Canadian Catholics seemed happy with the arrangement, for they even hired an American Protestant minister to teach their children.[5]

Despite the apparent and mutual goodwill, a minority of French Canadians desired Catholic priests to minister to their spiritual needs, and they repeatedly called upon church authorities to send some. By 1837 they were growing impatient. In March they informed the vicar apostolic of the Northwest District, Bishop Joseph Provencher, who resided at present-day St. Boniface, Manitoba, that they were surrounded by "every religion" but their own. They even implied that most of their fellow Catholics had already converted to Protestantism. Though they did not wish to follow, they warned that, due to the lack of priests, it was becoming very difficult to raise their children in the Catholic faith. In closing what they said would be their final plea, and probably in hope of at last being heard, the 16 signers assured the bishop that they had already built a chapel-residence for their expected pastor.[6]

Initially, George Simpson, governor of the HBC rejected the idea of introducing Catholic missionary priests to the area since only a handful of adherents had requested them. He considered that such a move was both "impolitic and imprudent" for there was ample past precedent that the subsequent religious denominational rivalry and dissension that was bound to ensue would interfere with trade and ultimately, and worst of all, with Company profits. McLoughlin warned Simpson that denying priests to even a few Canadian Catholics might undermine their loyalty to the Company and cause them to sow division among other Catholics. Not only, wrote McLoughlin, could a Catholic priest strengthen that same loyalty, far more importantly he would also probably weaken the growing American influence in the region. The last point finally convinced Simpson. Therefore, in 1837 he gave permission to Archbishop Joseph Signay of Quebec to send two of his priests and agreed to Signay's request to pay for their passage to the Oregon Territory.[7]

✤ The First Catholic Clergy

FOR THIS HISTORIC UNDERTAKING Signay selected Father Francis Norbert Blanchet and, to assist him, Father Modeste Demers. At 43, Blanchet was a very energetic pastor who had gained his early missionary experience among the French Acadians in New Brunswick. There, due to his additional ministry to Irish Catholics, he learned to speak English, an essential skill for his future work in the far west. During his next assignment in Cedars, a village on the St. Lawrence in the diocese of Montreal, he acquired first-hand knowledge of his future home from the fur trapping *voyageurs,* the manpower backbone of the HBC enterprise. Demers was 14 years younger than Blanchet, having only been ordained a priest in 1837. Added to inexperience and youth, Demers had never enjoyed robust health. While Blanchet possessed a strong, often very arrogant personality, Demers was an obsessive-compulsive worrier with very low self-esteem. It is no surprise that Demers would forever remain in Blanchet's shadow.[8]

Liberalism, one of the major fruits of the French Revolution, and then at its height in Quebec, often prompted clergy like Blanchet and Demers to become missionaries. Among liberalism's major elements were religious indifferentism and anticlericalism. The latter was especially strong in Catholic societies such as Quebec. There the official church, especially the hierarchy, not only opposed bourgeois liberalism, but with generous annual state incomes, which made them beholden to government, the bishops were also strong supporters of the British establishment. Such behaviour frequently and naturally resulted in very hostile lay reactions to their church's usual support of the status quo. Obviously these lay attitudes influenced church attendance figures. It was even noted that most of Demers's family did not attend church.[9] Therefore, many, like Blanchet and Demers followed Mazenod in seeking answers to local societal discontent in some form of ecclesiastical fundamentalism which, since the French Revolution, meant for the Catholic Church an ever-increasing emphasis on ultramontanism, Marianism and ultimately, papal infallibility. A major nineteenth century outlet for such a mentality was demonstrated in a missionary zeal to spread the gospel, particularly among the poor. In France, the poor would supposedly soon be "liberated" from liberalism, especially in its drive to subvert the old order and to replace it with that "horror," democracy. As for most missionaries to the far west, Oblate and otherwise, the Native people, or the "noble savages," as many missionary magazines then referred to them, personified the "poor."[10]

Soon after receiving Signay's commission, both priests began making plans for this major new chapter in their lives. Demers arrived in St. Boniface over a year before Blanchet and spent most of his time at the small French Canadian settlement on the Red River acquiring his first on-hands experience of mission work, as well as learning English. Finally, on 10 July 1838, Demers and Blanchet, who had arrived from Quebec a short time before, set off for the Oregon Territory. They began an exhausting as well as harrowing overland journey that lasted four months and ultimately claimed the lives of twelve members of their travelling party in a drowning accident on the treacherous Columbia River. On 24 November 1838, the two pioneer Catholic missionaries, reported to be happy just to be alive, finally arrived at Fort Vancouver.[11]

✤ *Beginning to Build a Catholic Church*

TENSIONS, in the form of denominational rivalry and prejudice, soon ensued, though the results did not justify Governor Simpson's earlier fears but, as McLoughlin had predicted, for a time actually enhanced the Company's regional control. Blanchet reported that most of the French Canadians were "happy and willing to obey" the two priests. In addition, both priests, in addressing Canadian Catholics, publicly characterised the American Protestant missionaries as "false prophets" and "wolves" who had come to steal the sheep of the "true flock." They also insisted that the Catholics who had been baptised or married by the American Protestant clergy must now repeat the same ceremonies according to Catholic form. In reply, the American Protestant clergy publicly equated Catholicism with "popery" and "pagan idolatry," and complained to the acting chief factor, James Douglas of this "Romish" interference in their ministry. Douglas, a Glaswegian, and at best, never more than a luke-warm Protestant, had no problem subordinating any religious loyalty he might have had to Company and to future British imperial interests. He refused to intervene but was quite happy to see the Americans losing their earlier influence over the French Canadians.[12]

As the number of American settlers gradually out-numbered the Canadians, increasing social strains developed between them. In 1841–42 when American settlers tried to establish some form of locally elected government, all of the settlers immediately took denominational sides with their clergy in the lead. Bitterness between the two groups escalated. The Protestant clergy began characterising all the Canadians as "foreigners...[in] opposition to all [the] American missionaries and all the American people." Blanchet and Demers were convinced that any type of elected government, given the ever-growing American Protestant presence, would strengthen their Protestant opponents. Much to the delight of HBC officials, the two priests publicly declared that the area was "too immature" for even a provisionally elected government, withdrew their support for such a plan, and encouraged Canadian Catholics to do the same.[13]

Yet despite their opposition to the threat of American political and social control of the region, Blanchet and Demers admired and adapted well to American ways. They particularly appreciated the determination of the new American settlers who arrived by land and sea with enough livestock and equipment to establish quite sizeable farms. Observing that nothing seemed to stop the Americans, Demers declared approvingly: "I do not think there is a people like them under the sun." Economically, at least, the Oregon Territory was very kind to the two priests. Through Blanchet's intelligent management and land investments, by 1844 the local Catholic Church, of which he was the head missionary, had become the fourth wealthiest enterprise in the region. Such a circumstance also encouraged Blanchet to think big in the matter of the church's future organization there.[14]

✤ An Ecclesiastical Province

IN 1843, following the suggestion of Archbishop Signay of Quebec, that because of the enormous distance Blanchet should be made independent of Quebec, the Holy See appointed Blanchet the vicar apostolic of the huge region under the direct authority of Rome. However, believing a report from the American hierarchy that the area was still too unsettled to merit the establishment of a diocese, Rome had initially refused making Blanchet an ordinary or head of a diocese. Yet, by 1845 Blanchet had concluded that, just as he had been so successful in building up the economic base of his vicariate, he could achieve similar results as an ordinary. That is if Rome were willing to create an ecclesiastical province out of the huge area and designate him as its first archbishop.

Certainly, the Catholic Church had experienced some progress during its first seven years of official establishment in the region. There were tiny wooden Mission chapels in Cowlitz, Fort Vancouver, and Oregon City as well as a reasonably large brick church in St. Paul, Oregon. Twelve Jesuits, who operated four Missions, the only regular clergy, represented most of the 16 priests working in the huge area. The four secular clergy, besides parish work, also ran a fee-based boarding school for 28 boys, which was mainly due to the small number of laity from whom they could expect financial support, and so they could not afford to devote themselves entirely to pastoral work. In addition, five Sisters of Notre Dame de Namur, the only community of nuns in the region, taught 47 girls in a day school. As to numbers, the nascent missionary church could claim no more than a thousand Euro-Canadians and Americans, most of whom rarely attended church. While Blanchet numbered Native adherents at over six thousand, most of them were only nominal Catholics and would remain so.[15]

As the evidence clearly indicates, Blanchet's plan to establish an entire ecclesiastical province in such an "immature" region was extremely ill conceived. However, despite the statistical realities, and no matter how preposterous the idea, he seemed determined to become an archbishop. Therefore, during a trip to Rome in 1845–46 Blanchet personally presented the Congregation of Propaganda Fide with a lengthy "Memorial" full of grossly exaggerated and misleading promises, population figures and predictions. In it he alleged that there would be tens of thousands of converts to the Catholic faith once an archdiocese and seven suffragan or attached sees were created in the immense region, which reflected the traditional structure of an ecclesiastical province. Furthermore, Blanchet warned the Vatican that any delay would mean that this mass army of prospective converts would most certainly become either "schismatics" in Alaska under the Russian Orthodox clergy or, even worse, "heretics" in the rest of the vast far west under Protestant pastors. Filled with such audaciousness, if not falsehoods, Blanchet's plan reflected a type of "propoganda" that the Vatican wanted to hear and probably because of this, Rome was deceived. It appointed Blanchet the second archbishop in the United States though sees in major cities such as Philadelphia, Boston, New York and St. Louis were still suffragans under the archdiocese of Baltimore. Thus, a new ecclesiastical province was established in a region that in 1846 had only a handful of villages, few roads, no postal system, and not even an elected government.[16]

Rome had based its decision largely on Blanchet's "Memorial." He had carefully avoided informing any bishops in North America of his precise plan since he was clearly aware of their inevitable opposition. Consequently, Oregon City, then a mere village in the Oregon Territory, now had an "archbishop." Rome's only insightful decision was to reject Blanchet's outrageous demand for seven suffragans, which would have required appointing almost half of the clergy then working in the region to fill such posts. Instead, the Holy See created only two dioceses, Walla Walla (later Nesqually and ultimately Seattle), making Blanchet's brother, Augustin, then a canon of the Cathedral of Montreal, its first ordinary, and Vancouver Island (eventually renamed Victoria), appointing Demers to be its first bishop. Therefore, because of Blanchet's totally distorted version of reality, Rome prematurely established a new ecclesiastical province in a region that was quite ill prepared to receive it. Given the region's general indifference to organized religion, the Catholic Church in the Pacific Northwest, including British Columbia would be plagued for many years by a paucity of both personnel and adherents.[17]

Bishop Modeste Demers (AD)

"Extravagance" was the quite understated response of Archbishop Samuel Eccleston of Baltimore when in the summer of 1846 he learned of the erection of the second American archdiocese. A few years later Rome would lament the haste of its decision, but by then, it was too late. Blanchet's coup was complete, however, his deception would ultimately cause him, and his colleagues only added hardship, and would prove a very empty victory. Yet writing to Eccleston in the fall of 1846, Blanchet could not help but "congratulate" himself, as, he said, did his two suffragans on now "being part of the Catholic church in the United States."18

Unlike Blanchet, Demers believed that establishing the new province had been a preposterous idea, but, always feeling intimidated by his older colleague, he never appears to have had the courage to confront Blanchet with this judgement. Since the Oregon Treaty of 1846 established the forty-ninth

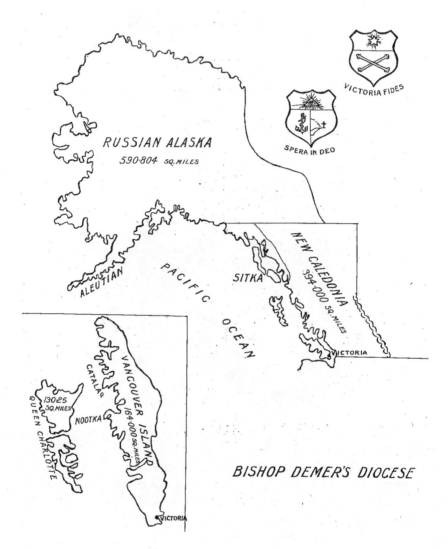

RUSSIAN ALASKA
590·804 SQ.MILES

VICTORIA FIDES

SPERA IN DEO

NEW CALEDONIA
394·000 SQ.MILES

ALEUTIAN

PACIFIC

SITKA

OCEAN

VICTORIA

VANCOUVER ISLAND
164·000 SQ.MILES

CATALA

NOOTKA

QUEEN CHARLOTTE
13025 SQ.MILES

VICTORIA

BISHOP DEMER'S DIOCESE

Bishop Demers's Diocese (AD)

parallel as the new border between British North America and the United States, Demers's diocese of Victoria, a suffragan see under Blanchet in Oregon, was now in a different country. In addition, although Blanchet showed some confidence in Demers's abilities, having put him in charge as his vicar general during the former's long absences in Canada and Europe throughout most of 1844–46, Demers felt poorly prepared for his new duties. His enormous diocese, which included all of British North America west of the Rocky Mountains and Alaska, was much more sparsely settled than the region south of the new border, a fact well-confirmed in his mind after his extensive travels in 1842–43 through a small part of the huge region.[19]

Both Demers and Blanchet had long maintained and would continue to give the impression that their missionary conversion work in the far west was producing abundant fruit, especially as reflected in the very glowing reports that they sent back to eastern Canada. These were later published in *Rapports*, a Quebec diocesan journal, which was devoted to encouraging lay financial support of Catholic missionaries. However, both men deliberately distorted reality, portraying the American Protestant missionaries as inept at best, unable and/or unwilling to comprehend fully the supposed "power" of the Catholic priests or "black robes" over the minds of all potential converts. Naturally such "exaggerations" had an intended purpose, namely, to impress present and possible future donors of how well their money was being and would be spent.[20] Like their Protestant American counterparts, by 1846 Blanchet and Demers had made no more than a handful of converts, a fact that was in direct contradiction to what their own propaganda proclaimed.[21]

By 1846, both Blanchet and Demers were at least familiar with the terri-tory to the south of the new international border, however, neither could say the same about the area north of it. Demers dreaded his new assignment and its largely unknown challenges, especially as a bishop in a new diocese which contained only a handful of Catholics and no clergy except himself, an absurd and almost unheard of predicament. At least Norbert Blanchet and his brother, Augustin had a handful of priests to help them in their new dioceses. In 1847, Demers, in a very depressed state of mind, wrote to a col-league in Quebec: "I do not know in what terms to express my misery!" For Demers was convinced that he had only "poverty," if not "destitution" to look forward to as the new bishop of Victoria.[22]

2

The First Oblates

✝ *The Historic Decision of 1847*

WHILE THE NEW ECCLESIASTICAL PROVINCE had few lay people, its lack of clergy was no less absurd. During his long travels around Canada and Europe, Blanchet was only able to attract eight priests—three Jesuits, five seculars and two deacons. This raised the number of clergy in the entire province to a only 16, with the regulars accounting for twelve, or 75 percent of the total. Demers had no clergy, and Blanchet, with very few clergy himself, did not offer to help, and too intimidated, Demers did not request assistance. Blanchet's brother Augustin, the new bishop of Walla Walla, had recruited even fewer clergy, but he had also gained Oblate assistance. His arrival in his new diocese in September 1847 coincided with that of the first community of Oblates in the far west.[1]

Initially, Bishop Mazenod was not at all interested in accepting the invitation to have his "spiritual sons" work in the Oregon Territory. The Founder had twice been approached by Norbert Blanchet in Marseilles, both on his way to and from Rome where he convinced the Holy See to establish the new province. In his repeated rejection of Blanchet's request, Mazenod told Bourget, the bishop of Montreal, that he could not spare the men, but he was certain that "Divine Providence" would send "help...from other sources." However, experienced missionary clergy in Canada had already rejected Blanchet's provincial scheme. Actually, no less a missionary authority than Bishop Provencher implied that the whole idea was badly planned and even harebrained. This reality goes far in explaining why Blanchet received no direct help from the two bishops of Quebec in staffing his new province.[2]

In effect, it was an Oblate, Joseph Guigues, who finally offered assistance, however, it was not to Norbert, but rather to his brother Augustin Blanchet. Augustin was one of Bishop Bourget's priests, and Guigues, the Oblate Provincial of Canada, was then in Montreal learning to speak English before becoming the first bishop of Bytown (later Ottawa). Guigues, unaware of Mazenod's refusal, though, remembering Eugene's strong criticism of him in 1844 for his initial hesitation to help Provencher by sending Oblates to St. Boniface, now hastily agreed to assist Augustin. Mazenod put the best face he could on the situation, and almost bragged to Bourget that he could not now refuse to Augustin the "feeble help" that Guigues had promised him. Given his theology, Eugene told Bourget that he viewed Guigues's "mistake" as a sign of divine "predestination" that now directed the Oblates to establish themselves in the United States.[3]

Mazenod appeared to be making the best out of what he believed to be a very bad situation. Countermanding Guigues's decision might undermine the authority of his Canadian provincial who was about to become a bishop, and thus confirm to the outside world that the Oblates were not united. However, Mazenod informed Guigues that the Founder alone would decide upon those to be sent. For while his criticism of Guigues was mild, Mazenod noted that the person who led the Oregon assignment must have "opinions comfortable to those of the head of the family," by which he naturally meant himself. Since the distance from Marseilles to Oregon was even greater, the person must thus act as the Founder's alter ego.[4]

Pascal Ricard (1847–57) was Mazenod's first choice, though after 18 years of Oblate ministry he was exhausted, and already suffering from the first signs of tuberculosis. Because of ill health, Ricard was in semi-retirement as the acting superior of Notre Dame de Lumières. However, he viewed the Founder's latest "request" as a "divine command." And reflecting a Jansenistic spirituality of suffering and emulation, according to Mazenod,

Ricard immediately resolved to "offer up his life to God" in Oregon. Mazenod also insisted that the three scholastics that he selected to accompany Ricard, Eugène-Casimir Chirouse (1847–92), George Blanchet (1847-1906), no relation to the Blanchet brothers, and Charles Pandosy (1847–91) evidenced a similar desire for being "sacrificed."[5]

✟ Fighting for a Foundation

SACRIFICE would certainly be their lot under the new bishop of Walla Walla, Augustin Blanchet, who was even more imperious and arrogant than his archbishop brother. Ricard got his first taste of his new predicament when he met Augustin in St. Louis on 16 April 1847, from whence they set out for the west together. After less than a month in the United States, and revealing his very difficult disposition, Augustin Blanchet found little to his liking: the cities were mere "villages," the people were all uncouth, and the Catholic Church was in "a very poor state." As for the Oblates, his initial welcome to them was very cold and with time got even worse. No doubt, his unfriendly behaviour was partly due to feelings of intimidation, since the Oblates already slightly outnumbered the secular clergy of Walla Walla. For besides his three scholastics, all of whom would eventually be ordained priests, Ricard was also accompanied by a lay brother, Célestin Verney (1847–89); whereas Blanchet had acquired only one secular priest, John Baptist Brouillet, a deacon, Louis Rousseau and a seminarian, William Leclair. When Blanchet finally reached Walla Walla on 5 September 1847 he was chagrined to find not even a mere "village," but only a forlorn HBC fur trading post now having the effrontery to be masquerading as his episcopal seat.[6]

In his first verbal agreement with Blanchet, Ricard quickly realised that the bishop was determined to create problems. As superior, Ricard insisted that the Oblates were not prepared to be parish priests nor function as secular clergy under Blanchet's control, and that any Oblate Missions would "belong to them alone," and not to Blanchet. Although he appeared to acquiesce, Augustin did not intend to give in that easily to what he quickly concluded to be just one more troublesome and disobedient priest. Determined to maintain a physical distance from Blanchet, Ricard had established the first Oblate Mission, dedicated to St. Rose of Lima, about 40 miles west of Walla Walla near Richland, Washington on land given to Ricard and the Oblates in perpetuity by Piopiomosmos, a principal elder and leader of the Walla Walla.[7]

When Blanchet tried to force Ricard to cede the Richland property to him, the Oblate superior refused. Blanchet tried to support his demand by providing Ricard with a copy of his brother's "Memorial," which had attempted to secure the approval of Propaganda Fide that in the new province, the regular clergy would be completely under local episcopal control. While Rome had never explicitly rejected Blanchet's request regarding regulars, given their canonical protections from interference by local ordinaries, it was ultimately bound to do so. As such, Ricard did not intend to oblige Blanchet on a point that the bishop could never win. Nevertheless, for about six months letters went back and forth between the provincial bishops and Ricard, all parties repeating their position as irrefutable and unalterable. Thus using the "Memorial" as proof, the three provincial bishops contended that only the local ordinary should direct and own any new Missions founded by the Oblates. However, Ricard insisted that such a position violated canon law, which supported the right of the Oblates both to own and manage their Missions.[8]

The Whitman massacre of 29 November 1847 would supply the cause of the next crisis in the escalating battle between the Oblates and the local bishops. Dr. Marcus Whitman, a medical doctor and lay Methodist missionary, had arrived in the Oregon Territory in 1836 as part of the American Protestant missionary enterprise in the area, which had begun two years earlier. By 1847, denominational rivalry had been raging ever since the arrival of Blanchet and Demers in 1838. Added to this there were the hordes of American settlers with their voracious appetite for land, who, if they attended church, were usually Protestant, and thus Native hostility over the loss of their land was much more likely to be levelled at Protestant rather than Catholic missionaries. Such a factor was further compounded in the Walla Walla region by the terrible winter of 1846–47 when more Natives than usual died from European diseases. Whitman, being a physician, tried to minister to the sick. However, when his remedies failed, several Cayuse braves, accusing him of actually poisoning them with the intent of acquiring more land, attacked his Mission at Waiilatpu near Walla Walla, murdering him, his wife and eight other Euro-Americans.[9]

The tragedy had an immediate impact on everyone. The most lasting one was the further souring of relations between Protestants and Catholics, since for years the former accused the latter of being in collusion with the Cayuse. For its part, the American government used the massacre as an additional excuse to continue removing Native peoples from the area, usually by force, which was often lethal. The Blanchet brothers both sensed the growing tensions around Walla Walla, and, like the Oblates, they rightly blamed the problem on Euro-American hostility towards Native people and Catholics that had greatly escalated after the Whitman massacre. As a hoped-for solution, the bishops decided to petition Rome to create the diocese of Nesqually and transfer Augustin there. The two Blanchets argued that Augustin would be west of the Cascade Mountains and near the larger European settlements, where, both bishops insisted, his ministry was bound to be far more successful. In making their request, the Blanchets stressed the need for additional secular clergy on the pretext that they were "more zealous" than religious priests in the exacting task of missionary work. They exemplified their intended policy by recommending that the Holy See transfer the entire Yakima district, then under the Jesuits, to the care of the future bishop of Nesqually and substantiated their request by accusing the Jesuits of not doing enough to promote the Missions there and elsewhere. Then, clearly referring to the recently arrived French Oblates, all three French Canadian bishops warned Rome against appointing any "strangers" to local sees.[10]

Realising that the "Memorial" alone would never provide sufficient support for their cause, Norbert Blanchet decided to use the first provincial council to strengthen episcopal authority over the regulars. The proceedings, held at St. Paul's Oregon, lasted from late February until early March 1848. In reporting to Rome, Norbert Blanchet carefully avoided mentioning the precise number of clergy who took part. Instead, he referred to the eleven priests and three bishops who attended only as "a large number." After following the French-Canadian model and approving a multiplicity of days of fast and obligation far in excess of what was then in force in the rest of the United States, the three council "fathers" addressed the matter of regular clergy. Long before the arrival of the Oblates in 1847, the regular clergy had greatly outnumbered the secular clergy in the region by more than two to one. The disparity kept increasing, especially as the secular clergy sought admission to the Jesuits, initially with the hope of obtaining greater financial security, and later as a means of escaping from the increasingly tyrannical authority of the Blanchets.[11] In a vain attempt to both legislate against this continued haemorrhaging of their secular clergy to transfer and to bring the regulars under their effective control, the "fathers" passed a decree composed by Demers who still had no clergy. The decree stipulated that the regular clergy could continue to open local noviciates, but only on condition that they "brought their novices from Europe rather than accept [local] secular priests that the Oregon bishops had procured at great expense."[12]

The Oblates were determined to have an Oblate appointed as bishop of a local diocese in order to insure their independence from the Blanchets. With the support of the Jesuits, Mazenod insisted that Rome should appoint an Oblate to Nesqually. Giving the precedent of his own situation in France, the bishop of Marseilles justified his request with the recent appointment of an Oblate, Joseph Guigues, as the first bishop of Bytown. Ricard was the candidate favoured by Mazenod as well as by the Jesuit procurator general, Emilio Pellegrini. Writing to Canon Lowenbrük, a friend who apparently had considerable influence in Rome, Mazenod was blunt in his criticism, insisting that the Blanchets and Demers were far more interested in being masters than pastors. Although Mazenod avoided such direct fault-finding in writing to Propaganda Fide, he clearly implied that the appointment of Ricard would definitely improve conditions in the province. It seemed both fair and logical to Eugene since the regular clergy, Oblates and Jesuits, already dominated the regional clergy there, he believed that they deserved to have one of their own as a local ordinary.[13]

Rome, however, sided with the Blanchets. While the Holy See was certainly not prepared to criticise either the Oblates or the Jesuits, it insisted that Ricard was far more valuable as a missionary priest, and therefore should not abandon that role to become a bishop, either in Nesqually or Walla Walla. Even so, Rome did not close the door to the possibility of a regular being appointed a bishop to a local see. In defending the logic of its decision, Propaganda Fide insisted that their position was actually based on local tradition, at least among the Jesuits who had always refused episcopal appointments. In fact, in 1843, the American bishops had asked the Jesuits to appoint one of their own as vicar apostolic of the Oregon Territory, but they had declined. Never realising that he would become their future enemy, the Jesuits ironically recommended Norbert Blanchet for the position. For his part, at first Blanchet had refused episcopal office because he felt that, as the dominant clergy in the region, a Jesuit should become vicar apostolic. Actually, only a few years before, Blanchet, in reflecting upon the few secular clergy in the Territory, had even considered joining the Jesuits himself, since he felt that by so doing he would "secure unity in action in the spiritual government of all the missions."[14]

The most likely explanation for Rome's position was its fear that a regional diocese headed by a regular bishop, whether an Oblate or a Jesuit, would soon attract the bulk of the local clergy, secular as well as regular. Thus, such a circumstance would probably leave the other dioceses, except for their bishops, with no clergy at all, which was then the actual situation in the diocese of Victoria. By then, Rome was also well aware of its mistake in having created the province in the first place, but the Holy See was probably concerned that appointing Ricard a local bishop would only further worsen an already unfortunate reality.

Rome's decision not to appoint an Oblate bishop to Nesqually only further aggravated relations between the ordinaries and the Oblates, who, with the Jesuits, increasingly complained about their treatment at the hands of the local bishops, especially Archbishop Blanchet. A clear sign of the escalating tension was the continued and growing determination of the secular clergy to join the regulars. The most notorious example among others was Fr. François-Jean Jayol (1849–1907) whose priestly ordination by Norbert Blanchet on 19 September 1847 was the first in the new province. By December 1848 Jayol had had enough of his archbishop's dictatorial behaviour and decided to join the Oblates, requesting that Blanchet allow him to enter the noviciate at St. Joseph's Mission at Olympia, Washington. As could be expected, a furious Blanchet demanded that Jayol return immediately to Oregon City; however, with Ricard's full support, the priest delayed doing so until he had made his permanent vows as an Oblate. Upon hearing this, Blanchet, believing Rome supported his assumed right to control regulars, again ordered Jayol's compliance under pain of suspension. As the Jayol incident coincided with word of Rome's decision not to appoint Ricard to a local see, the Oblates were in no mood to bend to what they regarded as Blanchet's latest arrogance. Rome was ultimately drawn into the imbroglio, each side complaining to it of the insensitivity and lack of co-operation of the other. Propaganda Fide finally agreed with the Oblates and approved Jayol's decision. While Rome supported Blanchet's right to refuse to allow his clergy to join religious orders, it admonished him that the problem would not likely have arisen if he had treated his own clergy with greater respect.[15]

Tensions between the Blanchets and the Oblates continued to worsen. The archbishop was faced with increasing financial problems due to a decline in the Catholic population, which, though never large, became even worse after the 1849 California gold rush. As usual, Blanchet refused to accept his own role in compounding his difficulties, but remained convinced that his problems were due to insubordinate clergy, especially regulars. Blanchet's blindness to his own grave shortcomings was made clear in 1850 when he even advised Rome to place the newly created diocese of Monterey, California under the Oregon Province since, he wrote, it would then be "far better administered." In frustration, Propaganda Fide replied that, while it had not yet decided upon Monterey's suffragan status, Blanchet had still not forwarded his long overdue report on the conditions of his own see, clearly implying that he was doing a less than satisfactory job of administering the archdiocese.[16]

Mazenod and Ricard continued to complain bitterly of the Blanchets, especially Norbert, and persisted in advising Rome to remove Augustin from Nesqually in favor of Ricard. By then (1850–51) the Oblates considered their request even more crucial, since both Blanchets now decided to interpret as rigidly as possible the Holy See's requirement that secular clergy have permission from their bishops before entering religious life. As such, they threatened to close all of the male noviciates in their dioceses, and thus prevent the secular clergy from escaping their authority. Such machinations infuriated Mazenod, so much so that he even threatened to withdraw the Oblates from the region.[17]

By the early 1850s most of the clergy of Oregon, secular as well as regulars, were in full revolt against the Blanchets. Almost everyone began to look south to California where, given the gold rush, many of the Oregon settlers had already migrated.[18] The Jesuits felt the situation, especially with the Blanchets, made expansion of their ministry impossible. While Propaganda continued to plead with both the Jesuits and Mazenod to reconsider their threats to abandon Oregon, when Rome finally suppressed the diocese of Walla Walla in 1853, it privately admitted that the province's creation had translated into "little or no regional progress for religion."[19]

Although Mazenod was unable to obtain a diocesan foundation in Oregon, which he had long believed was the best security for his "spiritual sons," he finally, and very grudgingly, agreed to let the Oblates stay. In so doing he and the local Oblates again tried to reach some kind of understanding with Augustin Blanchet to give the Oblates effective control over their ministry and Missions. While the bishop of Nesqually agreed to this in writing, as in the past, he continued to oppose Oblate influence in his diocese. In defending his position, he cited the now tired argument of the "Memorial" that supported the notion that the bishops of the province should have complete control over all the clergy. Thus, Augustin continued to insist that ultimately he was not bound by any arrangement he might make with any regulars.[20]

Added to their problems with the Blanchets was the growing violence against the Native population in the Oregon Territory, which only increased the apparent futility of their ministry in the region. Ever since the Whitman massacre of 1847, the Americans had been waging war, official and otherwise, on the Natives of the area. In May 1850, five Cayuse braves came to Oregon City supposedly under safe conduct in order to explain to the American authorities that the Native murderers of the Whitmans were now all dead. Not surprisingly, the five were immediately arrested, and, in a sham trial, were found guilty and subsequently hanged. Such gross injustice only fuelled further racism among Euro-Americans. For while the U.S. government ostensibly opposed the summary slaughter of the Native people, it tended to turn a blind-eye to Euro-American vigilantes or "volunteers." Such people, following a racist philosophy of general extermination, continued to attack the Native population where and when they pleased, ignoring any evidence of whether or not they were friendly or hostile.[21]

This placed the Oblates in the impossible situation of trying to support the American government's suppression of violent Natives, while at the same time opposing the murder of innocent Natives by American vigilantes. Increasingly viewed by both sides as the enemy, many Americans blamed the Oblates for siding with the Natives, whereas a growing number of Natives saw the Oblates as defenders of American genocide.[22]

✣ The Oblate Decision to Leave

DURING LATE 1855 AND EARLY 1856 several Oblate Missions were attached and heavily damaged by both Americans and Natives. While no Oblates were killed or injured, Mazenod was convinced that it was only a matter of time before they were. He based his judgement on a recent canonical visitation by Fr. François-Xavier Bermond (1856–59) that concluded that the

Bishop Louis D'Herbomez (AD)

ongoing Native-American hostilities made Oblate neutrality ultimately impossible in the area.[23]

By then Ricard, who was dying of tuberculosis, and determined to return to France, had relinquished the leadership of the Oregon Missions into the hands of Louis D'Herbomez (1850–90) who became the acting-superior. A logical successor, D'Herbomez had arrived in the Territory in 1850, and since 1856 had been an extraordinary visitor to the Oregon Mission, a form of special advisor to Ricard. By then, both men were persuaded that the Oblates had to leave the United States. For while they might barely maintain some of their Missions in the Oregon Territory, the tensions between the Natives and Americans as well as between the Blanchets and the Oblates meant that it would be years, if even, before they had a secure foundation south of the forty-ninth parallel. As an added incentive, by 1855, Bishop Demers, who, though he shared his episcopal colleagues' prejudice against regulars, was desperate for clergy, and as such was prepared to take them from whatever quarter they came. By 1860, except for a small Mission at Tulalip in the Washington Territory where the government had established a large Native reserve, the Oblates had abandoned their American Missions and turned their attention northward to British territory.[24]

✤ Trying to Lay a Canadian Foundation

INITIALLY, the Oblate decision to come to the diocese of Victoria made no immediate improvement over what they had experienced in Oregon, since organizational problems were worse there than they had been in Oregon. For if folly best described the creation of the two dioceses south of the forty-ninth parallel, then the establishment of the diocese of Victoria was even more absurd, since, except for its bishop, for years there were no clergy, or only a few, to minister to a handful of laity, mostly French Canadian Catholic employees of the HBC. Geographically, the diocese covered the immense region of all of western British North America and Alaska, which was still part of the Russian empire.

To add further to the problem, Demers, who had always considered the creation of the ecclesiastical province to be a preposterous idea, was never more than a very reluctant bishop, and therefore a quite poor one; also Demers was a bad administrator who had great difficulty with organization, finances and people, particularly clergy who universally complained of his "quick temper." When he was able to acquire priests, few stayed with him for very long, usually drawn away by greener pastures elsewhere, particularly California, where, although bishops may not have been much better, certainly parishioners, and therefore money were both in far greater supply. While Vancouver Island would ultimately become the gateway for the Oblates in gaining their independence from the local secular ordinaries in the far west, before that became possible they would have to deal with one more secular bishop.[25]

✝ The First Priest in the Diocese of Victoria

HONORÉ-TIMOTHÉE LEMPFRIT (1847–52) was the first priest and Oblate to work in the diocese of Victoria, and had received his assignment from Ricard in 1849 in answer to a request from Archbishop Blanchet. Lempfrit's task was to begin establishing a church during Demers's long (1848–52) fund-raising and clergy recruiting trip to Canada and Europe. Like most Catholic missionaries, Lempfrit's ostensible objective was to convert the "heathen" Natives. However, unlike Demers, who, due to deep prejudices, viewed all Native people as more or less "sub-human brutes," Lempfrit saw genuine value in the Natives and their culture. While he founded a one-man school for the French Canadian children at Fort Victoria, he spent most of his time visiting and ultimately baptising hundreds of Native children and marrying thousands of adults on both Vancouver Island and the mainland.[26]

Viewing such Christian ceremonies as added expressions of their spirituality, the Cowichan and coastal Salish tribes, among whom Lempfrit worked, integrated them with their own rites of purification and blessing, demonstrating a form of culture assimilation similar to all of the Native people of the far west and elsewhere. However, the Europeans were incapable of grasping this understanding due mainly to their arrogant certitude of the infinite superiority of western civilization, including Christianity.[27] Lempfrit certainly was unable either to comprehend or even make the slightest accommodation with Native spirituality. Rather, an incurable paternalist and romantic, he quickly became convinced that his thousands of baptised and married "savages," or his Native "children," were now totally committed Catholics ready to become loyal "parishioners" by financially supporting their new pastor. His Cowichan "parishioners" did not share his attitude. Apparently angered by his assumptions, and in an attempt to be rid of him, they accused Lempfrit of fathering a Native child. Although no evidence has been found supporting the charge, in 1852 the HBC, which viewed the Native people as major suppliers of furs, and had no wish to irritate such vital clients, quietly ordered Lempfrit to leave the colony. In 1853, reflecting a self-righteous theology that emphasized sexual obsession as well as almost masochistic suffering, Mazenod declared that Lempfrit, because of his unsubstantiated "sins" was now unworthy of the priesthood. In consequence, the Founder advised his "former son" to lock himself away in some remote monastery, there to do penance for the rest of his days. Instead, Lempfrit chose a more positive path, and spent the last ten years of his life as a secular parish priest in France.[28]

Demers finally returned to the region in 1853 after having spent four years (1848–52) traveling in Canada and Europe in a largely fruitless attempt to raise funds and recruit clergy for his diocese. The reports of Lempfrit's supposed behaviour only further convinced him that his episcopal colleagues' complaints against the Oblates were well founded. Yet, Demers's inability to work with people, and his unhappiness at being a bishop meant that he was never very successful in retaining the few clergy that he did attract. By 1855, despite his continued prejudices towards the Oblates, with the only secular priest about to depart, a desperate Demers was willing to accept almost any priests, even Oblates.[29]

✣ The Decision to Come North

NEITHER DEMERS NOR THE OBLATES were particularly eager to embrace. By initially insisting in 1855 that the Oblates had an obligation to come north in order to repair the public damage supposedly caused by Lempfrit, Demers obviously did not endear himself to those from whom he now sought assistance. Again, his attitude demonstrated his serious lack of tact, and, like the Blanchets, his tendency to see himself as the "victim" and others, especially priests, as the cause of all his misfortunes.[30] Rome, in attempting to rectify its mistake in having created the diocese, also pressed the Oblates, even insisting that Pius IX expected the Oblates to work on Vancouver Island. Mazenod, however, was in no hurry to act, rightly sensing that his spiritual "sons" would ultimately be treated by Demers much in the same way as they had been by the Blanchets. And although Demers insisted that he would abide by any arrangements he made with the Oblates, the Blanchets had made similar promises and then had repeatedly broken them. In fact, while Demers was pleading with the Oblates to come north, he was also complaining to Rome that the Oblates alone were at fault in their continued disagreements with the Blanchets.[31]

Perhaps initially despairing of their assistance, in April 1856 Demers implied that he no longer needed the Oblates, however, by then the Oblates were definitely looking north.[32] In order to investigate its potential as a future Oblate Mission, that summer Charles Pandosy and Louis D'Herbomez traveled to Fort Nanaimo, then a small HBC coal mining settlement about 95 kilometres north of Fort Victoria. Perhaps they thought that if they came to Vancouver Island, it would be best to keep their distance from Demers as they had attempted to do with Augustin Blanchet. Yet, Victoria was then the only significant population center on the Island, and by 1857 D'Herbomez thought that it was imperative to return to British territory, a decision confirmed the following year by the canonical visitation of François-Xavier Bermond.[33]

By the end of 1858, except for the Mission at Tulalip, the Oblates had bid a less than fond farewell to the United States and the Blanchet brothers. True to form, in November 1859 Archbishop Blanchet wrote to Rome complaining bitterly that, after over ten years, the Oblates had abandoned his brother, although he illogically contended that in any case they had "achieved nothing" during their time with Augustin. In the face of such supposed failure, he argued that Propaganda Fide continued to provide the Oblates with the "greatest share" of its missionary funds, while it neglected the local bishops. Coming from Blanchet, whose initial dishonesty had lead to the premature creation of the province, such faulty reasoning and falsehoods were hardly surprising. Still dissembling, in the same letter, Blanchet insisted that he had just returned from Canada with personnel for all three dioceses, notwithstanding the fact that he assigned no one to assist Demers, and kept most of his recruits for himself. Like Blanchet, Demers also repeatedly complained that he too was not getting his share of the mission funding from either Rome or the Propagation of the Faith in Lyon. Demers was always convinced that everyone, the Oblates and the Blanchets included, were receiving far greater financial support, although there is no evidence to support his contention.[34]

While each party appeared willing to cooperate, clearly both Demers and the Oblates knew that the latter were determined to gain in British North America what they had never been able to achieve in the United States, namely, independence from the local secular ordinary. From 1858 until his death in 1861 Mazenod made no secret of his desire to see the Oblates obtain in the far west what they had already achieved in the east with Oblate bishops in Ottawa and St. Boniface. With such an eventuality in mind, throughout their time on Vancouver Island, the Oblates openly made plans to establish Missions on the mainland, despite Demers's growing need for clergy in Victoria. Thus, 1858 marked a most important turning point for the Oblates, for it was the official beginning of their ministry in far-western Canada.[35]

Part Two
The Native People

"Most of the savages are still plunged

into the darkness [of superstition]

and the shadow of death."

FATHER LOUIS D'HERBOMEZ, OMI, 1861.

MISSION BOYS' BAND CRANBROOK

3

Respecting Spiritualities

✤ The Christian Shadow and the Native People

EXAMINING THE INSTITUTIONAL SHADOW of the Roman Catholic Church was one of the aims of the Second Vatican Council (1962–65). "*The Declaration on the Relationship of the Church to Non-Christian Religions,*" also known under the Latin title of "*Nostra Aetate,*" though the shortest, was also one of the Council's most revolutionary documents. For the first time in its long history, the Catholic Church officially recognised not only the existence but, far more importantly, the inherent value of other, non-Christian religions. While still maintaining the church's claim to contain the fullness of revealed truth through the revelation of Jesus Christ, "*Nostra Aetate*" at least declared that other religions "nevertheless often reflect a ray of that Truth which enlightens all...[people]."[1]

"*Nostra Aetate*" does not mention North American Native religion/spirituality by name, but it declared that from ancient times a "certain perception" of God has instilled in the lives of all people "a profound religious sense." In an historic precedent, it defended religious freedom, insisting that the

Catholic Church rejected "any discrimination against...[people] or harassment of them because of their race, colour, condition of life, or religion." Yet, after admitting that the Catholic Church had made mistakes in its relationship with other religions, sadly "*Nostra Aetate*" then urged "all to *forget the past* and to strive sincerely for mutual understanding." But how can such understanding be achieved if the past, and especially its shadow parts, are forgotten? For as the philosopher, George Santayana noted "progress, far from consisting in change, depends on retentiveness," and that "those who cannot remember the past are condemned to fulfil it."[2]

✦ North America: The "Promised Land" for Europeans

G.K. CHESTERTON'S OBSERVATION that Christian ideals have not been tried and found wanting, but rather that they have been "found difficult; and left untried" would certainly be one reason for the failure of relations between the Native and European peoples of Canada.[3] A central reason for this failure was that most Christian European settlers in North America believed that "truth" and God were on their side, and thus the Native people and their culture, especially their spirituality, were of little or no value, and certainly contained no "truth." In short, most Euro-Canadians and Euro-Americans, including the Oblates, viewed Native culture as essentially "meaningless," if not "evil."

Another important element in explaining such bigotry, including its accompanying racism, was the European inability to live with either cultural ambiguity or diversity. Historically the cultural roots of this tragedy began in the fourth century when by the edict of Milan of 313 the Emperor Constantine I legally recognised the Christian church's right to exist. In a little more than a century the church had successfully "convinced" the Roman state, who by then already viewed religious uniformity as a vital foundation for its survival, that Christianity must become the sole imperial religion. By the sixth century, it had become a legal fact under the Justinian Code, which outlawed all other non-Christian religions in the empire, thus finally abandoning a religious pluralism that, until then, had been one of the great strengths of Roman civilisation. So in the interest of supposed social "harmony," Christianity long ago destroyed the healthy religious diversity that for many centuries had been a major part of the cultural vigour of the ancient Hellenistic world. In fact, it was into such a religiously pluralistic world that Christianity had been born, and which its gospel, in such parables as the Good Samaritan, appeared to both support and defend.

However, by the time of Constantine I (D. 337) Christian theology had long held that under the "great law of divine right" it was the only "true religion" in the world. Therefore, they believed, that before the world could experience the long expected second-coming of Christ, all of its peoples must be converted to Christianity, even, if necessary, by force. During its first five centuries of existence, the Fathers of the church, its earliest and most formative theologians, used as proof texts for Christianity's supposed superiority the Jewish scriptures that the Fathers now claimed as their own. Thus, Jewish scripture was now interpreted by the Fathers to prove that, through Jesus' coming, God had disinherited the Jews, since they had not only rejected their "true" Messiah, but they had even "killed" God. Subsequently, God had elected Christians to be his "new chosen people." In so doing, Christianity laid the foundation of western anti Semitism thus making the Jews the first in a long list of Christian-inspired "out" groups. When, centuries later, such a "theology" was applied to the Native peoples of the Americas, it theorised that "in fact," like ancient Israel's view of the Canaanites, the first immigrants to the Americas were actually in "wrongful possession" of these "new promised lands." And so the "Christian God" now demanded that, like the ancient Israelites, his "truly chosen Christian people," the European Canadians and Americans should take, by whatever means necessary, "their promised-land." As justification for the use of force, many, if not most Europeans theorised that such was "required by the superior right of the white man...founded in the wisdom of God." In the secular realm, the social Darwinist "law of progress" was cited as the central reason, which meant that "all opposition" must ultimately be "hushed in the perfect reign of the superior aggressive principle." In effect, a "manifest destiny," whether it was viewed as divine or human, had preordained that North America now, as *always,* belonged to the Europeans.[4]

✤ The First Immigrants and Their Spirituality

CROSSING AN ICE SHELF that then covered the Bering Strait, the first immigrants to the Americas apparently arrived from Siberia between 50,000 to 20,000 BCE gradually moving south and southeast. During much of this period most of far-western Canada, including British Columbia was covered by the great Wisconsinan glaciation. This enormous glacier only began to recede about 9,000 BCE allowing the first explorers to enter from what is now Alaska and the Yukon which ironically, due to its "milder" climate, had been inhabited as early as 20,000 BCE. By about 8,000 BCE, as the ice continued to disappear, human settlers moved into the region in greater numbers. Because of continuing glacial melting, the region which now comprises far-western Canada reached its present geographical configuration by 3,000 BCE.[5]

Over many millennia, the first immigrants to the Americas developed as profound a sense of the spiritual as any other inhabitants on this planet, then or now. Certainly early French Oblate missionary ethnologists such as Émile Petitot and Adrien-Gabriel Morice attested to this fact as well as to their great diversity. But both men remained inextricably tied to their western European and Christian prejudices. Still, in their groundbreaking studies, which saw the myths of the Native people of Canada as proof that they were the "lost remnants of Israel now [finally] converted to Catholicism," both at least admitted a spiritual integrity in Native beliefs *almost* equal to their European Christian counterparts.[6]

After many years of dismissing Native culture as irrelevant, today there is an awareness, even among Christian leaders, that the Native people of North America already possessed a powerful spirituality long before any European contacts. Through it they had a profound sense of what was wise and good that was equal, if not sometimes superior to the Europeans who would not only take their land, but who would also try to destroy their culture.[7] Such wisdom is evident in the advice of Chief Seattle to European immigrants recorded in the 1880s: "The white man must treat the beasts of this land as...[their] brothers and sisters....Every shining pine needle,...every mist in the dark woods,...every humming insect...is sacred. The sap which courses through the trees carries the memories of the red [people]....This shining water that moves in the streams and rivers is not just water but the very blood of our ancestors."[8] Perhaps time has helped the Europeans, among the latest immigrants to North America, to see more clearly the profound insight and contemporary wisdom in such words, which actually reflect the spirituality of St. Francis of Assisi as well as the culture of the peoples who first settled this land.

The spirituality or religious worldview of the Native people who formed the initial inhabitants of the area that would become British Columbia contained innumerable variations. The Coast Salish religious legends and myths differ significantly from those of the interior Kutenai. Even so, there were also basic similarities, which demonstrated a definite regional syncretism as well as the apparent collective unconscious unity of all human spirituality. The Native people believed that the powers of all living things differed in degree, and that except for this fact, they were identical, sharing consciousness, culture, spirits and even physical forms. Native spirituality held that nonhumans were capable both of assuming human form and of preying upon humans for food and for the spirits necessary for their continued existence. While residues of these beliefs continued, gradually, particularly through contact with other Native cultures, new insights and patterns arose that recognised the strengths and weaknesses of all things and beings, human and nonhuman, and so developed the basic principle of reciprocity or mutual dependence with its cyclic view of history. Therefore, the Native peoples of the region, through their rich variety of myths and legends, did not consider humans as the dominant species. They believed that they shared their powers with other creature-spirits upon whom, through the performance of sacred rites of initiation and blessing, they likewise depended for their mutual well-being, ultimate survival and happiness both here and hereafter. This view was not dissimilar from many mystery religions of the Hellenistic world that had a significant influence on the early development of Christianity.[9]

The shamans or holy persons were the central figures in Native spirituality throughout the region. They could be a man or a woman, who, through a personal and triumphant experience with nonhumans, and which was recognised by their community, had gained important power in the spirit world and who represented the central human-divine force behind all Native spirituality. Though they could employ their power for evil as well as good, shamans were generally considered "helpers," and their power was usually employed to assist other humans. This would mainly consist of driving out evil forces, especially a physical or psychological illness, that had inhabited the body and/or spirit of their client.

Shamanic power died with the individual, but certain powers could be passed on from one generation to the next and could be possessed by anyone. Among the coastal peoples these hereditary "gifts" from the spirit world were often embodied in crests, as on totem poles, in regalia or on longhouse facades. The crests explained how an ancestor acquired such powers and represented hereditary "deeds" to certain territories.

The potlatch had a profoundly spiritual character among the coastal Natives. Reflecting the bounty of nature, during the potlatch the hosts gave away much of their wealth to their guests and thus gained in social and political prestige. Such celebrations were an extremely important means of maintaining tribal relations and marking important events, such as puberty, marriage, and especially death. Belief in an after-life was universal among the Native people of far western Canada. Funeral rites were crucial in separating the dead from the realm of the living. Because the death of a principal elder was especially critical, his successor was expected to hold an elaborate series of potlatches before assuming his new authority. Marriage was also accompanied by such feasts and was contracted only by persons from a different clan or extended family group, since marriage within the clan was considered incestuous. Though polygamy was practised, it was a sign of high rank and was only permissible for those who were financially capable of supporting more than one wife.

Spiritual powers, whether Shamanic or not, were always vulnerable to human error and injustice. The social order was reflected in the cosmic. The stability of both depended upon the protection of the moral order and the recognition that all life was sacred and interconnected.

Myth narratives, as in all cultures and religions, reflected on the problems, solutions and reasons of existence that then, as now, perplex humans everywhere. Raven, wolf, beaver, mosquito, frog, eagle, whale—the narratives employed the nonhuman as well as the human to teach the profound wisdom of past ages. Creation was a central story, and in every version stressed the integrity of all life.

Despite the long efforts of Euro-Canadians to destroy it, aboriginal spirituality never completely died. Though damaged by many years of European prejudice, which then prompted Native neglect and conscious and unconscious repression, Native religious rites and ceremonies of the far west have survived. In fact in the last few decades Native spirituality has made a remarkable recovery and has attracted a reasonably large number of Native participants. Perhaps Native spirituality's greatest contemporary role is in helping to safeguard Native cultural identity and with it, individual Native self-respect.[10]

Franz Boas, the father of North American cultural anthropology, did some of his earliest fieldwork studying the Native cultures on the west coast of Vancouver Island. Boas believed that with the gradual "increase in knowledge," all peoples would free themselves from their "traditional fetters" and experience an "emancipation from...[their] own culture," and develop a greater appreciation of and respect for other cultures, while enhancing their knowledge and appreciation of their own culture. In the ever-increasing globalisation of the planet, both Western European civilisation and Christianity have much to learn and gain from other cultures and religions, and this would obviously include Native spirituality. No one has all the truth.[11]

4

Initial Encounters

✤ *The Hudson's Bay Company*

CERTAINLY THE HUDSON'S BAY COMPANY, one of the first major European incursions into the far west, was representative of the arrogance of Western ways and, unlike the Native people, mirrored the consistent inability to either adapt or appreciate the inherent diversity and value of other, nonwestern cultures. Profit from furs was the Company's prime interest, and it embraced whatever methods enhanced that objective. Therefore, in working to win British government approval of its control of a given trading territory or department, the Company fully supported the "conversion" of the Native population to European civilisation. The HBC embraced any means as long as it improved profits, particularly in its commercial arrangements with the Natives, who were among its major suppliers of furs. The Chrisitianisation of the Native peoples was implicitly part of such "civilising," and also an additional reason that the Company used to gain government approval to open a new area. This was clearly the case when the HBC gained London's permission to establish itself on Vancouver Island and the lower mainland.[1]

In line with this aim, in 1843 the acting chief factor of the HBC, James Douglas invited Jean-Baptiste Bolduc, a secular priest from the diocese of Quebec, to accompany him on his initial survey trip to Vancouver Island in order to "convert" the local Natives to Christianity. Bolduc obliged and became the next recorded Christian clergyman to visit the Island and its Native inhabitants, after the brief, historic encounters of the Spanish, the English and the Nootka.

In describing his brief experiences in the usual genre of missionary magazine propaganda, Bolduc noted that the local Natives, the Songhees "entreated" him to baptise all of their children. Bolduc reported that the Songhees were aware of Demers's presence on the mainland where he was then visiting several tribes on the Fraser River. An unnamed tribal elder told Bolduc that the children baptised by Demers "died almost immediately" after receiving the sacrament. In what appeared to be a death wish for his own children, at least as reported by Bolduc, the Native leader now "begged" the priest to do the same for the offspring of the Songhees. In Bolduc's missionary "logic," the elder had obviously realized that, such an act "will make...[the children] see the Master on high after death." Therefore, the elder reportedly asked Bolduc to "baptise all...[the children] in our camp; do this charity; they are to be pitied; almost all [will] die."[2]

If the incident is true, the Songhees would have viewed baptism as a form of cultural syncretism, and even perhaps as a means of protecting their children from physical death, but certainly not in the same way that Bolduc would have interpreted baptism. Bolduc, given his own cultural blindness, could never have grasped such cultural blending. In any case, the priest satisfied the elder and baptised over a hundred children. Obviously the early deaths of the Native children, both on Vancouver Island and the mainland, were caused by their weaker immune system than Native adults, which was not able to withstand the diseases contracted from their initial contacts with Europeans, including Demers and Bolduc.

Naturally, like Demers, Bolduc also reflected strong prejudices towards the Native people that were common to most missionaries. He feared that, except for such children who might "receive the grace of an early death soon after baptism," such Songhees customs as polygamy, which he described as "hell's abomination," would prevent most of the Native adults from receiving the "good news" of Christianity. However, for Douglas the central purpose of his visit was that Bolduc's baptisms gave the chief factor and the HBC two additional reasons, namely, "civilizing" and "Christianizing" the Natives, that could now be used to justify their future control of the region.[3]

✤ Early Proselytizing and the Consequences

BOTH THE PROTESTANT AND CATHOLIC MISSIONARIES, represented by Blanchet and Demers, saw the conversion of the Native peoples as a central aim of their ministry. Since many French Canadian Catholics who had settled in the Oregon Territory had married Native women, Blanchet initially believed, naively, even arrogantly, that converting their Native wives to Catholicism would open the way to the conversion of other relatives and ultimately of the entire tribe.[4]

For while American Protestant settlers continued to come in increasingly large numbers, both Blanchet and Demers persisted in the foolish belief that they could make up for any loss due to French Canadian converts to Protestantism by being more successful than the Protestants in evangelising and converting the Native peoples. Since, though they had ostensibly come west at the request of the French Canadian employees of the HBC, evangelising and saving Native "souls" remained at least their official and even primary objective. In his letter commissioning the two priests, the major directive from their ordinary, Archbishop Signay of Quebec, was "to withdraw the savages [of the region] from barbarity and the disorders" that such behaviour produces.[5]

Both Demers and Blanchet made ample use of the preached mission in their early work among the Native people. Since the time of the Catholic Reformation, and like the early Oblate ministry among the poor of Provence, the church mission had been a major tool in trying to re-evangelise Europeans and also in the struggle to evangelise the Native people in the early Spanish and Portuguese colonies in Latin America. It also played a part in attempting to acculturate indigenous populations in Asia and Africa as part of European expansion there during the nineteenth century. Consisting usually of a series of fire and brimstone sermons and other religious celebrations, especially confession, the mission normally lasted several days to a few weeks. However, apparently convinced that the longer it lasted the greater the impact, especially on the Native people, Blanchet and Demers decided to extend it. At least one Native mission reportedly went on for 140 days.[6]

Europeans, including Canadian and American missionaries, unwittingly brought to the Native peoples another far more frightening reality than their peculiar interpretation of Christian "truth," namely, disease. The Native people, without the hereditary immunity of the Europeans, and so unable to cope, were usually overwhelmed and died from European diseases, especially smallpox, which Demers called the "fever-and-ague." Yet like other European settlers, the two priests were ignorant of their essential role in spreading the disease. Instead, like most missionaries, Catholic and Protestant, they self-righteously saw smallpox as God's judgement on the Native people for the "abominable lives" that they lead before the coming of Christianity, and for their continued refusal to convert. Certainly, similar to other missionaries, both priests also made efforts to vaccinate the Native population. Although unknown then, such undertakings actually had little or no impact once the disease had been contracted. Since the Natives continued to die even after vaccinations, Demers and Blanchet concluded that only universal Native acceptance of Roman Catholicism could "insure their survival," if not in this world, then at least in the next.[7]

For Demers and Blanchet, however, the contagion of "heresy," contracted from the American Protestant missionaries, was far more threatening than any earthly malady that killed only the Native "body," for "heresy," they were certain, also destroyed Native "souls." The Protestants harboured similar feelings regarding "Romish idolatry," and, given a choice, all the denominations in the region would have preferred that the Natives remained "pagan" than convert to their opponents' version of Christianity.[8] Therefore reports, which later proved false, that American Protestant missionaries were "threatening" to proselytise among the Natives in New Caledonia, the mainland of future British Columbia, prompted Demers to spend almost nine months there during 1842–43. Travelling as far north as the HBC Fort George on the Fraser River, Demers met no Protestants along the way, but he did baptise a very small number of Native people, mostly children, and memorised a handful of words in two Native languages.[9]

A racist, like most Euro-Canadian and Euro-American settlers, Demers found the Native "customs and habits" in the north as "inveterate" as those in the south, though he cited polygamy as their "greatest...death-dealing scourge." Such a complaint reflected the cultural and racial misunderstanding of most European settlers and their difficulty in overcoming it. Again, like most of their race, Blanchet and Demers were unable and unwilling either to live or deal with ambiguity or diversity, and instead retreated into their extremely narrow philosophy of life. Thus their racism made them very intolerant of any differences and incapable of even beginning to comprehend the religious syncretism of Native culture. As a major consequence of such studied ignorance, these early and hasty missionary endeavours usually had little or no impact on their Native audiences and ended in failure, although Demers would have been oblivious of the true reasons, especially of his cultural blindness.[10]

Christianity, like capitalism, has usually placed a very high priority on conversion figures, since for both, profit and loss were and still are all part of their most central objective, the bottom-line. As to early Native conversions, Blanchet officially set it at over six thousand. Yet since most converts consisted of children, many of whom apparently soon died, actual numbers of adults were extremely small, and most of whom, if baptised, remained only nominally Catholic. Throughout their ministry, the two priests, eager to gain financial support for their work from the readers of such missionary magazines as *Rapports*, sent glowing accounts of their success, especially of their supposed superiority over Protestant rivals due to the "power" of the "black robes" over the minds of the Native people.

However, the Protestants did appear to be somewhat less successful in proselytising among the Natives. In part, this may have been due to the Catholic emphasis on ceremonies and artifacts such as the Mass and processions, as well as statues, vestments and incense that the Natives probably found more accommodating and which, unknown to either Demers or Blanchet, they often syncretised with their own spirituality. Yet this in no way meant that by doing so the Natives had accepted Christianity to the exclusion of their own religious traditions. Rather, Protestantism, with its emphasis on scripture and preaching, was far more interested in written and spoken English, which did not hold the same attraction for the Native imagination.[11]

Nevertheless, like their Protestant American counterparts, the two priests soon realised that converting the Native people was far more difficult than their own propaganda often implied. Certainly such an attitude seems clear in Demers's words to a colleague when he contemplated his future in his new diocese of Victoria, for he noted that he was now "charged" with the conversion of "more than 30,000 savages, plunged for the most part in the darkness of infidelity!" It was becoming increasingly evident to some

Catholic clergy that most of the Native peoples of the region were not really interested in accepting any form of Christianity.[12]

✦ Early Oblate Views of the Natives

EVANGELISING THE NATIVE PEOPLE remained the ostensible reason for the Oblates coming to the far west and they remained the major Oblate audience until the end of the nineteenth century. Numerically, the Natives were dominant. Until the beginning of railway construction in the early 1880s, they represented well over half the population of British Columbia. In his first report to Mazenod of 1861 on the state of the Oblate Native Missions, their local superior, Louis D'Herbomez admitted that they had still only scratched the surface, and that most Natives were "still plunged into the darkness and the shadow of death." He also noted that the first requirement for converting them must be to learn their "barbarous language," which, he insisted, the Oblates had already achieved "with as much facility as their mother tongue."[13]

The "barbarous language" to which D'Herbomez referred was the Chinook Jargon, which the Native peoples of the region had used for many years as a lingua franca and a means of communicating and trading with other tribes who spoke one of the six distinct languages in the far west that had evolved by the late eighteenth century out of "fifty-four mutually unintelligible languages," reflecting the rich cultural diversity of the area. Because of its intended narrow use, Chinook had little grammar, no more than 700 words, and was relatively easy to master. The earliest European visitors to the far west quickly learned Chinook, and, like the Natives, had mainly done so for trading purposes.[14]

The preached mission, as it did among European Canadians, remained a major Oblate tool in their attempt to convert the Native people. In 1861 D'Herbomez referred to a six-week long mission he had preached in the summer of 1859 to the Saanich people whose central settlement was on a peninsula north of Victoria. Declaring it an enormous success, D'Herbomez reported that "over four hundred [Native] infants" were baptised, and "over two thousand [adult] Indians" amended their ways by renouncing "gambling, shaman medicine, murdering and drinking, etc." He was convinced that their transformation was now complete and that the "beautiful example of their conversion" could be used to impress the other Native peoples of the region to follow suit.[15]

This early mission was preached in Chinook, a practice some Oblates were still following as late as the 1950s. In so doing, the Oblates were merely following a method used by most Christian missionaries in the region. Being a jargon and with little nuance, Chinook had never been intended for such a purpose. However, most Christian missionaries, like D'Herbomez, believed it enhanced their authority with the Natives, and so they usually had Native interpreters translate the priest's mixture of Chinook, French or English into the local language. In time, more circumspect missionaries realised that Native comprehension of what they were actually saying was usually quite limited and so their attempts to communicate were largely meaningless.[16]

Nevertheless, Oblate mission techniques did impress some local Europeans. One Protestant missionary noted that because the Oblates had "the art of making themselves understood and feared by the Indians," they possessed "considerable influence over them." Bishop George Hills, the first Anglican bishop of British Columbia, claimed that, while the Oblates were extremely active and had lessened drunkenness among the Natives, they had essentially done so by playing on the "excessive superstition" of the Native in order to "create reverence" for the Catholic priest.[17]

Even so, and while initially the Oblates spent only a few years on Vancouver Island, their brief presence apparently left an indelible mark, particularly on the Island's secular clergy. Due largely to their far better organization and the discipline of their rule, the Oblates did appear to be much more successful in their ministry to Natives. As to the actual depth of Native conversion to Christianity, few Europeans would then have asked the question. Paternalistic assumptions reigned supreme and when challenged, the evidence indicates that the Natives did what they had to do in order to survive in the face of the overwhelming dominance of European culture. Total acceptance of Christianity by the Native people, especially if this meant rejecting their own culture, remained quite rare.[18]

✟ Early Oblate Mission Settlements

BY 1861, due to their determination to establish themselves on the mainland and gain their independence from Demers, the Oblates had founded Missions at Okanagan Lake (1859) and at New Westminster (1860) and Mission outposts at Port Douglas, Hope and Yale on the lower Fraser River. The two major Missions gave the Oblates a prominence in these regions and an early, strong and independent presence among the Native people in the far west.

Father Charles Pandosy (AD)

Charles Pandosy founded the first permanent Oblate Mission on the mainland in October 1859 when he inaugurated the Oblate district of the Immaculate Conception with its central Mission in the large and fertile Okanagan Valley. Over ten years before, in May 1847, John Nobili, along with another Jesuit, Anthony Goetz, had been the first Catholic missionaries to visit the Valley where he founded St. Joseph's Mission, but due to personality conflicts between the two men as well as the physical hardships, they had abandoned the Mission a year later. This would not be the case with Pandosy who would spend many years there and who almost immediately recognised the valley's great agricultural potential, especially as a centre for fruit production. He deserves major recognition in planting some of its earliest orchards, a fact that, among Europeans, ultimately made him something of a local folk hero.[19]

Earlier in his career, Pandosy had also been a personification of the Oblates' initial presence in the interior of the Oregon-Washington Territories and their subsequent move to British North America. He had been among the first Oblates to arrive with Augustin Blanchet in October 1847 and he had soon turned his attention to the conversion of the Yakimas of the region and had remained there despite the warfare that followed the Whitman massacre of 29 November 1847 and the subsequent withdrawal of other Oblates. Until 1859, he tried to act as a confidant and advisor to the Natives and as a mediator between the Yakimas and Americans. Ultimately it was to prove an impossible situation, since the judgement of both sides constantly shifted between viewing him as a friend and then a foe. Such ambivalence, when added to local racism, especially among the Americans, and the constant battles with the Blanchet brothers who had tried to deny the Oblates their canonical right to be largely independent of the two local ordinaries, all this constituted an unresolvable predicament for both Pandosy and the Oblates.[20] In the end, with Pandosy's departure for far western British North America in 1859, the Oblates lost their local Mission to the Yakima and also sustained over twelve thousand dollars in property loss and damage, for which they were never compensated by either the Blanchet brothers or the American government.[21]

Within a few months of closing their Mission to the Yakima, and against this depressing backdrop, Pandosy and another Oblate priest, Pierre Richard (1854–1907) arrived at what would be a far more hospitable location in the Okanagan Valley. A packer, William Pion, and a settler, Cyprian Laurence had also joined their little company. Their first six months, though spent in tents, were reasonably comfortable due to the relatively mild winter. In the spring, the two priests located a suitable site for their Mission on the banks of the l'Anse su Sable River, later named in their memory

Okanagan Church (AD)

"Mission Creek." Late in November 1860, Richard filed papers at the Rock Creek land office for "160 acres of land near the shore on the eastside of Okanagan Lake." With the help of a recently arrived Oblate Brother, Philippe Surel (1859–1908), Richard immediately began construction of a house, that also served as a chapel. All of the initial necessities of the new Mission were covered by their first annual allocation from D'Herbomez of $800. These included building equipment and materials as well as seed which consisted of one minot (i.e., 8.58 gallons) each of oats, barley, wheat and peas, a small quantity of corn and eight minots of potatoes. In all, it seemed a very promising beginning for the first permanent Oblate Mission on the mainland of what, with Confederation into Canada in 1871, would become the province of British Columbia.[22]

The next establishment there, and destined to be their headquarters, was St. Charles Mission at New Westminster with Port Douglas, Hope and Yale as outposts. Léon Fouquet (1859–1912) and Charles Grandidier (1860–82), together with Brothers George Blanchet (1859–1906) and Gaspar Janin (1858–80), were the founders of this historic Mission. Such early foundations were based on an agreement that the Oblates had signed with Demers on 1 September 1860 that officially permitted them to found permanent Missions on the mainland of his enormous diocese. Log structures at New Westminster and Hope, where Grandidier had settled, served as initial house-churches. As in the Okanagan, the Oblates at New Westminster planted crops, mainly potatoes, although there are no details regarding the size of their first crop. However, since they were near a growing European settlement, they could readily purchase food supplies, unlike the situation at their far more isolated Okanagan Mission.

By 1861, under Brother Blanchet's direction, the Oblates had built two churches in New Westminster on small lots, which the government had previously granted to Demers in 1860. The larger church measured 40 by 20 feet and was designated for the use of the hundred or so local Europeans; it was blessed and dedicated to St. Peter by Demers on 12 July 1861. About 300 yards from there, a second church, dedicated St. Charles was set aside for the area's three to four thousand Native peoples of the Stó:lô tribe. Later that year a second Mission church, named St. Mary's, was built nearer the centre of the Stó:lô settlements about 30 miles east of New Westminster.[23]

For months, Fouquet and Grandidier preached Native missions from New Westminster to Yale and baptised hundreds of Native infants. The focus of their missions was on temperance. European influence in the region, as on Vancouver Island, was wreaking havoc on Native society. Fouquet complained that since the Fraser River gold rush the Natives were in a "state worse than barbarism." He blamed their plight mainly on "unprincipled white men" who had "infected them with horrible corruption...and the foul practices which accompany the scum of a degraded civilisation." As a consequence, he asserted that hundreds of Natives were "never sober," since they regularly drank a concoction supplied to them by European traders made of alcohol, camphor, and tobacco juice. Fouquet wrote that they went around the area in bands "fighting, killing one another and howling like wild beasts." But even more horrible than this, he reported, "brothers kill brothers and drunken fathers stab their innocent children."[24]

As propaganda and as signs of past success, Fouquet and Grandidier used Native converts from D'Herbomez's Saanich mission as witnesses of what could be done once temperance became an established way of life. By 1862, Fouquet noted that four thousand Natives had joined Oblate inspired temperance societies. To enforce temperance pledges, after the mission was over, the Oblates enlisted local elders or leaders to act both as judges and to impose public humiliations upon those individuals who strayed by breaking their promises.[25]

The Oblate temperance campaign was certainly not that significant nor lasting, yet many Europeans seemed impressed. Governor James Douglas, who had prohibited the sale of alcohol to the Natives in 1858, publicly supported the Oblate efforts in 1863, noting that he had "never seen the Indians so sober." *The British Columbian* praised and congratulated the Oblate efforts for the increased "cleanliness" among the Natives, and especially in "their marked abstinence from drink and disorderly conduct." Fouquet believed that Oblate progress had been possible because the Native people viewed the Catholic priest as "God's ambassador." Yet, many Natives continued to drink and ultimately rejected conversion to Christianity, temperance, and other "white ways." But in the early 1860s, these realities were rarely mentioned. The Europeans, including the Oblates, remained largely unable or unwilling to comprehend the reasons for the persistent resistance, which was probably largely prompted by feelings of despair in many Native people, especially when faced with the conflicting realities of European racism set against the Oblate plan of acculturating them into "white" civilisation.[26]

Although Demers insisted that he wished the Oblates to remain, his behaviour did not support that conclusion. He did not even respond to D'Herbomez's repeated requests to inform him of Demers's future plans for the Oblates, a fact that confirms Demers's very poor administrative skills. The two men also had several angry confrontations over their irreconcilable differences, especially regarding the canonical independence of the Oblates from Demers. By 1863 Demers knew that D'Herbomez was only waiting for word from Rome regarding the establishment of a vicariate apostolic on the mainland that would finally allow him and the Oblates to leave both Vancouver Island and Demers for good.[27]

At last, on 14 December 1863, the Oblates made their official break when Rome formally divided Demers's huge diocese by erecting the mainland into the vicariate apostolic of New Westminster. With Louis D'Herbomez as its first vicar apostolic (1863–90), the new ecclesiastical district would remain directly under first Rome and then Quebec until 1871, when it became a suffragan see in the newly established ecclesiastical province of St. Boniface, Manitoba, which was headed by another Oblate, Archbishop Alexandre Taché (1850–94). A new chapter was about to open for the Oblates and the Catholic Church in British Columbia. Its ultimate implementation also fulfilled Mazenod's plan that "his sons" in British Columbia be under the episcopal authority of their "brother" Oblates so that they would be finally freed from the interference of any local secular bishops.[28]

5

Trying to Transform a People

✤ *Early Attempts*

WHILE THE OBLATES FELT A NEW SENSE OF INDEPENDENCE, this feeling was certainly not true for the Native people of the region. While Natives were the majority population throughout the province until the early 1880s, even for those who lived closest to European settlements, this fact provided them with little protection from a far more technologically sophisticated and aggressive culture. The Stó:lô of the Lower Fraser Valley, living near New Westminster, were particularly vulnerable to the effects of "white" culture. This also meant that they were the closest to the new Oblate headquarters and would thus become the first Native people on the mainland to experience an organized program of Oblate ministry, which, in effect, meant European acculturation.

The cultural invasion by the Oblates and other Europeans could best be described by the anthropological term: acculturation, which has many possible interpretations. It can be passively directive, such as through encouraging the observance of the moral behaviour of those from one culture who wish to influence another culture with regard to the inherent superiority of the former. This would certainly be one way of defining the gospel-culture of nonviolent change through individual and communal love as laid down by Jesus. An historic example of this approach was undertaken by the seventeenth century founder of Pennsylvania and Quaker, William Penn, who tried to implement such a vision of acculturation in his own colony. Another and far more usual understanding of the term would be that of bringing about cultural change through aggression, such as military subjugation or even slavery. This approach normally sees no value in the culture of the "conquered" group, and so gives them no right of effective control over their own lives, and might even segregate them from the dominant culture. A third and presumably more "benign" application of this interpretation of acculturation was by means of "re-education" that either demeaned or dismissed the subjugated culture, and that still had as its ultimate aim the total destruction and then assimilation of the "conquered" society. It was this last understanding of acculturation that was almost always followed by the Oblates and most other missionaries.

The Oblates hoped ultimately to make the Stó:lô into "good" European Canadians by some form of "reduction." Most missionaries had always considered such an approach to be a more compassionate, less racist and violent form of acculturation. It was probably only more dishonest, for, by essentially dismissing or demeaning Native culture, its final objective was equally destructive. What the Oblates really wanted to do to the Stó:lô and the Native people in general was to "save" them from being who they already were, or, in a word, themselves.[1]

✣ The Coast Salish Culture

THE CULTURE OF THE COAST SALISH, and of the Stó:lô people in particular, that is their entire way of life, including language, history, religion, technology, is part of a much larger Native cultural area that extends from Alaska to northern California. Although there was much diversity in each culture, and while interior tribes, due to their harsher climate, found the need to minimize cultural complexity, still, because of frequent contacts, there were also many similarities. The Stó:lô personify many of the elements in the complex cultural web that makes up the Native peoples of this vast region. The lands of the Coast Salish stretched along the Lower Fraser

Valley from the European settlements of Yale to Roberts Bank, and contained 14 independent tribes of which the Stó:lô were one.[2]

Prior to the Fraser River gold rush of 1858, which brought the first great wave of European settlement to the area, Stó:lô culture had retained much of its precontact integrity. The complex political and economic elements of Stó:lô culture were all based on a strong social cohesion. Stó:lô politics was also cooperative and kinship based. Prestige and social station were founded upon wealth and rank, such as the largest plank dwelling, number of wives, weapons, and masks. The most respected person in this regard was the *siam* or principal elder, a man who obtained and kept his position through his recognized natural abilities, which included both knowledge and honest admission of failings. However, the *siam* did not rule like eastern Native chiefs, but rather arbitrated or helped to direct social and economic events such as marriage or potlatching arrangements, dealing with property exchanges, including spiritual artifacts. Masks were especially important in this regard, since by their transfer they symbolized a corresponding shift in power within the value system of kinship, rank and wealth. The warrior who protected the village was also considered a type of *siam* since his unique skills too were viewed as being based upon acquiring, keeping and using special spiritual powers.[3]

The extended Stó:lô family was the economic heart of each Stó:lô settlement, which meant the leading families, their relatives and slaves. Slaves were usually acquired during raids on other tribes, and were often bartered in return for Stó:lô slaves who had been captured in a similar manner. Each nuclear family lived in large plank houses that formed the core or "winter" village of between 50 to 75 or more adults and to which they returned from less substantial seasonal dwellings that were established for the sole purpose of fishing, berry and root gathering. Their economy depended upon women, the elderly and the young as gatherers and able-bodied men as the hunters and fishermen, essentially of salmon, the major food staple. Salmon was a local staple that was shared with other Native people throughout the region. Warfare for fishing stocks occurred, although it appears to have been quite rare due largely to their great abundance.[4]

Siams, as heads of villages or families, were not in theory hereditary, though the *siam* usually selected and trained his successor, often a relative. However, this was not always the case, either because a *siam* was childless or, due to perceived spiritual powers, someone in another family was judged to be called to such a position. The possession of more than one wife, perhaps the most frequent criticism leveled against the Native people by all missionaries, usually indicated high rank and wealth, especially in the case of a *siam*. Divorce was rare and viewed as a sign of insecurity and inferiority, and, when practiced, was usually limited to the "lower" classes, who as a sign of their status, normally had only one wife.[5]

Europeans, in later imposing their own cultural interpretations, misconceived the position of the Stó:lô *siam* who were not owners but only guardians or protectors of a particular community's wealth, especially land. However, the Europeans concluding that the *siam* "owned" such wealth, confused the *siams* with the chiefs of eastern tribes whose powers were closer to that of European monarchs. This error began with Simon Fraser, and, until recently, due largely to the deep-seated cultural prejudice and ignorance among Europeans, both Indian agents and missionaries continued to hold such views.[6]

Class structure was maintained by the fact that the children of the socially prominent were more carefully trained in such areas as spirituality and tradition when compared to those in classes below them. The potlatch, which comes from a Chinook word meaning "to freely give," was an important means of maintaining or increasing such class prestige, particularly at major events such as marriages and funerals. It was also used to reinforce social position at times of communal celebrations by which a rich person, man or woman, would give away much of their wealth, usually in the form of food and clothing, and by so doing heighten their class standing in the community.[7]

Social ethics among the Stó:lô were not directly linked to spiritual or religious sanctions, but rather were based on the powerful influence of public opinion. As a result, by means of such social instruments as public shaming, which heightened social approval or disapproval, a person, of whatever rank, was compelled to conform or could be excluded, which in the extreme, such as capital crime, could mean complete social ostracism from the community. In theory, at least, such a circumstance could lead ultimately to death from starvation.[8]

Stó:lô religious power, though often founded on property and blood, had to be acquired through spirit quests and then publicly recognized and socially accepted by the tribe. Thus, indicating a definite form of monotheism, the Stó:lô believed that the "Great Spirit" chose and equipped certain people who had the inclination (grace) to search for their own personal "guardian" spirit, and, who, in turn, were expected to guide others to do the same. These persons were the healers or shamans, who could be male or female, and who usually helped others in need. The shamans were of three classes or orders: doctor, seer and witch; and, while roles could overlap, usually they remained distinct. Normally the first two classes were made up of men and the third of women. While any of them could impose curses, this appeared to be a rare use of their power. Their activities were especially prominent during the winter dance season, but they also assisted throughout the year in curing spiritual or physical illness as well as acting as midwifes and predicting future events. They also conducted funerals, which included preparing, burying the body and praying over and for the dead in their journey to the afterlife. If they were not already from a prominent family, then those who possessed such powers gained in social importance.[9]

As for cultural religious syncretism, the Stó:lô were as comfortable as other coastal and interior peoples, and had already begun to adapt and adopt Christian blessings as part of their own spirituality long before the arrival of Christian missionaries such as the Oblates. Native guides and employees of the HBC appear to be the earliest transmitters of Christian ideas among the Native peoples of the far west. This was certainly true of baptism, and there is even evidence that they introduced "confession," usually to a shaman or *siam* as part of their syncretic borrowing. While Christianity, during the early centuries of its own development, had itself borrowed very heavily from other religious traditions, especially Jewish and Hellenistic, by then there was no social memory of that fact. Thus syncretism, the essential basis of all religions, including Christianity, would have seemed anathema to almost all Europeans, and certainly this would have included the Oblates.[10]

The education of children among the Stó:lô was both structured and ongoing and contained a common philosophical and spiritual orientation. Thus the spiritual, personal and material worlds were not divided but integrated. Schooling was a part of children's everyday existence. They were constantly taught how to behave, the importance of the spirit world, what happened at puberty, how to hunt, to carve, to weave, to cook, and how to determine a person's rank or station. In addition, folk tales were related to the next generation through Native "bards" who traveled about and received room and board in exchange for imparting their wisdom. In short,

Stó:lô education, like all Native education, stressed instruction that essentially depended upon looking, listening and learning, or "the three Ls."[11]

Even before the Fraser River gold rush of 1858 their initial contacts with earlier European traders had brought about some changes in Stó:lô social, political and economic realities. When the HBC fort at Fort Langley was established in 1827, some Stó:lô moved nearby in order to take advantage of trade, employment as well as protection from potential Native enemies. The Fort's journals relate how the Stó:lô as well as other tribes felt shielded by the Fort's defenses, lessening their fear of raids from traditional enemies. In the case of the Stó:lô, this would have been the Cowichan of Vancouver Island, who appear to have frequently intercepted Stó:lô fur hunting expeditions. Forts were also viewed as convenient locations at which tribes could "corner the market" in trading with the HBC, and so they highly resented it if a fort were moved or closed without their knowledge. In the coming years other HBC forts at Victoria, Hope and Yale attracted the Stó:lô and other Native peoples for similar reasons.[12]

These early interactions between the Europeans and the Stó:lô as well as other Native peoples influenced social, political, economic and general cultural blending and enrichment. They increased intermarriage between the Europeans and the Stó:lô and between the Stó:lô and other coastal peoples. European staples such as the potato were also added to traditional Stó:lô root diets, as were less desirable items such as tobacco and alcohol, but especially diseases that would be introduced by Europeans, which no doubt included the Oblates.[13]

✤ The Basis of Oblate Methods for Converting the Stó:lô

FROM THE OUTSET D'HERBOMEZ hoped to achieve among the Stó:lô a level of control, essentially by means of preached missions, that would ultimately turn a Stó:lô village into a type of reduction. The classic and most extreme examples of Mission reductions were those operated by the Jesuits, especially in sixteenth and seventeenth century Paraguay where well over fifty such self-supporting, church-centered and missionary-controlled villages were founded. The governing principle of such reductions was that the Natives could be converted to both Christianity and western civilization only if they were isolated from their own former culture and such evil influences of western civilization as drinking and gambling, or any contacts with bad, immoral Europeans. Instead, they were subjected only to what the missionary judged was "good" in western civilization. In what was a very paternalistic system, their Native "children" were expected to learn what was ultimately "best" for them from their missionary "fathers."

Central to such a system was the destruction of the entire Native culture, which almost all missionaries had always generally believed promoted laziness and moral corruption. As such, heading the list of those things that had to be destroyed was the "idolatrous" system of Native spirituality. Therefore, the Jesuits sought to turn the essentially nomadic Natives of Paraguay into model "western" Christian peasant farmers who would be under the care of their "feudal" missionary priest overlords. This strict, top-down constitution of absolute control is reflected in the fact that no Native was ever allowed to become a priest. So, when in 1767 the Jesuits were finally expelled from Latin America by the governments of Portugal and Spain, the reductions quickly disintegrated.[14]

The Oblates adopted and adapted such methods, but they never achieved such extreme levels of control due mainly to Stó:lô proximity to European settlers as well as Stó:lô resistance, both direct and indirect, to such programs. The general concept of the reduction, especially its central element of total clerical control, formed more or less the basis of all Oblate Missions. Among the many tools that the Oblates employed to achieve such control were the public celebrations of feast days, especially Marian ones, including Eucharistic processions and other pageants.

Reflecting their Jansenistic spirituality which emphasized the "virtue" of suffering, the Oblates placed special stress upon Stó:lô participation in passion plays. By means of a series of tableaux that represented various stages in Christ's passion, a Native person portrayed Jesus "from Bethlehem to Calvary." According to one eyewitness account, and reflecting, rather than a strong Jesus who challenged the status quo, especially social injustice, instead a milk toast portrayal of Christ seemed the norm, for all the Native persons selected for these roles were "strangely alike in face and figure; less sturdy than their companions,...with a plaintive, loving sweetness so well suited to the character they represented." Also in the final tableaux, Christ was not played by a Native, but by a large crucifix on which was affixed a "white" European-featured statue. It reflected what was true of most attempts by Europeans to acculturate Natives, namely, that "God" was "white," and so no matter how hard a non-European might try, a major

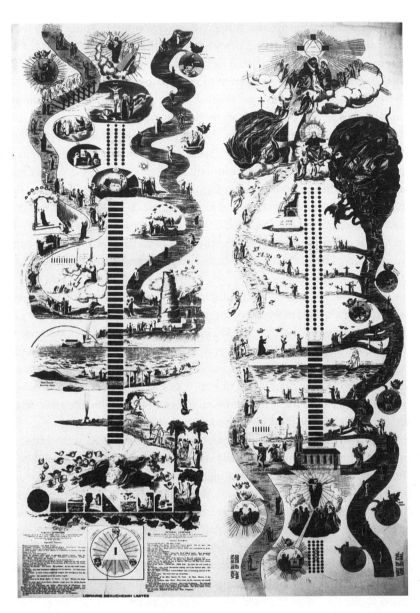

The Catholic Ladder (AD)

implication of such an approach was that "non-whites" could never be truly equal to their new "masters." Whether consciously or not, the Oblates too promoted such racism.[15]

Ultimately the residential school would be the major means of gaining cultural control, especially among the next generation of Stó:lô. Unlike day schools, which were never very successful, mainly because of very sporadic attendance, ideally students at a residential school were to be isolated from both Stó:lô and secular European influences. Besides religion, they were to learn manual skills and basic education. While the Oblates would have liked more schools throughout the region, they could not afford to do so until the federal government began to finance them in the 1890s. While other denominations would participate as well, the Catholic Church and the Oblates would become the major partners with Ottawa in making such institutions a reality throughout Canada, and British Columbia would have a major share of such institutions. Yet almost every method of acculturation, and especially the residential school, had its roots in the concept of the reduction that the Oblates tried to firmly establish on the local Stó:lô reserves.

In attempting to put the reduction into operation, one of the Oblate's most important teaching tools was the Catholic Ladder. Its inventor appears to have been Norbert Blanchet who saw its major potential as a Native catechetical instrument. The Ladder consisted of a chart painted or printed on cloth or paper or carved into a Sahale stick, Chinook for "a stick from above." At one end of the chart or stick were forty marks representing the 40 centuries before Christ, then there were 33 marks standing for Christ's life, followed by 18 marks each representing a century, plus marks for each year of the nineteenth century to the present. This simple and ingenious device was essentially a time line beginning with creation and continuing with the fall of the angels, Adam and Eve, the coming of Christ, and his death and resurrection. Completing the Ladder were the major events since the beginning of Catholic Church history. The Ladder became an important instruction device, particularly during missions, and afterwards it would usually be taught to Native leaders, such as the Stó:lô *siam*, with the expectation that they would continue to impart its message.

The Ladder also intensified local sectarianism, dragging centuries-old European religious conflicts into the far west. Printed versions of the Catholic Ladder referred to the Reformation by depicting Protestants, such as Luther and Calvin, being literally dragged down to hell. Protestants responded with an equally bigoted brand of the Ladder which, not surprisingly, echoing Catholic theology, showed Roman Catholics, especially popes, being consigned to eternal flames. No doubt, when Native people compared both versions, this element of the Ladder must have seemed at least a strange, if not a humorous one, as well as a very graphic contradiction of the supposed Christian "love" for one another.[16]

The Ladder had played an important role in the earliest visits of Catholic missionaries to the Stó:lô. Norbert Blanchet first used it in 1839 in preaching a mission to the Whidby Island Salish, and in the following year he employed it in his only contacts with the Stó:lô. At that time he described several elements of Stó:lô culture, and, as usual among most missionaries, Blanchet judged the practice of polygamy, which, as observed, in Stó:lô culture was a sign of social standing and responsibility, as an "abomination." Such prejudices revealed more about Blanchet and his fellow missionaries, including the Oblates, than it did about the Stó:lô, especially the European obsession with "pelvic morality."

This incident was also important, since it was the first time that Catholic missionaries visited the mainland, prompted essentially by their fear that Protestants had already arrived. This was the central purpose of Blanchet's visit to the Stó:lô in 1840. In the following year, fearful that Presbyterians from the Walla Walla area intended to convert the Stó:lô to "heresy," Demers again traveled there, though he discovered no "heretics." However, Demers reported that he preached in Chinook to about 1500 Stó:lô at their summer camp near Fort Langley, presented them with the Catholic Ladder, sang several hymns in Chinook, baptized about 400 infants, and finally taught them to make the sign of the Cross. In 1842, in the face of similar rumors that the "heretics" were again on the march into New Caledonia, the Jesuit missionary, Peter DeSmet visited the Stó:lô, though the Protestants were still nowhere to be seen.[17]

The Oblates, like Blanchet, Demers and DeSmet before them, believed that the Stó:lô were essentially "heathen," because they did not believe in a Supreme Being, which was not true, nor in such western, Hellenistic concepts as the soul, as well as "mortal" sin or salvation through Christ. D'Herbomez was convinced that before he could convert them, he had to first civilise the Stó:lô, whom he initially described as "savage hordes whose many vices degraded human nature." To do this, he hoped to establish among the Stó:lô a "model reduction" that would include both schools and a hospital, so that they might ultimately become both "good" Catholics and "good" Canadians.[18]

In achieving their aim, which meant the ultimate destruction of Stó:lô culture, the Oblates definitely had some understanding of that culture. In preaching early missions, the Oblates apparently hoped to enhance their position and gain respect and spiritual power among the Stó:lô. They tried to convince their listeners that they too were *siams* whose Christian God, or "the great one from on high" in Chinook, had far greater power than the Stó:lô spirits, who the Oblates tried to convince their Native audience were all "demons"; objectives which the priests also attempted to accomplish through the use of Oblate hymns and other Catholic rites. To communicate these ideas to their audience, the Oblates used Chinook and French, which was then "translated" by Saanich interpreters. Since these interpreters spoke a dialect quite different than Stó:lô, much of the meaning of what the Oblates were trying to teach was undoubtedly lost on their hearers. As they had done on Vancouver Island and in the United States, in the interval between missionary contacts, the Oblates appointed Stó:lô men as catechists and/or watchmen who were expected to lead regular prayer services and teach their tribe by using such tools as the Catholic Ladder. They were also expected to report any lapsed participants to the priest whenever they were able to visit. Such reporting was especially important for those who wished to be baptised.[19]

The Oblates baptised Native infants immediately, since they frequently died soon afterwards, mainly through contracting European diseases such as smallpox, often from the very missionaries who had baptised them. But the Oblates would only baptise those Stó:lô adults, like Saanich adults, who, for at least a year, had kept their temperance pledges, were clearly following the directives of the Oblate appointed Native watchmen and/ or catechists, and who were giving good example by publicly performing daily prayers. This was not an Oblate innovation, but had been considered prudent Catholic missionary practice for centuries in order to avoid the "superficial" Christianization of the Native people. However, given the propaganda value of the "numbers' game," it was often practiced more as the exception than the rule. Nevertheless, Mazenod took such a practice very seriously, and it was certainly the recommendation of the Oblate Canonical Visitor, Bermond, who in 1858 suggested that "the longer the wait the better." Bermond believed that a year should be the absolute minimum preparation for the baptism of Native adults and at least a second year should pass before their reception of first communion.[20]

A key element in the early Oblate ministry to the Stó:lô, as it had been to the Saanich and other Natives in the United States, was the establishment and maintenance of temperance societies. At the large annual reunions, or whenever the opportunity presented itself, there were meetings at which a missionary preached and Natives made bold public declarations of abstinence and equally open admissions of failure. Most Europeans, including the Oblates, believed that Natives, because of "their childlike nature," were more "easily led astray by unprincipled [white] men," and so it was assumed a weaker moral character lead them to "more naturally" succumb to the "vile drink" than "whites" would. While "public shaming" was a traditional method of moral control and betterment in Stó:lô as well as other local Native cultures, it was based on individual responsibility and was never intended to deliberately patronize, which was a central element of the Oblate temperance agenda. The idea of public confession and public penance represented a major means of shaming those who had fallen, and of teaching those who had not the consequences of failure. The Oblates, Demers and Blanchet had all used such methods, including the appointment of a watchman, often a *siam*, to maintain surveillance over everyone between meetings and to report any lapses to the priest. Those "converted" to temperance, after a communal pledge were given a "ticket" that symbolized their commitment and which, in a public shaming, would be ceremoniously taken from them if they failed to keep their promise.[21]

The task of the watchman, who often doubled as a catechist, was essential to the maintenance of a temperance society. Not only did they report to the priest regarding those who had "fallen," but even more importantly they were expected to conduct daily morning and evening prayer services and special services on Sunday. If they were *siams*, the watchmen naturally held a superior position, but whoever filled the role, their major task was to represent the priest and report to him all "sins" upon his next visit, and so they would provide the Oblate missionary with a method of control of a Stó:lô group between visits. Besides drinking, a vigilant watchman might also report adultery, failure to repay debts, gambling and especially resorting to shamans, which the Oblates saw as a "very serious" sin. In addition to public humiliations, sinners were also fined money or some other penalty at special "trials" that were presided over by the *siam* and/or watchman, but,

Our Lady of Lourdes, St. Mary's Mission, Mission City, British Columbia (AD)

reflecting the paternalistic nature of the traditional reduction, whose "verdicts" were under the final control of the priest.[22]

Clearly, good behaviour for the reception of baptism went well beyond only temperance and required a whole new lifestyle similar to the Jesuit-inspirited reductions of Latin America which were now to be replicated in British Columbia. This was to mirror both western and "Catholic" ways including the renunciation of polygamy, refusing marriages with Europeans that had not been blessed by the Catholic Church, and, apparently the most serious of all, calling upon a shaman in time of illness. All were part of a continually growing Oblate list of requirements of what it meant to be a "good" Canadian, and ultimately, and far more importantly, a "good" Native Catholic. In fact, even consulting with elders as teachers of traditional Native ways was viewed as practicing superstition, and so the Oblates considered such behaviour to be serious and sinful. Over time, farming as the Oblates did, "proper" Sunday dress, and even living in European-style homes were added to the list of acculturation.[23]

Trying to Transform a People

The Oblates constantly struggled to expand upon the ways western "Catholic" culture could be imposed upon or translated into Stó:lô culture. As with other tribes, the Oblates tried to "translate" Stó:lô into a combination of Chinook Jargon combined with either French or English prayers and hymns that were then printed in Roman lettered transliterations. Easter and Christmas celebrations, as well as a summer reunions, reflecting the times of traditional Stó:lô gatherings, usually twice a year in the late spring and early summer, were celebrated with great festivity at the central Mission of St. Mary's, and reportedly such celebrations brought out large numbers of Native peoples. At this time catechism lessons were given, and those Stó:lô who had been judged faithful by the Oblates for at least a year were baptised. This was also considered "good example," so that others present would ultimately want to follow the example of these new Christians. In addition, these gatherings were used to administer smallpox vaccine, especially to the children.[24]

In 1869 a Sister of St. Ann, Mary Lumena Brasseur described one of these large meetings. The Stó:lô *siams* along with their entourage arrived at St. Mary's Mission by boat, each group being greeted with salutes of gunfire, and then they proceeded in a more or less formal procession towards the church. When they reached the front of the church they first shook hands with each other and then entered the building for a brief time where D'Herbomez and other Oblates welcomed them with more handshaking. After the opening ceremony, sufficient tents were erected on the grounds to hold upwards of two thousand people. In precontact times, such gatherings would have been devoted to commemorating important natural or community events, such as the inauguration of a new *siam*, and which, like other tribes of the northwest coast, would have centered on potlatching. Under the Oblates, such "superstitions" had now given way to Catholic celebrations such as Corpus Christi processions and passion plays.[25]

✤ Early Oblate Schools Among the Stó:lô

THE OBLATES VIEWED FORMAL EDUCATION as a vital means of gaining influence over and future control of the Native people. St. Charles Mission at New Westminster, which would become their headquarters, became an important initial testing ground for Native residential education. For it was near St. Charles that the first local model Residential School of St.

Mary's for Stó:lô boys was founded in 1862 by a 28-year-old French Oblate, Florimond Gendre (1862–73). Again using a reduction model, D'Herbomez considered such schools as essential means of forming Stó:lô youths into future "Catholic citizens," or, essentially, "docile and obedient" followers of the Catholic clergy. Such a Stó:lô would ideally be separated forever from the evils of both the surrounding European culture of New Westminster as well as the Native or "pagan" superstitions that the Oblates hoped would eventually become part of a forgotten Stó:lô past.[26]

St. Mary's Mission Residential School began with 42 boys. Though Gendre taught them reading and writing in English, the thrust of the school was to prepare future Native farmers, so gardening and general farming methods formed the core of the curriculum. With the desire of making them good "Canadian" citizens as well as good Catholics, he took them on annual outings to New Westminster to celebrate Queen Victoria's birthday. In trying to adjust his teaching skills, the priest also studied Stó:lô education methods, especially the three L's of looking, listening and learning. As for discipline, the school approved of physical punishment ranging from writing, kneeling, extra work, confinement, public humiliation, whippings, and the ultimate one, expulsion. However, as an alternative to such traditional methods, to reinforce good behaviour, Gendre also used a rewards system. Prizes were given for such things as reporting mischief, taking good care of tools, or tutoring other students. D'Herbomez presented such prizes, one of which allowed the recipient to use the title: "Captain of the Holy Angels" for a term during which he had the right to carry a flag on which the words: "Jesus Christ *Rex Angelorum*" were emblazoned. With the hope of passing on their faith, if not also their practical learning, Gendre expected that during their summer holidays with their families, his pupils would act as catechists and instruct their relatives in the faith. A few years later, before his tragic death in a hunting accident in 1870, another Oblate, Denis Lamure (1868–70) started a brass band at the school. This particularly impressed the European settlers in the area, who apparently found it hard to even imagine that "savages" could learn such skills.[27]

Stó:lô girls were the next to be included, along with Europeans, in these early educational plans at New Westminster. To achieve this, on 4 January 1865 D'Herbomez asked the Sisters of St. Ann for help. The first sisters had been brought from Quebec by Demers in 1858 and by then had established several schools and an orphanage on Vancouver Island. Now D'Herbomez

Sisters of St. Ann in the yard of the View Street Convent (School), 1863:

(l-r) Sister M. de la Croix, Sister M. Romuald, Sister M. Praxîde,

Sister M. des Sept-Douleurs. (ASSA)

wanted them to do the same in New Westminster by supplying "a definite number of subjects" to provide for "schools, orphanages and hospitals [among the Europeans] as well as establishing similar institutions for the savages." Perhaps the bishop believed that, by simple fiat, he could have an immediate and balanced complement of religious women equal to or even greater than that of the Oblates. The Mother General of the Sisters of St. Ann, who resided in Lachine, Quebec, Marie Jeanne de Chantel responded that the Oblates and D'Herbomez would first have to demonstrate equal willingness and responsibility in these areas before the Sisters of St. Ann would even consider such a request. The letter undoubtedly implied the tensions between the nuns and clergy, regular and secular, especially with regard to the clergy's inclination to dictate. Clearly, the sisters were not prepared to be at anyone's beck and call. In June 1865 the local superior in Victoria, Sister Marie de la Providence, however, finally did send two nuns. Sister Marie de la Conception, who had arrived in the area in 1858, was from

Students and Sisters in front of View Street School circa, late 1860s (ASSA)

an Irish family in Quebec, and thus could speak English. She was joined by Sister Marie des Sept-Douleurs, who, following the pioneer nuns of 1858, had come west with the second group in 1863. Together the two laid the foundation of St. Ann's Academy in New Westminster.[28]

The nuns had already learned in Victoria that local European racism demanded strict segregation of their schools, therefore, they followed such a policy from the beginning in establishing their school in New Westminster. When the school finally opened in September 1866, Sister Marie des Sept-Douleurs taught the initial 20 European students, of whom eleven were boarders. Her colleague, Sister Marie de la Conception instructed the 30 Stó:lô and Métis girls to whom she taught general learning and domestic work. As such, she held her classes in the school kitchen where her students helped to prepare the meals for everyone else, including the boarders and the two nuns. Reflecting the slow growth of the local "white" population and resulting competition for students, Mr. Burr, a teacher in the public school, which had been started in the same year, tried to convince the European day students and their parents to abandon the Academy for his institution. However, according to Sister Marie des Sept-Douleurs, the nuns ultimately triumphed by bribing the day pupils with promises of regular treats of candy.[29]

Reflecting the reduction model, and wishing to segregate the Stó:lô girls from the Europeans, as they had always done with the Native boys, in 1868 the Oblates opened the female division of St. Mary's Mission School, an event that demonstrated some of the early tensions between them and the Sisters of St. Ann. In line with these preparations, in 1867, the Mother General of the Sisters of St. Ann, Sister Marie Jeanne de Chantel, who was then making her first year-long visitation of the community's houses in British Columbia, visited the mainland. At St. Mary's Mission she entered into a more formal agreement with the Oblates to establish a Stó:lô girls' school. Each of the two founding sisters, Marie Luména and Marie de Bon Secours, would be paid $200 a year as well as an initial payment of $400 to cover convent furnishings, the building of which would be done by the Oblates. However, by the time the school opened in late November 1868, while the structure was ready, D'Herbomez had failed to supply the promised funds for furnishings, which the nuns had to provide for themselves. As a result, this meant, at least initially, that they did not even have the barest necessities each as beds, tables or chairs. In addition, during the first year the diet, which was limited to potatoes, was both unbalanced and in short supply because of miscalculations by the Oblates in planting the initial crop. When, due to a faulty scale, the two sisters and their charges consumed "too many" potatoes, the Oblates cut the already miserable rations still further. Not surprisingly, this early incident did not strengthen the initial relationship between the nuns and the Oblates, and reflected those disagreements between them that sometimes weakened the effectiveness of their ministry.[30]

In an attempt to improve conditions in the following year, the nuns worked to expand the diet at St. Mary's, both for themselves and their Stó:lô students. First, produce from a convent garden was complemented by a planned increase in the Oblate potato crop. Occasionally the two Sisters had flour to make bread for themselves, and, though rarely, they also made some extra bread as a reward for "good" students. Though no tuition was charged, Stó:lô parents were asked to give ten dollars a year to cover soap, thread, needles and other domestic supplies, including the sugar, which was used to flavour the herb tea that was drunk by both the students and staff. The Stó:lô also agreed to provide the nuns with two large barrels of fish, and after learning to smoke them, the sisters were able to provide fish for themselves and their "best-behaved" students.[31]

Each girl was expected to follow a strict code. Dress was one of the early examples of this. Some girls began to wear "fancy dresses" provided by their proud relatives. In order to avoid jealousy and counteract what their teachers viewed as unnecessary display and wastefulness, as well as to instill conformity, the Sisters introduced a school uniform consisting of a white bonnet, a brown blouse, and a calico skirt.[32]

The girls' curriculum included reading and writing, but the major emphasis was on domestic skills, especially sewing. This lead to the establishment of a small shop, which was funded from student profits from making and selling men's shirts, and where the nuns sold calicoes and flannel materials to Stó:lô women. As the girls' sewing skills improved, they were soon making altar linens, which lead to the establishment a Stó:lô Altar Society.[33]

In cooperation with the Sisters of St. Ann, the Oblate objective was to make Stó:lô children permanent and contented members of a "Catholic reduction." There they would learn to live in basic isolation from the western world around them. Such institutions were intended to prepare their students for this life, but especially for the next. The Oblates assumed that only a Catholic education was sound. Ideally, the family and state would, when they accepted its great value, became willing partners with the church in bringing such a hoped-for "reality" into being. In essence, it was again a type of model reduction or a "subculture within a western culture" stressing "Catholic theology and the moral taboos," especially sexual ones. And it was expected to transform its graduates into exemplary signs of the Christian life, especially when contrasted with the supposed less fortunate non-Catholic members of the larger society. Grounded on working class, French equivalents, a fact reflected in their basic curriculum and industrial nature, in the end the Stó:lô schools for both girls and boys were very similar to others that the Oblates would found throughout the region with the essential help of the Sisters of St. Ann as well as other female religious communities. Ideally, all such institutions were to create a "totally controlled environment" that would develop citizens for the only "true" civilisation, a Catholic-Christian one.[34]

After completing their studies, graduates were expected to return home to teach and lead their own families into a similar controlled, Catholic and ultramontane, or, in other words, into truly civilized patterns of community.

Such a scenario was doomed to failure because most Stó:lô refused to cooperate with such a plan. Moreover, after the coming of the railroad, the larger world would just not go away. In the end, neither the Oblates nor the Stó:lô could live in, what was in essence, a fantasy-like version of reality. Nevertheless, D'Herbomez was convinced that the schools were the major means of preparing a future generation that would be ready for such a "reality." And while probably fewer than five percent of Stó:lô children ever attended the two schools, they were expected to be the light, the salt, the leaven that would achieve such a "miracle" among the rest of the Stó:lô. By it the Oblates would create a "totally indigenous Catholic population." The Natives' ways, those "heathen beliefs that were the enemies to the truly Catholic ones," would be successfully discarded, or so the plan hoped. After this the Native people would be ready to join with the Métis and Europeans to become the ultimate "triumph of holy Church" in British Columbia. And in trying to achieve this final objective, the residential school would become the major engine.[35]

Such predictions were also intended for the Oblate and conservative French Catholic readers of *Missions*. The Oblate magazine, which began in 1862, was designed to increase communication between Oblate Missions around the world and to garner as much financial help as possible from lay subscribers. Though reports were supposed to be "simple and *true*," some "deliberate exaggerations" did "creep in," undoubtedly to impress lay readers. Although some Oblates later challenged some deliberately distorted accounts, especially the often extraordinary "success stories," most Oblates, and their lay supporters did believe and trust in the "truth" of what was frequently and carefully crafted Oblate propaganda.[36]

6

Early Influences

✤ *The Native People and the Secular Clergy*

UNLIKE THE OBLATES, only a very small number of secular clergy ever took any real interest in ministering to the Native people, for while Demers appeared to show some early interest in such work, it was never as consistent nor as committed as the Oblates. Demers had a serious problem seeing any value in Native culture, and his views, if anything, were certainly negative. He always claimed that most of the Native people respected him. If so, this attitude was certainly not reciprocal, for he believed that most of them were ignorant, even stupid; and that their culture was at least irrelevant if not evil, and as such must be totally eradicated if they were to survive in Canadian society.

Demers's missionary approach reflected a stifling, patronizing paternalism that essentially confused western civilization with the Christian gospel, however, he always suffered from much stronger feelings of racism than most Oblates. Given this attitude, he was bound to reject everything Native, especially their spirituality. He described their music at a potlatch as

---

73

"monotonous" and "boring." Unable to understand or appreciate anything about their culture, he was equally mystified by their early "indifference" to Christianity, and yet their simultaneous tendency to integrate it with their traditional "pagan" beliefs. He admitted that Europeans often cheated the Native people, but blamed this primarily on the Native person's "childish greed," especially for blankets. His major hope was that, under his guidance and that of his clergy, their "brutish," "uncouth" and "sexually insatiable" ways could be conquered so that they could finally become "something...at least approaching the human." Then, perhaps, he concluded, they might finally be converted to Christianity. Nevertheless, he was convinced that progress would be "very slow," especially among the present generation of Native adults. As for the future, his hope was with the children, whom the clergy must "prevent" from "taking on the customs and following the super-stitions of their ancestors."[1]

Unlike the Oblates or Demers, most Europeans either ignored Native cul-ture and their rights, or assumed that European diseases, such as smallpox, would eventually, even conveniently, wipe them out. European settlements and incursions into Native territory often lead to Native hostility. In 1863 two Cowichan braves, furious over how Europeans took Native land with apparent impunity, killed three settlers. Demers blamed the incident on the Europeans for selling liquor to the Natives. Boasting to the Quebec Catholic readers of *Rapport*, Demers asserted that his intervention had been a major factor in avoiding more bloodshed, especially European reprisals. He insisted that, such was his influence over the Natives, he had single-handedly convinced the Cowichan tribal elders to cooperate with government author-ities and to surrender the two Cowichan braves allegedly responsible for the murders. The two were tried and subsequently sentenced to hang. In addressing the condemned, Demers noted in *Rapport* that he admonished them: "I wished to make you good, but you did not wish to be good!" Hoping the executions would mark the end of Native attacks on Europeans in the area, Demers predicted that the Natives would finally be "reformed either by...[their] fear of the noose or by the [Catholic] church." However, he was certain that readers' donations would permit him and his clergy to watch over the Native "children of the forest" so that none of them would be lost to the Catholic faith.[2]

While propaganda in such magazines as *Missions* or *Rapport* often seemed to indicate that the Native peoples were eagerly awaiting conversion, private reports, not intended for publication, often gave a very different impression. In 1869 Charles John Seghers, a Belgian and destined to become Demers's successor, related the story of the execution of a Chemainus man for murdering an African American. Although the man had repeatedly refused baptism, Seghers decided to accompany him to the place of execution in the hope that he might change his mind at the moment of death. He did not. However, Seghers was appalled when, after the device intended to hang the man failed and only slowly strangled him, the executioner jumped on the poor man's head until his neck was broken. A deeply disgusted Seghers noted that while the Chemainus man was "only a savage, he was still a creature of God and his soul was as valuable as...[any European's,] since Christ died for us all." Preaching in Chinook to the Chemainus who were present at the execution, Seghers revealed his own intellectual blindness when he wrote that they seemed "surprised to hear of a loving Christian God!" Due to the lack of Catholic missionaries on Vancouver Island, Seghers lamented to a friend that the Native peoples there would probably have to "remain unbaptised and thus go to hell."[3]

Peter Rondeault, another early secular missionary and native of Montreal, had arrived on Vancouver Island in 1859 where he would live and work among the Cowichan for over forty years. As paternalistic and patronising as Demers, Rondeault counselled the Cowichan that if they did not obey him in all things, the European settlers would ultimately destroy them. Like the Oblates, Rondeault was assisted in his work by the Sisters of St. Ann, who opened a day school for Cowichan girls in 1864 to complement the one that Rondeault had established for boys in 1860.[4]

Time would prove that Native cooperation with the missionaries of all persuasions was very often, if not totally motivated by a desire to survive in the European culture that had been thrust upon them. As intelligent as Europeans, most Natives soon realized that this new reality was driven very largely by a lust for individual wealth, especially land and all that it could provide. When an unnamed Cowichan elder accused the Europeans of robbing his people of their land, an anonymous Sister of St. Ann assured him that the Europeans were only doing it for his ultimate "good." "Oh no," he retorted, "they are only doing it for themselves!"[5]

The influence of the early ministry of the secular clergy and religious women in trying to evangelize the Native people was far less significant than most of them could or would admit. This was clearly true in the Cowichan Valley. As early as 1870 the Sisters of St. Ann reported that all the "generally well behaved" Cowichan were by then devout and practicing Catholics. Yet, over a generation later, when the Methodists began to work among the Cowichan, there was strong opposition from Catholics who insisted that they were already members of their church. Nevertheless, the Department of Indian Affairs agreed with the Methodist contention that "a very large number" of the Cowichan were in fact still "pagan."[6]

✤ Disease, the Native People and the Missionaries

CONTACT WITH EUROPEANS had long affected the Native people and their culture, however, these threats tended to pale before the greatest enemy, European diseases. For thousands of years shamans, both men and women, had been seen as the principal defenders from illnesses caused by such things as splinters of bone, duck claws, or pebbles that were accidentally introduced into the body, as well as other precontact maladies. The skills necessary to achieve such cures took many years of training in order to acquire both the practical knowledge as well as the spiritual inspiration, especially in experiencing a successful vision quest. Before encountering Europeans the cure of all sicknesses, both physical and psychological were usually occasions for public performances—as a form of celebration—by shamans who would demonstrate their skills before an admiring patient and their family members. While herbal remedies were part of the shaman's arsenal as well as prayers, chants and songs, Native immune systems must have also played a major role in many recoveries. Still, the shaman was usually highly respected due to past success rates, and were as honoured in Native culture as any Western physician of the period. Given the small size of their constituencies, too many failures would have led to rejection, therefore shamanic cures were publicly celebrated. However, shamans had no remedies for veneral diseases, especially syphilis, or smallpox. Unfortunately, neither did the Europeans once such diseases has been contracted.[7]

Outbreaks of smallpox in the far west were reported as early as 1782 and again in the 1832, but the first truly devastating epidemic occurred in 1862. The Spanish and HBC employees were probably the main carriers in the first two incidents, limited respectively to the west coast of Vancouver Island and the mainland. The disease would gradually burn itself out, leaving its survivors with some immunity. While there are no figures on the first and no accurate statistics on the second epidemic, the impact of both was probably considerable.[8]

The great outbreak of 1862 started in Victoria, the central administrative and European population base. Native people were lured there by trade and what appeared to be easy money. Overcrowding in nearby Native settlements resulted in deteriorating sanitary conditions in which diseases of all kinds flourished. Alcoholism and veneral disease also took their toll.

In March 1862 smallpox came to Victoria, probably brought there by a sailor from San Francisco. European ignorance regarding smallpox was widespread and little was then known about how the disease was either contracted or spread. Due to Edward Jenner's work at the end of the eighteenth century, it was believed that serum made from cowpox virus was an effective vaccine against the disease, but in order to be effective, it had to be administered *before* an outbreak. Local newspapers also recommended that people clean any refuse that smelled, since for centuries Europeans believed that infectious diseases were spread by bad vapors causing "miasma." When it was apparent that the Native peoples in the area were extremely ill from the disease, Europeans demanded that they be sent away. By May, city authorities had evicted the Natives and burned their shack dwellings. As Natives from the north returned home, they spread the disease up the coast and from there it apparently expanded into the interior, resulting in the gradual infection of much of the Native population of both colonies reaching the southeastern corner of the mainland where it was reported to have been "particularly devastating." Some Europeans, especially Americans living in Victoria and New Westminster, judged the outbreak as either nature's or God's way of "exterminating" a nuisance, and as an ultimate fulfillment of the supposed "divine" plan of "manifest destiny." In the end, estimates of deaths varied from thousands to tens of thousands, probably accounting for an estimated death toll as high as a third of the region's indigenous population, or, in effect, a holocaust. The outbreak was undoubtedly the single most catastrophic event in local Native history since first contact.[9]

Many people responded to the disaster, but the missionaries were in the forefront, since, except for fur traders, they had long appeared to be the only Europeans who took an interest in the welfare of the Native people. The press reported that the clergy, especially Anglicans and Catholics, were involved in hundreds, and some reported thousands of vaccinations, particularly in Victoria and New Westminster. But few physicians at the time had any notion of germs, much less how they were spread. It is now known that vaccinations were irrelevant as afterthoughts, whereas real "cures" were probably due to the body's natural immune system, which was gradually strengthened after repeated exposures to such diseases.[10]

Still, missionary "doctors" took great pride in believing in the "miracles" their treatments had supposedly wrought, and they must certainly take credit for risking their own health in vaccinating infected Native populations. Bragging about what they had presumably accomplished in missionary magazines was bound to impress other clergy as well as potential contributors. Like the laity, however, the clergy also saw the disease as a "sign of God's wrath." Demers wrote in *Rapport* that smallpox was undoubtedly "a punishment from heaven" upon the Native people, both for their lack of conversion to Catholicism and their ongoing sexual liaisons with the Europeans. Still, he said, the disease was "more glorious for the church," since, he noted that during the summer of 1862 the Catholic clergy on both Vancouver Island and the mainland had vaccinated "approximately 8000." In fact, their labors were so successful, Demers reported, that they "had to record but two deaths." "Even the most narrow-minded Protestants," he declared, "have been forced to accord us a tribute of praise and recognition." As for the Protestant clergy, Demers assured the readers of *Rapport* that they did "nothing at all" to arrest the spread, but merely "buried the savages as fast as they died."[11]

Demers's exaggerations regarding numbers and "Catholic" success perhaps impressed his Quebec readers, but would have had little impact upon eyewitnesses, though the Oblates followed a similar approach. Certainly D'Herbomez did not fully believe in such "miracle" cures, for, with apparent tongue-in-cheek, he noted in 1861 that a missionary could become "a good doctor" with "no lengthy studies," but merely provide a constant remedy of "purgative salts" for whatever ailed a Native, and they were "almost certain" to get well. However, in reporting upon the 1862 smallpox epidemic, the Oblate *Missions* magazine, much like *Rapport*, noted that the Oblates, in this case Fouquet, had "8,000 [Natives] pass under...[his] lancet." And that Pandosy, Chirouse and Durieu were also said to be very active in vaccinating the Natives against the "terrible epidemic." Yet, there were no press reports that came close to such large numbers being vaccinated, and it must be assumed that such very high figures were intended to impress either other Oblates or potential French contributors to their foreign missions.[12]

✤ The Stresses of Early Growth

THE MARKED DEVELOPMENT AND EXPANSION of the 1860s and 1870s, especially on the mainland of British Columbia, brought with it enormous responsibilities for the Oblates. In 1864, when the vicariate apostolic was established, the Oblates gained complete jurisdiction over a huge area; to minister in it, the Congregation had only seven priests and four brothers. By the early 1880s they had 19 priests, including two bishops, eight brothers and the help of nine Sisters of St. Ann. Even so, the immense region placed a great burden upon what would remain a relatively small body of workers, and in turn created further tensions that constantly taxed their limited resources, financial, but particularly human.

As the years passed the Oblates were continuously challenged to spread themselves more and more thinly among their growing and complex ministry: serving the Native peoples, the growing European population, attending to diocesan responsibilities, managing the needs of their farms, and fulfilling their individual spiritual duties. As their voluminous correspondence demonstrates, wherever they chose to concentrate their energies, they would regret the time taken from other activities. The need for more Oblate clergy in British Columbia also coincided with the Franco-Prussian war (1870–71) which in France had increased the demand for military chaplains, and by promoting nationalism, lessened the desire of many French Oblates to serve in the foreign missions. Given their very strained resources, especially in personnel, which was further compounded by a spirituality of Jansenistic perfectionism and "silent suffering" that encouraged denial and lack of communication, the Oblates discovered there was no truly satisfactory solution to any of these problems.[13]

By 1880 the Oblate Missions had just about reached their final level of development. They had seven major Missions in British Columbia: St. Charles (New Westminster, 1860), St. Mary's (Mission City, 1860), St. Louis (Kamloops, 1859), the Immaculate Conception (Okanagan, 1859), St. Joseph's (Williams Lake, 1867), Our Lady of Good Hope (Stuart Lake, 1873) and St. Eugene's (Kootenay, 1874). Except for the almost 20-year (1887–1916) period when Holy Rosary in Vancouver held that position, New Westminster remained their headquarters until 1926 when the English-speaking Province of St. Peter's was founded with its center in Ottawa, and which covered all of Canada.[14]

Due to personnel shortages, personality conflicts, and the requirement that a person must always bend to the will of a superior, imposed by the vow of obedience, reassignments could be frequent and stressful. Charles Pandosy, who was the first and most famous missionary in the District of the Immaculate Conception in the Okanagan Valley was assigned to various Missions in western Canada from 1858 until 1891. For health reasons, Pandosy withdrew after only two years from the Okanagan, then served at Esquimalt (1861–63), Fort Rupert on Vancouver Island (1863–64) and New Westminster (1864–67). He returned to the Okanagan in 1868, where he planted his famous orchards and remained there as superior until 1882. He then became head of the Stuart Lake Mission (1882–87). Returning for the fourth time to the Okanagan, Pandosy served there until his death in 1891.

Pierre Richard, the Mission's other founder, remained in the Okanagan from 1859 until 1868 when he was transferred to the last Oblate Mission in the Washington Territory at Tulalip (Priest Point) where he worked with Eugène-Casimir Chirouse until the Oblates relinquished the Mission in 1878. Richard then went to Kamloops, but left in 1883 for Cranbrook, though 1890 found him back in the Okanagan where he stayed until 1894 when he left for New Westminster, staying there until his death in 1907.[15] Despite these many moves, Richard and Pandosy were the longest serving priests in the Okanagan-Kamloops region. During the remainder of the century the Mission witnessed the ministry and transfer of many others.[16]

As in other missions, the frequent change in staff often reflected disagreements and resulting stresses, and a transfer was the only solution. This highlights an inherent instability in the Oblate method of assignments. It was an extremely paternalistic system, grounded on a form of blind obedience. Therefore, superiors, such as D'Herbomez, frequently referred to priests under them as "my child" or "my son," while Oblate subordinates, whether priests or brothers, often addressed him as "your most obedient child." Superiors expected and usually received instant compliance from subordinates. Such a system was not designed to address interpersonal problems, which were further compounded by the fact, that, being men, Oblates were very unlikely to share in any intimate way with each other. Thus personnel and personal problems were most often allowed to fester, increasingly undermining morale, which either lead to yet another reassignment or, worse, through suppression, only further poisoned staff relations. And while a handful of Oblates did leave the Congregation, again their Jansenistic spirituality constituted a major barrier. For Jansenism demanded that one must always follow the will of the superior and not one's own will, which was judged to be sinful. Since a good Oblate was supposed to believe that the will of his superior was indeed the will of God, and so to question it was to question God and even possibly to endanger one's personal salvation. Consequently, such distorted spirituality, which practically celebrated the need for suffering, tended to encourage a terrible shame in anyone who would "abandon" their vocation, especially for such a "minor" reason as personal happiness.[17]

Personnel transfer and rotation also created new problems. In a new Mission, experienced personnel were naturally considered a prerequisite, thus younger clergy were usually placed under the tutelage of such people until they had proven themselves. Lay brothers were also moved to areas where their particular manual skills were in demand, so a carpenter would find himself in a Mission that needed a house, a church or a barn. Other brothers who specialized in cooking, farming or livestock would be assigned more permanently to a Mission. Some brothers were also well trained not only in manual skills, but also in intellectual ones. Joseph Buchman, who spent five (1863–68) years in the Okanagan Valley, and being very literate in English, taught boys in its Native school. As personnel in a highly hierarchical system, brothers tended to be viewed as "inferior" beings, less intelligent than priests, or in a real sense "the serfs," "the proletariat" of the Missions. Again, these attitudes compounded staff stresses, which continued to be a significant reason for the transfer or, in extreme cases of lay brothers and sometimes priests, even the dismissal of personnel from the Congregation.[18]

As was often true of the other Mission districts, due to shortages, the staff was never large enough to adequately serve the massive Okanagan-Kamloops region. Only two priests were expected to serve the entire district, until, that is, 1865 when a third was added. In 1868, the day school was closed due to lack of interest, staff shortages as well as Oblate personality conflicts, which meant the number was again reduced to two. By 1871 the figure had again risen to three because of expansion into the Thompson River area. Yet, by this time Gendre was dying of tuberculosis, and his death in 1873 left only two priests in the area, one of whom took care of the northern part of the Mission and the other the southern. The division was also determined by the attempt to learn the region's two Native languages: Shuswap in the north and Okanagan in the south, thus the priest who worked in each region would be expected to specialize in that language.[19]

Oblates in the Okanagan-Kamloops Missions had a heavy daily schedule, which when not completed, added to feelings of disappointment, stress, and burnout. The Oblates who worked there frequently complained that, before coming to the Okanagan Mission, they had not experienced such physical and psychological fatigue nor been so personally frustrated by so many conflicting demands. Mass, mediation, chapel visits, the rosary, and reading of their office were supposed to be routine activities. But according to the season, each priest also undertook a certain amount of manual work. The farm on the Okanagan Mission provided food for the personnel and some cash from the sale of surplus that was used to support the school and outlying Missions, especially St. Louis at Kamloops. In addition the priests were expected to preach missions, hear confessions, teach catechism, baptize, marry and bury people. The Mission "Econome," always a priest, was expected to perform all of the above duties as well as keep the accounts. In addition, they oversaw the work of the Oblate brothers; traded with Natives and Europeans; managed seasonal lay workers; oversaw any construction, and marketed livestock and produce. The "Econome" also instructed Natives on crop management and anything dealing with farming. In addition, he would have to make at least two and sometimes even five journeys a year to Hope in order to direct the transport of the needed goods that the Mission could not produce on its own. In all it could be a very trying, tiring, and when a form of Jansenistic perfectionism is added to the mix, a quite disheartening, and even a depressing existence.[20]

7

Founding More Missions

✤ *Expansion in the Okanagan Valley*

STRESSES CAUSED BY THE OBLATE SYSTEM did not encourage a prosperous or contented Mission; but they did not necessarily prevent the Mission from progressing. Okanagan missionaries Richard and Pandosy tried to work with the Europeans in the mining settlement of Rock Creek, but its population being mostly male had a very limited interest in organized religion. Therefore, the two priests concentrated on the Native population. Durieu, in his four years (1860–64) in the Okanagan supervised the construction of a priest's house at the Head of the Lake and tried to learn the local Native language. Within six years the Oblates had established small, outlying Mission stations situated near Native settlements throughout the Okanagan Valley from the international boundary in the south to the North Thompson River in the north, extending to the Nicola, Similkameen and Thompson Rivers to the west. In 1866 D'Herbomez, on his first visit to the region, blessed a total of ten chapels built by Natives on Native settlements. All were small, poorly constructed buildings; however, such structures were rarely an accurate reflection of Native enthusiasm but rather their main purpose was to "prove" to the Oblates that there was a Native interest in Catholicism, and so "convince" them that their ministry had a firm foundation. Consequently, the Oblates interpreted a Native refusal to build a chapel as a lack of readiness or their inability to fully abandon "paganism." By 1874 the Oblates reported that in their Okanagan and Kamloops Missions they counted over 1300 Native Catholics who, divided between the Shuswap and Okanagan, represented a total of 15 separate tribes, each containing between 50 to 150 Catholics. Until the coming of the railroad in the 1880s, there were barely a hundred Europeans in the same area.[1]

Because of the harsh winters in the Okanagan-Kamloops region, the lack of manpower, and the time and distances entailed in visiting Native villages, the Oblate ministry's central work among the Native communities was usually very seasonal and haphazard. Therefore, each village was visited only about two or three times a year. Thus the early contacts between the Oblates and Natives of the region were very sporadic.[2]

The Oblates in the Okanagan, as in their other far western Missions, often gave the impression of sharing in the lifestyle of the Native people, especially their poverty. Such images were very strong in the pictures portrayed in *Missions*, since both Oblate and lay readers expected it, as it reflected their vow of poverty and their need for financial assistance. In fact, in the Okanagan Valley, unless it was a personal choice, the Oblates were quite well feed and clothed. Indeed, given their self-assumed leadership position among the Natives, they would have rejected the notion of identifying in any way with Native poverty. Although the Natives were their sole parishioners for many years, the Oblates could not have depended upon them for much financial assistance. Contrasted with the local Natives, the Oblates lead solid middle-class lifestyles and were better housed and fed than almost any of the Europeans in the region. This was largely due to their very successful farm of over two thousand acres, which by 1871 had large herds of cattle, horses and sheep, and produced vegetables, grain and fruit in abundance. Within a decade the Okanagan-Kamloops Missions were self-sufficient and able to assist in supporting other Oblate enterprises in the vicariate.[3]

Obedience, like poverty, was another vow that influenced Oblate behaviour and especially their attitudes towards others. This mentality was certainly translated in their dealings with the laity, whether Native or European, though it flowed from a very different perception of the two races. From the Native people, as reflected in the reduction ideal, they expected blind acceptance whether it was of church teachings or of the Oblate-imposed vision of reality, since in Oblate eyes, being "weak in mind and heart," "the Indians...[were] only big children who...[could therefore] be naughty sometimes." As for the handful of European Catholics in the region, while the Oblates frequently complained about their lack of religious practice, bad marriages, drinking, gambling, stealing, especially of Native land, they made no attempt to moderate European behaviour, mainly because most Europeans would have totally rejected such control. Certainly the Oblates accepted such attitudes from the Europeans, but never in their dealings with the Native peoples.[4]

The Natives were far wiser, however, than the Oblates were willing to concede. For although the Oblates strove to limit what they viewed as abuses of power, an elder could often buttress his own authority by citing the support he had from a priest. Thus it appears that elders could gain considerably from the new arrangement of having Europeans, whether Oblates or Indian agents involved in tribal politics. Europeans, ignorant of local Native traditions, mistakenly understood the Native "elders" as being "chiefs" in the eastern Native tradition. In fact, in far-western tradition, the "elders" had limited power and were essentially protectors of past wisdom. As "chiefs," however, they began to try to assume far more power and control over their band. When difficulties arose, the Oblate intervened. So when in September 1867 Petit Louis of the Kamloops lost a church collection as a result of gambling, Grandidier tried to reduce his power by appointing a Native "treasurer" who would be responsible for future funds and a village council that would decide "democratically" what a "chief" could do. When a "chief" disagreed publicly with the priest, the Oblates would try to counter by openly criticizing his authority, thus hoping to gain support from other tribal members. However, in the case of Petit Louis this backfired. Not only was he not removed, but his influence was enhanced by his opposition to the priest's interference, which produced additional Native resentment towards the Oblates. Clearly, Native-Oblate relations were a delicate balancing act. The Oblates, in their desire to create reductions, by giving the Natives more authority over the local Catholic communities and then, in order to retain their influence, by playing sides in the process, could often unwittingly strengthen Native independence, and thus resistance to Oblate control.[5]

Racism, perhaps often unconscious, was a major reason for the Oblates' conduct. The Oblates assumed that the European was controlled by "natural forces," like the fear of bankruptcy or the desire for excessive profits, which could admittedly lead to extreme ambition and it accompanying excessive materialism. Therefore, though Europeans would be better for being religious, in Oblate reasoning they did not need a strong belief in religion to retain a basic moral equilibrium. However, this was not possible for the Native, unless totally governed by Catholicism. So as long as they were "only big children," or until they became "adults," that is the equivalent of European Catholic Canadians, then the Native was supposedly "doomed" without the Oblates to look after their needs.[6]

Even so, Oblate influence over Native affairs in the Okanagan-Kamloops as well as other regions was very rarely absolute, and was often in conflict with both the Native and government authorities. Native elders in their role of "watchmen" were essential in order to have effective control over a particular tribe. Viewing their position as a type of feudal overlord, when an elder died, the Oblates tried to name his successor, or at least have some say in his appointment, so he would be beholding and thus hopefully become an obedient Oblate "child." Although, heredity could play a part in succession, tribes usually selected elders for their perceived abilities, especially wisdom. But, given many additional factors outside Oblate control, their choice was often countermanded or ignored by other tribal members or influenced by other Europeans in the region who had no intention of defending Oblate interests. In 1865, John Hayes, the local Indian agent had Moise Cinq-Coeur appointed an elder among the Kamloops. On hearing the news, the Oblates were quite upset that Hayes was determined to prevent them from having a formative influence over the Natives. When Cinq-Coeur died some years later, the Oblates complained that another Indian agent, Forbes Vernon had confirmed the desire of the Kamloops to have Basile of the Head of the Lake as his successor. While it certainly did not stop them from trying, the Oblates at the Okanagan-Kamloops Missions seem to have had very little real or lasting impact in influencing such significant processes.[7]

Whether or not their efforts were actually having a marked influence in their control of Native behaviour, the Oblates in the Okanagan-Kamloops region usually sent fairly glowing evaluations to New Westminster, indicating that, despite some problems, ultimate success seemed certain. In 1875, Baudre reported very positively on the moral, social and religious state of the

Natives people at Spallumcheen and at the Head of the Lake. His sermons always tried to avoid wrathful images of God. He was convinced that his sermons, given in a mixture of Chinook and French and translated by a Native interpreter, were all well understood by his audience, and that his approach had and would continue to work wonders. According to Baudre, Mass attendance and confessions, especially among the young, the church's future hope, were all excellent. He was confident that, largely due to his work, the region's future was bright for the Catholic Church and the Oblates.[8]

Other more experienced Oblates, such as Pandosy, were usually highly critical of such heady optimism and of the clergy who indulged in it. He complained that priests like Baudre were always too much in haste, especially in baptizing Native adults. Pandosy believed that if they were honest with themselves, they would have to admit that they were actually building their religious house on quicksand. Baudre admitted the problem, but, given the infrequency of his visits, implied that there was really no alternative. He hoped that the elders and/or "watchmen" who were left in charge would perform their duties well. Actually there is a rather humorous example of Pandosy's own effort in 1877 to transform Natives into practitioners of a western "work ethic." Trying to wean them off "Indian time," he introduced the use of a clock at Penticton to better regulate daily religious routines by the watchmen.[9]

While the Oblates did have some influence and even success, it was very limited. Certainly the nomadic hunters, gatherers and fishermen refused to cooperate with the plans of Oblates and other Europeans to transform their lives by making them settle down, plant crops and behave like Euro-Canadian farmers. Even so, by 1876 there were some "signs of success." Baudre reported that the reserve of "Chief" Cinq-Coeur contained a burgeoning French style village with commodious western style houses, with even a sizable one for the priest. Such "progress" seemed good to Baudre since in his view the Natives were becoming more and more obedient to "God's plan" for them. Such "successes," however, were the exception.[10]

Nevertheless, the Oblates working in the Okanagan-Kamloops Missions believed that their plan for the Natives was for their own good and ultimate betterment. They did try to limit some of the worst aspects of European encroachment such as alcoholism, promiscuity and disease. The Oblate control over the lives of the Natives in their missions was intended to "save" the Natives. The question is from what and at what price? The central aim of acculturation as interpreted by the Oblates meant denying the Native peoples the right to be themselves. Although they saw their aims as largely benign, like most other missionaries, the Oblates were often implicitly more cruel than the worst European racists. Explicit racists tended to ignore the Native with the sole expectation that disease, despair and other factors would eventually destroy them. Whereas the Oblates, by confusing Christianity with western civilization, were determined to destroy the Native's culture in order to save them and turn them into "whites"—all in the name of a gospel that makes no mention of western civilization. Instead, the Christian gospel insists upon mutual and radical inclusion and love. If the Oblates had followed a healthy attempt at transformation, it would have been reciprocal and collaborative, and it would have encouraged and even celebrated Native independence and ultimately total freedom from any Oblate control.[11]

✤ A Failed Residential School

EARLY ATTEMPTS by the Oblates to educate the Natives of the Okanagan-Kamloops region demonstrated just how independent the Native remained. As they were doing at Mission, the Oblates opened a residential school in the Okanagan in September 1866 with three boys; by Christmas its enrollment had reached eleven. Although initially more Natives were interested in attending, the Oblates tried to accept only the children of elders or "chiefs," members of the Native "ruling classes," whom they expected would become champions among their people of both the school and the church. By 1867 total attendance figures had reached 21 and seemed very promising. Though their early expenses were considerable, the Oblates expected that in time the colonial government would compensate them. Food from the Oblate farm, on which the students worked, was plentiful, and Native parents supplied many basic necessities, such as clothes and farm implements.[12]

In the end, however, the school failed. For most parents and children the basic and insoluble problem was their separation from each other. Added to this, given the very confined living arrangements at the school, was the very real threat of tuberculosis or other European diseases. The school recorded two deaths in 1867–68. Used to a free life, in which looking, listening and learning played the major roles, Native children refused to conform to the rigid Oblate discipline of blind obedience and rote memorization of seemingly meaningless "facts." In trying to explain the failure, Richard blamed it on the Okanagan who had become at best, he declared, "mediocre Christians." Since there were few Protestants in the Valley, perhaps, he concluded, the Natives of the region did not have the threat of "heretics" who he believed inspired conformity to the Catholic faith among the Stó:lô on the lower mainland. Worst of all, Richard thought that the Native parents "loved their insolent children" too much to send them to the school, thus, like disobedient children anywhere, the Native students had failed to "properly honor" all that the Oblates had been doing for them. It would take almost 25 years (1890) before another Native residential school at Kamloops was established with essential federal government funding. It would again present the local Natives with such a choice, and once more most Natives rejected it. However, unlike the Natives, the Oblates appeared to learn little, if anything from their first educational experience in the Okanagan-Kamloops Valley.[13]

✤ Williams Lake and St. Joseph's Mission

Father James McGuckin (AD)

St. Joseph's was the fourth Oblate Mission established on the mainland. Unlike Pandosy, James McGuckin, its founder, spent a far longer (1867–82) period at the Mission, and had a much more formative role. While he was less colorful than Pandosy, McGuckin could also be independent in his views, perhaps reflecting his Northern Irish birth. Although strictly adhering to the Oblate rule, he did not hesitate to respectfully oppose his superiors if he disagreed with a decision. A confirmed educator, after his ordination to the priesthood by Demers in 1863, and as one of the very few anglophone Oblates then in the region, he became a teacher and administrator (1863-66) at St. Louis College, Victoria. Within six years of leaving St. Joseph's, McGuckin became the rector (1889–98) of the University of Ottawa.[14]

St. Joseph's Mission had its beginnings in a gold rush at Williams Creek (1861–62). When he arrived in the area, McGuckin was already apprised of the situation from previous Oblate visits to the region. Fouquet, Gendre, Baudre, Jean-Marie LeJacq, and Grandidier had all traveled in the area and

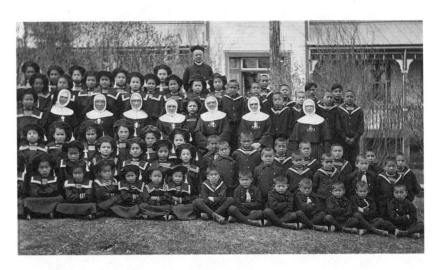

Native children at St. Joseph's Mission in Cariboo, Williams Lake (AD)

sent back reports to D'Herbomez regarding the practical considerations of founding a Mission there. The Chilcotin, Carrier and Shuswap were their central concern. Unlike the Coast Salish, they had had no significant contact with Europeans until the gold rush. But by 1866, most Europeans had left the Cariboo, taking with them what the Oblates called the "evil influences" of "white civilization," especially alcohol. Even more important, with their departure, the non-Catholic clergy went with them. The Anglicans re-established themselves at Barkerville in 1868, but they represented the only regional Protestant presence, and made little or no attempt to work among the local Native peoples.[15]

The depressed times certainly affected the sale of land, and the Oblates hoped to benefit. After looking at eight different sites for the future Mission, McGuckin recommended the purchase of the Pomeroy farm to D'Herbomez. It was very central to a number of bands, being about half way between Alkali Lake and Soda Creek, which was near the Shuswap, and was not far from the Quesnel tribe. The Chilcotin and Carrier also used the area as a meeting ground. Because the farm was about 70 miles from Richfield, the nearest European settlement, an isolated, reduction type Mission was quite feasible. It even came with some equipment and livestock, and most important of all the land was very fertile. McGuckin hoped that it would not only support the Mission, but, as was always a major consideration in Oblate farming, also produce a surplus, the sale of which would assist in funding other Missions in the vicariate.[16]

McGuckin thought the local economic downturn would allow a "steal," however, Pomeroy, a non-Catholic, suspected that despite their protestations to the contrary, the Oblates were not poor. He must also have known that McGuckin had collected considerable sums from his parishioners in Richfield. Therefore, Pomeroy believed $1,500 a reasonable price. While McGuckin encouraged him to pay, D'Herbomez stood firm at $600. Finally two Catholic laymen came to the rescue, Dennis Murphy and a Mr. Toomey. Since Pomeroy was desperate to sell, the two men purchased the 160 acre farm for $600 and then resold it to the Oblates at cost. By the end of 1867 St. Joseph's Mission was finally a reality.[17]

McGuckin was determined to create a farm in the Cariboo that would not only solve their local financial problems, but would ultimately rival their enterprise in the Okanagan. Durieu and a fellow Irishman, the vicariate's bursar, Edward Horris, did not agree and insisted that preached missions and education, especially to the Native peoples, should be the Mission's highest priority, and that the local Europeans should support it. Convinced of the land's great potential, McGuckin disagreed. During much of 1869–71, while his most enthusiastic supporter, D'Herbomez was in Europe attending Vatican Council I, Horris and Durieu had their way. But upon D'Herbomez's return McGuckin convinced his superior of the farm's importance to the Mission's financial future. Through McGuckin's management, the farm became a ranch-farm whose livestock and crops made it one of the most productive in the region. Building on the original 160-acre farm of 1867, within little more than a decade McGuckin had expanded the Oblate holdings in the Cariboo to 1600 acres. As he predicted, it became a major source of income for the Williams Lake Mission and the entire vicariate until well into the next century.[18]

While he spent much of his time ministering among the nearby Europeans and building up one of the most prosperous farms in the vicariate, McGuckin had the "brightest hopes" regarding his ministry among the "poor savages." He reported that every Native band he visited in the summer of 1866 had made requests for priests. In 1867 he used the occasion of the execution of several Chilcotins at Fort Alexandria, south of Quesnel, to preach in Chinook to the relatives and band members of the condemned men. The Chilcotins had been tried and convicted of murdering a number of

Euro-peans who settled upon what the Chilcotin considered were their hunting grounds. For several years many European Americans, especially in Victoria, had demanded a bloody retaliation against the Chilcotins, preferring, as they had in the Oregon Territory, a vigilante-style solution to the region's Native "problem," namely, extermination. However, unlike the American government, British colonial and Canadian authorities had a policy of not giving even tacit approval to genocide, though as the executions indicated, they had finally taken action.[19]

Under the watchful eye of the local government authorities at Fort Alexandria, McGuckin had a safe environment for his initial contact with the Chilcotin. Unique among the region's Athapaskans, the Chilcotin were the most overtly hostile and resistant Natives to European contact and control. While other tribes shared such views, the Chilcotin made no secret of their judgement that European settlers were simply thieves whose only desire was to steal Native land. They usually made no distinction between missionaries and other Europeans, apparently viewing the former as only precursors of much worse to come. However, McGuckin reported, the Chilcotins were finally interested in obtaining a "black robe." At Quesnel he wrote that a "Carrier Chief" was even ready to set up an Oblate style reduction by having "two watchmen and two policemen" elected, and that "all the Indians desired it." He noted, "I have the brightest hopes for these poor savages."[20]

Not all the Oblates shared McGuckin's optimistic views. In the previous summer Charles Grandidier correctly observed that the Chilcotin "seemed ill-disposed towards [the Christian] religion." By 1870 even McGuckin had to admit that he found "none so savage as the Chilcotin," a judgement based largely on their lack of interest in any form of Christianity, and that their conversion, if it ever came, would be very slow. Still, other local tribes, especially the Shuswap and Carrier, did seem to demonstrate a willingness to convert. Even if they were not always as enthusiastic as McGuckin and others would have hoped, most Oblates appeared to believe that given time Catholicism would finally triumph among all the Natives of the region.[21]

In May 1868 D'Herbomez made his first visit to the new Mission. McGuckin had been encouraging this for months, with the expectation of gaining his superior's support to extend the Mission further north to include the entire Carrier nation. After a five-month stay in the region visiting the various tribes, and especially the Carrier, D'Herbomez approved the extension. The visit seemed a great success, for after traveling throughout the area, D'Herbomez reported to the readers of *Missions* that not only did everyone he meet, especially the Natives, greet him with great enthusiasm, but he blessed no fewer than "ten churches or chapels."[22] To be fair, it would be an exaggeration to call any of these buildings "churches *or* chapels," for even St. Patrick's in Richfield, the European parish, was then merely a converted house, though by then the parishioners had added a bell. The other nine, which all stood on Native settlements were built by very seasonal and inexperienced Native labour. The enumeration by D'Herbomez of such structures there, as well as throughout the vicariate, was usually a central element in Oblate reports to their European headquarters since they gave a graphic impression of significant growth. These reports in *Missions* would have encouraged Oblate readers and especially lay subscribers that their funds were indeed working miracles with dozens of "chapels," especially "among the savages." Therefore, though poor in appearance, the "chapels" provided a physical assurance, no matter how tentative, that the Native settlements they represented would soon contain "good" Catholics.[23]

✤ *Staffing Problems*

SUFFICIENT OBLATE STAFF was essential if such a "dream" were ever to be realized, however, lack of manpower remained a major problem in the central interior. Rapid turnover and internal tensions also contributed to staffing problems. McGuckin's first assistant, François Jayol, was the first priest ordained by Archbishop Blanchet in 1847 and the first to abandon him for the Oblates in the 1848. Arriving in the spring of 1867, Jayol became the temporary superior of the Mission, living in a small cabin where he taught catechism to a handful of Shuswap. This freed McGuckin to spend more time visiting the Natives and trying to raise money among the Europeans for the Mission and vicariate. Accompanying Jayol was Brother Philip Surel, who would remain for 17 years (1866–83) at Williams Lake. Surel soon had serious personality conflicts with the priest. Naturally favoring a priest over a brother, McGuckin tended to blame Surel, although he also found fault with Jayol's behavior. Seemingly taking his Jansenistic spirituality to extremes even by Oblate standards, Jayol, in McGuckin's opinion, was far too serious, "breaking his heart about everything," for while Jayol said "little," according to McGuckin, he "suffers much."[24]

McGuckin, not happy with the situation, believed assigning additional staff to Williams Lake would provide Surel and Jayol with alternative relationships. In the summer of 1867 when he heard that there had been new arrivals from France, he immediately made a formal request that staff levels be raised to three priests and three brothers. However, instead D'Herbomez decided to replace Jayol with Jean-Marie LeJacq and Brother George Blanchet, both of whom would remain for five years (1868–73), and ordered a despondent Jayol to St. Michael's Mission at Fort Rupert. There he spent four fruitless and difficult years (1868–72) trying to convert the totally disinterested Kwakiutl, an undertaking which only further increased his depression.[25]

For McGuckin, D'Herbomez's announcement of Jayol's departure was made much worse by even sadder news, namely, that the Oblates had suffered their first "apostate" in the vicariate. Father J.X. Willemar, whom McGuckin had worked with in Victoria, had joined the Anglican church. In July Bishop Hills appointed him the rector of the parish at Alberni, on Vancouver Island. McGuckin found the news "heart-rending." Leaving the Oblates was bad enough; that Willemar had become a Protestant was "almost incredible." McGuckin went on, "when a poor soul loses the grace of God, it is capable of anything." He concluded: "My our dearest Lord, through the intercession of the Immaculate Mother, convert him!"[26]

McGuckin had LeJacq, who appeared very successful in his work among the Native peoples. Possibly this seemed true since LeJacq was far stricter than McGuckin in his adherence to a classic reduction system. LeJacq believed that every aspect of Native life must be under clerical control. By means of watchmen, any infractions were to be carefully reported to and punished by the priest. For years stories circulated among the Natives that LeJacq was a "miracle" worker who could impose deadly curses upon those who violated his prohibitions, especially the cardinal "sin" among Oblates of apparent Christian converts calling upon Native shamans for healing or advice.[27]

During his years at Williams Lake, LeJacq traveled extensively among the Carrier, Chilcotin and Shuswap. Since the Shuswap lived closest to the Mission, they had the greatest contact with local Europeans, and therefore fit the reduction stereotype of requiring the greatest protection from bad influences. In trying to put such a plan into operation, LeJacq was able to use a band of Shuswap whom the government had consistently refused to assist in establishing a reserve because they had been accused of murdering several miners. Hoping to establish a model reduction, LeJacq encouraged them to form a village on Oblate land just opposite the Mission's headquarters. This group, both heavily dependent upon and grateful to the Oblates, became a local showcase for the proclaimed success of the reduction system, and for some years provided LeJacq with a constant solace that his work was indeed bearing fruit.

In time experience taught LeJacq that he was far too sanguine. For years later, after his time at Stuart Lake (1873–80), a more objective LeJacq reached very different conclusions. He noted that though the Shuswap on the Mission reduction appeared to be the most dedicated of Christians, "little by little,...such goodness would evaporate," and they would ultimately return to their former "savage practices." Alas, he lamented, the original seed he had planted had indeed fallen upon "stony ground."[28]

While McGuckin had also been initially enthusiastic about his own work among the Native peoples, he too soon changed his mind. As early as 1869, McGuckin, using the "terrible Chilcotin" as an example, admitted that even among them there were probably "some excellent" Natives "well-disposed and most anxious to become good." However, he was convinced it would require much time and effort to achieve such an end.[29]

Initially, when LeJacq vehemently disagreed with such a viewpoint, McGuckin complained of him to D'Herbomez. Unable to bring up their central problem, for fear of seeming to be insensitive to the need to convert Natives, McGuckin chose to criticize his colleague for his lack of "cleanliness." He stated that the situation was so bad that after LeJacq celebrated Mass, the altar linens always had to be washed. Insisting that cleanliness was indubitably next to godliness, he wondered that LeJacq's dirty habits might also "ruin the good" in his ministry; in a far more ominous tone, he was even concerned that they might ultimately "ruin not only his [missionary] labors, but even his soul." LeJacq apparently made no strong accusations against McGuckin, but instead stayed away from the Mission and McGuckin as much as possible by visiting the most far-flung tribes. Such frequent absences were not unusual among Oblates missionaries. However, given the much deeper issues that plagued their relationship, it meant that there was little hope of improving, much less maintaining any real cooperation, nor for that matter any real sense of community. Much worse, left unresolved, such attitudes could also undermine the purpose and spirit of their ministry.[30]

✤ *Stuart Lake and Our Lady of Good Hope Mission*

FOR SEVERAL YEARS, Jean-Marie LeJacq had looked forward to working at Stuart Lake. The first Oblate contact with a Carrier, the major tribe in the region, had been made by McGuckin in 1867 when he reported meeting one from the Fort St. James band who begged him to return with him. The Carrier informed McGuckin that he had orders from his village to bring back the first priest he saw, "and if he be not willing to come," he was told, then "bring him by force." In 1868 D'Herbomez had extended St. Joseph's Mission at Williams Lake to include the Carrier; the following year LeJacq became the first Oblate to visit Fort St. James. His initial experience amazed him, since he wrote that the Carrier were so desirous of baptism, that they either feigned illness or, by exaggerating their age, insisted they would soon die. So great was their desire to become Catholic, said LeJacq, that they even insisted that he hear their confessions and impose harsh penances upon them. This first encounter convinced LeJacq that a Mission must be established at Stuart Lake. Given his desire to be his own authority and freed from McGuckin and Williams Lake, and also his strong love of ministering to Native peoples, LeJacq was also drawn to the remoteness of the location.[31]

The Carrier had an affinity for imagination and myth usually far exceeding that of most European Christians. Tied largely to reason and science, Western Europeans had long ago forgotten their own syncretistic use of Hellenistic and Judaic myths to enrich early Christian theology. Unlike the coastal Natives, who were far more negatively affected by European settlement, the remote Carrier remained much freer to choose or reject what Christianity had to offer. Like most other Natives in Canada, the Carrier had their first contacts with Christianity through the European fur traders and the Christian Iroquois personnel of the HBC.

By the middle of the nineteenth century the Carrier were radically reinterpreting their ancient mythology. Although there is evidence of monotheism in their earlier belief structure, their contacts with Christianity helped centralize it. Their previous animistic spirituality was enriched by belief in a God whom they now referred to as *Utakke* or "He who dwells on high." The genesis of these Christian influences seem to be rooted in the cult of the Prophet Dance, which originated in Oregon in the 1830s about the time the first Christian missionaries arrived there. The principal tenets of the cult consisted of a belief in a supreme creator spirit, a sacred circle dance, the

Native Mission at Stuart Lake (Fort St. James), ca. 1917 (l-r: school, church, mission) (AD)

confession of sins, the performance of harsh penances, such as public scourgings, the coming of a millennium and a bodily resurrection or rebirth. The fleeting visits of the "black robes," such as Demers, Blanchet, and the Jesuit, John Nobili, apparently produced more "native prophets" who spoke of confession, baptism and even of "proper marriage," or monogamy. Through this process a number of Carrier prophet sects gradually arose that all predicted that, after death, the Native person would become a "European." Combined with the acquisition of new wealth expressed in guns and metal pots as well as European skills, such as carpentry and husbandry, spread mainly by the HBC, the Carrier ingeniously developed a syncretised form of Christianity. Much as the Native peoples in other parts of the Americas had done, the Carrier were thus able to adapt to and make sense of the ambiguity and diversity of this "new world" that had been suddenly thrust upon them.[32]

This was the Native world into which LeJacq now entered, and which he planned to work, with the assistance of Georges Blanchet (1873–82) who had recently been ordained. A master carpenter, Brother Blanchet had laboured for five years at Williams Lake (1868–73), having come there with LeJacq. Clearly both men felt close, and showed an unusual concern for each other that was and remains rare among men, including Oblates. Blanchet had pre-

Founding More Missions

97

Fort St. James and Native Village (far left: church and the priests' house) (AD)

viously refused ordination after he concluded the loss of a finger in a shoot-
ing accident made him unworthy to celebrate Mass. However, LeJacq, a man
Blanchet deeply respected, encouraged him to seek ordination if he wished
to join him in the north, for LeJacq insisted that he needed a second priest
even more than a master carpenter. And so on the 1 November 1872, at 54,
Blanchet was finally ordained a priest by D'Herbomez. Though almost 20
years his senior, Blanchet continued to view LeJacq as his superior in both
name and fact. Clearly Blanchet could not fully accept the status of his new
role, for during their eight years together at Stuart Lake, Blanchet continued
to act more as the lay brother than the priest. Still, LeJacq's kind and familiar
manner created a very pleasant atmosphere and further strengthened their
relationship.[33]

Fort St. James was still a HBC town in 1873. As the only resident clergy,
LeJacq and Blanchet were viewed as definite assets, especially in their
potential influence over the Native population. Chief Factor Gavin Hamilton
received word of the two priests' arrival from Charles Graham, the HBC
agent in Victoria. Graham and Hamilton were especially concerned about
the widespread practice of Native gambling and the potlatch. Both were
considered a nuisance, since the Natives would often gamble or potlatch
goods that had been extended to them on company credit in exchange for

furs that they had yet to provide. HBC officials hoped the arrival of the Oblates might end or greatly lessen such "foolish" behaviour.[34]

Such feelings were mutual, for the Oblates had always viewed the HBC, other businessmen and secular authorities in general, as potential allies. Since the aim of the Oblate missionary was essentially the conversion of the Natives to Catholicism, unless a trader or other European did something to hinder this, superiors directed them to follow a pattern of respect, and, if possible, cooperation. The obvious logic was that to do anything that angered local Europeans, especially those in authority, such as HBC factors, might hinder their mission. In fact, LeJacq went out of his way to impress HBC officials; for one of his first acts at Stuart Lake was to inform the Natives that he could not baptize nor marry anyone who had an outstanding debt with the HBC. Clearly, LeJacq was determined to be most cooperative, and he remained on quite friendly terms with the Company throughout his time there. Such a prudent approach benefited all, but especially the Oblates. One of the first results of LeJacq's policy and his good relations with the HBC was that within months of his arrival he obtained an official pardon for an escaped Native who had been wrongfully convicted of a crime and sentenced to six months on a chain gang.[35]

This good relationship was further demonstrated in the location of the Mission on a 320-acre site provided by the HBC near their post. Over the next five years, under Blanchet's direction, the local Natives built a church and Mission house, which contained a chapel, a *"salle des sauvage,"* as well as living quarters for the two priests consisting of a large kitchen and two bedrooms. By 1879 the church was almost complete, its interior having been finished free of charge by Simon and Billy, two Carrier carpenters from Fort George. To complete the work, the local Native band paid for a bell.[36]

The two priests spent most of their time visiting the various Native settlements, both near and far. Blanchet's age kept him near the Mission, thus he ministered to the three villages surrounding Stuart Lake: Pinché, Taché and Yekhuche, whereas LeJacq spent a good part of the year traveling to the most distant and dispersed bands of Carrier, Sikani and Babine trappers. Blanchet also planned a new village near the church and encouraged the Natives, who chose to live there, to plant vegetable gardens. Nevertheless, except for such minor adaptations, which were viewed as healthy supplements to a diet that was almost exclusively meat and fish, neither priest made any attempt to convince the local Natives to establish reduction-style settlements. In any case, the harsh climate did not permit either the large farms or population concentration that were essential to such a system.[37]

Learning the very difficult Carrier language was of central importance to any missionaries who hoped to make any lasting impact. From the beginning McGuckin had warned his superiors that the Oblates' usual reliance on Chinook would be of no use in communicating with the Carrier. Both Blanchet and LeJacq repeated the warning, though Blanchet, given his age, found the language was far too difficult to master. LeJacq reported that such was its complexity, that many HBC Métis employees, even after many years in the region, had still not learned it.[38]

Both LeJacq and Blanchet certainly took the language question very seriously. LeJacq had unsuccessfully tried to adapt the Carrier language to a Cree syllabic, which had been invented by James Evans, a Methodist missionary. Yet it was clear that any European who was able to teach as curious a people as the Carrier to read and write in their own tongue would subsequently gain enormous influence among them. When he was preparing to leave the Mission in 1880, LeJacq was quite insistent that whoever replaced him must be willing to master it if he wished to have a prosperous Mission. Blanchet warned D'Herbomez that to truly minister to their "six hundred savages," a thorough knowledge of Carrier was vital. Otherwise, he feared that the title of the Mission's patron, Our Lady of Good Hope, would soon become a song of lament, for there would be no hope for its future.[39]

✤ The Kootenays and St. Eugene's Mission

THE KUTENAI PEOPLE of the southeast also benefited from their remoteness from European contact. Thus the Kutenai, like other interior Native peoples, retained a far more romantic attraction to Europeans than those of the coastal people. While many Europeans viewed the Coast Salish as stupid, lazy fisherman, many "whites" viewed the Kutenai as "noble savages" well into the twentieth century. Remoteness was the Kutenai's greatest asset. The Kootenay River and Lake, and the great Columbia River demarcated their lands, providing water for the forested mountain slopes and fertile valleys. Although it had semi-arid regions, the land abounded in big game, fish and edible bird life.[40]

Kutenai culture was rich and complex. Villages were politically autonomous, although linked by familial ties. Though they differed from the coastal Natives in dress, economy and social mores, resembling more the Plains people, in other ways they were akin to the Coastal and Interior Salish. While the Kutenai had no crests or totems or mask dances like the Northwest coastal peoples, they had shaman and warrior classes and a system of elders who had a role in electing leaders and in making important decisions. The Upper and Lower Kutenai formed the major tribal divisions. The Upper Kutenai lived along the northern reaches of the Kootenay River and took part in the bison hunts on the Prairies, whereas the latter inhabited the southern expanses of the river and relied heavily upon a fish diet. However, by 1861 both groups, according to the Jesuit, Peter DeSmet, also cultivated small crops of corn, barley, oats and potatoes. The Kutenai language was one of the six distinct tongues spoken in the Canadian far west. Total population reports of the Kutenai varied from 1000 in 1835 to 625 in 1885, which undoubtedly reflected European contact and diseases, especially smallpox. As late as 1888, the Oblates constituted one of the few outside influences on the Kutenai.[41]

Spirituality and the supernatural formed a central area of Kutenai culture. They borrowed or contributed to both Plains and Interior Salish mythology. The Sun Dance, probably adapted from the Plains peoples, con-

St. Eugene's Mission Boys' Band, Cranbrook (AD)

tained elements of monotheistic belief, although many guardian spirits also demanded fasting, prayer and other ceremonial rites. Due to their relative and continued isolation, the Kutenai, when faced with the new challenges of western civilization and Christianity, were able to practice a more judicious and careful syncretism. DeSmet, one of the earliest missionaries to visit them in the 1840s, found them the "best disposed of all the mountain tribes."[42]

The Kutenai had their first exposure to Christianity from amateur catechists, such as Christian Iroquois guides who worked for the fur trading companies. There were also important influences from the Flatheads of Montana Territory, especially stories of an eighteenth century prophet, Shining Shirt who announced that a new religion would soon come. By the nineteenth century the Prophet Dance, which had originated in the Oregon Territory in the 1830s, had become intermixed with Christian teachings that together emphasized prayer, penance, baptism and a resurrected life after death. By the time the first Oblate, Léon Fouquet arrived among them in 1874, the Kutenai had evolved a system of beliefs from many different sources that contained a rich mixture of both Christian and non-Christian elements.[43]

Before his arrival in the Kootenays in 1874, Fouquet, the 43-year-old Oblate founder of St. Eugene's Mission had already spent 15 years in the Missions of British Columbia on both Vancouver Island and the mainland. Within a year of his arrival among the Kutenai, a Victoria newspaper was singing his praises as a man who was "wholly devoted to his calling" and taking "the country by storm." While such a report seemed to reflect a marked improvement over his previous experience at Fort Rupert (1867–74) where the Kwakiutl had totally rejected his efforts, ultimately Fouquet's many personality shortcomings would seriously hinder his work among the Kutenai.[44]

Fouquet, who possessed a rigid disposition, was neither an innovator nor did he have a very strong imagination. Although he could be quite forthright in opposing a decision that he did not agree with and publicly defending one he did, as he had in a 1864 pamphlet on the value of religion based schools, he remained an almost obsessive follower of Oblate rules and regulations. Any deviation for him was usually sinful. Thus he tried to convince the Kutenai to settle into reduction-style settlements and become sedentary farmers. Although they had gone into cattle and horse ranching at least a decade before his arrival, they were not prepared to settle permanently anywhere. During his time there, in an almost blind drive to continue to pursue his plan, Fouquet oversaw the completion of 77 Kutenai houses that accommodated almost 600 people. However, the Natives thwarted his reduction plan by settling in half a dozen places, most often near traditional village sites. By 1884, there were close to 50 houses on Mission property, but the Natives gathered there "only during winter months," and so the buildings of the hoped-for reduction remained unoccupied throughout most of the year.[45]

The Kutenai, however, did not require the supposed protection of the reduction system, since their isolation remained their greatest barrier between the worst elements of western ways, especially land speculators and settlements. There were the more "normal" problems of drinking, gambling and other dissipations that could occur when any human beings gathered in large numbers, especially when trading horses or cattle. Fouquet used the preached mission to try to address such behavior. Those who publicly admitted such wrong doing, such as drinking, gambling or seeking the advice of a shaman were given penances and pledged to refrain from such activities. In keeping with well-established Oblate tradition, Fouquet also established temperance societies and gave badges to participants. Not until 1880, did he select Natives to act as watchmen and catechists who, during his long absences, were expected to conduct regular prayer services and report any infractions to him upon his return. The long delay in such appointments resulted from a serious communication problem, for Fouquet, whose English was poor, neither spoke nor understood much of the Kutenai language, nor had Chinook ever been widely used by the interior Native population. By the 1880s, due to the gradual increase of Europeans in the area, the Kutenai had begun to learn some English as well as Chinook. Thus it was not Fouquet but the Natives who first adapted to change.[46]

Probably reflecting his own very rigid mindset, especially his adherence to Oblate regulations, Fouquet was quite strict in administering sacraments and expected his colleagues to reflect a similar mentality. During his 17 years at Cranbrook, he only baptized 69 Natives and only married about 60 couples. Actually, such were his extreme demands upon adults, most of his baptisms were of infants or little children. He was equally strict in admitting any Native to first communion, requiring that before its reception they had to pass a lengthy oral examination. Both of his initial assistants: Louis-Napoléon Grégoire (1875–78) and Edmond Peytavin (1879–86) fought such policies, but most of all they complained about his authoritarian manner, which was usually accompanied by angry outbursts.[47]

In line with vicariate policy, Fouquet had a strong desire to found a residential school for Native boys at Cranbrook. On paper he was well qualified for such a task. His first assignment (1854–59) after ordination was teaching in two seminaries in Europe, and he had been involved in founding and teaching (1860–67) in the Native Residential School for boys at Mission City on the Lower Mainland. His numerous attempts to establish a school among the Kutenai, however, failed, probably due to his frequent tantrums and his general inability to work with other Oblates who might have helped to balance his obsessive personality. Native schooling at St. Eugene had to wait until 1890 when his successor, Nicolas Coccola (1887–99) opened a federally funded industrial Residential School.[48]

The Mission farm was to be an important source of income for St. Eugene's, but, under Fouquet's direction, it soon proved to be almost more trouble than it was worth. Within five years of his arrival, Fouquet had purchased over 700 acres along the south bank of St. Mary's River. It was a very considerable undertaking. This was especially true given his poor health, the very limited help of one lay brother, and his unwillingness to pay for hired help. Therefore, Fouquet found himself tied to an enterprise for which he had very little liking, although, since he wished to see it succeed, he had to devote much of his time working in the fields. Far worse for him, it prevented him from doing missionary work, especially visiting the Kutenai.

In 1882 an official visitation by Aimé Martinet found that both the farm and the Mission were being poorly run. Fouquet's very limited knowledge of Kutenai and English made basic communication very difficult with both the local Natives and the growing Euro-Canadian population. As a possible solution, especially with regard to Fouquet's inability to delegate, Martinet suggested that Fouquet's latest assistant, Father Adolphe Martin (1880–83) be appointed bursar. Nevertheless, while Fouquet promised to make amends, little would come of it.[49]

Brother John Burns,
First Companion of Father Fouquet
at St. Eugene Mission (AD)

His interpersonal problems represent almost a textbook example of staff stress and how such issues could undermine Oblate missionary activities. The Dublin born Brother John Burns, who had been with Fouquet at Fort Rupert (1866–74), spent the rest of his life (1874–1908) at St. Eugene's. Each man complained of the unwillingness of the other to cooperate. In 1882 Burns insisted that when Grégoire and Peytavin were there, Fouquet's inability to get on with them had meant that the director treated Burns like "a honey-comb," but after their departure, with no priest colleagues to attack, Fouquet turned on Burns, who then received "only black face" from Fouquet. Grégoire, a Quebecois, and Peytavin, a Frenchman, were just as critical. Both priests had completed their theology under Fouquet, which might explain their later tensions, since Fouquet's view of theology was as conservative and inflexible as his personality. Grégoire was not suited to the constraints of religious life, and he finally left the Oblates and the Catholic Church around 1883. Apparently his major reason was his desire to marry, and he eventually became a Protestant minister in Quebec, though he reportedly had a death-bed return to Catholicism in 1908. As for Peytavin, circumstances were so bad, that he also threatened to leave the Oblates if he were not transferred. However, after his time with Fouquet ended, Peytavin appears to have spent a productive career in the Congregation.[50]

There were few, if any signs of improvement. Adolphe Martin, a Quebecois was the next (1880–83) assistant. Although the two got along for about a year, Fouquet soon complained of the young priest's "hardened liberalism." Finally in 1883 Pierre Richard (1883–92), a seasoned missionary and Fouquet's senior by several years, replaced Martin and eventually succeeded him at Cranbrook. While the two seemed to relate well, much of the credit no doubt must go to Richard who had the wisdom to ignore the continued testy behaviour of his colleague. Actually Fouquet felt so alienated from the Oblates in British Columbia, that when he left St. Eugene's in 1888, he was finally transferred to work with the Oblates in Alberta. It was a decision that both he and his superiors supported, and he ministered there for over ten years (1888–99), though he would spend his final years (1899-1912) at Mission City.[51]

Like quite a number of missionaries, whether Catholic or not, Fouquet possessed a maverick, lone-ranger mentality, that often made cooperation with colleagues very difficult. The famous Anglican missionary, William Duncan had similar conflicts with his associates, as did the well-known Oblate ethnologist, Adrien Morice. Lack of compatibility was one cause, and in the case of Cranbrook, as elsewhere, everyone began to complain of being misunderstood by everyone else, which then lead to multiple illnesses. Fouquet and most of his associates endured horrible health problems throughout their years at St. Eugene's, but when they separated, they seemed to "miraculously" disappear. The Jansenistic-inspired Oblate spirituality encouraged suffering and victimhood, but discouraged the one solution to such interpersonal tensions, communication with and the willingness to listen to others. When these critically positive attitudes were present, communities and the Mission seemed to flourish, as at Stuart Lake. However, though perhaps not as extreme elsewhere, it seems that the circumstances at St. Eugene's were in some ways far more common than the situation at Our Lady of Good Hope. Thus, petty human disagreements were too often allowed to grow and ultimately hindered, if they did not destroy the Oblate raison d'être, "ministering to the poor," particularly to the Native people. Actually, when compared to the Natives, often it was the Oblates who were truly "poor."[52]

8

The Native People
and
the Diocese of Victoria

✤ The Secular Clergy

UNLIKE THE OBLATES, the secular clergy never had the same interest in working with the Native people. When compared to seculars, a high degree of almost military-like organization was expected of the regular clergy, and was reflected in their many rules and regulations. A major result was a certain sense of community. Due to a lack of dialogue or consensus, this notion of community was usually quite artificial, which often caused considerable staff stress, and was largely unsuccessful. Nevertheless, it did require its members to at least *appear* to be willingly acting in unison. When the community leadership emphasised participation in a ministry, such as working among the Native people, co-operation was demanded. For while such participation may not have been enthusiastic, it was not only expected, but it was required under the religious vow of obedience to a superior. However, there was no such organization among seculars. Rather, although not officially encouraged, a "rugged individualism" dominated their relationships with one another and greatly influenced their ministry. Based on individual

Father August Joseph Brabant (ASSA)

ability and whim, the ministry of seculars was frequently inefficient and haphazard, which strongly impacted their work, particularly in the evangelisation of the Native people.

Since there was no "system," or even the pretence of one in the secular modus operandi, Catholic missions to the Natives on Vancouver Island "never recovered their momentum," after the Oblates withdrew in 1866; although a tiny handful of seculars took this ministry quite seriously. A young Belgian priest, Charles John Seghers, who, in 1873, would become the second bishop of Victoria, was far more committed to this challenge than his predecessor, Demers. For while Demers did not ignore the Native people, he clearly considered such a ministry as far less important than that to Europeans. Seghers's enthusiasm was definitely shared by his colleague and fellow Belgian, August Joseph Brabant.[1]

Brabant was unique, since he was the only secular priest in the diocese of Victoria who spent most of his life working among the Native people. His decision turned him into something of a celebrity, especially among his secular colleagues, which would have been unheard of for an Oblate. By the 1870s, ministry to the Natives on Vancouver Island was part-time and limited to the regions around Victoria, the Saanich Peninsula and the Cowichan Valley. When Seghers succeeded Demers, in an attempt to expand their work, in 1874 Seghers and Brabant visited the Nootka in the relative wilderness of the westcoast of Vancouver Island. Since the eighteenth century, when the Spanish and English had made their initial contacts with the Nootka, few Europeans had attempted to return there, since its remoteness made commerce, such as fur trading, unprofitable. Consequently, as in the interior, until the 1870s their relative isolation had also protected Nootka culture.

Lack of contact also increased ignorance, especially among Euro-Canadians who erroneously blamed the situation on the supposed "savageness" of the Nootka. Like all prejudice, it was undeserved, though Seghers and Brabant were influenced by it. On the eve of their departure, Seghers, who had always

The Lord's Distant Vineyard

longed for "martyrdom," remarked that a missionary's "real happiness" was "to die in service to God." Apparently expecting, if not hoping for a violent death, Seghers concluded "so much the better."[2]

Perhaps somewhat disappointed, the two clergymen found the Nootka quite friendly. Seghers, evidencing a "noble savage" romanticism that was also tinged with racism, misinterpreted Native hospitality towards himself and Brabant as reflecting a form of "holy timidity" by the Nootka when faced by their supposed "white" superiors. Given the lack of recent contact, their trip was historic. So when they returned the following year, they brought gifts to the Native leaders from the provincial government. Demonstrating a naïveté common among most missionaries, including the Oblates, Seghers reported in 1875 that besides visiting "twenty-one villages," he and Brabant had converted "thousands of savages" to the Catholic faith. Brabant reported, in a not uncommon fit of cultural arrogance, that he and Seghers had erected a huge cross to mark their "conquest," that Brabant insisted symbolised "Christ's triumph over paganism and superstition, and...his peaceful conquest of the poor, forsaken children of the forest."[3]

Brabant began a ministry among the Native peoples of the westcoast that would last for over 30 years, making him probably the most famous Catholic secular priest missionary at that time in British Columbia. Initially, as the first European to live among them for generations, his major contribution to the Hesquiat, the Nootka tribe with whom he spent most of his time, was to introduce smallpox. Like many Oblates, he tried to treat the terrible disease with vaccine, but he also saw it as God's curse upon these poor people for their lack of interest in and/or continued resistance to the "Catholic" faith.[4]

However, one of their leaders, Matlahaw, realising the reason for his people's suffering, tried to murder Brabant with the priest's own rifle. Unlike Matlahaw, who was dying of smallpox, Brabant not only survived, but the incident resulted in his lionisation by many in the Euro-Canadian community on Vancouver Island. As for Matlahaw, "whites" viewed him as an "assassin," and almost totally ignored the deadly consequences of smallpox among the Hesquiat. Instead, after five months in the capital recuperating from a hand wound, the press in Victoria trumpeted Brabant's return to the Hesquiat as a "white" triumph of "Christian civilisation" over "heathen barbarism."[5]

The Victoria press no less naively and arrogantly reported that the Hesquiat were "very anxious" to see Brabant return. If Brabant had dared to do the same among Euro-Canadians, they would no doubt have murdered him for his central role in their terrible plight. In fact the Hesquiat did express the fear that the priest had indeed come back in order "to kill all the...Indians," but they did not murder him. No doubt they realised that such an action would result in "white" reprisals. In not seeking revenge, the Hesquiat appeared to be far more Christ-like than most of the so-called Christians who were attempting to indoctrinate them.[6]

Determined to convert his "savages," Brabant immediately inaugurated a type of reduction system and, though largely unsuccessful, for years he struggled to implement it. Initially he appointed three watchmen to "spy" on other Hesquiat and report to him any infractions, especially sexual ones. In order to "distinguish" the watchmen "from other savages, and as a mark of their authority," Brabant provided them with "pants and a coat." Hoping to gain future control of Hesquiat leadership, he also named the three watchmen as "regents" to the young son of their dead elder and leader, Matlahaw. Besides his very haphazard reduction system, the "Catholic Ladder" was probably the major weapon in Brabant's proselytising arsenal.

His primary handicap in trying to evangelise the Hesquiat remained his inability to communicate. Jean Baptiste Brondel (1879–83), the third bishop of Victoria, strongly encouraged Brabant to learn Nootkan, but he never did. He conducted missions, preached to the Hesquiat, as so many missionaries before him, through interpreters who tried to convey his ideas in a mixture of English, Chinook and Nootkan. Although Brabant's Native audience may have appeared to be listening, in time it became clear that the preacher's inability to communicate meant that his efforts were largely a waste of time.[7]

Certainly, after many years of effort the ultimate impact was minimal. There was some degree of change, which could loosely be described as acculturation, but it seems to have influenced Brabant more than the Hesquiat. Their extreme isolation from Euro-Canadian society certainly made their acceptance of Christianity or western ways conditional, especially in deciding if such changes would be beneficial. Brabant was somewhat successful in encouraging young men to marry whom they wished, thus partially undermining tribal traditions that placed considerable restrictions on how a suitor must proceed, and that were also intended to protect the rights of Native women. Again, his home remedies, such as mustard plasters, appear to have been quite popular, although they in no way ended the important influence of the shamans. In fact, by 1900, after almost 30 years of living near them, except for a handful of fervent adherents, Brabant had "Christianised" very few Hesquiat. A rather incompetent educator, in time even Brabant would grasp the reality that reasonably regular or, more likely, quite sporadic church attendance did not translate into "conversions."[8]

Brabant did experience some success in his work, yet it was neither orderly nor permanent. His published *Reminiscences* reflect a person who was always an outsider, but this was less true in 1899 than in 1877. Perhaps Brabant's initial contacts with Seghers gave him unrealistic and even naïve expectations. Except for a handful of dedicated followers, most Hesquiat were either never baptised, or if they were, only when they were near death. Infant baptism was quite common, but did not guarantee that the recipient would continue to practice the faith as an adult. Brabant always proclaimed eagerly that his work had finally seen the successful triumph of both Catholicism and civilization among the Hesquiat. However, his ultimate determination to build a residential school on the westcoast before the Methodists and Presbyterians "perverted" his "poor little Indian children," clearly indicated his predicament. Also, in so doing he provided a clear recognition that the Catholic faith that he had tried to engender for almost a generation (1877–1900) did not have a very solid foundation.[9]

✤ Another Westcoast Missionary

JOHN NICHOLAS LEMMENS, the fifth bishop of Victoria (1888–97) was the only other secular priest of the diocese, besides his fellow Belgian Brabant, to work (1883–86) among the Native peoples on the westcoast of Vancouver Island where he founded a small mission at Clayoquot. Little is know personally of Lemmens, but he kept a journal, apparently the only other one, in addition to Brabant's, to have survived among the diocesan clergy of Victoria. The title of his sketchy, though illustrated account reveals a man with at least a sense of humour: "*Haps & Mishaps, Accidental Incidents, Eventful Casualties, Adventurous Occurrences, Casual Events, Occasional Fortuities and Contingencies, Detailed Minutes, Minute Details of Solid Facts.*"[10]

Lemmens, admittedly only after several years of trying, had only a few faithful Native adherents, however, unlike Brabant, he admitted that fact and even speculated on the reasons for his lack of success. He reported that after three years he could count only two adult baptisms, two marriages, 25 funerals, and 33 first communions. While he had some knowledge of

Bishop John Nicholas Lemmens (centre) and his clergy (AD)

Chinook, and "commanded" a few words in Nootkan, he admitted that, unless he composed and then very carefully read his sermons, his Native audience found him almost impossible to understand. Like Brabant, he tried to run a little day school, but attendance was extremely poor. He acknowledged that the school's existence was due solely to the annual allowance he received from the Department of Indian Affairs towards its operation, for, without that subsidy, he said that he could never have remained on the westcoast.[11]

At times Lemmens was somewhat inventive in trying to win greater Native interest in Catholicism. As most missionaries, he saw his main task as bringing the "blessings of Christianity and western civilisation to the poor Indians," yet occasionally he tried to make the experience interesting, if not even enjoyable. Thus, in an effort to increase attendance, at his first Christmas midnight Mass he showed "magic lantern" slides during the celebration.[12]

Still he found Native culture unattractive, meaningless, and even "evil." Describing a male initiation ceremony, where a young man received a wound, in this case on his arm, a practice almost universal among aboriginal peoples, Lemmens, in his cultural ignorance, could only describe it as an "awful scene."[13]

Lemmens's reaction to failure, and fail he did, was typical of many, if not most missionaries. His Jansenistic spirituality helped him almost celebrate his failure as the will of God and thus, his few surviving sermons reveal a dualistic, "other worldly" view of reality, describing this one as largely a "continual and painful experience." When faced with opposition or rejection, he tended to blame the "ignorance" of the Native people in not being open to accepting the "truth." He also believed that there would be consequences for what he saw as their continued obstinacy. When a Native father, who had fought his presence, later lost three sons in a drowning accident, Lemmens attributed the tragedy to divine retribution because of the father's behaviour.[14]

One incident in particular seemed to summarise his feelings and to underscore the general lack of Native acceptance. After the death of a young boy, which Lemmens blamed on the "interference" of a shaman, the boy's family accused Lemmens of causing the tragedy by filling the child's head with "too-much-study" at the day school. With a sense of almost depressed resignation that revealed his own gloomy view of his ministry, he concluded: "Such is life in the far-west" of Vancouver Island.[15]

Despite his admitted failure, like Brabant, Lemmens was lionised by his fellow priests and the Catholic laity of the diocese. Largely because of their "heroic" Native ministry, both men were recommended to succeed Seghers. In promoting Lemmens to the Vatican as a fit candidate for the episcopacy, referees repeatedly cited his "valiant" work among the "rude, ignorant and superstitious savages" as a major reason for his selection. In 1884, while he was still working on the westcoast, his fellow priests, largely because they were impressed with his labours, elected him to represent the diocese at the Third Council of Baltimore. There he met Cardinal Gibbons and Archbishop Gross of Portland, Oregon. Such personal contacts, added to his missionary work, helps explain his ultimate selection by Rome as the fifth (1888–97) bishop of Victoria and successor to Seghers.[16]

✣ Seghers, Alaska and the Native People

SEGHERS HAD LONG HAD AN INTEREST in converting the Alaskan Eskimo, which until 1894, when it would become a vicariate apostolic, remained part of the diocese of Victoria. His fascination with Alaska ended in his murder there in November 1886, at the hands a paranoid, schizophrenic Irish Catholic named Frank Fuller. Seghers's almost obsessive interest in Alaska certainly ranks as one of the strangest, and one of the saddest stories in the history of the Catholic Church in the far west.

Seghers's fascination with Alaska began in 1863, but his first visit came in 1868 when Demers sent him there to relieve another priest and Frenchman, Joseph Mandart, who had recently made an unsuccessful attempt to found a small parish at Sitka, in the Alaskan panhandle. In 1878, as bishop of Victoria, Seghers tried to establish another parish, this time at Wrangell, also in the panhandle; assigning a fellow Belgian, John Althoff as its first pastor. However, by 1881 inadequate finances, resulting from the lack of a congregation of either Europeans or Eskimos, ended the second attempt.[17]

Even after he became the second archbishop of Portland, Oregon in 1881, Seghers remained obsessed with the evangelisation of the Alaskan Eskimo. Therefore, in 1885 he asked Pope Leo XIII to allow him to relinquish Portland in order to become the fourth bishop of Victoria (1885–86). By then Seghers had begun to view Alaska as almost his raison d'être. A world-wind trip back there in September 1885 had left him in a state of shock. The little church of St. Rose in Wrangall, lacking a congregation and abandoned since 1881, was becoming a ruin. But much worse for Seghers, Presbyterians, who had arrived since his last visit, appeared to be "perverting" the Eskimos. With the help of substantial subsidies from the American government the Presbyterians had established church schools. Since most Euro-Americans in the region resented tax money being spent on the education of "savages," they had started an anti-Presbyterian campaign, which Seghers was very willing and eager to support.

While the Presbyterians continued to be a major religious force in Alaska, Seghers was convinced that his return had heralded their final downfall. For he had long "fantasised" that the Eskimos of Alaska were the last people on earth to hear the gospel preached, at least by the Roman Catholic Church, despite the fact that the Russian Orthodox Church had been in the region since 1784. Still, Seghers believed that, if Roman Catholicism were finally proclaimed there, this singular event might well usher in the end-time, and with it the second coming of Christ! Like a man already pitying a vanquished foe, Seghers termed the Presbyterians "poor unfortunates" who were actually neither educating nor converting the Eskimos. Instead, he wrote, "like the hypocrites of whom Jesus spoke, neither they nor the people to whom they preached would ever go to heaven," noting that "even the Protestants, Jews and infidels asked for Roman Catholic missionaries in order to destroy Presbyterian control." Seghers was certain that the Native people would soon be "tired of the Presbyterian

Archbishop Charles John Seghers (AD)

yoke." Although some Eskimos had long been members of the Russian Orthodox Church, given the competitive behaviour of all denominational-ism, most were reluctant to join any of the "new" churches.[18]

Headstrong and romantic, at times in the extreme, Seghers rarely consid-ered any objections or alternatives once he had made-up his mind. All he wanted now were priests, he said, who "would rather pluck out their eyes than quibble," and who had the "courage to undertake anything and the con-stancy to persevere." He apparently found them in two of his diocesan clergy: John Althoff, the Alaskan veteran, and William Heyman, then an assistant priest at St. Andrew's Cathedral in Victoria. Rising to his challenge, both Belgians left for the Alaskan panhandle where they would work for 17 years, although their efforts produced few lasting results. Nevertheless, like a Siren, Alaska continued to lure Seghers towards it and his ultimate doom.[19]

Seghers admitted that it was a "foolhardy undertaking," but he was determined to found Catholic Missions in the Yukon River Valley and Alaskan interior. Impressed by their missionary work in the United States, he asked the Jesuits for help. In response, their provincial superior, Joseph Cataldo eventually chose two priests: Pascal Tosi and Aloysius Robaut to accompany Seghers to Alaska. However, Seghers was not satisfied, and despite strong opposition from the Jesuits, he insisted on adding "Brother" Frank Fuller to the missionary team. Seghers had met Fuller while he was archbishop of Portland, and for some inexplicable reason had developed what would become a "fatal" attraction for the Irishman who, when approached, "happily volunteered" his services for Alaska.[20]

Fuller was a deeply troubled man. Born in Dublin, Ireland, by the 1880s he had settled in the Washington Territory where he "attached" himself to several Jesuit Missions. He gained credit for his skills as a mechanic and hunter, but his paranoid personality made him suspect the very worst of everyone and he would quarrel over the slightest matter. The Jesuits repeatedly dismissed him, but, because of his practical skills, would rehire him. While finally rejected as a Jesuit aspirant, his mechanical talents appear to have been in such demand that he became a Jesuit "hanger-on."[21]

✤ The Murder of an Archbishop

SEGHERS'S LAST TRAGIC JOURNEY began on 13 July 1886 when the 46-year-old archbishop, together with Tosi, Robaut and Fuller, left Esquimalt Harbour for the Yukon on the "Ancon." Early in the trip, Tosi warned Seghers about Fuller's increasingly strange behavior in that he believed that someone was going to kill him. Given Fuller's history, Tosi strongly recommended allowing Fuller to return to Portland. Seghers disagreed. Referring to him as "Brother" Fuller, although he was not, nor never had been a professed religious brother, Seghers assured Tosi that the Irishman would be fine once their party had left "civilization." Seghers's patently illogical reasoning only further undermined the confidence and respect of the two Jesuits. Tosi, who was Robaut's superior, in his later assessment of Seghers's behavior, was far more critical than his colleague, Robaut, who blamed the archbishop's very poor judgement on a genuine, though naïve desire to befriend Fuller. Although none of the clergy appear to have further discussed their feelings about Fuller, Seghers continued to refer in his diary to "the good-hearted Brother." Finally, after weeks of very arduous trekking down rivers, through mountain passes and over harsh, forbidding terrain, on September 7th the weary travellers reached a trading post at the mouth of the Stewart River and where they planned to spend the winter.[22]

Seghers soon changed his mind about remaining there after he heard that the Anglicans would soon enter the Alaskan interior. Determined to arrive before them, he insisted on continuing their journey. Tosi, long angered over Seghers's decision to bring Fuller, and adamant that they did not have enough supplies to sustain them, refused to leave, and ordered Roubaut to remain behind as well. Convinced that he was in the right, undaunted, and accompanied by only three Eskimo guides and "Brother" Fuller, Seghers pressed on. Within a fortnight of his "foolhardy" decision, Seghers ominously began noting in his diary that "Brother Fuller" was showing "evidence of insanity." By late November Fuller was insisting that the party stop for the winter, but Seghers, within days of Nulato, his ultimate destination, refused to listen. On the evening of November 27th the party reached Yesetltor, which was only ten miles from the mouth of the Yukon River. Seghers's spirits were now as high as Fuller's were low. Together with the Eskimo guides, they spent the night in a smokehouse. The following morning, a Sunday, sometime between six and seven o'clock, while Seghers was reaching down to put on his mittens, Fuller shot him through the chest with the archbishop's own Winchester rifle. Adding another bizarre twist to the whole tragic incident, despite Seghers's clear awareness of Fuller's apparent insanity, the night before, the archbishop had left his loaded rifle lying on the floor between himself and Fuller. Charles John Seghers apparently died instantly.[23]

Immediately overpowered by the Eskimo guides, who turned him over to the American authorities, Fuller remained in jail until his trial, which began at Sitka, Alaska in September 1887. Fuller always maintained that he had shot Seghers in self-defence, claiming that the Native guides, under Seghers's direction, were plotting to murder him. The Eskimo witnesses rejected Fuller's story, and the court-appointed doctors testified that he was suffering from delusions and melancholia. Cost and a desire to avoid further delays prevented the government from calling additional witnesses. After deliberating for over 40 hours, the jury seemed hopelessly deadlocked apparently due to what some jurors saw as Seghers's very poor judgement, and therefore his own responsibility in the affair. Finally, the jury asked if

Fuller could be found guilty of manslaughter. Judge Lafayette Dawson replied in the affirmative, as long as the jury "believed that when the rifle was fired the prisoner had no intention of killing the Bishop." Thus Fuller was found guilty of manslaughter, sentenced to ten years at hard labor and fined $1,000 which, after he indicated his inability to pay, was commuted to 30 additional days in prison. The verdict also implied that Seghers, knowing Fuller's mental problems, for some inexplicable reason, perhaps arising out of an unconscious desire to die, or even possibly an unexplored attachment to Fuller, had quite willingly decided to travel in his company.[24]

There were many reactions to the murder. The Victoria press condemned the U.S. government and American justice for not finding Fuller either innocent, by reason of insanity, or guilty of first degree murder. The diocesan administrator of Victoria, John Jonchau, a fellow Belgian and veteran priest of the diocese, convinced that the archbishop was a "martyred saint," called for a definitive response to the tragic death of a man he now called the "apostle of Alaska." Namely, he wanted both the Jesuits and Sisters of St. Ann to dedicate their lives, as Seghers had, to laying a solid foundation for the Catholic Church in Alaska. Certainly the Jesuits were embarrassed in having a dead archbishop on their hands. For, no matter how foolhardy his own behaviour, Seghers had been murdered by a man who, the newspapers, picking up on Seghers's published diary entries, referred to as a "Jesuit Brother," which he was not. Even so, Fuller had been a Jesuit postulant for a brief time. Very reluctantly the Jesuits did accept Alaska as their latest missionary assignment. The Sisters of St. Ann were considering a permanent Alaskan ministry, and three Sisters, Mary Zenon, Bonsecour and Victor had opened a small hospital in Juneau in September 1886, but there was still no definite determination to stay. Thus, they too were extremely hesitant to accept Jonchau's romanticised suggestions, due mainly to practicalities, such as the great distance involved and staff shortages. However, Jonchau, together with Archbishop Charles-Édouard Fabre of Montreal, cajoled and mortified the nuns into accepting. Evidencing definite signs of Jansenistic spirituality, both clerics insisted that Seghers's "great sacrifice" only proved that it was the "will of God" that was calling upon the Sisters to also "sacrifice" themselves in making a final commitment to Alaska.[25]

While he expressed many of his views in the extreme, Seghers was still a man of his age. The longing he frequently expressed of experiencing a "martyr's death" in some far off country had first been fed by Belgian missionary magazine propaganda that usually pleaded for people to work among the "poor savages" in some remote land. Such enticements had been a major factor in Seghers's decision to leave Belgium and come to distant Victoria. In 1864, shortly after he arrived there, a youthful Father Seghers wrote that he hoped that he would "make the necessary preparations to die as a soldier of Christ on the scene of war, with the weapons in the fist; at least if His [God's] will be so." On the eve of his final departure for Alaska in 1886, Seghers told a colleague that he was looking for priests who were "ready to shed their blood in Alaska."[26]

A talented man, though at times far too headstrong, Frank Fuller interpreted Seghers's unbending, even obsessive determination as life-threatening, and so he killed the archbishop. Ironically, given Seghers's hostility towards all non-Catholics, a Presbyterian minister conducted his funeral, and his body, which could not be returned to Victoria for over a year, was temporarily buried in a Russian Orthodox church in Sitka, Alaska.[27]

Although definitely not a martyr, Seghers's tragic death did leave a mark on the history of the Catholic Church in the far west. Certainly the circumstances of his demise embarrassed and thus forced the Jesuits and the Sisters of St. Ann to accept an Alaskan mission. Therefore, his death, which common sense could easily have avoided, prompted an earlier than otherwise likely establishment of the Catholic Church in Alaska. Perhaps a comment made by an anonymous Sister of St. Ann in May 1973 sums up the life and work of Charles John Seghers: "How wonderful and strange he was."[28]

Native Girls in Concert Costumes, Williams Lake (AD)

9

Oblate Approaches
to the Native People

✟ *The Residential School*

THE RE-EDUCATION OF NATIVES by Euro-Canadians is one of the most painful experiences in the long encounter between these two peoples. Residential schools could never have existed without the vital encouragement and funding of the federal government of Canada and the willing cooperation of the major denominations. The Catholic Church had a very significant role in conducting such institutions and the Oblates, more than any other Catholic religious order, were charged with carrying out their policy.

The Oblates, in their formal published *Apology to the Native Peoples* of Canada, made in 1991 by Douglas Crosby, President of the Oblate Conference of Canada, expressed sorrow for their central role "in setting up and...maintaining" the residential schools. Referring to the abuses against the Native people, physical as well as cultural, Crosby noted that "the biggest abuse was not what happened in the schools, but that the schools themselves happened." In their reaction to the *Apology*, almost all the Oblate members of British Columbia's St. Paul's Province were decidedly hostile. Using such words as "stunned," "shocked," "too harsh," they almost unanimously rejected the contention that the schools should never have existed. Instead, most believed that, while mistakes were made and wrongs committed, it was done in what most Euro-Canadians long thought was in the best interests of the Native people.[1]

✤ The Oblate Vision Behind the Schools

CERTAINLY THE OBLATES working in British Columbia always believed in the essential need for such schools. Writing as recently as 1942 about the education of Natives, an Oblate Bishop, Émile Bunoz had no doubts about their importance. The first vicar apostolic of the Yukon and Prince Rupert (1909–1945), Bunoz noted that the "Indian is weak in mind and heart." As a means of altering this situation, in order that the Native peoples might obtain the "wonderful fruits of salvation," he concluded that the residential school had a vital role in reinforcing the reduction.[2]

The Oblates' policy in British Columbia was that all Native Catholic leaders should receive their education in residential schools, and, in turn, they should be willing to support the importance of both the school and the reduction. Further, to enhance the Native leaders' role in achieving those ends, the Oblates believed that the dominant society should also recognize their importance by making Native leaders provincial magistrates or judges. By doing so, the Oblates were convinced that Native authority figures could then lay the groundwork for molding the reduction and residential school into essential tools for the ultimate transformation of Native culture into a mirror image of the local Euro-Canadian culture.[3]

Only a few secular authorities saw any wisdom in the idea. Chief Justice Matthew Baillie Begbie thought it an interesting concept, but preferred the present system, since he believed that the only social problem that could not be effectively controlled by the provincial judiciary was drunkenness. However, Begbie concluded that "the laws of Moses," together with organized Christianity, were best suited to deal with what was really a question of moral behavior. He certainly did not believe that a native judiciary could be founded upon a "single social problem." Though he rejected the notion of Native judges or even magistrates, Begbie was prepared to consider the possibility of Native constables who would have been responsible, as their Euro-Canadian equivalents, to local magistrates. However, none of these suggestions was ever implemented.[4]

As for Christian missionaries, the government, whether provincial or federal, viewed them as relatively inexpensive custodians and teachers of western civilization to the Native people, with acculturation as the final goal. Thus, if the churches were successful, either through the use of the reduction or residential education, or a combination of the two, the Native peoples would ultimately be totally absorbed into the larger society, and eventually nothing would remain of their former selves, not even their memories.

✣ Native Land Claims and the Oblates

FOR THE OBLATES OF BRITISH COLUMBIA, the question of local Native jurisdiction also touched upon the issue of Native land rights. Both were important elements in maintaining the reduction and residential schools. As long as the Native peoples had no control over their land, the Oblates believed they must remain subservient to the larger society. Unlike the nomadic Natives of the prairies and plains, those in British Columbia had settled village sites, many of which were far older than most Euro-Canadian or Euro-American cities in North America. Therefore, they had a sense of belonging to the land, similar to their eastern counterparts, that was not dissimilar to the notion of European property rights.[5]

For many years European authorities had largely ignored the land issue in British Columbia, with the notable exception of James Douglas who signed a handful of minor agreements with Native tribes near Victoria that he hoped to expand and extend to other parts of the province. Yet, none of his successors, whether colonial governors or provincial premiers took the matter seriously. In the rest of Canada there had long been treaties between the Natives and Europeans designating land transfers and specific compensations, such as reserves. Instead, the European authorities in British Columbia acted either as though the Natives did not exist, or that they would very soon disappear through assimilation or disease.[6]

The Oblates did make a definite effort to address the land issue, since they realized its importance to their overall aim of acculturating Natives into following "white" ways. As early as 1869 Durieu tried to convince Governor Anthony Musgrave to provide the Natives on the lower mainland with substantial reserves. After his advice was ignored, Durieu complained that everything possible was being done by the local colonial authorities "to deprive the Indians of their land." Durieu noted bitterly in 1892 that the few attempts made by Douglas to set aside land for reserves on the lower mainland were now being totally disregarded by both the provincial and federal authorities, since Europeans were settling on them with apparent impunity.[7]

D'Herbomez also tried to address this serious injustice and, by doing so, to foster both the reduction and residential school. In 1871, he expressed his frustration and hope to Joseph Howe, federal minister for Indian Affairs, and Hector Langevin, federal minister for Public Works. He told Howe that the government had refused to establish reasonably large reserves and even ignored the reserves granted to the Natives by Douglas. He admitted that, perhaps the government, fearing the legal consequences, did not wish to draw attention to the old reserves by formally revoking them, but noted that the few existing reserves were mostly tiny parcels of ten acres or less, and thus nearly useless. Yet, he noted that land hungry Europeans could usually settle even on these plots without concern for any legal consequences. Since the Native village was vital to the reduction and residential school, he feared that the Native peoples would ultimately be driven from them and forcibly settled on American-style reservations. If this should happen, he warned Howe that violent Native reprisals might cause a Euro-Canadian backlash, with disastrous consequences for the aboriginals. However, if the government recognized, protected and expanded Native land rights, with the help of the reduction, residential education and the Catholic faith, D'Herbomez believed that the Natives would soon become exemplary Canadian citizens.[8]

With the hope of achieving this objective, D'Herbomez recommended to Langevin that each Native village be granted a reserve large enough to meet the needs of its population, and that treaties, extinguishing Native land claims, should be immediately formalized. In exchange, the Natives should receive all the supplies and financial support necessary to establish settled farming communities, including, by implication, residential schools. In short, D'Herbomez was encouraging the federal government to support a formal reduction system.[9]

For the next 40 years, recognizing its vital importance to their reduction plans, the Oblates tried to convince federal and provincial government officials of the need to settle the land claim issue in British Columbia, but to no avail. When the federal government seemed ready to grant larger reserves to the Natives, the provincial authorities refused to cooperate. Native leaders publicly complained of government indifference and even racism. The Oblate, Charles Grandidier, like D'Herbomez, warned of possible Native reprisals, especially in the interior, if their claims continued to be rejected. Hopes and investigations of land settlements came and went with no progress. Some reserves were enlarged, but they were few and far between, so much so that by 1927 Ottawa altered the Indian Act to prevent Native people from using any money "for the prosecution of any [land] claim." The amendment was directed specifically at British Columbia and was "intended to suppress political activity" on the issue. Land security was a vital ingredient for achieving a successful reduction system, so its success was doomed from the outset in British Columbia. But this did not stop the Oblates from at least trying to implement such a concept.[10]

✣ Preparing for Residential Schools

THE OBLATES HAD ALWAYS ACCEPTED the great value of residential schools in their ministry to the Native people. Beginning in 1867, they had established schools at St. Mary's at Mission for both Native boys and girls. There, the boys, under the Oblates, and the girls, under the Sisters of St. Ann, received a basic academic education. However, in setting up the schools, like those they founded for the French poor of Provence, with regard to Native children the Oblates had a similar classist assumption namely that they were forever destined to be working class. The Oblates were convinced that, if they were ever to prosper by obtaining gainful employment in Canadian society, Native children must concentrate their education in nonacademic areas. For, although neither of the early Oblate schools at Mission was classified as an industrial residential school, they stressed domestic skills for the girls and industrial skills for the boys, such as carpentry, blacksmithing and shoemaking, although general husbandry was also included.[11]

With British Columbia's entry into Confederation in 1871, D'Herbomez hoped to obtain federal funds in order to expand the residential schools at St. Mary's and open new ones in the other Missions, though his pleas would find little initial support in Ottawa. Writing in 1871 to Hector Langevin, then minister of Public Works in the Conservative Macdonald government, D'Herbomez emphasised the great value of residential schools, especially when compared to day schools. According to D'Herbomez, the day schools that the U.S. federal government had founded in the Washington Territory did not work since the Native children, because of the almost daily need to gather or hunt for food, usually attended them very sporadically. However, the residential school, by denying students this opportunity, held out the best hope of helping them establish the virtues of "order and discipline" that were absolutely essential if they were to survive, much less prosper in Canadian society. Yet D'Herbomez was convinced that without federal government help St. Mary's could never be enlarged nor could new schools be founded. He was certain that both Canadian society as well as the Native people would gain enormous mutual benefit from such an enterprise. Still, except for some tiny annual subsidies, neither the Conservative nor Liberal parties, and certainly no provincial governments, were then interested in "wasting" much money on the education of "savages."[12]

Eventually, however, the federal government, concluding that it was "good politics" and "essential" to "civilising" the Native people, decided to fund residential schools. The new policy very much reflected the social Darwinism that had become a major justification for later nineteenth century western imperialism. Earlier theories that the aboriginals would ultimately either adapt on their own or perish did not appear to be working, since they had neither disappeared nor, to any significant degree, had they been willing to embrace western ways.

Ottawa policy makers long believed that Native culture was extremely inferior to its western equivalent, and must ultimately be eradicated. However, if this were ever to happen, it was now believed that the government had a "duty" to intervene. Although Ottawa remained loath to spend money to achieve that end, by the 1870s the federal Department of Indian Affairs was beginning to realise that its objectives could best be realised in a highly controlled, residential school system. While they would operate at a far more inferior level, such schools would be similar in nature to English public schools, such as Eton or Rugby, which were training the future leaders of the British Empire. It was theorised that, if these schools helped the upper class gentleman "take his place in the world," it would be relatively simple to use them to achieve a similar objective among "savages."[13] Such a plan reflected the reasoning of many, if not most Euro-Canadians who believed that, despite their "dubious morality," Native children had an "innate intelligence" that made them capable of reform. This thinking was based on a very "crude evolutionary dogma" that took no notice of the long historical journey of Western Europe out of its own "barbarism" that had lasted, after the fall of

Rome, for almost a thousand years. Yet such racist "logic" was believed unassailable during the last quarter of the nineteenth century.[14]

It was the Anglicans who were the harbingers of such a policy in British Columbia. Like St. Mary's at Mission, which received most of its funding from a missionary organization, the Propagation of the Faith in Lyon, France, the Anglicans obtained their support from a similar body, the New England Company in London, England. Its support was essential to the survival of the Anglican Native Residential School for boys at Lytton, which was started in 1867 by Reverend John Booth Good. This school came into being after the local Natives had had a falling out with the Oblates. This was certainly not an uncommon happening, since the Native people often "shopped-around" for the denomination that was willing to meet their demands. In Lytton, they wanted a residential school close to their reserve so families could visit their children more frequently.[15]

The first Anglican to call upon Ottawa to become more involved in Native schooling was Acton Windeyer Sillitoe, the first bishop of New Westminster, which had been established in 1879. Sillitoe began his campaign in 1883 by challenging the federal superintendent for Indian Affairs in British Columbia, Dr. Israel Wood Powell, to fund a new residential school for Native girls at Lytton. However, Powell, a crony of Prime Minister Macdonald, saw his main function as superintendent to be the avoidance of spending money on Natives, and it was a position that Ottawa encouraged. When Sillitoe failed to get a satisfactory response from Powell, he went directly to Macdonald. This resulted in a lengthy investigation into the matter, and, when in 1885 Powell informed Macdonald that it would cost well over $200 per pupil per annum to fulfil Sillitoe's request, Ottawa rejected the idea. Thus the Anglicans, like the Catholics and other denominations, had to be satisfied with a small annual grant, which was, in effect, a charity that could be easily stopped.[16]

Sillitoe's insistence however did help to promote a major change of thought in Ottawa. By 1883 Macdonald and his government had finally become convinced that federally funded residential schools, run by the churches, which would be cheaper than any state-run equivalents, were essential to the task of "civilising" the Native people. This change began in 1879 after Macdonald had Nicholas Flood Davin, a backbench M.P. for Regina, study residential schools in the United States. Greatly impressed by the "aggressive civilization" of the Native Americans that had been initiated under President Grant in 1869, Davin recommended that, besides funding existing church residential schools, the government should encourage and fund new ones. His reasoning and intentions were two-fold: first, that the "simple Indian [religious] mythology" must be eradicated and replaced by something "uplifting," such as Christianity, and secondly, church people could far more easily provide teachers who were already possessed of the "learning and virtue" necessary to achieve the first objective. Macdonald agreed, for though he believed that secular education was fine for "white men," he told the House of Commons that the Native people needed to be made "better men, and, if possible, good Christian men." Again, and dear to the heart of any Conservative, such an education would be far less expensive than any secular alternative.[17]

Therefore by the mid 1880s Ottawa had become convinced that church-run residential schools would guarantee that the "Indian child" would "be disassociated from the prejudicial influence by which he is surrounded on the reserve of his band." In keeping with the androcentricism of the English public school model, all of the residential schools were initially limited to male pupils. Within a year, however, Macdonald conceded that the schooling of girls was "of as much importance as a factor in the civilization and advancement of the Indian race as the education of the male portion of the community." Reflecting a policy that was common among the existing church schools, including the Oblates, the schools were to be located off the reserves, since it was assumed if they were to be successful, students must be kept entirely "separate...from their families."[18]

By 1887, Ottawa was ready to begin funding new and existing schools. In an interview that spring in Ottawa with Louis Vankoughnet, the deputy superintendent general for Indian Affairs, D'Herbomez was initially confused by Vankoughnet's assurance that the schools would be denominational. The difficulty probably sprang from D'Herbomez's belief that as the one "true" church, Roman Catholicism was *not* a denomination. The bishop reacted by insisting that Protestant Native children be allowed to go to Protestant schools and Catholics Native children to Catholic schools. Vankoughnet naturally agreed, and they next discussed the funding and locations of the two projected Oblate residential schools at Williams Lake and in the Okanagan. By the fall of 1888 Parliament had agreed to fund three new Catholic residential schools in British Columbia on Kuper Island under the diocese of Victoria, and at Kamloops and Cranbrook under the soon (1890) to be established diocese of New Westminster.[19]

Bishop Paul Durieu (AD)

✤ The Durieu System and Its Role

THE DURIEU SYSTEM, named for the first bishop of New Westminster, Paul Durieu (1890–1899), was a formalization of the reduction that Durieu hoped, with the advent of federal funding of residential schools, could finally be implemented in tandem with such institutions. The Oblates had long supported the use of the residential school as a vital support and reinforcement of the reduction. But except for St. Mary's Residential Schools at Mission, until 1890 and the advent of federal funding, they could not afford to realise such a plan in their other Missions in British Columbia. Now that it was possible to do so, Durieu was certain that his "system" could be more thoroughly implemented, since it would be reinforced and complemented by the residential school. For Durieu, both were vital in reforming the Native people and preparing them to become productive and loyal members of both the Catholic Church and Canadian society.[20]

The Durieu system was something its author had been developing ever since his arrival in the Washington Territory in 1854, but its first recorded use came sometime in the late 1860s when he began working among the Sechelt at Pender Harbour. Although there had once been 5,000 Sechelt, the 1862 smallpox epidemic had been devastating, and by 1876 the village had only 167 people. It was this sad remnant that became a sort of living laboratory for Durieu, and all of his anecdotes about the success of his system are drawn from the Sechelt.[21]

The initial element in the system, the "Indian court" had as its major objectives avoiding "white" interference in Native affairs and creating a "peaceful atmosphere favorable to the practice of religion and piety." To be held at night, "after...prayer," its judges were the elders or other important members of the tribe. There they passed judgements on the violators of church law and on "family quarrels,...neglect of children by parents, on the disobedience of children, on rowdyism of some young men, etc. etc."[22]

The elders or "chiefs" and watchmen were essential to the smooth operation of the courts and the other elements of the system. While the priest was to select the watchmen, the village was expected to elect the "chief," although the priest could correct both, and, if he believed that they were inadequate to their task, remove them. The Durieu system directed that each Native village should have "two chiefs," one approved by the Indian agent and the other by the priest. The first was a "mere figure head," while the second, called the "Eucharistic chief" by Durieu because of his much greater importance, could be deposed by the priest "as he saw fit."[23]

The central element of the Durieu system, the Catholic religion was the "hinge on which [the system] turned." To impart memorized doctrine, the priest appointed at least two catechists, a man for the boys and a woman for the girls from among the "most competent." They were trained to baptize both adults and children who were near death in the "absence of the missionary." Sunday was the central day of religious observance, and when no priest was present to say Mass, under the catechist's direction, the whole community would engage in morning and evening prayers, the rosary, catechism classes, vespers and stations of the cross. However, such practices were not to be a "joy-killer," for "ample time" was given to communal amusement, such as games and sports, which were expected to produce an atmosphere of "general glee." If a priest were available, the Natives were expected to attend daily Mass. In addition, regular confession was mandatory, which, accompanied with a careful examination of conscience, would recall the sins of even "the dullest minds." After confession they would be ready to take part in the central religious event, Holy Communion, which Durieu stressed for all, but especially for the "newly-converted" who were being rescued from the "mire of paganism," so that they could enter "the purity of a Christian life."[24]

After the Sechelt, the Stó:lô were the next tribe to experience the implementation of the system and so, Eucharistic celebrations soon became the central experience at their "great gatherings" in spring and early summer. In fact, in 1894 Durieu brought together an assembly of over 3,000 Stó:lô at St. Mary's at Mission where the Native people spend the enormous sum of $2,000 erecting altars, buying candles and building great fires to represent the Sacred Heart and the Blessed Virgin Mary. After a week spent in such activities, everything was pulled down and burned. When a Euro-Canadian asked why the Natives would spend such a large amount of money and then obliterate their handiwork, Durieu replied, because it was "for the Holy Eucharist."[25]

Marriage under the system was to strengthen the Catholic religion and break down tribal traditions that might hinder that objective. Since the idea of marriage was based on Catholicism's long, if sometimes unofficial tradition of moral dualism, it is not surprising that Durieu concluded that, even more than Euro-Canadians, the Native people had "giant passions" that only Catholic marriage could properly channel. While he was incorrect, Durieu was convinced Native marriage traditions produced a sexual degeneracy, which was reflected in the supposedly little regard they had for either consanguinity or affinity in their marriage contracts. In order to insure strict consistency, which was vital in the creation of a closely-knit church community, essential to the system, Durieu placed great emphasis upon determining the time and age of marriage, usually between 18 and 21. Traditionally Native marriages were arranged, which Durieu believed was really the "root of the evil," since parents, for "personal interests," chose the mates for their children and always from among their own tribe, which again was wrong. Rather, depending on their class, since unions between

St. Joseph's Residential and Industrial School (Williams Lake) (AD)

members of the lower class were not as restricted, Native marriages, as in European tradition, were viewed by families as a central means of acquiring wealth and position for them and the newlyweds.[26]

Durieu, through arranged "Catholic" marriages, was determined to encourage the development of a pan-Indian community that, by destroying tribal loyalties, would help pave the way for the Native people to more easily join the larger society. Ideally, such marriages would encourage the Native people to remain separate from, though equal to Canadian society. To insure this objective and also to reinforce Catholic teaching, he stressed that such inter-tribal marriages were to be indissoluble and only between Native Catholics, for Durieu believed mixed marriages with a Protestant Native would endanger the faith of the Catholic. Yet, even marriages with European Catholics were to be avoided, since this would lead to an increase in "half-breeds" and, given the secular nature of far western society, might lead to "no religion" and thus, he believed, add to "the decadence of the race."[27]

To further strengthen the internal integrity of the system, Durieu tried to foster Native vocations to the religious life and priesthood. When the Native people showed no interest, Durieu tried to "make some" Native nuns. In 1896 he selected eight girls, all "daughters of the best families" at St. Mary's

Mission and graduates of the Residential School there, who, for six years, had expressed a desire to become nuns. When they reached the age of 15 Durieu created a novitiate for them at Williams Lake Residential School, and which was placed under a French community, the Sisters of the Child Jesus who were also in charge of the School. Once there, however, the Native novices "almost immediately asked to go home, saying that they did not want to be Sisters any more." In the end, all the women became "good Christian mothers" instead of consecrated virgins, which for Durieu was "a sign that they had no vocations." As for Native boys, they apparently never showed the slightest inclination to be priests. Like other Oblates, when no vocations materialized, Durieu concluded that it was probably "providential." Certainly there was always a sense of foreboding among most Oblates, fed by a stifling paternalism and implicit racism that ultimately it was most likely best not "to take chances with Indian priests" or even nuns, as long as there were "enough white priests and white nuns." Apparently basing such a conclusion upon the importance of complete acculturation, there was a general conviction that Euro-Canadians would have a "more beneficial influence on the Natives than would priests and nuns of their own race."[28]

Durieu also considered Native financial support of the local church essential in their preparation to join the larger society. Though some Oblate missionaries opposed the idea as "dangerous," since such a demand "might lead to the loss of the Indians" by making them too independent of the priest, Durieu insisted that they must be encouraged to do so. To demonstrate Durieu's methodology in this regard and to impress upon Natives the need to be self-reliant, he told a story of some Sechelt men who were assigned to transport him by canoe during a mission that he was preaching among them. Although he had supposedly warned them to bring their own lunch, the men had failed to do so, since they expected that Durieu, as he had always done, would feed them. When they complained that they were hungry, the bishop replied: "why,...didn't I tell you to bring food? Eat wood, it is good enough for disobedient boys as you are." Publicly shamed, Durieu believed that the Natives "boys" had learned their lesson. Because of such experiences and the discipline they engendered, Durieu reported "goodly collections" from among the Native people that took care of the priest's needs and helped to build "fine churches" and "catechism halls" in Native villages throughout the diocese of New Westminster. However, the evidence does not confirm these rosy conclusions, for both Durieu and his successors continued to depend

Pemberton Native Band, Williams Lake (AD)

very heavily on the support of missionary societies, both European and Canadian, in the essential funding of their Native Missions.[29]

In order to maintain such an elaborate system, clearly Durieu needed to impose a rigid, almost monastic-like discipline on each Native reserve. Thus, while residential schools were expected to transform "Indian boys and girls...into white people," this would only work if such attitudes were reinforced in the reduction that was to epitomize the Native village, and again public shaming played a central role. As an example of what he meant, Durieu again used his experiences among the Sechelt. There to preach a mission, when he arrived at the reserve a watchman reported that the young men had purchased a football and uniforms and planned to play the Nanaimo. Although their action did not breach the letter of any law in the system, by not asking permission from the priest, they had broken it in spirit. Thus in his first address to them, Durieu told the young men that they were only "poor ignorant Indians." Taking the football from them, he ordered them to stop wasting their money on such things. Rather, he noted their "football" was the "pick, the shovel, the axe, the saw, etc." He then ordered them to use such tools to drain a village swamp that was breeding "frogs, mosquitoes and sickness." Reportedly they immediately obeyed because they had been told to do so by Durieu, "their wise and loving 'papa.'"[30]

The Lord's Distant Vineyard

Play or entertainment, however, was also essential in the system, since Durieu believed that there was a "great deal of the child in the average Indian," yet only "Christian" play was permitted. Durieu demanded that the Natives destroy all of their "old fashioned amusements," including "totem poles...rattles, expensive coats, [and] other paraphernalia of the medicine men" and discontinue potlatches, "gambling, dancing and some winter festivals," since they "contained some traces of paganism and superstition." In the place of such "pagan" things, Durieu substituted "Christian ones."[31] In addition to long processions in honor of the Blessed Sacrament and the Blessed Virgin Mary, Durieu also established brass bands in each village to accompany religious celebrations. A famous example of this were the Passion plays, especially those at St. Mary's at Mission, which were reportedly so well done that they "drew tears from the eyes of many spectators, including bishops and priests." The Oblate Superior General, Louis Soullier, after witnessing a play during his Canadian visitation of 1904, noted that "he had never expected so much from the Indians."[32]

However, the ultimate question is did Durieu's system work? An important incident, which occurred in 1892, seemed to indicate that when any serious implementation was attempted, the Durieu system failed badly. Referred to as the Lillooet affair, the event revolved around a young, unmarried Native couple from the Lillooet reserve who had engaged in intercourse. Brought before a tribal court after Johnny, a watchman had reported them, the old "chief," Killapowtkin, with his council, decided that both should be publicly flogged. Since Eugène-Casimir Chirouse (1879–1927), nephew to the older Oblate of the same name had just completed a mission in the village, Killapowtkin asked for his advice. Chirouse approved, though trying to be lenient, limited the usual 30-to-50 lashes to only 15. The following day Lucy, the girl involved, was seen leaving the reserve with another girl and two boys. Johnny pursued then, since the watchman was convinced that all four were "bent on evil." Though he captured the girls, the two boys escaped. Angered that Lucy had broken her word, the "chief" ordered her to be flogged again, though this time the lashes apparently exceeded the previous number. Lucy was also ill at the time from a bout of the "la grippe." In reaction, a Thompson woman, who had witnessed the affair, reported it to the local justice of the peace, Captain Martley. After apprehending Killapowtkin and his council, Martley discovered that Chirouse had allowed the first

Illustration of a Passion Play in British Columbia (AD)

flogging, so he also ordered his arrest. By then Chirouse was in Pemberton Meadows, some 60 miles from Lillooet. The arresting constable denied Chirouse the right to ride his horse and instead forced the priest to walk most of the distance back to Lillooet.

Martley decided to turn the case against the priest and the five Native defendants over to local county court where, on May 3rd it was tried by Judge Cornwall. Basing his judgement mainly on the first flogging, Cornwall found all six men guilty and sentenced them to prison terms: Chirouse to one year, Killapowtkin to six months, and the four members of his council to two months each. The case was soon the topic of newspaper editorials throughout the province. In Victoria, Bishop John Lemmens (1888–1897) told a reporter for the *Daily Colonist* that it had left him "deeply grieved and perplexed." The press generally believed that the Natives had a right to "carry on their own moral code," and that the Catholic clergy should not be "unnecessarily" interfered with for only doing their duty. In July the federal minister of Justice, Sir John Thompson, a Catholic, apparently agreed, and dismissed all charges against the six defendants. The Oblates would appear to have triumphed, for the Vancouver *World* noted that the whole case had only reflected a pure and simple "bigotry" and "hatred" towards the "Roman Catholic missionaries [who were working] among the Indians of the Province."[33]

Although Durieu would no doubt have concurred with this assessment, he could not ignore underlying issues in the controversy, especially with regard to the Native people and the Durieu system. Writing to Lemmens on 9 May 1892, in a letter intended for publication, Durieu lamented the negative publicity and possible fall-out that might ultimately damage his system. Durieu was convinced that the system was calculated to aid the Native people in their "upward march of progress." Yet, because the Native had always identified the Oblate missionary with other "whites," the incident had prompted a "cry of hatred" and a "spirit of rebellion" to arise among "many tribes" against all Euro-Canadians, including the Oblates. This was due largely, Durieu believed, to a Native "fear" that they would now be "deprived entirely of their immemorial rights to regulate the private affairs of their people." Even so, as evidenced by the recent editorials in their favor, he believed the majority of the "white population" in the province was in sympathy with the Native desire to change and become "good" Canadians, which, in addition to becoming "good" Catholics, were the central objectives of his "system."[34]

In private, however, Durieu had other, far deeper concerns regarding his system. He feared that the scandal from the Lillooet affair could jeopardize federal funding for the newly established residential schools. As Judge Begbie had advised D'Herbomez years before, except for alcoholism, federal or provincial law already covered the domestic issues over which the Natives assumed they had effective control. Therefore, by its almost unlimited power to intervene, the secular law made the Durieu System practically unworkable.[35]

It was becoming increasingly clear that the system was also ultimately doomed for internal reasons, since, in order to work effectively, it depended upon a thorough knowledge of Native languages. Nevertheless, by 1892 at least three out of four Oblates then working in British Columbia could not speak well, if at all, any of the aboriginal languages. Instead, the missionaries depended upon Native interpreters to communicate with most of their congregations. It was hardly a satisfactory arrangement, for it meant that Native culture remained essentially closed to most Oblate missionaries.[36]

Given these factors, the Durieu System could never be implemented as planned. Even so, for years thereafter those Oblates, who did not wish to admit such a reality, would continue to follow it. Many Oblates stubbornly reminisced about its supposed value well into the twentieth century, a few as late as the 1950s. However, nostalgia could not alter the facts, nor would denial of reality change anything. The only hope, as Durieu admitted to Lemmens, was for the Natives to willingly abandon their culture for "white" ways. By 1892 for the Oblates, though certainly not for most Natives, the residential schools, still tied to some form of reduction, seemed to hold out the best and perhaps the only hope for achieving that objective.[37]

The year 1899, when Augustin Dontenwill (1899–1908) succeeded Durieu, marked a major shift in Oblate approaches towards the Native people. For Dontenwill had little sympathy with the Durieu System, and as an educator, viewed its aims as naïve, if not actually cruel, but certainly bound to fail. Rather, Dontenwill believed that if the Native people were to be acculturated into the dominant society, the process should be on their own terms. Thus, the strict isolation from "white" society, and the public humiliations of the "Durieu System," were, he believed, counter-productive, if not unethical or even immoral. He thought that in its desire to control, by demanding public disclosure of wrong doings, it perhaps even violated the sacramental seal of confession. However, he did champion residential schools, for as an educator he believed they continued to hold out the best hope for Native integration. Naively, he also assumed that most Native people shared his optimism.[38]

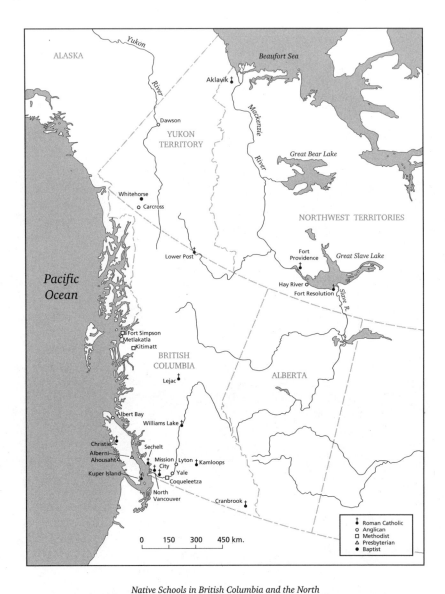

Native Schools in British Columbia and the North

Based on J.R. Miller's map of "Schools of British Columbia and the North" from Shingwauk's Vision:
A History of Native Residential Schools *(Toronto: University of Toronto Press, 1996), p. xiii.*

Used with permission.

10

The Residential Schools

✦ *The Kamloops School*

AFTER THE FIRST OBLATE NATIVE SCHOOL in the Okanagan valley
closed in 1866, provincial authorities insisted that Native education was
primarily the responsibility of the federal government. Reflecting Euro-
Canadian racist attitudes, the province implicitly banned Native people
from attending the tax supported provincial public schools. But for years the
province illegally collected a poll tax from Natives who took jobs outside the
reserve, which was supposed to go towards supporting segregated Native
public schools. These institutions were very few, and where they existed,
very poorly funded. It was not until after the First World War, in the face of
a successful court challenge, that the poll tax was abolished. Occasionally
Native children attended classes in public day schools alongside Euro-
Canadian children, but usually only when the province threatened to close a
particular school because of poor "white" enrolments. For when Natives
were admitted to such schools, Ottawa paid an annual tuition of $12.00 for
each Native student, which was crucial to their survival. However, if Euro-

Canadian numbers increased sufficiently, Native children were then excluded.[1]

Still, Native peoples in the Okanagan repeatedly attempted to obtain public schooling for their children. In 1874 the Shuswap asked Superintendent Powell to provide them with public schools, although nothing came of it. Again, in 1879 the Thompson expressed an interest and even applied for an annual federal grant, which they agreed to supplement if the government allowed them to build and manage their own day schools. As usual, there was no response from Ottawa. In an apparent attempt to address the issue, in the 1870s Charles Grandidier started a small day school at the Kamloops Mission, but poor

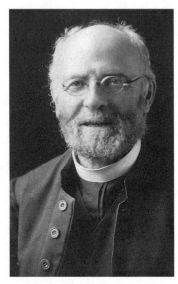

Father Jean-Marie LeJeune (AD)

attendance and lack of funding soon caused its closure.[2]

However, Jean-Marie LeJeune (1879-1930) made a unique attempt to help Native peoples of the region adapt to "white" ways. During his 38 years (1892-1929) at the Kamloops Residential School LeJeune translated the Chinook Jargon into a form of shorthand based on the French Duployan system, which he called *Kamloops Wawa*, after the Chinook word for "speak" or "talk." In the hope of encouraging Natives to learn his shorthand version of Chinook, LeJeune published several books that contained hundreds of words in both Chinook and English, mainly in the form of basic prayers as well as a catechism. Though well intentioned, the shorthand invention never appears to have had much of an impact on the local Natives, due mainly to the limited value of Chinook, given its small vocabulary.[3]

In 1886, the Department of Indian Affairs conducted a survey in the Okanagan valley and found little improvement in education for Natives. Out of approximately 700 local Native children in the valley, only about ten were attending small, church supported private day schools. In 1880, out of a provincial Native population of over 25,000, only about 500 Native students were receiving any formal western schooling, mainly in church-sponsored day or residential schools. In 1886 the local Indian Agent, Charles MacKay advised Ottawa that Native parents wanted schools for their children, and, therefore he believed that a federally supported residential school should be built at Head of the Lake as well as in Kamloops. Again, nothing was done.[4]

Ottawa was clearly in charge. Although the Oblates were open to other possibilities, reflecting their isolated reduction model, when the federal government finally agreed to provide funding, the Oblates tried to have the residential school located on their Okanagan Mission. There they had a large farm on which the Native students could work and a building that could house a boys' school; all that they required was a facility for girls. Yet when this attempt failed, the Oblates eagerly accepted Kamloops as the local alternative. Reflecting Ottawa's preference for lay personnel, the first principal was a Mr. M. Hagan. His appointment was apparently a political one made through J.A. Mara, MP. The Sisters of St. Ann, whom Durieu had obtained as the teaching staff, disliked having to answer to a layperson, and, far worse, a Protestant. Whoever was at fault, and no doubt there were problems on both sides, early in the first academic year (1891–92) Durieu reported to Ottawa that the nuns were determined to have Hagan removed. Not pleased to have its policies questioned, the government informed Durieu that if anyone were to go, it would be the Sisters. However, with an uncooperative staff, Hagan found his position untenable and resigned at the end of his first year after which the government temporarily closed the school. Mara then proposed another layperson, Alfred Morris. But Durieu wanted an Oblate named to the position, and recommended the superior at Kamloops, Julien-Augustin Bédard. At first Ottawa was not prepared to budge, but in January 1893 finally accepted as principal, another Oblate, Alponse Carion (1893–1916) with whom the Sisters of St. Ann were prepared to work. Again demonstrating who was in control, although Ottawa agreed to pay for 50 students instead of the original 25, they further reduced the first figure to 19 by the time the school opened again on 4 April 1893.[5]

Actual numbers attending, as was true in all the residential schools, were never large when compared to the overall Native population. At Kamloops the 19 students enrolled represented only between one to two percent of the region's school-aged Native children. While 1901 saw the number increased to 53, this figure was less than eight percent in the region, and most of these were limited to the Shuswap. Many reasons explain the low attendance. While "white" children paid nothing to attend public schools, the Oblates tried to impose a noncompulsory $50 per capita fee on Native parents to off-set their expenses which, as in their other schools, were never covered by the government's annual grant of $130. The most glaring problem was parental resistance to sending their children to a school that had, as its ultimate objective, the destruction of Native culture. In trying to combat parental obstructions, the Oblates at Kamloops, like other residential authorities throughout British Columbia, gradually imposed a government-supported policy that denied children the right to leave the School for at least six years. This naturally resulted in constant attempts by many Native families to rescue their offspring from the School.[6]

The Kamloops Residential School, like all others, was intended to remove Native children from their culture and, by so doing, transform them into "civilized" Canadians through a form of cultural genocide. As elsewhere, the speaking of Native languages among students was allowed until government policy forbade the speaking of "Indian." Carion reported to the Department of Indian Affairs that by means of strict discipline, especially through public shamings, he and the Sisters of St. Ann were doing all in their power to wipe out Native ways and instill only "good [western] ones." As in their other schools, the Oblates tried to put into effect an educational version of the "Durieu system," except that their students were now a captive audience.[7]

There is also the important question of what did Native parents really expect from the schools. As at other schools, there were high truancy rates at Kamloops, which resulted from runaways and parents' refusal to return their children to the School. Indian agents reporting on Kamloops and other institutions came to the general conclusion that Native parents had only one desire, namely, that their children receive just enough "white" education so they at least could cope with the dominant culture.[8]

When faced with all of the many negative consequences of the residential schools, the Native people gradually intensified their demand for day school equivalents. Yet those in charge in Ottawa, convinced that residential schools would eventually achieve their intended aims, long dismissed both Native parental rights and objections.[9] Certainly no one would question that western learning was supposed to be the major objective at Kamloops and other residential schools. Yet the evidence indicates that most Native children left Kamloops with few educational benefits for the time that they spent there.[10]

When all of the factors were combined, such as low attendance, student and parental resistance, cost, and poor education, it was clear as early as 1910 that Kamloops was a dismal failure. By then inspectors, both provincial and federal, had begun to recommend that the authorities should listen to Native demands for alternatives, especially "Day schools, on or near the Reserve." Rev. John McDougall, the provincial inspector suggested that such schools, with skilled and committed teachers, be founded throughout the region. In short, McDougall recommended five day schools, which, he reported, were both required and desired by Native parents. A few years later a federal agent complained of the obvious that Native parents in the Okanagan, as in the rest of British Columbia, were being denied the basic right to educate their children, a right that was taken for granted by their Euro-Canadian neighbors. However, Ottawa saw no need to change its policies, and so such pleas continued to fall on deaf ears.[11]

The Kamloops Residential School saw many physical changes over the years. By the early 1900s, the complex had reached its final form, being situated on a 200-acre site on the north bank of the South Thompson River, about two miles from Kamloops. It consisted of a main two-story structure and two one-story buildings, one for the boys, the other for the girls. There were several outbuildings, including a laundry. Again, government grants were never sufficient, and were even cut at times, although living expenses continued to rise. One of the major results was that building repairs were delayed until some structures had to be condemned, as happened in 1927 when a house for small boys had to be pulled down due to its dilapidated condition. The Sisters of St. Ann worked with the Oblates throughout the school's history and, like them, had to make up for annual deficits from their own resources. Kamloops Residential School ceased being under the Oblates in 1974 when it was placed under a Native administrator. It closed a few years later.[12]

✤ The Cranbrook School

ST. EUGENE'S RESIDENTIAL SCHOOL at Cranbrook opened in 1890 with the Oblates in charge of the boys, while the girls were under the care of the Sisters of Providence. A major factor in its creation was the sudden influx of European settlers into the Kootenays during the 1880s, which was due to a local hardrock and silver-lead mining boom. Before this, the region's rugged geography had long protected the Kutenai. Even with the boom, the high cost of transportation made mining tremendously expensive. Also, because of its location in the southeastern corner of British

St. Eugene's Mission in Cranbrook (l-r: church, school, barn) (AD)

Columbia, the Europeans in the region tended to look south to Spokane and the United States.[13]

Because the mining boom of the 1880s was close to the international boundary, Euro-American prospectors were among the first to arrive. Given their well-established hostility towards Native Americans, this hostility spelled serious trouble for the local Kutenai. The first Native leader to challenge the invasion was "Chief" Isadore. His stature among his people on both sides of the border was such that he could probably have gained support for an all-out war against the American and Canadian invaders. He certainly had reason, for within months of their arrival, the "whites" were killing Kutenai and taking their land, and to many, they appeared to be doing so with the tacit support of the provincial and federal governments. Nevertheless, with the wisdom of a true leader, Isadore soon realised that any violent opposition from the Natives would only serve to justify their summary slaughter by either "white" vigilantes or government troops. By the spring of 1888, he agreed to leave his ancestral lands for what amounted to a government reserve. The Europeans, with their assumption that might almost always makes right, had won; the only positive aspect for Isadore was that his people had not been butchered in the process.[14]

In 1887, the colourful Corsican Oblate, Nicolas Coccola (1880–1943), the founder and first principal of the Cranbrook Residential School, arrived at St. Eugene's Mission. In his *Memoirs*, Coccola gives the impression that his actions, as the "essential" mediator between Isadore and the government, represented by Major S.B. Steele of the North West Mounted Police, then stationed in the Kootenay, were crucial in saving the situation. As was usual with the Oblates, Coccola had remained neutral or, until violence threatened, sided with the government and counselled an already convinced Isadore, who was also a Catholic, either to capitulate to superior forces or risk annihilation. Still for Coccola, Isadore's decision was a "victory," especially for the church. Almost immediately after these events, Coccola asked Ottawa to fund a residential school at St. Eugene's. He assured them that with its advent, "the Indians would never after that give any trouble to the government."[15]

Yet, despite his importance, it was Paul Durieu, the first bishop of New Westminster (1890–99) and not Coccola, who finally convinced Ottawa to add St. Eugene's to its initial list of new residential schools. As for staffing, it was a given that the Oblates would be involved, especially in assisting in the boys' school. Regarding the principal and those who would be in charge, Durieu turned to the Sisters of Providence who had arrived in the diocese in 1886 to establish St. Mary's Hospital in New Westminster. Durieu's initial negotiations with the Sisters also indicate his naïve notion that he was in control, especially in telling the federal government what to do. He assured Sister Jean de la Croix, their provincial in Vancouver, Washington, that the school would be totally under church authority, that the government would merely fund building construction and pay the staff that Durieu chose to appoint. Thus, he explained, the sister principal would receive $800 per annum and the sister matron, who would head the girls' school, would get $400 per annum, the sister cook $250, and the two teaching sisters $200 each. However, the layman, who was to teach trades to the boys, would receive $600 per annum. Their major source of income and expansion would be the annual per capita funding of $130 per student. As for numbers, according to Durieu, there was no limit, the school might begin with about 30 boys and girls and increase as it wished in subsequent years. Accepting this arrangement, in May 1890, the superior general of the Sisters of Providence agreed to run the school and appointed Sister Pacifique as its first principal. She had been head of the Residential School at Walla Walla, spoke both French and English, and thus was considered well qualified for the position.[16]

Durieu soon learned that he was not really in charge. When the bishop wrote to Ottawa in order to complete the final preparations, Vankoughnet informed him what was to be taught at the new school. The boys were to learn carpentry, blacksmithing, shoemaking and general husbandry; the girls were to concentrate on domestic areas, and both were to receive a basic education, including the use of written and spoken English. As for numbers, Ottawa decided that for the time being, the school would be limited to 25 students, as reflected in its funding. Yet the directives did not end there, for soon there were further bureaucratic restrictions, namely, that Sister Pacifique was unacceptable as principal since in Ottawa's eyes only a man should hold such a position. As for the co-educational character of the school, while the government assured Durieu that it supported the education of girls, for the first year, at least, only boys could be admitted. A frustrated Durieu made a somewhat empty show of being in control. He informed Coccola that, due to government restrictions, the priest would be the first principal of St. Eugene's, though Durieu insisted that the Sisters of Providence would really be in charge of the school.[17]

Although Oblate policy stressed the use of Native languages, Native students at St. Eugene's were only permitted to memorize a few prayers in "Indian" or Chinook. While the Oblates encouraged the children, like their parents, to confess in their Native tongue, Oblate confessors rarely understood what was being said. Only one in four Oblates ever came close to mastering a Native language. Three separate Native languages were spoken by the students at the Cranbrook school but none of the staff could speak any one of them. While Ottawa expected all students to learn English, and Coccola and the Sisters of Providence encouraged its use, their teachers' first language was French, which they spoke among themselves and sometimes even to the students. As such, the staff was not an ideal model of spoken English.[18]

Funding the school was an added headache. During this early period, the *per capita* annual grant was $130. Yet, in 1892 Coccola complained that the actual annual average cost for each of the 25 students came to $192, out of which clothing and feeding each student accounted for the greatest proportion of the expenditure or $149. However, the annual $130 grant did not change until 1905, although by then the student numbers had increased to about 50. Thus, there was always a deficit which the Oblates were forced to cover out of their own pockets.[19]

Adding even further to their problems, the school's clients, the Natives also had serious misgivings. Coccola saw no reason to involve Native parents in his plans since for him they were the problem that the school was to solve. There their offspring would learn to abandon their past and ultimately become good Catholics and good Canadians. Native opposition appeared to center on the very notion of a residential school. Parents were unwilling to entrust their children's upbringing to "whites," especially European women, no matter what they were called. Determined to open the school on time, Coccola sent three of his "best" watchmen to the Columbia Lake Reserve with orders to direct the parents to attend Mass at the Mission that Sunday. After Mass, Coccola selected the children, whose parents, he believed, were "favourably disposed toward the school," although he added others to the rolls in order to have a full complement. Then, with their parents following, he had them marched to the school where the waiting sisters took the children inside and then closed the doors. Coccola was convinced that his plan had worked, and that his "triumph" was now complete.[20]

The surviving reports regarding student ages, grades and studies do not reflect this early optimism, and at best provide a very mixed picture. Probably reflecting their relative value in their parents' eyes, there were no boys at the school over 15, but there were several girls as old as 20. As for their studies, both genders took basic academic classes, and records indicate that the girls achieved slightly higher grades than the boys. As for vocational skills, the girls concentrated on gardening, sewing, and housekeeping, and all over the age of eight did washing, ironing, cooking, and milking. The boys, who were eleven or younger, cut wood and gardened, while the older ones learned carpentry and minded cattle.[21]

Time would prove that early optimism was very ill conceived. In fact, by the end of the first year, even Coccola was expressing his doubts regarding the whole idea of the school and Sister Pacifique complained to Durieu of the priest's apparent second thoughts in having initiated it. Yet, even Pacifique was concerned over the high rate of illness among her students, especially after 40 students became quite ill during an influenza epidemic in the fall of 1891. In fact, by 1897 a horrifying figure of 67 students had been discharged for health reasons, and of these a total of 47 later died. Such terrifying statistics were also reflected in attendance records, which provide ample and graphic proof that most parents and students were extremely unhappy with the school. By 1892, only seven or little more than a quarter of the original 20 students who entered in 1890 were still enrolled. Faced with such high turnover rates, the teachers rarely got to know their students well, and felt they were constantly beginning anew. By June 1894, only five of the original 20 were still attending.[22]

Nevertheless, despite all these serious shortcomings, the School continued to develop. By 1915 it had a main building of concrete which, besides dorms and classrooms, contained wings devoted to a chapel and staff accommodation. By then the facility had its own water supply from the St. Mary's River; it used hot water heat and had its own electric power station. Student numbers grew from 51 in 1895 to a high of 133 in 1955. Per capita grants rose to $320 by the 1950s, but, as usual, it never keep pace with expenses which had to be met by either the Oblates or the other religious that worked with them. When the Sisters of Providence left in 1929, they were spending about $1,000 per annum from their own funds. Unable to find religious replacements, the Oblates hired lay staff until 1936 when they were able to obtain the services of the Sisters of Charity of Halifax who remained until Cranbrook closed in 1970.[23]

✣ The Williams Lake School

ST. JOSEPH'S RESIDENTIAL AND INDUSTRIAL SCHOOL at Williams Lake Mission was opened in 1891, although until then the Oblates had made little attempt to establish a school there for Native children. In 1872 they had opened a fee-based boarding school for Europeans and "half-breeds," and four years later the Sisters of St. Ann joined the staff. "White" racism and the inability of their parents to cover tuition barred Natives from attending. Still, due to the advent of local tax supported public schools, declining enrolments gradually equated into heavy financial loses and the "white" school finally closed in 1888.[24]

By early 1890, with residential schools at Mission, Cranbrook and Kamloops, Durieu decided to add Williams Lake to the list. In promoting his scheme, Durieu insisted that the idea had originated with the local Natives who, knowing of such schools elsewhere, now wanted their own. Durieu noted that he was also responding to a local crisis in the Cariboo. Until recently the Native population had depended upon local salmon as their major food staple, however, the continued growth of canneries at the mouth of the Fraser meant few fish returned to the upper areas of the river and its tributaries. In response, the Natives had been forced to take up farming and ranching, though Durieu insisted that they would need further training if they hoped to excel in these new undertakings. Thus a residential school would become an invaluable asset in achieving this vital objective.[25]

In his determination to achieve his aim, in February 1891 Durieu presented his plan to William Meason, the Indian Agent at Williams Lake. Durieu offered to sell the abandoned convent building to the government or to rent to them any of the other buildings. As he had done elsewhere, the bishop asked for an annual student per capita of $130 for 50 students. He told Meason that he was negotiating with the Sisters of St. Ann with the hope that they would return. In 1888, when they closed their school for "whites," the Sisters said they would be more than willing to return. However, they now declined, pleading other commitments and staff shortages. He then turned to the Sisters of Providence, but they sent a similar response.[26]

So Durieu decided that, until he could obtain another community of religious women, he would hire lay people for both the academic and trade areas. Naturally this added to the initial costs. In the meantime, LeJacq was put in charge of the boys' school and a Catholic lay woman oversaw the girls. Yet finding lay people of good character, especially men, who were not alcoholics and who were prepared to live and teach in remote areas for relatively little money, was a perennial problem. The school was open for an entire year before either a blacksmith or a carpenter was hired. Hiring and retaining good lay male employees continued to plague the school well into the next century. Consequently, while lay staff were used when they could be found, by 1902 the Oblates had resigned themselves to using Oblate brothers as trade instructors and disciplinarians, which meant they had to curtail or ignore commitments elsewhere.[27]

Due to the inability to gain a female religious community that was willing to teach at Williams Lake, the future of the girls' school remained in doubt until 1896 when Durieu finally secured the services of a French order, the Sisters of the Child Jesus. The first difficulty the Sisters faced was language. Naturally they could not speak Shuswap, Carrier or Chilcotin, the three Native tongues that were used by the student body at St. Joseph's, however, neither could they speak English. Since it was a government requirement that Native students learn English, both teachers and students had to try to acquire a new language.[28]

Most of Durieu's other problems at St. Joseph's Mission could be traced to his poor business decisions. Since he was determined to have total control of the residential schools in the Cariboo, Durieu made a contract with Ottawa by which the diocese would take full responsibility for running everything in exchange for an annual capitation grant of $130. His only stipulation was for a government allowance to cover 50 children, but only "for the first year." If that were done, he agreed to provide "board, clothing, care, education and training in two or three trades, the Government being at no further expense than the capitation grant."[29]

Needless to say, the government was quick to accept, and Parliament voted $6,220 to cover the *per capita* grant for 50 students for 1891–92 or "the first year." However, in the following year, Parliament reduced it to $3,250 or the amount necessary to cover 25 students, the figure Ottawa had initially set for the school. When Jean-Marie LeJacq, the first principal (1891–98) submitted his second annual report in June 1893, the school's enrollment had already reached 30, so he naturally complained when Ottawa reimbursed him for only 25 students. In July he was told that the larger sum had been given only for the first year to fulfill Durieu's contract, and that government was not prepared to pay a larger sum in the future. As the Oblate deficit continued to rise, in May 1894 LeJacq received word that Ottawa might consider increasing the *per capita* figure to cover 50 students. Yet when the fourth school year (1894–95) approached, the new deputy of Indian Affairs, Hayter Reed, citing the lack of government treaties with the Natives of British Columbia, wrote that the different denominations should be "prepared to carry on these schools without totally depending" on Ottawa for support. Instead, he suggested they seek future funding increases from nongovernment sources. Although the *per capita* grant was finally increased to cover 50 students in 1895, by then, due to an enrollment of 42, the Oblates had spent almost $11,000 of their own funds on the Residential School at Williams Lake. By 1895, Williams Lake had cost Canadian taxpayers less than $14,000, but Durieu's need to believe that he was in control, had saved Ottawa from expending almost twice that amount. Although it is doubtful, given his somewhat rigid personality, perhaps Durieu had finally learned that, since it held the purse strings, the federal government was *always* in charge.[30]

Certainly local Euro-Canadians saw the school as a business competitor. The school's harness making and butcher shops caused the greatest number of complaints that Native talents and crafts were threatening to put "white" craftspersons and merchants out of business by producing quality products that undercut their prices. Perhaps anti Catholicism also played a part in the opposition. In either case, determined to get Ottawa's attention with the hope of closing the School, a number of local Euro-Canadians accused the Oblates and sisters of ill-treating their pupils, who they said were badly fed, "dirty and not properly clothed," and severely beaten when they misbe- haved. After several unannounced visits, local Indian agents highly praised the school for their training and care of their students; the only caution was that "corporal punishment as a form of discipline needed to be modified."[31]

Native opposition to the school, as at other residential institutions, cen- tered upon the continued inroads of European civilisation. By the 1890s the local aboriginals had lost their land, their traditional government, their dependence on nature, or, in short, their entire culture; now they were being told that they must also lose their children. It was too much. One result was that initially the school only attracted twelve students. Certainly the Native people resented the strict atmosphere and the often brutal disci- pline which the Oblates and sisters judged as only "necessary suffering" on the way to becoming "good Catholic" and "good Canadian" adults. Again, such a policy reflected a repressively Jansenistic spirituality that had an obsession with pelvic morality. Based on the constant fear of and supposed terribly inherent "evil" in "sexual misbehavior," it also insisted upon the total separation of boys and girls that usually only heightened the problem it was intended to resolve.

While some graduates would later express positive feelings regarding their time at St. Joseph's, most felt otherwise. Frustrated, lonely and even angry, students expressed their opposition in the only way they could: they ran away. By 1900 the problem had reached epidemic proportions, espe- cially during the summer months when they were forced to remain at the school, with the result that over 50 percent would leave and not return. Native parents supported, and may have encouraged such behaviour, for they were rarely prepared to return runaways.[32]

Three Native nations attended the Williams Lake School: Shuswap, Carrier and Chilcotin, however, the Chilcotin, ever since their first contacts with Europeans, were the most resistant to "white" ways. One sister remarked that, though the Chilcotin were "very intelligent," they were not ready to accept the need for western education. At the center of this attitude,

The Residential Schools

she concluded, was their strong sense of cultural pride. Yet by the 1930s, with the economic depression making life miserable for everyone, but especially Native people, even the Chilcotin concluded that their children were better off in such schools where they would at least be fed. Still, even when the enrollment reached its peak of 120, 34 of whom were Chilcotin, the Williams Lake Residential School, like its counterparts elsewhere, never educated more than about five percent of the local Native children.[33]

As other residential schools, Williams Lake faced similar problems and challenges in its later history. However, because of its profitable farm, the usual shortfalls in government payments were far more easily covered than at other schools. The Sisters of the Child Jesus continued to teach there. The complex was similar to other institutions, in that it contained a main building, which was replaced in 1952 and several adjoining ones that served various purposes, including a kitchen, dining room and several industrial shops. It closed in 1981.[34]

✤ The Kuper Island School

FOUNDED UNDER THE AUSPICES of the diocese of Victoria, the Kuper Island Residential School was opened in June 1890 with 17 students. Following Ottawa's preference for lay principals, the first head was a Mr. McKinnon. Yet, because of early disagreements with the local Belgian secular priest, George Donckele, McKinnon soon left to be replaced by Donckele who remained in charge until his death in 1907. By then, and with the help of the Sisters of St. Ann, the school had a total enrollment of 68 with the usual annual *per capita* federal grant of $130.[35]

Donckele stressed that the Native peoples had demanded that the federal government give them a residential school run by the Catholic Church. An early "official" history of the school quotes the Natives as shouting: "We want priests," to which the author concludes: "the Government, realizing that the Indian mind was right for once, secured priests and sisters to replace the lay teachers already in charge." The same source insisted that Father Donckele had a "knowledge of Indians" that was both "accurate and deep, his love for them heaven-born." As was also the norm, such dualistic thinking was connected to a Jansenistic worldview, for again the brief historic account assures us that "like all enterprises undertaken in the name of God, the Kuper Island institution was destined to thrive but in the shadow

Native boys employed in the Bakery, Kuper Island Industrial School (AD)

of the Cross." It was a "Cross" that was imposed by the conqueror, whether church or state, upon the conquered, but, naturally, always for the "good" of the Native child.[36]

Denominational infighting also took place between Kuper Island and the Protestant Methodist school at Coqualeetza. Donckele complained to the government of how the parents of several pupils threatened to remove them and put them in the Methodist rival because of the poor food and general treatment they were supposedly receiving at the Catholic one, which the priest vehemently denied. Again, in 1914 a Marist priest at the school, William Lemmens, was furious over the fact that while the government refused to permit Methodist Natives to attend Kuper Island, it allowed Catholics to go to Coqualeetza.[37]

Although founded by the secular clergy (1890–1907), the De Montfort or Company of Mary Fathers dominated (1907–57) most of the school's history. Yet, as early as 1899, for those who were willing to read them, there were already clear signs of its failure. As in other schools, high incidences of pupil illness and disease were reflected in a very high truancy rate. When these were added to the poor food, harsh discipline, the deliberate repression of Native languages and culture and growing Native parental opposition, it is not surprising that on several occasions students attempted to burn the school down.[38]

Despite Native opposition, given Euro-Canadian racism, such views were dismissed as irrelevant. An excellent example of this mentality can be found in a brief history of the Industrial Residential School published by the diocese of Victoria in 1914. Written by M.M. Ronden, a De Montfort, the short piece breathes all the arrogance of "white" certitude. Referring to the Native peoples as "great children," Ronden contended that "due allowance" had to be "made for their slowly evolving mentality." Still, Ronden insisted that graduates of Kuper Island, while still below the "high mark" of "white" children, were at least better off than the Native children who never had the "good fortune" to attend the school. Nevertheless, Ronden admitted that even Native graduates, because of their "inborn lack of steadiness and ambition," never really gained the level of ability that "one would expect" among non-Natives. For Ronden in 1905 noted that even though "Kuper Island girls carried off the first prize for needlework at the Dominion Fair held in New Westminster" their competition was only Native. Reflecting a similar racist mentality, in 1897, when Mary Celestine, a Sister of St. Ann and the first nun superior of the school died, the *Colonist* reported that "none will sincerely grieve for her more than the dusky little pupils" she had taught.[39]

The Oblates were the last clergy to run the Kuper Island Residential School which they took over in 1957 when the De Montforts left, although the Sisters of St. Ann remained there throughout. A new school had been constructed with government funds in 1914–16 and a new dormitory added in 1954. The Oblates left two years before the school finally closed in 1975. It was demolished in the early 1980s.[40]

✤ The Christie/Kakawis School

ALEXANDER CHRISTIE, a former priest of the archdiocese of St. Paul, Minnesota, served briefly as the sixth bishop of Victoria (1898–99) before becoming the fourth archbishop of Portland, Oregon (1899–1925). The school that bears his name, located at Kakawis on the westcoast of Vancouver Island, was probably his most lasting legacy to the diocese of

Victoria. Until 1890, when the Kuper Island Residential School was established, the diocese had relied solely on day schools in the education of Native children, which, due to poor attendance, were largely failures.[41]

Both Lemmens and Brabant, diocesan missionaries on the westcoast of Vancouver Island, had admitted their inability to establish successful day schools, but, like the Oblates, they believed that residential schools would produce very different results. Brabant and Christie certainly believed this would be true of the Kakawis Residential School. The school, opened in 1900, was funded by the federal government and managed for most of its history by the Benedictines, including priests, brothers and nuns, of Mt. Angel Abbey, Oregon (1900–1938). Like all of its predecessors and contemporaries, it would try to "appreciably alter the cultural patterns of...[its] pupils."[42]

Another encouragement for Brabant to establish the School was a steady increase of Euro-Canadian settlers on the westcoast of Vancouver Island, which meant by the 1890s that for the first time he had to face Protestant, especially Presbyterian competition for Native "souls." In 1898, a Presbyterian residential school was begun at Ahousaht on the westcoast. In response, Christie warned Brabant to act quickly in obtaining a federal grant for its establishment, otherwise, Christie feared the Catholic "Indian children would all be perverted" by the Protestants, and thus the priest would "lose the fruit of all...[his] labours." Catholics and Protestants alike would have preferred to see the Native people on the westcoast remain "pagan" rather than convert to a rival denomination. The Department of Indian Affairs, although it welcomed the "civilising" influences of the churches, considered denominational rivalry, wherever it occurred, as counter-productive, disruptive and a general nuisance. Yet, Natives, by sometimes deliberately pitting one denomination against another, often viewed such "contesting for their souls" as an excellent means of getting the most they could from a particular church in terms of social assistance or education. Such wrangling by competing churches also led many Natives to reject Christianity, at least the model presented to them by most Euro-Canadians. However, the accusation against Brabant by a Presbyterian church official in 1901 concerning the recently established school at Ahousat that the priest was "doing little or nothing" to provide the Hesquiat with a western style education, was true.[43]

The Kakawis Residential School, like all such institutions, set about trying to make good "Roman Catholics" and "white" people out of its Native charges. In working towards this end, both Brabant and the Benedictines were, from the start, determined to suppress Native languages. For children who insisted upon speaking "Indian," Brabant set a "penance" of writing English verse and prose. Such a penalty, the Belgian priest claimed, worked "like a charm," and within six months, according to Brabant, the children had "totally abandoned" their mother tongue.

The school was touted as a great success where everyone, teachers and students, were all on "friendly terms," reflected in the "fact" that there was no "serious homesickness," although a month's holiday was allowed after the first year. Like its counterparts, the focus was on an industrial, and not an academic education. Therefore, girls were taught to cook, bake, sew, and knit, while the boys were trained in carpentry, shoe repair, and house painting. Although sports and drama were included as social enrichment, the central aim of the school was to turn all of its graduates into staunch, committed Roman Catholics. In fact, present and former pupils were expected to become "crusaders for the Christian [Roman Catholic] cause," by bringing back any lapsed relatives to the faith. In 1950, at the celebration of its fiftieth anniversary, the administration declared the Kakawis Residential School to be a marked triumph.[44]

Yet, less subjective evidence is not so glowing. From the beginning there was serious illness at the school. During its first two years, four deaths resulted from tuberculosis due, apparently, to very poor living conditions, harsh discipline and over work. Outbreaks of measles were also a grave problem. Though disease affected Native children outside the school, close confinement increased and promoted the spread of infection. While vaccines were administered, antibiotics did not exist, and, in addition, many, highly contagious diseases were erroneously thought to be hereditary. Because of so much illness, parents kept their children at home, which meant that attendance during the early years (1900–1905) was well under 50. By 1957 the enrolment reached its high point of 150. At Kakawis, this figure of those who attended the school represented only four percent of a mostly nominal Native Catholic population on the westcoast of approximately two thousand.[45]

Therefore, as an evangelising agency, the Christie School was hardly as successful as official statements indicate. The Benedictine clergy who ministered along the coast, and those who taught at the School privately lamented the continued lack of interest in church attendance among the older Natives, including the parents of both students and graduates. Ex-pupils were expected to re-evangelise their lapsed relatives and friends, and a school organization was established to achieve that objective. The evidence proves however that such efforts met with very little success, since forced religious conformity and compliance while at the School did not translate into either voluntary church attendance nor did it make proselytisers out of students once they had returned home.[46]

Despite or perhaps because of the strict discipline, the Kakawis School left its mark. Students gradually became more independent and even critical of what they considered were unreasonable demands. Teachers, realising that the parents could remove students or transfer them to the Presbyterian alternative at Ahousat, and thus deny the School its raison d'être, adjusted to such student behaviour, albeit very grudgingly. Records show that a few students did write back thanking their former teachers for their education. A very small number went on to high school and a handful to university.[47]

After the Benedictines priests left in 1938 and the nuns in 1960, the school was taken over respectively by the Oblates and the Immaculate Heart of Mary Sisters. The complex was located on a 175-acre site on Meares Island. The central building was a two-story construction, which also contained a basement and measured 144 x 52 feet. There were also a number of outbuildings, each of which served as a laundry, woodshed, warehouse, barn, and staff cottage. The School closed in 1971, and in 1973 the Oblates opened an alcohol treatment centre there. The Oblates left in 1976 and the school burned down on 10 July 1983.[48]

✤ St. Mary's Mission Schools: A Case Apart

BY 1890 ST. MARY'S, the oldest Oblate Native residential school in the far west, seemed an obvious candidate to join the other Oblate schools in British Columbia in gaining annual federal funding. In calling for such support, in 1888 D'Herbomez pointed out that the Native Anglican boarding school at Yale was already receiving an annual capitation of $60. In a rare show of ecumenism, D'Herbomez included the Methodist's Native boarding school at Chilliwack as a possible partner with him, for he believed that the Catholics and Methodists should receive equal treatment with the Anglicans. After D'Herbomez's death, Durieu continued to plead for St. Mary's and

St. Mary's Mission, Mission City, 1924 (AD)

specifically that the $500 annual grant, which had fluctuated greatly over the years since it was first begun in 1875, be raised to at least to $2,000.[49]

Prompted by the Oblates, the local Native leadership made similar pleas to Ottawa. Some Euro-Canadians, mainly those who did not wish to pay taxes to support such institutions, insisted that the Native people were not interested in seeing their children educated in residential schools. In response, encouraged and lead by the Oblates, in 1891, 25 Native elders or "chiefs" on the Lower Fraser, in a signed petition, rejected this assertion. Rather, they were emphatic that they were determined to see that their children had the same quality of education as Europeans, but, since they were Catholics, they did not wish to use Protestant schools. For several years repeated attempts to gain an annual capitation of $60 for St. Mary's failed. Finally, in 1894 James McGuckin, who was then Rector of the University of Ottawa (1889–98), was able to obtain the $60 target. However, he failed to get federal approval for raising the schools' population from 40 to a hoped-for 100 students.[50]

Using denominational rivalry, certainly more the norm than ecumenism, in 1896–97 Durieu and his coadjutor, Augustine Dontenwill began to complain to Ottawa of the unfair treatment of St. Mary's by making comparisons between federal grants to Protestant and Catholic schools. In compiling their statistics, they calculated that there were then 34 schools in British Columbia. These included seven industrial schools (Alert Bay, Coqualeetza, Kamloops, Kootenay, Kuper Island, Metlakatla and Williams Lake), four boarding schools (Alert Bay Girls' Home, Port Simpson Girls' Home, St. Mary's and Yale), and 23 day schools. There were four Catholic, two Anglican and one Methodist industrial schools. As for the boarding schools, two were Anglican, one was Catholic and one was Methodist. Of the many day schools, the Anglicans ran eight, the Catholics operated two, the Presbyterians had three, and the Methodists ran ten. Both Catholic day schools were in the diocese of Victoria at Esquimalt and in the Cowichan Valley, since the Oblates had long rejected such schools, given the migratory nature of Native life, and certainly government attendance statistics would bear out this contention. Province-wide, the two bishops calculated that the Canadian government was then spending about $29,000 per annum on Catholic schools and $22,060 per annum on Protestant ones. Breaking the costs down for the entire province the two bishops came to the seemingly shocking conclusion that Protestant Natives were receiving well over 40 percent more per capita than their Catholic counterparts. Most extraordinary of all, by 1897 they insisted that the Anglican Residential School of All Hallows at Yale was receiving $31.91 per student, while its Methodist equivalent at Coqualeetza had an even higher per capita rate of $43.05. However, St. Mary's, they declared, still was only getting a miserable federal grant of $1.30 per student.[51]

While the evidence was impressive, and certainly calculated to startle, the methodology being used was certainly not accurate. The large Methodist schools at Coqualeetza and the Anglican one at Yale drew Native students from the entire province, whereas, the student populations in the Catholic institutions, whether in the Fraser Valley, in the interior or on Vancouver Island were all local. Also, Catholic schools were far more numerous throughout British Columbia, since, being largely run by celibates who had also taken vows of poverty, their cost was much lower than their Protestant counterparts where staff were usually married and had families to support. Not surprisingly, Ottawa ignored such argumentation.[52]

However, St. Mary's saw many developments in the ensuing years. It was not until 1911 that the federal government finally began to pay a per capita grant that was equal to the other Oblate residential schools. New buildings were constructed in 1883–84 in order to give a right of way to the railroad. The property consisted of 310 acres on which there were separate complexes for the boys and girls. In 1965, the old complex had been pulled down after a last reconstruction in 1960–61. St. Mary's produced its first high school graduates in 1952. Due to staffing shortages, the Oblates and Sisters of St. Ann gave up running the school in 1973 which closed in 1980. In 1984 the Stó:lô leased the facility from the federal government for use as a Native training centre.[53]

✤ Later Native Residential Schools

WHILE SOME HAD LONG QUESTIONED the value of residential schools, until the 1960s the Catholic Church, including most Oblates and certainly Ottawa, saw residential schools as the last great hope of transforming Native people into "good" Canadians. In British Columbia, over the years a total of ten Roman Catholic residential schools were established; six were founded before 1899. The four founded in the twentieth century were very similar to the earlier schools.[54]

Of these four, the first to be opened in 1900 was the North Vancouver or Squamish School. Émile Bunoz, OMI, was the founding principal and the French Sisters of the Child Jesus completed the initial staff. The School was located on the north shore of Burrard Inlet, about four miles from central Vancouver. By 1915, its ten-acre site, owned by the sisters, consisted of a main building, which contained dormitories and classrooms, a cottage, which served as a hospital and a number of outbuildings. The school had electricity, city water and hot air furnaces. It opened with 19 students and by 1905 had 62, its highest attendance figure. When it finally closed in 1959, it had an average annual student body of 53. Federal grants were initially $60 per capita, which, by the time it closed, had risen to $311.54. Part of the building, known as the Durieu Convent, was then opened as a student hostel.[55]

Although the Sechelt reserve was the first to experience the "Durieu System" in the late 1860s, the Sechelt School did not begin until 1904 or possibly 1905. Like North Vancouver, it was under the Oblates and the Sisters of the Child Jesus. Fire destroyed the original building on 25 May 1917, and, though several temporary structures filled the gap, it was not until 1922 that a new School was completed at a cost of $140,000. It was

Sechelt School Workshop (AD)

Students and teachers, Sechelt School (AD)

The Residential Schools

located on four acres, on part of the Sechelt Reserve that had been purchased in 1915. Besides the main building, another contained a laundry and workshops. For many years water from a small stream about four miles away was piped to the School, however, the supply was very unpredictable. The early school was heated by wood stoves and lit by coal oil lamps. It opened with 46 students in 1906, and in 1954, at its highpoint, had a 114 residential and 47 day school students. Government per capita grants were $60 in 1906, and by 1956 had reached their highest figure of $320 per capita for 90 students. The school finally closed in 1975.[56]

The Lejac School, named after Jean-Marie LeJacq (1862–99), the founder of Our Lady of Good Hope Mission at Stuart Lake (1873–80), was opened in 1922 and replaced the nearby Stuart Lake Boarding School at Fort St. James. Nicolas Coccola (1922–34) was its first head. As at both North Vancouver and Sechelt, together with the Oblates, the Sisters of the Child Jesus comprised the teaching staff. The School was situated on Fraser Lake between the Stellako and Nautley Reserves, or several miles from Fraser River Village. It opened with 151 students and reached its highest enrolment in 1969 with 185 residential and 41 day school students. A new classroom wing was completed in 1954–55. By 1956, the federal per capita grant was $360. The school closed in 1976 and was demolished around 1983.[57]

The Lower Post School, the last Native residential school to be founded by the Oblates in the far west was built in 1950 and opened in the following year. Archibald Fleury (1937–56), a Quebecois Oblate was its first principal; his teaching staff was the Sisters of St. Ann. Within a few months, the enrolment had risen from 90 to 102 students. In 1958, a new wing was added, which contained classrooms, a chapel and a gymnasium. By 1954 the per capita grant for its 120 students stood at $480. However, within four years, and reflecting a gradual change in federal policy regarding residential schools, while student numbers had risen to 170, the annual per capita grant had been reduced to $456. The school was closed in 1975.[58]

✤ An Assessment

RESIDENTIAL SCHOOL GRADUATES react with very mixed feelings regarding their experiences and many of the educational results were equally mixed. Most graduates recognized that the school had been founded upon the very wrong, even evil premise of trying to destroy a peo-

Student performance, Sechelt School (AD)

ple and their culture. However, in another sense, as with the Oblate institutions throughout British Columbia and Canada, certainly some Natives admitted that the Catholic missionaries had, in usually unintended ways, contributed in some degree to the survival of their people. Ironically, by drawing children from several tribes together, who, though they may have remained rivals, all the schools helped to promote a type of pan-Indian identity both locally and nationally. Thus, by trying to eradicate them, the schools assisted not only in sustaining traditional customs, but also in building a sense of Native solidarity, which would eventually be used to fight both the federal government and the churches. Certainly, most Native graduates did not receive much of a western European education, but probably a little was better than total ignorance of "white" ways. The few students who did succeed intellectually were given tools to challenge both the federal and provincial governments in demanding their people's rights, especially in the areas of Native cultural identity, compensation for abuse and land claims.[59]

As the Oblate leaders did in 1991, many today lament the fact that the residential schools ever existed, however, others would continue to support them. While not approving all that took place, many would say that the Oblates and others who ran such institutions were part of an era. Thus, such

The Residential Schools

logic would conclude that the present has no right to stand in judgement on the past when people then did the best they could with the lights they had. Many Christians would say they have a consistent guide, the gospel of Jesus Christ, and though, as G.K. Chesterton observed, that it has essentially been "left untried," still, its challenge remains. So it is not only history that stands in judgement on the schools, but especially the words of Jesus, particularly his insistence, as in the parable of the Good Samaritan, that we must give equal treatment and respect to all peoples and their cultures. In other words, that prejudice of any kind has no place among his followers.[60]

Certainly racism, both implicit and explicit, played a major role in bringing the schools into existence. The federal government, which ran the Department of Indian Affairs, must bear the major responsibility, for without its encouragement and financial assistance such institutions could never have existed. Yet so strong was that racism, even government officials believed that the Native was so inferior to "whites," that nothing, not even residential schools, could help. In 1904 Clifford Sifton, minister of the Interior noted in the Commons: "I have no hesitation in saying—we may as well be frank—that the Indian cannot go out from school making his own way and compete with the white man." For Sifton the reason was simple: the Indian "has not the physical, mental, or moral get-up to enable him to compete. He cannot do it." The last phrase has a chilling finality and encapsulates the entire problem. For with such a "mental" preconception, which bedeviled the thoughts of most "white" Canadians, it was impossible to recognized a Native person as equal to their European counterpart in "physical, mental" or "moral" ability.[61] And such an attitude persists to this day.

Given such racism, it is not surprising that a supposed "separate but equal" but strictly segregated educational system would evolve which, for the most part, failed miserably in preparing Native children for Euro-Canadian society, a society which in reality did not wish to see them either well-prepared nor treated equally. In truth, the schools, if anything, made the situation far worse for Native people by demeaning them as persons through the demeaning of their culture. The schools were not set up to assimilate or help Native people to enter the larger society, though that was their ostensible objective, but rather their unspoken, yet effective and real intention was to educate Natives so that they could ultimately return to their reserves. There they were expected to recognize their true station in life, and where they were to form those patterns of "deference and obedience to the

Indian agent." For it was the Indian agent who personified the supposed superior "white" society. While Euro-Canadians society continuously complained about such dependency as a central proof of the problem, at the same time it did everything possible to keep the Native person dependent upon it. It was a classic catch-twenty-two situation, and like all racism, it produced an increasingly irrational and immoral scenario. However, the Catholic Church, in defending it, even indirectly, helped to perpetuate the evils. And the Oblates and the secular clergy who ran them were sometimes as racist in their views of Natives as any others in the larger society. In fact, the "Durieu system" demonstrates that, while the Oblates wished to see the Native in some way integrated into the larger society, this process was always to be under the guidance of the "white" priest, or the church equivalent of the Indian agent. The "Durieu system" also expected the Native "Catholic" to remain "separate," from, though "equal" to Euro-Canadians.[62]

In a very real sense the residential schools were indeed "successful." For the Native people continue to occupy the lowest rung on the social and economic ladder of all Canadians. If Euro-Canadians are honest and self-critical, this is exactly where the majority have always wished the Native to be. For although the residential schools were explicitly founded to help the Native people become "white," their implicit intention was to reinforce their continued exclusion from Euro-Canadian society.

II

The Native People and the Catholic Church

✿ *A Growing Awareness of Failure*

DENOMINATIONAL RIVALRY continued to bedevil the Oblate work about the Native peoples throughout British Columbia and the far west. While the Oblates were important in the Yukon, the Anglicans formed the first major missionary influence in this huge region and would eventually dominate it. The arrival of the Anglicans in the Yukon in the 1880s made a great impact on the Natives and prompted Archbishop Seghers's decision to make his last tragic journey north. As late as 1941, Albert Dréan (1935–67), an Oblate missionary in the area, complained that until the 1930s few Oblates could be spared to work in the region, and those who did, because of age and over-extension, had made little impact. Reflecting a traditional missionary style dominated by confrontation between other denominations in the hunt for "pagan souls," Dréan concluded that until then the major result had been that the "Indians became the prey of the Protestant ministers."[1]

By the 1950s, most Christian clergy were beginning to admit the persistence and survival of native spirituality, but most Euro-Canadians continued to dismiss it as "merely superstition." There were inroads into Native culture, for example Christian marriage ceremonies became more the norm, but only if a clergyman were readily available. Even then, although on a much reduced scale than in the past, such practices as polygamy, the trading of wives as well as the discarding of partners, continued. At best, the Native people, especially in the far north, yet also throughout the far west, were nominal Christians, accepting some of the outward trappings of the faith, while still refusing to abandon their own spirituality. Like most human beings, the Native people of the far north also used syncretism, blending what complemented their traditional beliefs and ignoring what did not. The failure to learn Native languages and the consequent ignorance and lack of understanding meant that Native spirituality remained largely unknown to most Christian missionaries. Except for ethnologists such as Morice, the Native worldview hardly touched any of the missionaries, Catholic or Protestant. Although they tried to revise the Native relationship with the Christian interpretation of the deity, most missionaries failed since they never truly comprehended Native "theology," especially its essential links to the surrounding environment. While some Natives remained ritually Christian, at least as long as the missionaries were present, outside of these narrow and infrequent encounters, the Native peoples were still wedded to their traditional culture. This attitude only reinforced the prejudices of most Christian missionaries, for in their judgement the Natives had a very "incorrect" view of "reality," dominated as Euro-Canadians were by their western ways and their obsessive insistence on the universal uniqueness of Christianity. Until very recently few Euro-Canadians, including missionaries made any attempt to challenge this serious lack of comprehension and its poverty of imagination.[2]

While a handful of Oblates always had their doubts about the effectiveness of their ministry to the Native people, they very rarely could see themselves as a major part of the cause of their continued failure. As early as 1861, this blindness lead people such as D'Herbomez to make exaggerated claims about the numbers of Native "converts" to Catholicism. In 1886, his coadjutor and successor, Durieu, taking pride in what he believed had been the miracle achieved by his "System," reported a "great success." For Durieu insisted that infidelity and drunkenness had been eradicated among Native Catholics, and even better, they were effectively supporting the church on their reserves. It is true that such extreme conclusions were intended to

Cariboo Indian Reserve School Hockey Team, 1940–41 (AD)

impress French lay contributors to Oblate overseas' Missions, yet Durieu always appears to have believed his own propaganda. As late as 1942, Émile Bunoz proclaimed the great benefits of the "Durieu System," and warned other Oblates "not to discard the past methods as useless[ly] antiquated things before giving them due consideration." Yet reductions, such as the Durieu System, which had been used by the Roman Catholic Church in various forms for well over 300 years, would certainly appear to have been given "due consideration." As late as 1947, the English-born Oblate, Joseph Scannell (1934–66) blamed any problems on nothing very new, namely, Native contacts with "whites." If the Oblates, he believed, were given greater financial resources by government, then they would be able to impress upon the Native Catholic the centrality of their church and faith, and the Native "problem" would be solved forever. In achieving his objectives, and while he does not mention it, Scannell would probably have favored a return to the old reduction missiology, perhaps even the "Durieu System." The words had changed, but the reality remained the same, for most Oblates continued to insist that the problems were all due either to the Natives or to the larger, Euro-Canadian society. For neither the Catholic Church in the far west nor the Oblates could comprehend that, in their inability to change, especially their very narrow, and often Gnostic, dualistically dominated worldview that fed their racism, they were also a major part of the overall problem, including their persistent nonsuccess.[3]

Night prayers in the dormitory at the Cariboo Indian School, St. Joseph's Mission (AD)

By the 1920s the Oblates, though still trying to "convert" the Native people, had increasingly concentrated their ministry among the "whites." However, when such over-extension is added to an aging, francophone dominated workforce in an increasingly anglophone society, it was clear to anyone who wished to see that they were fighting a losing battle. In an effort to address the issue, Augustine Dontenwill, in his first visit to the far west as Superior General in 1926, asked English-speaking Oblates in Saskatchewan and Alberta, who were now part of the new Province of St. Peter's, to volunteer for British Columbia, but they had their own staff shortages. Eventually, the new province did increase vocations, drawing most new recruits from Ontario, and by 1939 there were increases in personnel. But this merely delayed the ultimate admission that the inherently flawed method for evangelizing the Native peoples was ultimately doomed.[4]

Denial continued to dominate Oblate attitudes throughout this period. Whether it was the Oblates or female religious orders, such as the Sisters of St. Ann, consistent and glowing reports of success was reported throughout the far west. The Native people were supposedly continuing to move forward to the great objective of being acculturated into Canadian society, but especially into the Catholic Church, for their devotion to the church was seen as the core reason for such progress. This was reflected in the residential schools throughout the province, but even in some day schools in Homalco-Slaïamin, Chilliwack, Chehalis, Osoyoos and Ketzé. In 1944, in an official visitation of the region by the American-born Canadian Oblate, John Boekenfoehr attributed this "continued success" to the fact that the Oblates had retained a central element in the Durieu System: Native "responsibility." This Pollyannaish view of the Durieu System, which was extremely paternalistic, was balanced by the same visitor's observation that very few Oblates had mastered any Native languages, and the overwhelming majority still depended on a mixture of Chinook, English and French. Such skills were certainly important for their ministry, but were also an ideal laid down by the Durieu System. However, he also gave the lie to the supposed "responsibility" that he believed the Durieu System was engendering among the Natives. Noting that the training and general formation in the residential schools had failed to make the Native pupils either "self-reliant" or "self-supporting," he attributed the problem to the "false [Oblate] policy" that believed that it was perfectly acceptable to "to spoon-feed" Native children.[5]

✟ The Native People, the Oblates and the Catholic Church After 1945

AS THEIR 1991 APOLOGY STATED, if there is to be a future relationship between the Oblates and the Native people of Canada, it must not be based on a top-down, paternalistic, patriarchal, authoritarian model, but on a "reciprocal sharing of the Good News." Reciprocity is a vital part of such as process, not only between the Oblates and the Native people, but also in the latter's relationship with all Euro-Canadians, including the larger Catholic Church, especially if there is to be mutual healing.[6]

Racism continues to hinder that search. In January 1998, the federal government finally stated that it was "deeply sorry" for the abuse suffered by Native people in the residential schools set up to acculturate them into Euro-Canadian culture. Phil Fontaine, the grand chief of the Assembly of First Nations who accepted Ottawa's apology and the $350-million healing fund was especially moved by the event. Fontaine noted he had spent 40 years "trying to come to terms" with the physical and sexual abuse he suffered at the hands of some of the Oblate priests and brothers who ran the Native

Sports at the Sechelt Residential School (AD)

Students at Holy Rosary School (AD)

The Lord's Distant Vineyard

Residential School at Fort Alexander, Manitoba, which he entered at age seven. It was only in 1990 that Fontaine publicly revealed his experiences. He was prompted to do so in the wake of the 1988–89 revelations of Euro-Canadians who had been sexually and physically abused in the 1960s and 1970s by the Irish Christian Brothers at the Mount Cashel Orphanage in St. John's, Newfoundland. At the time, Fontaine encouraged other Native people to come forward, an invitation that, over the last decade, has triggered most of the public disclosures. The general public revulsion, however, at what had happened to the Native people was apparently only possible when it was first revealed that "whites" had also suffered such abuse, revealing the underlying racism that continues to bedevil Native-European relations in Canada.[7]

Public attitudes among Euro-Canadians towards race also showed marked progress after 1945. The large Asian population in British Columbia benefited from this change, where the Chinese and East Indians received the franchise in 1947 and the Japanese in 1949. However, it was the Native people, who had the furthest to go, and who experienced the greatest benefits. The residential schools, though terrible evils, especially in their intended destruction of Native culture, by forcing different tribes together gradually, though for the most part unintentionally, helped to create a pan-Native national outlook. Through such bodies as the Native Brotherhood of British Columbia, which was founded in 1931, the Native people began to take advantage of changing "white" feelings towards race. Even the Native birthrate, which, reflecting the onset of the worst period of racism, had begun to dramatically fall in the 1880s, now began to increase. By the late 1950s the Europeans were also beginning to accept that Native segregation, in all areas of life, but especially education, was serious and a fact. This resulted in a slow integration of public schools throughout the province, but also to a public recognition and a Native demand that they had a natural right to practice their traditions, such as the potlatch, which had been out-lawed in 1884. In 1966 it was reported that the Native people of British Columbia were "the most prosperous" in Canada, and in 1970 the federal government replaced Indian agents with local band councils, giving Native people greater control over their own lives. Nevertheless, like the Catholic Church, Ottawa and Victoria continue to practice a strong paternalism towards aboriginals. Certainly the recent "official apology" regarding residential schools by the federal government is hopeful, yet there is still a long way to go before it can be said that mutual respect, especially on the part of Euro-Canadians, is fully realized.[8]

Much must still change if there is hope for healing not only of Native people, but also of the Oblates and the Catholic Church. All are victims of psychological abuse, which for the Oblates is centered in the institutional dysfunctionalism and co-dependency of both the Catholic Church as well as their Congregation, especially in their continued, widespread denial of reality. In trying to confront such denial, James P. Mulvihill, head (1960–65) of the Oblate Commission on Indian Affairs in Ottawa and later bishop of Whitehorse (1966–71), wrote in 1963 that European and Native respect of each other, especially on the part of the Oblates and federal government, was essential. Mulvihill was adamant that Native people must be respected, not only for what was done to them in the past, but also for whom they are now. For, he noted, all Canadians were part of a "democratic, pluralistic society," which meant that, although Euro-Canadian support was vital, only the Native people could decide on the process of integration into that society. However, such a hope would never happen until the Native person "is shown...respect and sympathy in his [/her] efforts to work out a new way of life." Yet, in 1972 the National Office of Religious Education of the Canadian Catholic Conference was still insisting that such an undertaking must remain top-down. Therefore, "whites" remained in charge, and, reminiscent of the Durieu "System," in order to bring it about, "Native Catechists," should be "trained" by "whites" to assist in the process.[9]

This implicit paternalism was still evident in 1991. For in reacting to the Oblate *Apology*, denial dominated most responses of the Oblates in St. Paul's Province in British Columbia.[10] Virtually all of the members of St. Paul's Province had worked in the residential schools in the region. Although one Oblate in the province admitted that the schools were "just another way to kill the [Native] spirit," such a remark was the exception. Rather most insisted that the residential school had made it possible for the Native people to make "great strides" in breaking with the "problems" in their family systems, especially alcoholism. Most Oblates in St. Paul's also stated that the majority of the pupils they had worked with remained "very happy" with the schools. In an example of stifling paternalism, the Native people themselves were still the "problem" that the schools had only tried to address. This implicit racist attitude persists in most Oblates who ever worked in the far west. Its roots are in the dysfunctional system of the Oblate "family," not dissimilar to other clerical systems in the Catholic Church.[11]

Much of the problem seems to center upon an essential worldview, personality and spirituality differences between most of the Catholic clergy and the Native people. About 70 percent of all clergy, Catholic or otherwise, "fall within...authoritarian personality types." That is, they tend to see reality in "black and white categories," which also reflects a largely negative mentality that "my way of thinking and doing is the only right way." Instead of looking within to the unconscious, which has so much to teach the conscience mind in the formation of a healthy conscience, this personality type puts most "trust in externalised and dogmatised formulas" espoused by church authorities. However, largely because of their spirituality, Native people tend to operate out of an "egalitarian personality" type, which is "highly intuitive" and thinks in "both abstract and realistic ways." Thus, Native spirituality is grounded in service, particularly by looking at, listening to and learning from the other, instead of trying to dominate and control them. Yet, the authoritarian personality type, so evident among most clergy, that influences mainly negative, uncritical thinking, prefers to "play God" rather than allow "God to be God." In the end, as expressed in the Native shaman tradition, the only hope for the "white" missionary who wishes to "succeed" must be their willingness to be chosen and accepted by the Native people to whom they must be "present." Then they must allow the Spirit and the Native people to determine what form that "presence" will take. Any Native church therefore will depend upon the ability of the clergy to abandon an "assimilationist framework" and move into one of "effective interaction" with those who see the gospel, as did Jesus, "as a source of liberation and fulfilment."[12]

Under the control of the "authoritarian personality type," most Oblates and other clergy in their ministry to the Native people did not, nor do they now, spread the gospel, the "good news," but rather a form of denominational triumphalism for which there is no future in Canadian society. In August 1994, the Archbishop of Milwaukee, Rembert Weakland, OSB, spoke to the Catholic bishops of Canada regarding the future of religious life in the church. He noted that religious, both men and women, in their increasing disappearance, are a "weather vane" indicating that "the old order is passing away for the [Catholic] church and for how the church relates to the world." Like nationalism, especially as it is presently evolving in the European Union, the old rigid forms of denominationalism are also "passing away." And similarly, the Oblates in their *"present form"* have "no future." Yet, perhaps nowhere is the path towards that future better expressed than in the hoped-for Oblate relationship with the Native people. Particularly in their genuine desire to form "a renewed covenant of solidarity" with the Native people that, if realized, could become a model for them and the Catholic Church in their service not only to the Native people, but ultimately to all Canadians.[13]

Most Euro-Canadians still believe that they have little or nothing to learn from Native culture, however, many are beginning to realize that this is not true. Everyone has much to gain by abandoning a Judeo-Christian inspired linear, usually greed and consumption driven view of history which, especially over the last 50 years, has had much to do with leading us all towards an increasingly likely global ecological catastrophe. Instead, there is a great need to move in the direction of a cyclical worldview, which is still part of Native tradition, and that sees an integrity, wholeness and interdependency in all life, and as such is an essential concept for ecological survival. Through mutual respect by looking, listening and learning, we all have much to gain from each other for no culture has all the answers.

✤ The Beginning of the End of the "Old Order"

VATICAN II would indeed mark the beginning of the end of "old order" and its blind, unimaginative acceptance of the past, especially in the Catholic Church's centuries-long treatment of aboriginal peoples in Canada as elsewhere. And together with the federal government and other churches, Catholic authorities began to see the residential school as a major symptom of the *disease* of "exclusive" western acculturation. Still, it took many years of struggle and soul-searching for the Oblates even to begin to realize the damage that, despite their often best intentions, they and other Euro-Canadians had imposed on the Native peoples.

Reflecting this on-going debate, studies of Native residential schools continue the essential and critical examination of the past. In 1992, a Native writer, Elizabeth Furniss published a study of Williams Lake Residential School (closed in 1981) that was sponsored by the Cariboo Tribal Council, entitled: *Victims of Benevolence: Discipline and Death at The Williams Lake Indian Residential School, 1891–1920.* The title demonstrates the need for all concerned parties, but especially Native people, to explore the past honestly, particularly its shadow side and to learn to take personal responsibility in challenging and changing it. In her conclusion, Furniss notes that, despite their recent admissions of past wrongs, both the Oblates and the federal government retain "a paternalistic attitude" towards the Native peoples. The government still insists in "overseeing the decision-making of Band Councils in reserve communities," which is all done under the persistent belief that such a policy is in the "best interests" of the Native people. Still, Furniss believes that the Oblates and the Catholic Church have "begun to struggle internally to come to terms with...[their] own history and to modernize...[their] relationship with Native peoples." If this process is to be successful, however, Furniss insists that there must be a "fundamental reexamination of the assumptions that the Catholic church historically has brought into its relationship with Native peoples in Canada, both through the missionization program and through the residential school system."[14]

The Oblate desire for reconciliation with the Native peoples seems clear in their official *Apology* of 1991. In the *Apology*, Doug Crosby admitted past wrongs. That the Oblates had, indeed, played a part "in the cultural, ethnic, linguistic and religious imperialism that was part of the mentality with which" Native Peoples in Canada were treated by civil governments and by the churches. The *Apology* was issued on behalf of over 1,200 Oblates then living in Canada. It noted their sorrow for "the part" that they had all "played, however inadvertent and naïve that participation might have been, in the setting up and maintaining of a system that stripped others of not only their lands but also their" traditions. In conclusion, the *Apology* pledged the Canadian Oblates to a "renewed covenant of solidarity." Since the Oblates, the *Apology* said, still saw themselves as members of "the same family" with Native peoples, it noted the need to "come again to that deep trust and solidarity that constitutes families. We recognize that the road beyond past hurt may be long and steep, but we pledge ourselves anew to journey with the Native Peoples on that road."[15] Time alone will tell if the Oblates and the Native people have a future together. Yet, there is hope if there is also a willingness to dialogue in mutual respect, while still admitting, as Pope John Paul II recently reminded all Catholics, that "grave forms of injustice" have, indeed, been done in the church's past in the name of the gospel of Jesus Christ.[16]

Part Three

The Europeans

"When religion fails to integrate...

one's life experience, it should hardly

be surprising that...people find it 'irrelevant.'"

REGINALD W. BIBBY,
FRAGMENTED GODS,
PP. 270-71.

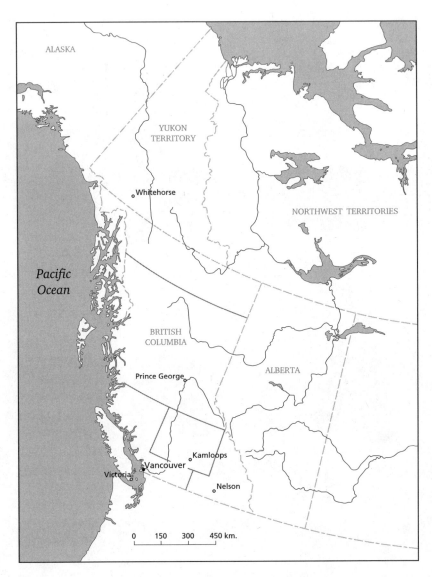

Ecclesiastical Province of British Columbia and the Yukon

12

The Years Before the Railroad

✢ *The Diocese of Victoria and Its New Bishop*

THE DIOCESE OF VICTORIA is the oldest (1846) Canadian diocese west of Toronto. St. Boniface, then the most settled area west of Upper Canada, did not become a diocese until 1847. However, its bishop-elect, Modeste Demers certainly had no sense of its historic significance, and early events would confirm the folly of its creation. While he privately opposed his new assignment, as he had the establishment of the ecclesiastical province, he lacked the courage to confront and challenge its architect, Norbert Blanchet. His administrative abilities were also poor, for when Blanchet left him in charge during his years (1844–46) in Europe, Demers had undertaken a building spree that nearly bankrupted the vicariate. Blanchet had "ordered" his colleague to construct the three rectories, two convents and a church, yet a stronger personality might have opposed the idea or at least have been more circumspect in its implementation. The church, St. Paul's in St. Paul's, Oregon, though it measured only 100 by 45 feet, since it was the first brick structure in the Oregon Territory, cost a staggering $20,000. On 30 November 1847, Demers was finally ordained a bishop there before a tiny congregation of a few dozen laity and eight clergy, a circumstance that only reinforced the ill-conceived nature of the new province.[1]

Early in the spring of 1848 Demers left for Canada and Europe where he spent four years in a largely vain attempt to obtain money and missionaries for his diocese. Quebec had changed during his ten-year absence. Nascent nationalism had weakened liberalism and strengthened ultramontane Catholicism, which had become a major element in the new francophone national identity. Earlier anticlericalism gave way to clericalism and soon produced a ready supply of local vocations. This did not benefit Demers, since, while he found funds there, few Quebec clergy were willing to trade such a relatively comfortable and congenial environment for the risks of the unknown in some remote area in far-western British North America. In October 1849, Demers left Montreal for Europe where he hoped his prospects for personnel would improve.[2]

Although Demers met with modest success in Europe, he found its ecclesiastical atmosphere to be quite unpleasant, especially when compared to Quebec. The revolutions of 1848 had left their mark on most of Catholic Europe, but especially France. The official church's usual opposition to progress and change, and its support of the status quo, particularly towards the working class, was reflected in a growing anticlericalism, especially in Paris. There the hostility against the clergy was so strong that it prompted Demers to condemn everything Parisian as "unbearable," including its cuisine. To make matters even worse, by 1851 he owed almost as much money as he had so far raised. News of the escalating financial crisis in Oregon, where the California gold rush was drawing tens of thousands away, stripping the new ecclesiastical province of laity, priests and money, hardly improved his disposition.[3]

Belgium provided a major ray of hope. Unlike the Catholic Church in France, due to its "strength and independence" from the liberal state, the Catholic Church in Belgium had "become a model, a kind of ideal for the other European [Catholic] Churches." This atmosphere lead to a definite popularity towards the church among conservatives, which meant it attracted far more vocations to the priesthood and religious life than the tiny Belgian church could possibly absorb. Demers was able to recruit four priests, the first who were willing to work in his huge diocese. Actually, Belgium was destined to supply most of the clergy there during the nineteenth and early twentieth centuries.[4]

Demers, even at the best of times, was a very difficult man to work with, a problem that got worse in his new position as a bishop, a role he had never wanted nor enjoyed. The four Belgian priests who worked with him complained of his "quick temper" and of being treated like slaves. As a consequence, by 1857 all but one, Louis Lootens, had left the diocese, mainly for California. Demers then tried to obtain Irish priests from All Hallows College in Dublin. While an Irish priest and graduate of All Hallows, Joseph Bowles did set out for Victoria in 1854, he got no further than Newark, New Jersey. Apparently hearing rumors of the difficult living and working conditions in Victoria, Bowles advised Demers that ill health would not allow him to continue with his journey, a condition confirmed by the first bishop of Newark, James Roosevelt Bayley. However, Demers, desperate for clergy, refused to believe the explanation, and was convinced that Bowles only wanted to remain in an "easier" place.[5]

Undoubtedly there were "problem" priests just as there were "problem" bishops. For it was not unusual for bishops and religious superiors in places such as Ireland or Belgium, which then had a significant surplus of clergy, to ship their "problem" priests, often alcoholics, as far away as possible, usually providing them with positive recommendations. Demers appears to have had his share of difficult priests, but the evidence indicates that even those who were "normal" and remained with him found him extremely hard to please.[6]

By 1857, with Lootens about to leave, Demers was desperate and looked to education as a solution, since he still lacked the laity necessary to support a viable diocese. As a financial alternative in 1856, Demers had begun a small fee-paying school for boys. Now he thought that if he could obtain religious women he would open a fee-based school for girls that would be equally popular among the local Europeans, especially the management class of the HBC. The two schools would produce desperately needed revenues, and at least give some justification to the existence of his diocese.[7]

✤ Victoria: From Fort to City and a New Religious Pluralism

THE DISCOVERY OF GOLD on the Fraser in 1858 changed everything in the far west. In the summer of 1857 Demers had gone to Quebec in search of personnel and money. There he was able to secure the services of three priests, four nuns, and two religious brothers, most of whom he planned to use as teachers. Upon his return to Victoria early in 1858 Demers expected to

The Years Before the Railroad

find the same sleepy HBC trading outpost he had left only a few months before. But the gold rush had begun and Demers was shocked to discover the beginnings of a city.

While the diocese of Victoria were founded in 1846, it was not until after 1858 that it became a serious reality. By then the British government had ended HBC rule in the region by establishing both Vancouver Island and the mainland as formal colonies, each with a directly elected assembly and a governor appointed by London. New Caledonia, as the mainland was known, was renamed British Columbia. The region had entered upon a new era, which would have profound effects upon its social, political and economic future. And certainly, this was true in the case of organized religion.[8]

While the HBC welcomed other denominations, being British, at its forts it always gave pride of place to the Anglican church and its chaplains. Demers had experienced this reality in Oregon, and resented it, but as a bishop it became even more frustrating. As official appointees, the Anglican chaplains expected special recognition both for themselves and their church. As at Fort Vancouver, this was true also at Fort Victoria. There the Company chaplain, John Staines and his successor, Edward Cridge, had each received a clergy reserve of 100 acres near the Fort in addition to their annual Company salary. Both clergymen considered themselves the representatives of an *unofficial* state church.[9]

Although Demers disliked this situation, there was a certain ambivalence in his feelings. His eight years in Oregon had convinced him of the value of American pluralism and its constitutional separation of church and state. Yet growing up in Quebec, he was accustomed to state support for the Catholic Church, and, in line with this, in 1850 he tried to obtain an annual pension for himself from the British government. His failure in this regard no doubt further fueled his strong hostility over the privileged position of the Anglican church on Vancouver Island. In 1855 he reported to a colleague that Cridge's perception of his special position over other denominations was "raising strong feelings against himself in public" and that "such bigotry...will not do in a country like this." The hoped-for special status for Anglicanism would eventually be challenged and rejected, and Demers would have a major role in achieving that objective.[10]

Reflecting Victoria's new importance, in 1860 it became the seat of the first Anglican diocese of British Columbia with an Englishman, George Hills (1859–92), as its first bishop. From the outset Hills assumed that his *was* the

Engraving of the Right Reverend George Hills (ca. 1859),
Bishop of British Columbia
(Courtesy of the Archives of the Ecclesiastical
Province of British Columbia and Yukon)

established church in the two colonies. His initial article in the *Columbia Mission Report*, the public relations organ of the London-based Anglican Society for the Propagation of the Gospel, which raised money for Anglican missionary activities throughout the British Empire, reflected this. Much like *Rapport* and *Missions*, the *Report* stressed "success stories" both to please its contributors and to gain new ones. Hills's first published account of his new ministry evidenced a certain triumphalism over Demers. He noted that his Catholic counterpart had "not seemed pleased" at the "cordial reception" given to Hills by the local crown authorities, nor, by it, the implied privileged position of Anglicanism in the two colonies. In reaction, Hills wrote that Demers had voted against the government at a recent election and in a sermon soon afterwards had also "incensed" Catholics against Hills. Nevertheless, Hills assured his English readers that all was well, and that Demers's behaviour had caused only a few "trivial" inconveniences. A short time later, Hills privately described Demers as "a coarse looking, but good-natured man." Still, his public statements reveal both the personal tensions between Demers and Hills and Hills's belief that, as in England, the Anglican church now enjoyed the status in the far west of an "established church." However, Hills soon learned he was no longer in the "Old Country."[11]

In October 1860, Amor De Cosmos, the Americanised, anticlerical and liberal editor of the first established newspaper in Victoria, *The Colonist*, published Hills's letter and a strong editorial condemnation of its views. Amor De Cosmos was rapidly becoming a local one-man institution and had assumed the leadership of the official opposition party in the new assembly. Certainly De Cosmos was determined to campaign against any notion of an "established church" in the two colonies, an objective shared by many, especially Demers, for while the two were extreme opposites in their attitude towards organized religion, on the matter of a state church they were in total accord. There were several early signs of their unity of purpose. Demers sold De Cosmos his first press, but more importantly, Demers voted for De Cosmos in the colonial assembly elections, mainly because he supported the bishop's anti-establishment views.[12]

Responding to *The Colonist* editorial, Hills almost immediately issued an *Occasional Paper* and, apparently trying to placate both De Cosmos and Demers, said that his offending statement had been published in the *Report* "without... [his] knowledge." Hills also apologised to any American readers who might have been offended by several critical remarks he had also made about them in the *Report*.[13]

Due to the gold rush, by 1860 American immigrants constituted the majority of residents in Victoria, especially among the "influential middle class," and thus were a significant force in helping to shape local public opinion. The American presence was so great, the fear of annexation of the region by the United States was a major factor that ultimately lead to British Columbia entering Confederation in 1871. This early reality was forever underscored in 1858. For in establishing the mainland as a crown colony that year, Queen Victoria deliberately chose the title *British* Columbia because, she said, the "citizens of the United States call their country also Columbia, at least in poetry."[14]

In the *Report*, Hills had criticised Victoria's American residents as "racists" for their prejudiced attitude towards both the Native peoples and African Americans. The latter had come to the area like other Americans drawn there by the get-rich-quick fever of the Fraser River gold rush of 1858. The U.S. Civil War (1861–65) would reinforce their desire to remain in Victoria. Hills now publicly apologised for this remark, but reminded any American readers that, while he had the "deepest interest" in their democratic pluralism, they were certainly "not free from criticism." Hills was incorrect in thinking that his published apology would end the controversy, for American influence on local public opinion was destined to effect the future unofficial status of the Anglican church in both colonies.[15]

Demers was so incensed by his episcopal rival's assumption regarding the privileged standing of the Anglican church, that, in order to demonstrate his opposition he sued Hills over public access to the local cemetery. The issue centred upon the right of other denominations to enter Victoria's only burial ground by means of a gate that was then solely accessible from a roadway that passed through the Anglican church reserve. Hills wanted another gate constructed so non-Anglicans would not trespass by crossing the reserve. It was a crucial issue, and Hills's enemies, especially Demers and De Cosmos, were determined to defeat him and by doing so champion religious pluralism in the two colonies.[16]

Governor James Douglas supported Hills, since he saw even an "unofficially" established church as a reinforcement of the government's right to govern. Fully realising the lawsuit's important implications, both Douglas and Hills privately attempted, without success, to convince Demers to drop his lawsuit.[17]

The trial took place in May 1861. Demers's lawyer asserted that though Hills was not "a wicked man," he was "misguided" and "badly advised" thinking, as he did, that since his church was *the* church in England, that the "same rule applied" in the two colonies. Hills's attorney attempted to prove that Demers would be trespassing if he insisted that he had a right to enter the cemetery through the reserve land. The jury disagreed with Hills, awarded the case to Demers, and assessed Hills a punitive $3,200 in damages. Much worse for Hills was the implication that the Anglican church had no legal claim to hold church reserves, or to assume that it had any kind of established status in the far west. Indeed, in an editorial published immediately after the trial, De Cosmos declared that the "verdict for Demers" in this "important suit" virtually settled "the vexed question of...the reserved lands...[in the two colonies] for all future time." By implication, De Cosmos believed the decision also rejected the Anglican church's "claim to be the established church" in the two colonies.[18]

Two months later, when several Anglican clergy attempted to set up church reserves on the mainland, Hills and Douglas expressed serious doubts about the wisdom of proceeding. Both noted the "wide-spread and deeply rooted objection" in both colonies against the idea of church reserves because of their clear connotation of privilege. Yet, while public "irritation and contention" might be the price, Hills refused to totally abandon his claim, for he was determined to protect the valuable reserve in central Victoria and the implied establishment status that it gave the local Anglican church.[19]

The Colonist and Demers kept the issue of the reserve before a public that already seemed predisposed to reject Hills's claims to the reserve that reflected the special treatment being accorded to the Anglican church. In an open letter in *The Colonist* in October 1861 entitled *"The Church in British Columbia,"* Demers again attacked Hills's *Occasional Paper* and expressed his resentment at Hills's reference to Catholics as "Romanists," and to Demers as a "foreigner." In July 1862 Demers expressed the belief, in *The Colonist,* that the state should, in principle, be completely "non-sectarian," as long as it treated everyone equally.[20]

By May 1863 Hills had lost local government support for his claims, a clear sign of things to come, for a year later the British government reduced the original 100 acre reserve to 22 and converted it into a Trust under government control. In Upper and Lower Canada church-state separation remained only nominal, since the churches there, especially the Anglican and Roman Catholic, continued to wield considerable social, political and economic influence. However, from its beginnings, British Columbia favoured a pluralistic "non-sectarian" society in which no church would have even a minor position of privilege, and the strong American presence there helped to strengthen and solidify this position. It was an early and groundbreaking achievement that set a precedent that would not be altered in the future. British Columbia was destined to be the most unchurched province in Canada. Ironically, Demers, influenced probably by his years in the Oregon Territory, and his failure to obtain an annual government pension, through his protests and lawsuit against Hills, enormously assisted in laying the foundation for this unique, Canadian reality.[21]

✣ *The Source of the Secular Clergy on Vancouver Island*

THE OBLATES FORMED THE BACKBONE of the clergy on the mainland throughout the nineteenth and most of the twentieth centuries. During the same period Belgian seculars would fill that role on Vancouver Island. This was largely due to the "strength and independence," of the contemporary Catholic Church in Belgium. As a by-product Belgium produced a glut of Catholic clergy, most of whom, reflecting their ecclesiology, were very reactionary. Belgian Catholicism was strongly ultramontane, and probably even more conservative than the church in France. Most of the graduates of Belgium's seminaries were strongly critical of their liberal society. Belgian cleric, John Charles Seghers, who became the second (1873–78) and fourth (1885–86) bishop of Victoria was a notable example. Seghers referred to Belgian liberalism as "imitating the madness of France" and he declared scornfully that it had reduced non church-going Belgians to the same intellectual level as "Darwinian monkeys."[22]

Like other Belgian clergy who came to British Columbia, Seghers had prepared himself to speak and read English at the American College in Louvain. Founded in 1857 by two American bishops, the College tapped the local clerical surplus there for its needy episcopal subscribers in North America. Demers, as one of the earliest subscribers, had a claim on a certain percentage of its graduates. Outside the mainland, until well into the twentieth century, Belgium and the American College provided Vancouver Island and Alaska, which was part of the diocese of Victoria until 1892, with four bishops and 16 priests, or the overwhelming majority of its clergy.[23]

While most of the secular clergy on Vancouver Island were Belgians, there were also some Irish. Initially, the Irish had a natural attraction for Demers, since Irish immigrants dominated the church-going European laity on Vancouver Island as well as the mainland. In fact, reflecting this reality, when he first thought of resigning in 1859, Demers suggested that Rome appoint an Irishman to succeed him.[24]

The terrible potato famines in Ireland during the 1840s and resulting death and emigration, as well as the influences of Irish nationalism, left the

Catholic Church there with far fewer laity and a clerical surplus. By the 1860s many Irish priests and seminarians had been radicalized by the politics of Fenianism, which was a mixture of American and European revolutionary liberal nationalism nurtured by an abiding hatred of all things English. Eager to be rid of their more radical priests and seminarians, and other "problem" clergy such as alcoholics, Irish bishops and religious superiors often "encouraged" them to volunteer for the foreign missions. North America, where so many Irish had emigrated, was naturally very high on their list. Thus, Irish superiors often provided such emigrant clergy with glowing recommendations, which, in some cases, only time and experience would call into question.[25]

By 1870 Demers had finally had his full of Irish clergy. Of the eight priests whom he had been promised and helped to educate at All Hallows College, Dublin, one quit the diocese almost before he had unpacked his bags. Another five either never left Ireland or, apparently scared off by horror stories of frontier poverty, found greener pastures in the United States. William Moloney, however, did stay and for five (1865–70) very long years. An extremely outspoken man, Moloney was soon infuriating the English and, no doubt, delighting many Irish Catholic laity in Victoria with his "sermons" on British "history." After tangling with Moloney more than once, Seghers, who naturally favored his far more conservative-minded fellow Belgian clergy, concluded that Moloney was indeed "God's curse" on the diocese of Victoria. Nevertheless, another Irish priest, Patrick Kirley (1868–78), the last of the original eight, eventually became vicar general of the diocese. However, by 1870 Kirley was the only secular Irish priest left on Vancouver Island, and, by then, a disgusted Demers had cancelled his contract with All Hallows College, Dublin. He appeared well-content with his Belgian clergy, at least as far as his difficult disposition would allow.[26]

✛ The First "White" Schools

DEMERS'S STANCE towards the Anglican church would be repeated in the matter of the state's role in supporting church controlled schools. The issue again reflected American influence over public opinion at the time. Historically, the Oblates, in the person of Honoré Lempfrit, had made the first attempt in 1849 to establish Catholic schools in Victoria. About then the HBC's Anglican chaplain, Robert Staines started a similar enterprise. Class played an important role in the type of students in these early schools. Staines's school was for the "better classes," namely, the English-speaking children of the Company's management, whereas Lempfrit's was for the "poor children of...[the] French Canadians" or the offspring of the Company's working class employees. However, Lempfrit's forced departure in 1852 put a temporary halt to Catholic education in the diocese.[27]

In the years before the gold rush of 1858, local schooling continued to be problematic. The HBC entered the education business in March 1853 when it established two schools to meet the needs of its working class employees, who were mainly, if nominally, Catholic. Though the Company rarely provided anything free of charge, tuition was quite low. There was no formal religious instruction, but there was Bible reading and prayer. Since all the schoolmasters were Protestant and most of their students were French Canadian Catholics, Demers considered this a grave danger to the pupils' Catholic faith, and desired to re-establish a Catholic alternative as soon as possible. Their francophone parents, however, were apparently far more interested in having their offspring receive a general education, especially in speaking and reading English, than in learning the tenets of the Catholic faith. By the end of 1856 Demers was able to open a small school for boys, yet since it was mainly intended to help support the diocese, and so charged fairly high fees, it would have been limited to the "better classes." Still, with his continued difficulty of obtaining and retaining clergy to run such institutions, especially ones who could teach as well as speak English, this fact meant that the school had difficulty attracting and keeping students. In 1858, with the arrival of the Oblates and the Sisters of St. Ann, both with members who had English as their first language, this difficulty was solved. St. Louis College for boys and St. Ann's Academy for girls were finally established, signalling the official beginnings of Catholic education in the far west.[28]

St. Louis College was a continuation of the school Demers had founded in 1856. In running it, the Oblates were assisted by two clerics of St. Viator, François Thibodeau and Charles Michaud, who Demers had brought back with him from Quebec in 1858. Then located on View Street, it showed considerable success during the next five years, growing from under 25 to almost 75 students. As a result, in August 1863 the Oblates moved it to much larger quarters on Pandora Street where it was renamed St. Louis College in honour of the patron saint of the local Oblate superior, Louis D'Herbomez. The earliest records indicate that D'Herbomez, Julien Baudre (1856–90),

James McGuckin (1863–1903), Edward McStay (1863–1907) and Patrick Allen (1863–1911) all taught there. The last three were from Dublin, with English as their mother tongue, which was vital for the college's continued growth and success.[29]

The overall curriculum, general standards and discipline reflected the makeup of a more or less typical contemporary boarding school. At first, due to a serious lack of space, the college functioned only as a day school, a condition that would not have recommended it as well to the better-off classes. By 1860 it had begun accepting boarders, though day students continued to attend. Board and tuition were $250 per annum, half that figure for day students, either amount indicating that the student body would have been limited to the well-to-do, for, though poorly paid, a good Chinese cook in Victoria then cost about $300 a year. The curriculum covered the general arts and sciences, but reflecting the importance of Victoria's growing business community, the prospectus emphasised that "particular attention" would be paid to the "commercial" area. As for religion, all denominations were welcomed, and students were left to follow their own religious profession. But it was stipulated that "for the sake of good order and regularity," non-Catholics were asked to "conform to the general regulations of the establishment," which included taking part in community prayers.[30]

The College ultimately produced considerable tensions between Demers and the Oblates. The Oblates had only assumed the enterprise with the clear understanding that Demers would compensate them for their investment when and if they relinquished it to the diocese. By the time they made the decision to depart in 1865, the Oblates had spent well over $10,000, including the cost of land and construction of the new facility on Pandora Street. For well over a year D'Herbomez and Demers contended over the final settlement; in fact, the latter even cited the dispute as a major factor in his deteriorating health. Though the Oblates never received the amount that they believed they were entitled to, Demers complained bitterly of the final settlement, especially since he had to sell a nearby farm to pay for it. So it was probably fair, especially when compared to the large amount that the Oblates had lost in their final negotiations with the Blanchet brothers.[31]

Complementing the Oblate college for boys, in 1858 the Sisters of St. Ann initiated St. Ann's Academy, the first formal Catholic educational enterprise for girls in the region. While the Sisters experienced definite tensions in their relationship with them, they would become important allies with the Oblates in their future ministry in the far west. Arriving with Demers in 1858, four sisters: Mary Valois, Angèle Gauthier, Lumena Brasseur and Conception Lane formed the first community and Convent School or Academy of St. Ann, which was located on Park Street. Classes began in November 1858, and, as the only exclusively girls' school in the city, the student roster even included the three daughters of Governor James Douglas. By 1863, when overall numbers had reached almost a hundred, part of school was moved to View Street and used the space resulting from the transfer of the boys' school to Pandora Street. While the arts and sciences were not ignored, as would be expected for the period, when "moral and domestic" training formed the backbone of a young lady's education, St. Ann's Academy was essentially a "finishing" school and remained so. It did have a "general" curriculum that stressed "practical" subjects, which by the turn of the century had developed into a commercial school for the training of secretaries. As at St. Louis College, all denominations were encouraged to apply, however, with the same proviso that students "conform to the general regulations of the establishment," which meant attending daily prayers.[32]

As in the very first schools founded by Lempfrit and Staines, class played an important role in segregating student instruction, but race was also important. Most Europeans were unwilling to associate with Native peoples or the several hundred African Americans who had come to Victoria because of the gold rush and tensions in the United States during the Civil War (1861–65). Since there were large numbers of Euro-Americans in both colonies, this fact heightened racism in Victoria, especially against African Americans. While the Oblates, given their desire to impose a reduction system, would naturally have excluded Native children, they did admit African Americans to St. Louis College. However, they soon reversed the policy because of Euro-American opposition. In 1865 they tried to readmit African Americans, but most African Americans returned to the United States at the end of the Civil War. This fact and continued Euro-American racism ended the second and last attempt. Like the Oblates, by 1862 the Sisters of St. Ann had accepted African American girls into their school, but in the "general" and not the "select" division, which was limited to upper class "whites" where French and fine arts were taught. Nevertheless, a number of well-to-do African American business people in Victoria insisted that their daughters had an equal right to attend the "select" school. Both Demers and the Sisters initially agreed. However, just as at St. Louis College, threats, especially from Euro-American parents that they would withdraw their daughters if they had to attend classes with "coloureds," finally moved the bishop and the nuns to exclude black pupils.[33]

The Anglicans, in face of the Catholic challenge, had soon begun their own schools, namely, the Collegiate School for boys (1862) and the Angela College for girls (1864). In recommending the establishment of the schools in 1860 to the English readers of the *Report,* Bishop Hills noted that while Catholics were not numerous in Victoria, they were "forward in the matter of education, both in the case of boys and girls." Nevertheless, Hills was certain that Anglican schools would be popular, especially among the many Americans then in Victoria who would appreciate the "more substantial" English system. Hills was also concerned that, lacking an alternative, "the boys of the upper class," who were mainly Anglican, were then going to the "Roman Catholic Bishop's school." Thus, Hills considered the matter of establishing Anglican schools to be "urgent." Regarding his personal view of the Oblates as teachers, Hills commented privately that their principal instruction appeared to be "the worship of the Virgin and hatred of the Americans and English, while the French," he added with disgust, "are exalted and extolled."[34]

✤ The Question of Religion in Public Education

AS IT HAD IN THE CHURCH-STATE SEPARATION ISSUE, the early American presence in the two colonies also greatly influenced public education, especially in the popular determination to keep organized religion out of the public schools. Apparently inspired by the writings of Horace Mann (D.1859), an important American pioneer in public education, in 1860 a group of Americans established the first common school system in Victoria. Although they were not truly public, since they charged a small tuition fee, strictly nondenominational common schools gave local parents the first clear alternative to the city's Anglican and Catholic schools.[35]

Due to poor management and financial problems, the common schools closed in 1864, but they had become so popular that there was a major public outcry for a tax-supported public school system in Victoria. In April, a large city-wide general meeting championed the creation of a free system of nonreligious public schools. Promoters of religion in public education in Victoria, realising the large American element in their audience, defended their position by referring to "an American work on education," probably by Mann, which supported the teaching of identifiable Judeo-Christian religious values in public schools since they were believed to promote general morality. Trying to further buttress their case, defenders of religion cited the example of "an American School in Massachusetts" which taught religion as part of its curriculum. Yet a resolution at the meeting advocating the inclusion of religion in Victoria public schools lost and "by a large majority," a defeat which "most in the audience" reportedly greeted with "loud cheers."[36]

Faced with such strong public support, the colonial government was forced to agree. Shortly after the general meeting, a delegation presented Governor Arthur Kennedy with a petition demanding a totally tax-supported public school system in Victoria that would exclude the teaching of religion. Kennedy agreed that such a system should be established and that the schools ought to be nonsectarian in order to insure class harmony and avoid "religious dissension," which, he said, should not be allowed "to creep into the public schools."[37]

From the outset the far west had very different attitudes from the rest of the country on public education and organized religion. Unlike eastern Canada where separate schools enjoyed broad public support, British Columbia opposed such an idea. By the mid 1860s public opinion there, greatly influenced by a significant American presence, had effectively rejected even the possibility. While this was certainly not an age of ecumenism, necessity can make strange bedfellows. For when British Columbia joined Confederation in 1871, both the Roman Catholic and Anglican churches there would make common cause in their vain attempt to initiate separate provincial school systems, or at least to gain tax support from their institutions. However, they would fail. This issue would continue to constitute the major focus of local public attitudes towards organized religion. And the overwhelming majority of the people in Canada's most secular province would persist in rejecting the idea of separate schools.

✤ The Separate Schools Question

LARGELY IN REACTION TO THE LIBERAL RADICALISM OF THE AGE, especially that which had been sparked by the French Revolution, the Catholic Church began to insist as never before that religious schools were essential in any healthy and truly "civilized" society. The Oblates and other

Catholic clergy saw eastern Canada as such a society since it was willing to support Catholic schools with its taxes. It was an assumption that was shared by many, though by no means all Christians in British Columbia in the years leading up to 1885 and the arrival of the CPR, but they hoped to be able to convince the rest of their follow citizens to agree with that position.[38]

By the mid 1860s the Oblates, the secular clergy and the Sisters of St. Ann were running more or less prospering schools for European students on Vancouver Island and the mainland. Also at this time, James McGuckin (1863–1903), head of St. Joseph's Mission at Williams Lake, had started schools for "whites" in the Cariboo. It demonstrated the hopeful temper of the period and that practicing Catholics, though low in numbers, were already prominent in education in the far west.[39]

The presence of denominational schools, especially Anglican and Catholic, reflected the fact that organized religion was well represented in the two colonies. Both colonies, which would unite in 1866, then had places of worship representing Catholics, Anglicans, Congregationalists, Methodists and Jews. There was little or no ecumenism but there was evidence of hostility. In Victoria, Father Seghers wrote in April 1864 that he had "to avoid conversation twice" with the "quite friendly" local Protestant clergy, "all of whom were impressed," he said, with the local schools in the diocese. Revealing a prejudice, that was often mutual, Seghers was "very distrustful of Protestant clergy" who he was certain were all "lying souls." He defined the typical Protestant minister as one who "preaches the gospel just like a lawyer pleads his case." As for the Anglicans, he reported they were attracting the "best" class of citizens to both their churches and schools. For though they had lost their bid to become "the established" church in the region, Seghers noted that they were trying to make up for that fact by a "self-imposed segregation, thinking themselves superior to others." Yet, most Catholics, especially their clergy, believed exactly the same thing.[40]

The forced closure of the common schools in Victoria due to bad management and financial problems in 1864 allowed the Catholics and Anglicans to dominated local education. It was a distinction, however, that was very short lived, for in the spring of 1865, the colonial legislatures responded to strong public support by establishing the first totally tax-supported public education system.[41]

Unlike his Catholic and Anglican clerical colleagues, Demers never championed the idea of a separate school system. Apparently influenced by his years of ministering in the Oregon Territory, Demers accepted the fact that the region was a highly secular and liberal society, and likely to remain so. For Demers, egalitarianism was fine, as long as it was truly equal. In the early 1860s he had requested a state subsidy to pay for books and other educational materials for two church day schools for Cowichan children. When the government replied that it could only supply funds to strictly nonreligious schools, Demers publicly replied that he had "no objection to non-sectarian principles among the whites, if they be fairly carried out." But he believed the Native people were an exception, since they were financially unable to support their own schools, so the state was "in justice bound to provide the means of civilizing and educating them." For Demers there was no such obligation on the province or its taxpayers when it came to funding separate schools for Euro-Canadians.[42]

Most, if not all, of his fellow clergy disagreed. Hoping to qualify as a separate school system, or at least for a tax exemption, the Catholics were the first to respond to this new, but hardly surprising development. In May 1865 the Oblate President of St. Louis College, Victoria, Julien Baudre (1863–90) petitioned the government for similar financial consideration, since, he argued, St. Louis College, like any future public school, was already open to all regardless of denomination, or even financial situation. Certainly, the latter description was a highly dubious contention considering the largely well-to-do clientele who were then attending the College. The attorney general, George Cary replied that neither St. Louis College nor any other denominational or private school in the two colonies could claim such status or have the right to any special treatment. Yet, the proposed public schools, Cary continued, qualified because "the public...[had] by law a perceived right to be educated," and only the courts could alter such a legal understanding.[43]

In reaction, another Oblate, Léon Fouquet (1859–1912) decided to go on the offensive. After consulting with D'Herbomez and Baudre, in the spring of 1865 Fouquet published a pamphlet championing the right of Catholic parents to educate their children in their faith. He insisted that the graduates of such an education, given its high moral character, would become major contributors to the betterment of society in general. Therefore, Fouquet set "forth the injustice of compelling...[Catholics] to contribute to the support of a system of [public] education to which they could not conscientiously send their children" while at the same time they felt morally obliged for the "good" of both their church and society to pay for a separate

Father Léon Fouquet (AD)

Catholic educational system. The liberal editor of the *British Columbian* in New Westminster, John Robson was quick to condemn Fouquet for "pretending" that Catholics, by their very existence, had a right to such special treatment. Robson, a Presbyterian, whose brother, Ebenezer was a prominent local Methodist minister, also challenged Fouquet's assumption that Catholic education was uniquely suited to contribute to the moral improvement of society. Rather, because of its implicit and frequently explicit encouragement of religious bigotry, especially against Protestants, Robson believed it produced just the opposite effect.[44]

That June a number of Catholic laymen met in Victoria and passed several resolutions calling upon the government to establish a tax-supported and separate school system in the two colonies. The government replied that such a plan would violate the recent School Act. The Anglicans issued a similar appeal, but their pleading also made no impact.[45]

As British Columbia prepared to join Confederation and become part of Canada in 1871, Bishop Hills complained to British readers of the *Columbia Mission Report* that the many American residents there had learned "to despise" the clergy as a result of attending the public education system in the United States. Like many Catholics, Hills feared that such a public system in British Columbia would have the same effect, and thus promote anticlericalism in the province along with "infidelity, crime and immorality."[46]

The Public School Act of 1872 settled the issue of separate schools in British Columbia. The official debate over the *British North America Act*, especially section 93 that dealt with the issue of public education, revealed a definite anticlericalism among some provincial legislators. Unique to Canada, the 1872 Act effectively ignored the very existence of denominational schools and carefully established a strictly nonsectarian character in the provincial public school system.[47]

Church leaders continued to try to alter the situation. Since they dominated the religious schools of the province, Catholics and Anglicans, while somewhat uncomfortable bedfellows, remained united on the issue. Both churches blamed the early American influence for creating what for them was this strange legislative contradiction that now opposed separate schools. In 1872, Hills repeated his dread warnings of the 1860s that the "purely secular schools" of British Columbia would soon rival their counterparts in the United States, which he believed were responsible for the "growing corruption" in America, even, he declared, to the "increase and impunity of the crime of murder." The Catholics, sensing their bonds, sided with the Anglicans on this issue. Father Charles John Seghers[48] argued that the Catholics and Anglicans "must" have their own system of education. Further, he insisted, it would be "unjust" to expect them to pay for two, and that it was therefore only "equitable" that church schools in the province should have a fair share of any public education funds. As in America, Seghers insisted, the Catholics in British Columbia were being expected to support their own system "at great sacrifice," as well as the public one, which was simply unfair. In short, it was the reasoning that had lead to the establishment of separate school systems in eastern Canada.[49]

Clearly British Columbia was the most secularized province in Canada and would continue to move in that direction. In Europe and North America the elementary school became a major international battlefield of church and organized religion pitted against the state and modern secular society. By the School Act of 1872 the public schools of the province were to teach the "highest morality and no religious doctrine." This was in contrast to the Vancouver Island School Act of 1865, which had permitted religious instruction by clergy, but only after school hours. In little more than a decade, the provincial legislature would exclude clergy from holding any position, voluntary or otherwise, in the public system. As for any religious exercises, by 1876 only teachers could conduct them, and they were limited to no more than the public recitation of the Lord's Prayer and the Ten Commandments.[50]

With the continued hope of being heard, in the early 1880s the Catholic bishops of British Columbia again raised the separate schools question. Their action was occasioned by new provincial tax legislation in the spring of 1881 to fund the first two public high schools in Victoria and New Westminster. While Seghers was by then archbishop of Portland (1881–85), he kept in close contact with events in British Columbia, and continued to share and support the views of his colleagues there. After several years in Oregon, he wrote that he had come to "hate American ideas" even more so than when he had first experienced them in Victoria, especially the belief in the strict separation of church and state. If anything, Seghers's time in the United States only heightened his loathing for American culture, particularly its rugged individualism and its extreme pluralism. It also hardened his ultramontane view of reality, especially the belief that the Catholic Church was the only natural educator of the young; whereas the state had no right to operate schools. However, he found that Oregon Catholics were even more indifferent to organized religion and church schools than those in British Columbia, which only strengthened his resolve. Shortly after becoming archbishop in 1881, Seghers made a dire prediction in an address published in his diocesan newspaper, *The Catholic Sentinel*, that unless the Catholic laity of Oregon funded and supported parochial schools, their children would "never enter into the Kingdom of Heaven." "I say it," he solemnly concluded, "without bitterness and without fear."[51]

Although they agreed with Seghers's theology, the three Catholic bishops in British Columbia, D'Herbomez and his coadjutor, Paul Durieu (1890–99) of New Westminster and John Brondel, the third bishop of Victoria (1879–83) were not prepared to go to such extremes, at least not publicly. Their petition to the Legislative Assembly did complain of the "sect of irreligionists" in the province whose only wish, they said, was to destroy all organized religion. They predicted that publicly funded schools would be a "source of evil," and would produce only "immoral youth." They also contended, as good ultramontanists, that the state, under natural law, had no rightful role in education. In an apparent attempt to demonstrate how "fair" Catholics could be when compared to "secularists," even when they were the overwhelming majority in a particular society, they cited Quebec. There they said the "Protestant minority" enjoyed the "educational advantages" of provincial funding, a situation that should now be extended to the Catholic Church in British Columbia.[52]

There was little response to their petition among the general public in British Columbia, perhaps indicating its ever-growing perception of the general irrelevance of organized religion. However, two newspapers in New Westminster did mention it. The editor of the *Dominion Pacific Herald*, John Robson, a future premier, who had long opposed such a plan, critiqued it.

He wondered how the bishops could compare British Columbia, which was so "thinly populated," with any other Canadian province. He also questioned, that, if permitted, most Catholics in British Columbia would even avail themselves of such an opportunity. He based his assumption on Ontario, where, he said, though the Catholic bishops had "fought and won" the "battle of separate schools," few Catholic parents seemed interested in sending their children to such tax supported institutions. D'Herbomez responded, though he ignored addressing the issue of Ontario, saying only that the present public school system in British Columbia was "partisan, oppressive and unjust," and that it had been made "Godless" with the sole purpose of favoring "irreligionists."[53]

By 1883 the Legislative Assembly was still unmoved. Again the three bishops petitioned it, and this time Brondel was so confident that he declared that even the premier, William Smithe now supported the Catholic cause. He told D'Herbomez that he was certain that the bishops would gain everything they hoped for "within a year." As the leader of the so-called "peace party" of British Columbia, which had been formed to accelerate the completion of the railroad, Smithe was trying to please all sides. However, Bishop Hills was equally convinced that the churches were about to triumph, for he could hardly imagine the alternative. In a rather dire warning to the receptive readership of the *Columbia Mission Report,* Hills predicted that without a separate school system to challenge it, public schools in British Columbia would soon produce a generation that was so morally corrupt that it was, he declared, "too lamentable to [even] picture." Except as an early and very mild example of ecumenism, such unity of purpose between the Catholics and Anglicans produced nothing. By the mid 1880s it was clear to all but the most obtuse that British Columbia was a thoroughly secular society and destined to remain so. Organized religion would certainly be tolerated there, but little more could be expected. Certainly the twentieth century would further confirm such a conclusion.[54]

✤ The Clergy, the Sisters of St. Ann and Health Care

THE SISTERS OF ST. ANN, after almost 20 years in British Columbia, had become indispensable to the life of the Catholic Church there. On both Vancouver Island and the mainland they conducted schools and orphanages for both Europeans and Natives, and without their unpaid labor, none of these institutions could have existed. Despite their absolutely vital role in the church, both the Oblate and secular clergy often treated them with suspicion and even disdain.

The sisters' success was often bought at a very heavy personal price. By the 1870s the long hours of work, financial difficulties and physical hardships had contributed to the deaths of three and the return to Quebec of two of the first twelve sisters to arrive in the province. Their spirituality had a part in influencing the situation, since it was based on a Jansenistic theology of silent, even desired suffering by an "avenging God" in supposed imitation of Jesus' crucifixion. As women in an institution that viewed even female religious "virgins" as partners in Eve's sin, and where the only female virtues were "obedience, deference, modesty and self-sacrifice," the sisters, given their unique commitment to the Catholic Church, suffered psychological stress. Much of their problem had its roots in their desire to always please a male hierarchical, highly patriarchal structure. "Good" sisters were expected to endure all suffering "with joy," and refuse to take sides or even disagree with others, especially the clergy. A "good" nun was not supposed to think but only to obey. This unhealthy spirituality usually resulted in overwork and additional hardships for the religious women.

In a description of what constituted a successful female religious, Seghers noted that such a person would always prefer "to do violence to herself, rather than to offend anyone." Catholic attitudes were so extreme in this regard, that Protestant parents, who were major supporters of the schools, sending their children to both St. Ann's Academies in Victoria and New Westminster, complained of the situation. For they felt that the Sisters lead "hard," even "unnatural" lives, and that they certainly seemed "especially oppressed" by the Catholic clergy. Except for such evidence, given their spirituality of silent suffering, there are apparently no complaints of any kind against anyone recorded by the nuns and surviving in their archives, indicating that such material either does not exist, is hidden, destroyed or edited out. Yet despite outside evidence that confirms their often harsh treatment and circumstances, the Sisters of St. Ann bore their "cross" and continued in their many indispensable occupations as teachers, clerical confidants, secretaries, general domestics and nurses. Even so, they were usually little appreciated, especially by the clergy, for their invaluable contributions to the life of the church in British Columbia. Nowhere was this more obvious than in their establishment of St. Joseph's Hospital in Victoria.[55]

St. Joseph's Hospital, with the grounds of St. Ann's Academy, Victoria, in the foreground (ASSA)

Over the years, the Sisters of St. Ann were to establish a total of seven hospitals in British Columbia, the Yukon and Alaska. St. Joseph's in Victoria held pride of place. For over a decade Demers and then Seghers had insisted that there must be a Catholic hospital in Victoria to reflect its growing status and to confront the only alternative institution, which was Anglican. Seghers, more determined and dedicated in his role than his predecessor, convinced the Sisters of St. Ann that it was indeed the "will of God" that they should undertake such a ministry. Far more than schools, denominations saw hospitals, where most people then came to die, as fertile ground for proselytizing. In 1873 Seghers noted that the Anglicans then dominated this "charity" in Victoria which, he wrote, "must cease." Thus over the next several years he purchased the land, raised the necessary funds, mainly from among the citizens of Victoria, and began the work on 22 August 1875 when the corner stone was laid by British Columbia's pioneer physician, John Sebastian Helmcken. It was an event witnessed by Seghers, four priests, three other doctors and "a number of citizens." Less than a year later, on 7 June 1876 St. Joseph's Hospital, named after the patron saint of the far-western Canadian province of the Sisters of St. Ann, finally opened its doors.[56]

However, filling the new 35-bed facility with patients was not easy. The ill-feelings between the very diminutive, mainly Catholic francophone community and their anglophone co-religionists in Victoria were then very strong, and would remain so—proving that culture often wields a far stronger influence over people than religious beliefs. For financial reasons, in 1884 the francophones had to close their "Benevolent and Mutual Society," which had been founded in 1865 to look after its sick members. In 1890 they chose to not join the Catholic hospital, St. Joseph's, but instead joined the Anglican hospital, which had become the Provincial Royal Jubilee Hospital in the same year. While the Jubilee had lost its specific Anglican atmosphere long before then, the Society was still a separate entity within the Hospital until 1949 when they finally merged with the Jubilee. Moreover, there was then a very strong social stigma against going to any hospital that most viewed as places were people, especially the poor, went to die. Instead, for anyone who could afford it, physicians administered medical care at home where patients, even the terminally ill, would be privately nursed. In fact Seghers described a Catholic hospital as a place "for the spiritual health of the dying." However, it took over six months before St. Joseph's admitted its first patient, a "Mr. Bowden." Described as a "very sick man without friends or means," Bowden "lingered for several weeks, though free from acute pain," finally dying, although the exact date is not recorded. The first operation at the new hospital was not performed until 1 September 1878. It consisted in the removal of a gallstone, "the size of an egg," from an unnamed sailor. Actually the procedure was considered so dangerous, that the surgeons attempted it only with "much reluctance." Yet it was successful, and the patient even survived.[57]

About the time Bowden died, St. Joseph's recorded its first success at proselytizing. The subject, a Mr. Law, who was "a Protestant," was described by an anonymous nun chronicler as someone who had "no esteem for our holy religion." "After many prayers," his nurse, Sister Mary Winifred "tremblingly placed a small pocket statue of St. Joseph in Mr. Law's bed," and then informed her patient "that his time on earth was short." "To her joy and astonishment, the sick man said: 'I want to die a Roman Catholic.'" The chronicle then continued: "St. Joseph had done his work—he had converted the worry, fatigue, and self-imposed sacrifice of the religious nurses into intercessory prayer, and Mr. Law's conversion was obtained. The newly baptized man died six days afterwards, aided in his last moments by our zealous Bishop [Seghers]."[58]

Although St. Joseph's never surpassed its Anglican rival, the Provincial Royal Jubilee Hospital, denominationalism continued to pay an important role well into the twentieth century in the development of both though not in the composition of its patients. The Jubilee founded a School of Nursing in 1891 and by 1900 the Sisters of St. Ann were able to provide a Catholic alternative, St. Joseph's School of Nursing. Though a Catholic hospital, its Catholic patients never numbered more than ten percent, which was also their approximate ratio, at least among practicing Catholics, to the general population in the diocese and city of Victoria.[59]

Yet by 1920 St. Joseph's was annually caring for well over three thousand in-patients. Due mainly to the self-denial and the generous financial support of the Sisters of St. Ann, local individual contributions, and fund raising groups, both Catholic and otherwise, St. Joseph's always operated "at a minimum of expense" to the larger community. Clearly, the first Catholic hospital in the province was a success story.[60]

✤ The Oblates: New Roots and a Final Break

DURING THEIR YEARS (1858–66) in the diocese of Victoria, the Oblate Missions were centred in or around Victoria. In addition to teaching at St. Louis College, they founded St. Joseph's Parish, Esquimalt, a short distance from Victoria, which became their first vicariate headquarters in the region. Initially they considered establishing their centre of command on the mainland at Fort Langley, near the Fraser River gold field and a comfortable distance from Demers. However, since Victoria was the only port of entry for the two colonies, and the principal city at that time, it seemed the logical place for the Oblate headquarters.

In 1861 D'Herbomez sent his first report on the state of the new vicariate to the Oblate superior general, Joseph Fabre (1861–92) who took Mazenod's place after the Founder's death on 21 May 1861. D'Herbomez began by describing the enormous variety of European gold-seeking newcomers to the region including English, Irish, French, Canadian, Americans, Italians, and even Spanish. The Oblates built a chapel in Esquimalt to serve the needs of the French, Italian, and Spanish sailors who frequented Victoria's major harbour. D'Herbomez noted, no doubt with a desire to impress his superiors, that the European settlers then numbered almost twenty-five thousand, a figure that he predicted would rise within a year to at least fifty thousand. Due to an economic decline in the 1860s, D'Herbomez's projections would not be realised, since ten years later in 1871, at the time of

Confederation, the province's total population stood at only 36,247, and over 70 percent of them were Native people.[61]

Although his report of 1861 does not mention a problem, by 1863 tensions between Demers and most of the clergy of his diocese, including the Oblates had become quite serious. The Sisters of St. Ann complained that the atmosphere was jeopardising their own ministry, so much so that they even thought of leaving Victoria. The laity were also unhappy. The French Canadians believed that Demers was only willing to supply the needs of anglophone Catholics, while he ignored the French. Dragged into the dispute, D'Herbomez tried to mediate. However, this only seemed to compound his own difficulties in trying to negotiate with Demers about the future role of the Oblates on the Vancouver Island. For though Demers insisted that he wished the Oblates to remain, his behaviour was not encouraging. He did not even respond to D'Herbomez's repeated requests for information about his plans for the Oblates. There were several angry confrontations between the two men over their irreconcilable differences. Of course, by then Demers knew that D'Herbomez was only waiting for word from Rome regarding the establishment of a vicariate apostolic in New Westminster that would allow him and the Oblates to leave both Victoria and Demers and probably for good.[62]

Demers's problems with the Oblates and his own clergy, and even with the Sisters of St. Ann, and the general difficulties in the operation of his diocese, all plagued him. He had never wanted to be a bishop, and as early as 1859 the work and worry appear to have worn him out. While recuperating in California that year he decided to resign just as soon as a coadjutor with right of succession could be appointed. Pius IX, however, refused to accept his decision, suggesting instead that Demers select an episcopal vicar who could eventually become his successor. Bishop Bourget of Montreal put forward an Oblate, Alexander Trudeau, but by 1860 Demers had had his fill of Oblates and vetoed Trudeau. By 1862, he had accepted a diocesan priest from Montreal, Charles Morrison as his vicar. Nevertheless, after more serious and, no doubt sober deliberations of what was expected of a missionary bishop, Morrison had second thoughts and withdrew, citing as his major reasons his corpulent physique and a dislike of riding horses. Nevertheless, by 1864 Demers had found his own replacement.[63]

Charles John Seghers, as seen, would eventually become the second (1871-78) and the fourth (1885-86) bishop of Victoria. He was born in

Ghent, Belgium in 1839 into relatively affluent circumstances, but by the time he was 20, tuberculosis had claimed his entire immediate family. This melancholy fact seemed to mark his entire life with "a certain fatalism" that he too would soon die. It also appeared to influence his belief that suffering, as expressed in Jansenistic spirituality, was the mark of a "good priest." Such thinking greatly affected his decision to become a missionary, preferably in some remote land where he could work with "the worst savages" from whom he ultimately hoped to obtain his "crown of glory" through a bloody martyrdom. After spending a year studying English at the American College, Louvain, Seghers accepted the offer of Demers, one of the college's sponsors, to come to Vancouver Island, which Seghers heard contained a European population that was as corrupt as that "Babylon of England."[64]

Seghers soon made a very definite and, what was extremely rare, a very positive impact upon Demers who referred to the bright, capable and amenable Seghers as his "excellent young priest." However, Seghers, who decided to stay, was not as complimentary. Though he saw Demers as "good hearted and zealous," like most who knew him, Seghers judged him as "quick tempered" and "certainly not a 'perfect' administrator." To make matters even worse, Seghers spent his first four years in Victoria, kept there by Demers for his considerable talents, compliant manner, and delicate health. Frustrated that Demers seemed deaf to his burning desire to be a missionary to the Natives, for a time Seghers thought seriously of leaving Demers and joining the Oblates.[65]

By the end of 1864 Demers was again sick. He decided to recuperate for a year in California and to travel and fund-raise for his diocese among the wealthy landlords of Central America. By then, however, he had decided he no longer needed a formal episcopal vicar, since he believed that in Seghers he had "all he could wish for." To demonstrate this he left the not quite 25-year-old priest in charge of the diocese.[66]

Such events were an indication of things to come. For on 14 December 1863 the Oblates had made their effective break with Victoria when Rome formally divided Demers's huge diocese by erecting the mainland of British Columbia as a vicariate apostolic, and naming Louis D'Herbomez as its first and only vicar apostolic (1863–90). A new period had opened for both Demers and the church on Vancouver Island, as well as for the Oblates and the Catholic Church in British Columbia.

On 9 October 1864 the ordination of Louis D'Herbomez, in St. Andrew's Cathedral, Victoria marked the official beginning of the Catholic Church as a separate jurisdiction on the mainland. Norbert Blanchet was the principal ordaining bishop, assisted by Demers. However, Augustin Blanchet, complaining of poor health, did not take part, although perhaps a continued feeling of ill will towards the Oblates in general and D'Herbomez in particular could have been the actual cause. Certainly, for the 42-year-old D'Herbomez his ordination was a type of liberation, since the new vicariate would be directly under Rome. After 17 very long years, D'Herbomez and the Oblates were now officially freed from the canonical jurisdiction and, far more importantly, the interference of the local secular bishops in the far west.[67]

By 1865 it was a fait accompli that the Oblates would soon leave, and Demers, feeling the victim, complained to D'Herbomez that the Sisters of St. Ann were also threatening to abandon him. Perhaps in an attempt to commiserate with Demers, D'Herbomez responded by implying that the sisters might leave New Westminster as well. Such reports also demonstrated some of the frustration that the nuns were experiencing in their dealings with the clergy in the far west, both secular and regular.[68]

As the time grew closer to the final departure of the Oblates, Demers became more embittered. In December 1865 he told the Oblate, Michel Baudre, who was then his vicar general as well as the president of St. Louis College, that Baudre could not preach at Christmas in the cathedral, since that right was reserved to the bishop. Within a few months he was grumbling to D'Herbomez that Baudre had been giving permissions that only the bishop could provide, such as allowing someone to be buried in the local Catholic cemetery. D'Herbomez responded by defending his colleague, especially after Demers told the vicar apostolic that he wanted the priest recalled. All of this was going on against the backdrop of negotiating a fair and final compensation for Oblate investments in the diocese, which goes a long way in explaining the prickly nature of these minor disputes.[69]

By 1866 the Oblates finally shifted the concentration of their ministry to the mainland colony of British Columbia and retained only two small Native Missions: one at Fort Rupert until 1874 and the other at the Tulalip Indian Reservation in the Washington Territory, which they left in 1878. The decision to remain at Fort Rupert was probably due in part to feelings of guilt in relinquishing their ministry on Vancouver Island. The Oblates did receive reasonable compensation from Demers for their major investments in St.

Louis College and the property that comprised their original vicariate headquarters at St. Joseph's, Esquimalt. In the spring of 1866, Demers received a letter from Léon Fouquet, then the pastor at St. Charles, New Westminster, who had been appointed by D'Herbomez to make the final arrangements for the Oblates to leave the diocese. In this capacity Fouquet informed Demers that the Oblates were also planning to close their Mission of St. Michael's, which had recently been moved from Fort Rupert to nearby Harbledown Island, and which was their last point of contact with the diocese of Victoria. A major reason for abandoning Harbledown Island was the growing Anglican Mission there, which Forquet sadly concluded seemed destined to dominate the area and thus teach "heresy" to the Kwakiutl. It was a conclusion that had also fed Oblate ambivalence over their decision to close their Mission there.[70]

Not willing to beg himself, and probably angry and hurt that D'Herbomez had appointed a "mere" priest to make the final plans for the Oblate departure, Demers ordered his new vicar general, a secular priest, Joseph Mary Mandart to reply to Fouquet. Mandart was a French recruit who had arrived in Victoria in 1862 after studying at the American College, Louvain. Described as an "eccentric sort of man," Mandart apparently "never slept in a bed," and only "wore stockings...once a year, on Good Friday, when he had to participate in the solemn ceremonies at the cathedral." Such a description might indicate how either desperate or indifferent Demers was regarding administrators. In his letter, Mandart noted that the diocese was hard pressed for manpower. After what the diocese had spent on St. Michael's and all the Oblate labors there, Mandart wondered who would "replace them," for he assured Fouquet that no secular clergy could be spared.[71]

An immediate result was that Fouquet volunteered for St. Michael's where he was to spend four (1867–71) quite frustrating years and in the end apparently achieved nothing. However, when the Oblates finally abandoned St. Michael's in 1874, Fouquet, always a strong critic of Oblate policy, still vehemently opposed the decision. Thus 1874 marked the end of the Oblate ministry in the diocese of Victoria until 1938 when they returned to take the place of the Benedictines from Mount Angel Abbey, Oregon at the Kakawis Industrial School on the westcoast of Vancouver Island.[72]

✣ Supporting a Mainland Church

PEOPLE OF EUROPEAN DESCENT, especially on the mainland of British Columbia, remained a decided minority until after the coming of the railroad in 1885. As late as 1887 D'Herbomez was still referring to the Catholic Church throughout the mainland as "this distant corner of the Lord's vineyard," one implication being this considerable imbalance.[73]

The preponderance of Native people heightened provincial racism. This was made even worse by the fact that, since the European population, mainly British, Canadian and American, contained only one woman for every three men, there seemed little likelihood that either the racial or gender scales would very soon be balanced. While this situation was less true in Victoria, where the ratio was about equal, even there racist fears were strong. In the 1870s, convinced that the Natives and non-Europeans might soon overwhelm the "white" population, the Legislative Assembly disfranchised the two most visible and thus, supposedly threatening racial groups in the province: the Native people and the Chinese.[74]

While the Native people remained their first priority, and although Europeans were then a definite minority, the Oblates did not ignore the latter's religious needs. Still, several factors, particularly on the mainland, militated against their ministry to Europeans. First, the gross imbalance of men to women meant that women's essential role in fostering the family and organized religion was largely missing, and until it was corrected, there seemed little hope of expanding or founding parishes, and, without family units, there was even less need for schools. D'Herbomez admitted this and noted that, even if they wished, most European Catholics, including the minority who attended church, were generally too poor to support it. Where there were enough parishioners and money, few Catholics were willing to contribute what was necessary to cover all the expenses. Though early church schools attracted Catholic students, they could never have survived without the admission of non-Catholics. However, with the advent of a public school system in the 1860s and 1870s few European Catholics were willing to spend their scarce income in educating their offspring, especially boys, in "private" church institutions. And certainly attempts to shame people into compliance proved counterproductive. Therefore, D'Herbomez reported in 1870 that the handful of church schools on the mainland for Europeans and "half-breeds" could only survive through the unpaid labour

Holy Rosary Church on Richards Street, Vancouver, 1887 (ASSA)

of the Sisters of St. Ann and the Oblates. Such schools were also heavily subsidized from Oblate farm incomes, most notably at Williams Lake and in the
Okanagan, and by the financial aid from lay supported missionary societies,
especially those in France.[75]

The major charitable body in France was the Society for the Propagation
of the Faith. From its centers in Paris and Lyon, it supplied everything from
cash to general church furnishings, including vestments, statues and religious items such as holy cards and rosaries for missionaries working among
both Natives and Europeans. Besides supplying a large share of the funds
needed by the European Catholic community in New Westminster as well
on Vancouver Island, the Society provided much of the interior decoration
for D'Herbomez's first cathedral, including most of the statues, the Stations
of the Cross, and even the sanctuary lamp, which initially had been just an
kerosene lamp. Another important charitable group, the Association of the
Holy Childhood, a subsidiary of the Society for the Propagation of the Faith,
raised money through the "purchase" and "baptism" of the "pagan" children

St. Ann's Academy, on the mainland, originally erected in 1888,
enlarged in 1903, sold and demolished in 1947. (ASSA)

of non-Christian Natives. This fund was mainly applied to the running of homes for abandoned and orphaned children, usually of mixed parentage. To encourage ongoing support, donors were asked to provide a child's baptismal name and, in so doing, become the child's "spiritual parent."[76]

New Westminster, the cathedral city of the vicariate apostolic, was also the center of European settlement on the mainland. The church, like the city, was strictly segregated. St. Peter's Church, D'Herbomez's cathedral, had been built in 1862 to serve European needs, while St. Charles provided for the Natives. However, indicating a growing local European Catholic prosperity, in 1886 a new St. Peter's, of a "better style," and over twice the size of its predecessor, was opened. St. Ann's Academy, begun in 1865 by two Sisters of St. Ann from Victoria, had only five boarders during its first year, although in 1866, during his first journey into the interior, D'Herbomez was able to gain seven additional recruits, mainly from Yale. By 1867 Sister Marie des Sept-Douleurs, the school's first head, had been replaced by Sister Mary Praxîde, under whom the school would gradually grow, and by 1877 a

St. Louis College, 1917, Victoria, front view (ASSA)

new building was needed. The Sisters purchased a site on Albert Crescent, as it was both closer to their convent and provided the school with a prominent location overlooking the Fraser River. While at first very grand architectural plans were proposed, prudence, based on the reality of poor finances, dictated that only about half of the design could be realized, although the completed building was described as "the most imposing and attractive structure" on the lower Fraser River. Compared favorably by many to its older sister academy in Victoria, its tower even boasted the first clock in New Westminster.[77]

St. Louis College, opened in 1866, like St. Ann's, also hoped to rival its namesake in Victoria. Still, the facsimile was a far cry from the imposing brick structure in the capital, being only a wooden building, 20 feet by 10, which one eyewitness described as a "shack." With only four pupils, it paled before the hundred or more boasted by its counterpart. Yet its student body gradually expanded and by the late 1870s represented many locations in British Columbia, but even as far south as Olympia in the Washington

Territory. Given such growth, like the academy, St. Louis also erected a much larger building in 1880 and added high school classes, which finally made it the equivalent of its competitor in Victoria. However, in August 1884, when the city opened its first public high school, St. Louis found its day student body considerably reduced since local parents, most of whom were not Catholic, saw no reason to spend money for their sons' education when a free one was now available. For while families, Catholic or not, viewed the Academy as a proper "finishing school" for young ladies, they saw the education of boys as a practical preparation, especially in business, and so St. Louis could claim no real distinction when compared to its public alternative. For years, local Catholics also viewed St. Louis as second best to its namesake in Victoria and that, and others factors, such as growing Oblate staff shortages, lead to its closure in 1917.[78]

A Catholic hospital for Europeans in New Westminster was opened in 1886. D'Herbomez had hoped the Sisters of St. Ann would undertake this ministry, but, with so many other commitments elsewhere, they were forced to decline his request. Finally he was able to attract the Montreal-based Sisters of Providence who established St. Mary's Hospital. While it slowly expanded, the first building was only a tiny 15-bed facility designed by Sister Joseph of the Sacred Heart. Certainly the early years were very difficult as "patients were few and dollars were fewer still." Through fund raising drives conducted by the Sisters and with local donations, especially from the city council, the hospital was able to survive, though barely. Probably its most important lifeline, then common among private hospitals, was an annual medical insurance program inaugurated by the Sisters, which charged $10 per year and covered all injuries and illnesses with the exception of those "brought on by alcoholism." In the end St. Mary's, like St. Joseph's Hospital in Victoria, not only survived, but grew.[79]

Though far less significant during this early period, the Oblates also attempted to address European needs in communities outside New Westminster. St. Gabriel's at Yale, the earliest example, was built by Grandidier and blessed by D'Herbomez in 1865. However, the most noteworthy parish church was in Richfield. St. Joseph's was the fourth Oblate Mission on the mainland after those in the Okanagan-Kamloops and the Lower Fraser regions. When James McGuckin arrived in the area in 1867 he had already been apprised of the situation there by other Oblates who had visited the region which had its beginnings in the Williams Creek gold rush (1861–62).

Richfield and Barkerville were the major towns and then boasted an array of places of worship, including Anglican, Methodist, Presbyterian, and Jewish, for at the height of the gold rush Richfield even boasted a synagogue.[80]

The welcome McGuckin received from European settlers seemed to bode very well for the future of Catholicism. He arrived on 18 August 1866 in Richfield, which, with Barkerville, were the only prosperous towns in the area, though, with the end of the gold rush, they were both in trouble, and their populations were steadily declining. Richfield's leading citizens, however, hoped farming might eventually take the place of mining and renew the economy. For them, a new, permanent clerical presence could be a very positive symbol of the town's present and potential prospects. A fellow Irish Catholic and shopkeeper, Patrick Kirwan immediately saw in Father McGuckin a ready-made parish. Within days Kirwan took up a collection, purchased a house for a fraction of its original value, turned it into an instant church-rectory, and even named the parish, St. Patrick's.[81]

At first McGuckin thought very well of his "new parish," and recommended to D'Herbomez that he send a letter to "Pat" thanking him for his "little mite," and the new "church," which had an average Sunday attendance of about 40. By the fall McGuckin had collected over $1200 from his European parishioners, which was intended for his own support, the founding of the Mission, and for the vicariate apostolic. Such collections, despite the financially troubled times, seemed so promising that they were a major theme of his early letters to D'Herbomez.[82]

Though McGuckin was still living in Richfield, by early 1867 the financial state of his European parishioners was rapidly deteriorating. It now seemed unlikely that they could provide a solid financial foundation for an Oblate Mission in the region, especially in their work among the Native peoples. McGuckin had deliberately begun his ministry in Richfield, in effect as pastor to the European Catholics there, and for a time he believed that they should remain an important focus for the Oblates. A sign of this early enthusiasm was his willingness to start a school for European boys in Richfield, apparently envisioning a new St. Louis College similar to the ones in Victoria and New Westminster. Such bright, though premature predictions of a European Catholic community with ready cash had even lead D'Herbomez to pressure McGuckin to raise money there for Oblate Missions in England. Yet because of the region's growing financial crisis, by the summer of 1867 McGuckin's assessment had become more realistic. For after predicting that Sunday attendance figures of well over a hundred, by July McGuckin had totally reversed himself, since by then he had less than a dozen parishioners, and he reported that he had never seen money "so scarce" among the local Europeans. What he had formerly thought would be a ready financial source for the Mission and that of the vicariate had evaporated. Therefore he saw no immediate future for a self-sufficient European parish in the area, and decided to turn his attention to the farm, which as seen, he eventually built into a major enterprise.[83]

Like St. Gabriel's parish in Yale, St. Patrick's in Richfield had seemed very promising in 1868 when D'Herbomez blessed the tiny church-rectory, which even boasted a bell. But both parishes vanished with the towns' economies. In fact, outside of New Westminster, until after 1885 and the coming of the railroad, the Oblate presence among European settlers on either the lower mainland or in the interior was virtually nonexistent.

13

The Years After the Railroad

✦ IN THE 1880s, the Europeans and other non-Native population in British Columbia tripled in size due to the arrival of the CPR in 1885, while the general population doubled. The 1891 census placed the total population of the province at 98,173, of whom 21,350 were Catholic, mainly Native people. Yet, the steady growth in the European population meant that there were now twice as many Catholics in British Columbia than in the 1881 census. In his final report on the vicariate before his death on 3 June 1890, D'Herbomez exaggerated these figures, stating that there were then 35,000 Catholics, 35,000 Protestants and 30,000 "infidels," or those of no religion. Still, the actual increase was impressive, and Catholics, at least nominally, were then the largest denomination (28.6%) in the province. It was a distinction that they would never enjoy again, for due to indifference, intermarriage and migration the figure continued to decline. By 1951, though the dominant denomination nationally, the Catholic Church in British Columbia had a far smaller percentage (14.4%) who claimed affiliation than its two regional rivals, the United (29.3%) and Anglican (27.1%) churches.[1]

✤ The Catholic Church on Vancouver Island

BRITISH COLUMBIA was and still is an urban-centered province, and until the coming of the railroad, most Europeans lived in Victoria. Until 1890, Victoria was the only diocese in the province when Rome created the second with its seat at New Westminster. Unlike the rest of Canada where well over half the European population then worked and resided on farms or in small towns, little more than ten percent did so in British Columbia where most Europeans settled in or near large coastal cities. This highly urbanized reality was largely due to the great difficulty of inland transportation before the railroads and a lack of good agricultural land in the interior, where only about four percent was arable. Most agriculture was carried on in small suburban farming communities in the Lower Fraser Valley and on the Saanich Peninsula north of Victoria, and whose main consumers were the residents of the nearby cities.

Until the early twentieth century, Vancouver and New Westminster on the lower mainland and Victoria and Nanaimo on Vancouver Island contained most of the European population of the province. Among these Victoria held at least the perceived economic, and certainly the real political and social dominance until about 1900. Throughout the nineteenth century, Victoria, with its strong British and imperial ethos, and its position as the provincial capital and major port of entry, well overshadowed any mainland rivals.[2]

Naturally the European Catholic Church in British Columbia reflected these social, political and economic realities, and class, race and religious distinctions ruled society in Victoria throughout the nineteenth century, especially after 1885. Among denominational affiliation, Anglicans, almost all people of English birth, comprised the ruling class, although there was a growing middle class of mainly English, Scottish and Irish made up of small businessmen and merchants from low-church Anglican and traditional dissenting churches, especially Methodists and Presbyterians. However, a growing number of Europeans, about 25 percent in the 1881 census, claimed "no religion." This percentage would continue to increase and insure that British Columbia remained Canada's most unchurched province. Catholics, especially people from the British Isles and particularly Ireland, made up the core of the working class. By 1881, due mainly to the dominant Native population and the large number of Irish immigrants, Catholicism had become the largest denomination in British Columbia.

St. Andrew's Pro-Cathedral, 1858 (ASSA)

As for race, the Chinese and Natives were at the bottom of the social scale and were denied even the right to vote for almost 75 years (1874–1947). The Chinese were mainly valued by Europeans for their ability to work hard for long hours and for very little pay. The Native people were usually considered at best a general nuisance. It was one that most Europeans hoped would eventually disappear, perhaps as the result of "white" diseases. Or as a minority still hoped, including the Oblates, that the Natives could finally be acculturated, that is, though still "separate" from, somehow "equal" to the general "white" population.[3]

While Catholics in Victoria were little visible among members of the privileged or powerful, nor even among the middle classes, they were determined to make their presence felt. One of the major symbols to achieve that visibility was through the construction of impressive buildings—an "episcopal palace" and a new cathedral. The original cathedral and its successor were dedicated to St. Andrew the apostle, for Demers had been ordained a bishop on his feast day (November 30th) in 1847. The first "cathedral" had been a 15 by 20 foot "mud house" that Lempfrit had built in 1852. Demers replaced it in 1858 with a small (30' by 75') wooden structure on Humboldt Street that was described at the time as "costly and handsome." It was the work of Joseph Michaud who designed, built and was finally ordained in it. However, in 1875 Seghers dismissed the building as an "old wooden shack," and resolved to build a much larger one on land he had purchased on the corner of Blanshard and View Streets. As a precursor of this grand plan, Seghers completed an "episcopal palace" on Yates Street in 1885, within months of his return from Portland, Oregon. The "palace" cost the diocese the then enormous sum of $25,000, which, when it was formally opened for public inspection, was described by the local press as the "most substantial, the handsomest, and the costliest" building in the capital. In fairness, the "palace" was never intended as a private episcopal residence, since it was expected to house all of the priests then living in the city, in effect, most of the priests of the diocese. By then the original wooden "palace" which Demers had built on Humboldt Street was said to be "near collapse." Certainly, after St. Joseph's Hospital, the new "palace" was Seghers's most significant monument in Victoria, providing Catholics there with a "presence." However, it did not long outlive him, since it was demolished early in the next century in order to enlarge the nearby Dominion Hotel. Seghers's tragic murder in Alaska in 1886 robbed him of the opportunity to build a cathedral, which fell to his successor, Bishop John Nicholas Lemmens (1888–97).[4]

Lemmens, like the majority of Victoria's secular clergy during the period, was a Belgian who had arrived in 1876. First pastor of St. Peter's Parish (1876–83) in Nanaimo, he also worked (1883–88) among the Natives on the West Coast of Vancouver Island where he established a small Mission at Clayoquot. His few surviving sermons reveal a traditional Jansenism, describing the present life as a "continual and painful experience" which only death could resolve.[5]

Certainly Lemmens was highly respected by Seghers and by his fellow Belgian priests, and he was their first choice to succeed Seghers. To underscore this, in 1884, when the diocese was without a bishop, the clergy designated Lemmens to represent them at the Third Plenary Council of Baltimore. This was required, since Victoria was a suffragan see of the archdiocese of Portland, Oregon until 1903. In effect, it was an American diocese, though it had been in British and later Canadian territory since its foundation in 1846. In Baltimore, Lemmens met James Cardinal Gibbons and his own metropolitan, Archbishop William Gross of Portland. Such experiences and contacts further advanced his career. It was no surprise therefore, when Rome finally selected him to become the fifth bishop of Victoria in 1888.[6]

The building of the present St. Andrew's Cathedral was no doubt Lemmens's most significant contribution to the diocese, which needed a new facility. To accommodate the growing European Catholic congregation, in 1884 a temporary or pro-cathedral, which was also used as a hall, had been built on View Street. The original, wooden cathedral, which, though only 30 years old, was described in 1888 as a "venerable relic," became the chapel of St. Ann's Academy, Victoria. When the cost of a new building was first seriously considered in 1885, it was thought to be "in the neighborhood of $70,000." By 1890 the figure had risen to $80,000, a massive amount for the period, especially when it is compared to the $600–$700 average annual wage then paid to a working class person in Victoria.[7]

The public announcement of the huge figure also aroused private jealousy among some Anglicans, as Christ Church, the "other cathedral," was still a modest wooden structure. Yet some Anglicans, especially those more comfortable with a low-church theology, were happy to keep it that way, and even resented calling Christ Church a "cathedral," since they judged the word to be "Romanistic." For the Anglican diocese, clerical salaries were the major consideration, buildings always came second; whereas the reverse was true for the Catholic diocese.[8]

While such a large outlay would challenge the resources of the local Catholic community, the contract for its construction was finally signed on 29 January 1890. The important church architectural firm of Maurice Perrault & Albert Mesnard of Montreal designed it, basing it on a parish church that the same firm had recently completed in Vaudreuil, Quebec. Christian churches, especially cathedrals, are supposed to face eastward towards the Holy Land, but St. Andrew's was forced to face westward due to its location. The final design of the brick, granite and limestone edifice was modeled in the neo-gothic style and given two asymmetric "east" towers in order to provide the finished building with the often "incomplete" look of the great medieval cathedrals of thirteenth and fourteenth century Europe.[9]

During the two years it took to erect the building, there were several noteworthy incidents, however, all paled before what is surely the most bizarre occurrence, a killing which took place within its walls on Christmas Eve 1890. The Dublin-born immigrant shooter, Clarence Whelan had been hired as a night watchman. Shortly after beginning his new position that December, Whelan, an ardent "Irish Free State" supporter, raised an "Irish-American Flag" on the building site. Immediately there were protests, especially from British sympathizers who demanded that it be pulled down, and that, if any flag were to take its place, it should be the Union Jack. The flag was removed, and while none was substituted, this did not end the dispute. For on the evening of the tragedy Whelan, while drinking in a nearby pub before reporting to his post, got into a violent argument with John E. Crawford over the flag issue as well as Irish independence. Returning to the cathedral site in an angry and drunken state, Whelan continued to nurse his wounded feelings. David Fee, who had just left Mass in the pro-cathedral, which was located behind the new building, was passing by. Curious, Fee entered the new cathedral grounds to inspect its progress. Fee was dressed in a white coat similar to Crawford's. Thus Whelan mistook Fee for the erstwhile critic of Irish independence, challenged him, and when he did not receive an immediate response, shot the young man dead.[10]

The sad event underscored the depth of public feeling and disagreement in Victoria over Irish politics, especially on the volatile issue of Home Rule. The subsequent trial revealed the reality of strong feelings and prejudices not only about Ireland, but also against immigrants generally, and even among Catholics. The Victoria press dubbed the poor 33-year-old immigrant Whelan, who lived in a small room at 55 View Street, as a "drunkard" and a "regular of some Irish [Free State] Society." However, in writing of David Fee, the oldest son of Mr. and Mrs. D.F. Fee of North Park Street, a native son, a graduate of St. Louis College and an apprentice carpenter, the *Daily Colonist* noted that "few young men made themselves more popular than the deceased and enthusiastic" Fee. At his trial, Whelan was not even permitted to defend himself, and Chief Justice Matthew Baillie Begbie, who tried the case, declared it to be the "worst in his thirty-two years on the bench." After the jury found him guilty of manslaughter on 31 January 1891, Begbie stated that, to "protect society," Whelan must experience "penal servitude for the rest of...[his] natural life." Surely the event was an unhappy prelude to the cathedral's construction. As a memorial to their son, the Fee family and their friends donated the "King David" stained glass window, the only one in the new cathedral to be dedicated to an Old Testament theme.[11]

While far less dramatic or serious, several other problems and difficulties arose during the cathedral's construction. One was a complaint between the contractor, John Teague, and the sub-contractor, Thomas Smith, over Smith's use of "inferior" stone in the building's foundation, which Teague insisted could threaten the "safety of the edifice." Claiming that the cathedral rector, John Durand had told him to proceed, Smith sued Teague. Chief Justice Begbie personally inspected the site, and sided with Teague who assumed the role of general contractor. Local bigotry also raised its head, for in the fall of 1891 several anonymous letters, claiming the building was a shrine to "godless popery," threatened to incinerate it before its completion, though, except for a minor "suspicious fire," work continued without further damage.[12]

The cathedral's location also proved a difficulty because it was not then in an "upscale" area of the city and its environs had long been favored by "ladies of the night." In August 1892 the new rector, John Van Nevel complained of the situation to the police, insisting that they "raid the brothels on the north side of View Street." When he received no immediate response, he took his demand to Mayor Beaven and the City Council as "guardians of the morals of the city," insisting that the "unfortunate creatures" be removed. Within a few days the ladies were forced to find another venue for their "business" activities.[13]

Finally on Sunday, 30 October 1892, Lemmens dedicated the new cathedral during a pontifical High Mass before a congregation of "at least 2000." The sermon was preached by Archbishop Gross of Portland, while the band of H.M.S. *Warspite* and the choir, which sang a Mass by "Marzo," provided the music. It was a triumph, and the press that covered the event declared St. Andrew's Cathedral the "most notable church in British Columbia."[14]

Lemmens had great difficulty paying for the construction of this new wonder, since a serious depression had gripped North America by 1893. The cathedral was the major parish in the diocese, in actuality the only truly viable one, and the diocese's most important source of revenue. The majority of its parishioners were Irish, who, though a minority in Victoria, formed the backbone of the parish. Perhaps hoping to gain further financial support from them, in April 1893 Lemmens publicly supported "Home Rule" for Ireland. It was certainly a controversial position to take in British-dominated Victoria and, in supporting such a liberal cause, it probably demonstrates how desperate Lemmens was for cash. Most of the Catholic laity were day laborers and shop assistants, though a few had small businesses, and there was a handful of professionals. Yet most were hard hit by the difficult economic times, and were certainly neither able nor prepared to contribute much towards the elimination of this huge new diocesan expenditure.[15]

Therefore, Lemmens had to look elsewhere for means to pay off the cathedral debt. To meet the immediate debts, on 23 April 1892 he had himself and his successors declared a corporation sole by act of the Legislative Assembly, and in consequence became the legal "owner" of all real property in the diocese. Consequently, a few months later he was able to borrow $50,000 in his own name at 7% interest secured on diocesan assets valued at over $80,000. On a visit to Belgium in 1894, his native countrymen contributed $5,000 towards the debt, which, while very generous, was not sufficient.

Lemmens decided to turn his attention to Guatemala. Since the middle of the century a liberal and anticlerical government had been in power there, which had tried with mixed success to gain the support of the peasantry or the mass of the population. The leadership of the church had doggedly supported the rights of the large landowners. In reaction, the government passed laws closing church schools. In response, in 1887 Archbishop Casanova y Estrada of Guatemala City excommunicated the country's President Justo Rufino Barrios, who in turn exiled the prelate. For almost a decade Guatemala was without a bishop and thus no one had been confirmed. Learning of this during a fund raising trip to Mexico in 1896, where he obtained his money by confirming over 50,000 people, Lemmens asked and was invited by Casanova y Estrada to go to Guatemala and perform the same service. In short, Lemmens was authorized to confirm the entire country![16]

Confirmations, as in Mexico, meant stipends, however, they were rarely paid in cash, but in candles. The Native people, who comprised the great majority of his confirmands, donated large and small candles, the former, when exchanged for cash, brought a dollar; the smaller ones about "two bits." What impressed Lemmens most was both the generosity and friendliness of all the people, even those who opposed the official church, for President Barrios received him warmly and only asked that he do his work "quietly." Nevertheless, there were serious, even threatening incidents. In one town Lemmens arrived shortly after the local priest had been murdered by a "liberal" faction. In another, the mayor and local officials had been jailed by a central government official after they dared to welcome Lemmens, although when Lemmens complained to the president, they were all released. Considering the fact that he had to confirm hundreds of thousands of people, Lemmens developed a scheme by which people first purchased a ticket, usually with a candle, that entitled them to receive the sacrament. When they arrived at the church they presented the ticket to the local priest before approaching Lemmens. Sometimes for six or seven hours at a time he confirmed until he could hardly stand. Everywhere he went his stamina amazed his hosts, most of whom were wealthy landowners. As a bishop, Lemmens was a symbol of the "old landed order," which the landowners intended to maintain, so they feasted him and lavished presents on him including cases of wine, boxes of cigars and jewelry.[17]

In gratitude to Casanova y Estrada for allowing him to make enough money to pay off the bulk of the cathedral debt, Lemmens made a decision that would cost him his life. He agreed to travel to the remote jungles of western Guatemala where, due to the great poverty, there was no expectation of stipends, however, people in the remote area had not seen a bishop for over two hundred years. It was to be his last journey, and in a prophetic mood he wrote to his vicar general, Joseph Nicolaye: "If I get out of this country alive, I will do well. Steaming forests and putrid marshes impregnate the air you breathe." Lemmens had already compromised his health, since he had suffered several serious bouts of malaria during his time in Guatemala, where his temperature had reached over 104 degrees. His body, its immune system no doubt already shattered, was finally overwhelmed by typhoid. On 10 August 1897 Lemmens died of gastroenteritis. At the last moment, taking the hand of his assistant, Jose Maria Fuentes, Lemmens uttered his final words: "I am going away." Although he died relatively young, since he was only 47, his enormous efforts in Guatemala had paid a large portion of the outstanding debt on St. Andrew's Cathedral.[18]

The construction of St. Andrew's Cathedral demonstrated the central importance of Victoria to the life of the diocese, for the only other city of significance on Vancouver Island, located about 90 kilometers north of Victoria, was Nanaimo. Until the beginning of the twentieth century, after Vancouver, New Westminster and Victoria, it was the fourth largest city in British Columbia. Originally, a HBC coal town that had been founded in 1853, by 1901 it had a population of well over ten thousand of whom at least 20 percent worked in the mines. The Vancouver Coal and Land Company, which had acquired it from the HBC, was definitely unique when compared to other mining companies, such as the nearby Dunsmuir mines, in that it believed that its best interests lay in having a satisfied work force. While Nanaimo was a neat, though not a pretty city, a nineteenth century eyewitness exclaimed that he had "never seen coal-miners so comfortably placed,...every miner has his own house and garden." The Company also provided a park and encouraged cultural and sporting events. "When, in the 1880s, two major mining disasters killed 170," their surviving families were all provided with free housing and fuel for "as long as needed." By the 1890s the Company had even recognized the right of its workers to organize.[19]

A contemporary described miners as "God-fearing,...basically good, hardworking [and] clean minded," however, for most of them, this did not extend to any serious interest in church-going, Catholic or otherwise. For miners, church, if attended at all, was something done as a child and then abandoned as soon as possible to be left thereafter to women or other "religious people." While the miners of Nanaimo rarely had complaints against the Company, when they did they found that the clergy, except for the Methodists, remained uninvolved, preferring, usually by their silence, to defend the status quo.[20]

The Catholic Church had little visible importance in Nanaimo, though the city's sizable population, as the second largest on the Island, certainly merited attention. The Anglicans had established their first parish, St. Paul's, in 1861. In 1876, Seghers, far more consciously determined than Demers to confront "heresy," founded the first Catholic Church, St. Peter's, and named his fellow Belgian, John Nicholas Lemmens as its pastor. The Sisters of St. Ann also started a small school in the following year, adding an orphanage a few years later, their third in the province.[21]

However, for many years the Catholic Church in Nanaimo remained no more than a shadow when compared to its counterpart in Victoria. Victoria continued to be the home of not only the overwhelming majority of

European Catholics on Vancouver Island, but also, where the bishop, its most important person, resided. While Alexander Christie (1898–99), the sixth bishop of Victoria, would be best remembered, at least locally, for the residential school that would bear his name, he had barely unpacked his bags when he learned that he had been promoted again, this time to become the fourth archbishop of Portland, Oregon. His eventual replacement, Bertrand Orth would become not only the seventh bishop of Victoria (1900–1903), but, three years later, Rome appointed him to be the first provincial metropolitan (1903–08) and the only archbishop of Victoria.

Then 50, Orth, a German by birth, had been a pastor in Portland, Oregon since his arrival there over 25 years before. Apparently selected because he was both "local" and "well-known" nationally as the editor of the Portland Archdiocesan newspaper, *The Catholic Sentinel*, he had also been a close confidant of the third archbishop of Portland and a German American, William Gross (1885–98). Gross was a crony of a major American bishop-maker, Cardinal Gibbons of Baltimore. Still, one of the most significant reasons cited by Rome in his appointment was that Orth could speak "Indian." That is, he had some knowledge of the Chinook Jargon, which, was an almost irrelevant skill in ministering to the Native peoples of the region, but was still erroneously assumed by Europeans in Victoria and Rome to be "very important on Vancouver Island."[22]

Bertrand Orth would be the last bishop of Victoria whose appointment would be determined by ecclesiastics in the Catholic Church in the United States. For due to its continued suffragan status with the American archdiocese of Portland, Oregon, the diocese's outright suppression had at least been rumoured in Canadian circles for well over a generation.

The idea of suppressing the diocese of Victoria and merging it with the mainland church, though not the last time, was first voiced in 1871. Rome rejected it because it rightly feared that the seculars on Vancouver Island would resent being under Oblate domination. Not surprisingly, D'Herbomez was decidedly in favour, an opinion shared by Alexandre Taché, the new Oblate archbishop of St. Boniface (1871–94), who, for the Oblates, had happily become D'Herbomez's metropolitan in 1871. By the 1890s, feelings in Canada regarding Victoria had further hardened, and the Liberal prime minister, Wilfrid Laurier (1896–1911) considered the situation of Victoria's suffragan relationship with the American archdiocese of Portland both a political embarrassment and an administrative absurdity that must be terminated.[23]

A more palatable suggestion instead of outright suppression was to make Victoria a suffragan of St. Boniface. When this was voiced in 1900, being a secular, Orth had no desire to be under a regular metropolitan. When asked for his views by the apostolic delegate in Ottawa, Orth delayed, asking for "more advice" in order to consider the question. Finally when he was confident that his counsel was a reflection of the majority conclusion, Orth stated that "in his opinion" St. Boniface was both too far and too French to be the metropolitan for Victoria.[24]

By March 1902, Rome had decided, under pressure from Ottawa and also because of its growing wealth in both human and material resources, that British Columbia should become a separate ecclesiastical province, the only question was which city, Victoria or Vancouver, should become the seat of the metropolitan. Even then, both civilly and ecclesiastically, Vancouver was dominant, though still somewhat marginally, when compared to Victoria. Victoria was the provincial capital, and, in contrast to Vancouver, had a certain "antiquity" about it. In addition, the mainland church was then still dominated by the Oblates, which fact, at least Rome believed, could lead to future tensions with the secular clergy of Victoria. Therefore, the Holy See decided that Victoria should become the first archdiocese of the new ecclesiastical province. And so, in 1903, Bertrand Orth became the first and last archbishop of Victoria.[25]

Orth had definite administrative abilities. Among his accomplishments, he introduced the Knights of Columbus to the diocese, and brought two religious orders of regular clergy to the area: the De Montfort Fathers and the Benedictines. He also founded the diocesan newspaper, *The Orphans' Friend*. In addition, he built a new "bishop's palace" at 740 View Street; completed the cathedral's stained-glass windows and installed its new organ; and finally in 1906 he retired the remaining debt on the cathedral, largely through fund raising and money donated by the Sisters of St. Ann.[26]

Bertrand Orth was not only the first archbishop of the new ecclesiastical province, he was also the first bishop in the region to be forcibly removed from office by the Holy See; an event strongly influenced by changes in Roman policies of church government. In 1903 the College of Cardinals had elected a new head, Pius X (1903–14) who, known in history as *the* antimodernist pope, was, after Pius IX (1846–78), probably its most reactionary leader in modern times. Modernism, as understood by its most "radical" supporters was intended to give the Catholic faith "a new form of expression" that would "do justice to the changes of the human mind," especially in modern science. However, to ecclesiastical authorities, particularly the Vatican curia and Pius X, such an approach seemed more "the beginning of an impending catastrophe," and was treated as such.[27]

While through the centuries its influence rose and fell due to historical circumstances, Rome had long been accustomed to having a degree of control over the universal church. However, by the mid nineteenth century such influence had been greatly strengthened through the theory and practice of the ultramontanism of Pius IX and culminated in Vatican Council I (1869–70), which approved the doctrine of papal infallibility. Under Pius X, the Holy See became positively obsessed with the need to manage every aspect of church life throughout the world. As a result, almost everything— Catholic lay societies, the size of stipends, the times of Mass, church music, the composition of Mass bread and wine, clerical formation, discipline and even dress—passed under Roman scrutiny and demanded Rome's authorisation. In 1906, for example, Orth had to obtain a papal rescript or permission before he was allowed to admit a "limit" of ten boys to attend St. Ann's Academy in Victoria.[28]

With Rome providing the lead, fear gradually replaced respect for church authority, and became the dominant mode of government on all levels. In 1905 Orth provided the Vatican with figures which, in effect, indicated that the entire region was probably the most irreligious, but certainly the most unchurched in all of Canada. In response, Rome counselled Orth to do his utmost to covert such "heretics," and to achieve such an objective, he was to have the seminarians of the archdiocese begin their studies as young as possible, so that they could be "thoroughly moulded" into "properly obedient" priests. In the Vatican's reasoning, so trained they would be much better prepared to win new adherents to Catholicism.[29]

Orth seemed to take very naturally to this far more "autocratic" form of church government, in which the bishop, while under the complete supervision of the Vatican, was in turn in absolute control of the local church. Reflecting such an attitude, his letters to his diocesan subordinates were couched in very imperious language. Requests became commands. Questions or hesitations were now normally interpreted as a form of insubordination. By 1905, in referring to himself, Orth had even begun to use the imperial plural: "we direct," "we desire," "we demand." When the provincial of the Sisters of St. Ann died in March 1905 and Orth received an invitation to attend the funeral, he wrote that "we were surprised not to be informed," and immediately ordered all plans to be cancelled because he had not been consulted first. His reason was simple: "to teach respect and obedience to episcopal authority." In approving the final arrangements, Orth dismissed the idea of having Protestant pall bearers who were friends of the sisters, but rather, he retorted, "we insist that they must be practical Catholic gentlemen." In another incident regarding two Sisters of St. Ann teaching at the Kuper Island Residential School, the words "we order" were in Orth's insistence that they be immediately removed due to "mysterious noises heard at sundry times." When their superior requested a further explanation for their dismissal, Orth replied: "we deem such unnecessary." Anytime contributions from the nuns or clergy were ordered, especially for the Holy See, Orth stated: "we deem it a must to ask you to contribute," and if the "donation" was not forthcoming, those who had been asked were required to give "the reason why it cannot be done." Such behaviour made him feared, but hardly respected. Not surprisingly, he was not popular with many, but especially with the clergy.[30]

These attitudes go a long way in explaining why Orth was the first bishop in British Columbia to be forced to resign and under a cloud of sexual scandal that centered upon "insinuations against [his] good behaviour" towards members of the opposite sex. Two women, Mrs. Godfrey and Miss Florence Crane claimed that Orth had sexually abused them. Each gave reports, which partly confirmed and partly contradicted the word of the other. In a statement to Archbishop Christie of Portland, Crane, though critical of Orth's behaviour, accused Godfrey of being both "immoral and dangerous."[31]

Yet, it was Joseph Nicolaye, a Belgian-born priest of the diocese, who would prove to be Orth's greatest enemy in the affair. Both men had very strong differences. Nicolaye, an influential and headstrong cleric, could be given to "exaggerations." He had been vicar general to Lemmens, Christie and Orth, before Orth dismissed him from that office in 1903 for his continued opposition to his ordinary's decisions. According to Nicolaye, the immediate cause of his removal was his discharging of the cathedral sacristan, "a young girl" who, Nicolaye insisted, was "flirting with the altar boys."[32]

Nicolaye, apparently still bitter over his dismissal, jumped at the opportunity of supporting the very serious charges of sexual misconduct against Orth. Determined to bring matters to a head, in February 1907 Nicolaye was prepared to call a general meeting of the diocesan clergy in order to "investigate" the whole affair. Furious, Orth threatened to suspend Nicolaye, who, in a letter to the apostolic delegate, interpreted such an action as "an additional proof" of Orth's "guilt." Officially accusing Orth of Jansenism as well as being extremely mean spirited, Nicolaye said that he had reported Orth to Rome for these lesser charges in order to have him removed, but especially that it could be done "without mentioning any [far more] serious crimes!"[33]

Rome was not amused. By nature slow to respond, particularly to accusations, and especially against bishops, given the anti-modernist and the highly prudish temper of the times, even the hint of sexual scandal moved Rome into almost immediate action. While the Vatican admitted that there appeared to be "contradictions, machinations, exaggerations and perhaps intrigue all hiding at the bottom of...[this] disgraceful affair," it still viewed it as "very dangerous," and certainly believed that a bishop had to be above all suspicion, particularly in areas of "moral rectitude." In March 1908, the local press mysteriously reported, with no further explanation, that Orth had left Victoria for Europe due to "reasons of health." Rome had ordered him to relinquish his office, although in May the Holy See announced that, since Orth was "seriously ill," Pius X had "permitted [him] to resign."[34]

Nicolaye was a hero among his fellow priests, and their favoured candidate to be the next ordinary of Victoria. This fact reinforces the conclusion that Orth was very unpopular, especially among the clergy as well as the Sisters of St. Ann. Nicolaye, as the vicar general to three bishops, must have had some leadership skills. Still, several groups of prominent lay Catholics in Victoria "energetically protested" Orth's removal. Certainly, such people would have been most upset if Nicolaye, given his well-know opposition to Orth, had succeeded the deposed archbishop. Also, and probably even more important in Rome's eyes, if Nicolaye were selected, such a fact would certainly lend considerable public credence to the serious accusations against Orth.[35]

It was also an era, given its strong anti-modernist stance, in which Rome was far less disposed to select local candidates for the episcopacy, since it might give the impression that the Holy See favoured that modernist "horror," popular democracy, and so it looked outside the diocese. The second candidate, Peter Masson, a secular priest was also an American citizen from the archdiocese of Philadelphia, and, Rome naturally concluded that his selection would upset Ottawa. Therefore, they finally settled on the third choice, Alexander MacDonald, also a secular priest, from the diocese of Antigonish, Nova Scotia. Described as a "capable theologian," having for years taught the subject at Saint Francis Xavier University, where he also had been rector, he was praised as a "very eloquent" speaker, and a "most distinguished" priest, being then the vicar general of his diocese. Perhaps most noteworthy, MacDonald was, after Demers (1846–71), only the second native Canadian to hold that office. Nevertheless, like Bertrand Orth, Alexander MacDonald (1909–23) would eventually become the second bishop of Victoria whom Rome would force to resign that see.[36]

Victoria had long been Canada's most "pagan" city, and by 1909 it also had the largest proportion of people of "no religion," and a Catholic population of only 6.87%, facts which led MacDonald to wish he had never left Cape Breton and its strong Catholic ethos. Still there was modest growth during his fourteen years there. Saanich and Sidney saw the construction of two tiny chapels in 1908 and 1911 under J.A. Vullinghs and a Marist, E.M. Sheelen. In 1870, Rondeault had built the first and only stone church in the diocese on the Cowichan reserve called the "butter church" since the money for its construction came from the sale of Native butter. Due to its remoteness from the centre of the reserve, vandals, mostly Native, had long before reduced it to a ruined shell. Selecting a site near the reserve, a new church, dedicated to St. Ann, was completed and pastored by P. VanGoetham. In Duncan, St. Edward's Parish got its first small chapel in 1902, which was enlarged in 1908. There two Marists, Francis Boshouwers and Henry Lemmens ministered. In Chemainus, the Marist, E.M. Sheelen supervised the erection of the first chapel in 1909 under the patronage of St. Joseph. During this period, Ladysmith, Extension and Cassidy, where lumbering was the economic backbone, saw chapels constructed and served by clergy from Nanaimo. Nanaimo was the first parish in the diocese established outside greater Victoria. By 1876 Nanaimo had a small church, which had originally been in Wellington, but after the mining boom ended, it was moved to Nanaimo to replace the church lost in a fire in 1910. The Sisters of St. Ann had run a school and orphanage there since 1877, but they also lost their convent in the same conflagration, though the building was replaced almost immediately. Due to the economic growth of the regions, Port Alberni, Comox, Cumberland and Campbell River all had chapels by 1914, though, because of clergy shortages, H. Mertens, who lived in Comox, was the only pastor in the area. Reflecting a local need, Comox and Campbell

River both had small hospitals opened in 1913–14 by the Sisters of St. Joseph of Toronto. In 1911 another community of nuns, the strictly cloistered Order of the Poor Clares founded a convent in Victoria (Willows). Outside Victoria, all the parishes were in effect Missions. Although there was some local support, they were also largely dependent upon the free-will generosity from either Victoria, or from the Catholic Church Extension Society. The latter had been founded in Toronto in 1908, and it still supplies significant financial support to the dioceses in British Columbia and the Yukon.[37]

It was during this period that the Catholic Woman's League (CWL) and the St. Vincent De Paul Society were founded in Victoria and Vancouver. The CWL was based on similar organizations in Germany and England, and it started in both cities in 1921, becoming a national organization in 1923. Intended to be a "well organized and loyally disposed" body, "in the hands of the clergy," it was assumed that CWL members would be, even after women gained the vote, at least "implicitly" anti-suffrage, that is leaving all public decision making to men, and it was a stance that was reflected in their description as "loyal and devoted children of Holy Church." By means of teas, bazaars or bake sales, they were to provide cash for whatever purposes the clergy judged to be important. For, as one unidentified Victoria priest advised a meeting in 1921, "Catholic women [of the CWL] must always put God first, [and] men second," or the church before all else, which then effectively meant its clergy. However, women who chose to come to British Columbia tended to be more independent minded than their eastern sisters, especially with regard to seeing their only role in life as home and family. Perhaps for this reason, the CWL had considerable difficulty in recruiting members, at least during its early years.[38] Less docile, since it was completely under lay control, the St. Vincent De Paul Society, which was initiated in France, began in Victoria and Vancouver in 1915. As its very limited means would allow, the Society mainly provided food, clothing, and shelter to needy families and individuals. This was very important during the depression of 1913–16. However, during the Great Depression of 1929–39, given its enormity, the Society was barely able to cope. In an overwhelmingly urbanised culture such as British Columbia, the Great Depression resulted in the highest unemployment (28 percent) in Canada. Voluntarist denominational bodies, such as St. Vincent's, despite their efforts, could never begin to fill the social need. Thus, though laissez-faire capitalists balked, the decade before World War II demonstrated that, short of a "red" revolution, serious economic hardship could only be adequately met by means of a tax-supported and provincially run social safety net.[39]

While MacDonald welcomed the work of such lay organizations, his real interests were in other areas. MacDonald was a prolific published author, with an excellent education. His printed works ranged from theology to popular piety, although he also dabbled in travelogues, evolution and even entomology.[40]

Like his predecessors, McDonald was a strong supporter of Catholic education. His most important contribution was saving St. Louis College, which had been threatened with closure since 1911. Tuition costs had risen because lay staff were needed after it became impossible to find diocesan clergy who were able to teach there. The local secular clergy had been running the school since the Oblates had left the diocese in 1866. Rising costs in turn lead to declining student numbers, so that by 1914 the college seemed doomed. However, MacDonald convinced the Irish Christian Brothers to assume responsibility for the school, and since the Brothers were bound by a vow of poverty, they were quite "cheap." They remained at St. Louis until, after over a century of operation, the school finally closed in 1968.[41]

MacDonald, as the second Canadian to be bishop of Victoria, combined with the fact that he was also an anglophone may explain his strong, jingoistic nationalism, and dedication to British imperialism. It is true that (excluding the Methodist pacifist, James S. Woodsworth, who lived briefly in British Columbia, and who broke with his church over the issue) chauvinistic patriotism was almost universal among the clergy of the major denominations throughout Canada. In MacDonald's case, besides encouraging Catholics to buy war bonds, he considered World War I as a "fight for God" in which, he declared, it was, indeed, "sweet and glorious to die for one's country." He also believed that by its participation in the war, "Canada...[had] sealed the covenant of Empire with the blood of her best sons." In fact, 17 members of St. Andrew's Cathedral Parish, including one woman, died in the "Great War," which was quite a large figure, representing over five percent of its registered members.[42]

It was, however, as a land speculator that MacDonald would best be remembered and the resulting financial disaster that resulted would finally end in his resignation. The single tax system then in operation in most western Canadian cities, including Victoria and Vancouver, made tax collecting in the wake of land speculation far more problematic. The single tax system, essentially invented and then advocated by the American, Henry George (1839–97), operated on the assumption that the growth of a community increased the value of property without the landowners having to make any effort. Thus the calculated increase in property values would form the basis of the single tax system. As such, "the tax would take from the public [i.e., land owners] the unearned increment of land value." However, "it would leave untouched with the individual holder the gains from labor or capital [improvements] which he might make upon his piece of land [or its buildings]." The major problem, more evident after 1912 when local land values plummeted, was that the single tax system could only adequately feed municipal tax coffers during times of rising land values.[43]

Hoping to make a killing for the diocese, in 1911 and 1912, when land prices were highest, MacDonald purchased three properties in Victoria for the then staggering sum of $80,000, which he hoped would soon double, if not triple in value. When prices began to fall and then collapsed in 1912, he owed over $100,000 at 6% interest. By 1915, a property in either Victoria or Vancouver was worth only 50% of its 1912 value, and by 1921 a mere 11.3%. Throughout the crisis MacDonald was unwilling to listen to lay experts on the issue, but insisted upon throwing good money after bad. Therefore, he secured additional loans, mortgaging what was left of the diocese's assets, raising another $50,000, which he would soon lose, since he was not even able to pay the principle, much less the interest. He ultimately was forced to default.[44]

By 1919 MacDonald owned $16,000 to the city of Victoria in back property taxes, most of which was on the land on which St. Andrew's Cathedral stood, since the building was exempt. Yet, due to the single tax system, in face of a deeply depressed real estate market, city hall found it increasingly difficult to collect. The city fathers, in their frustration, blamed land speculators, such as the bishop of Victoria, for their dilemma. To make matters far worse, Catholics were then a minority denomination (6.32%) in the city, and so fewer parishioners meant less income when it was most needed. Determined to get its money, in February city hall ordered the cathedral, then barely 30 years old, to be sold at public auction on 26 May 1919 unless the money owed to it was paid. MacDonald immediately went to court to block the sale, and eventually took his case all the way to the Privy Council in London, then the highest court in the British Empire. In August 1921 it ruled in his favour denying the city the right to tax the land on which any church stood. It was an historic victory for MacDonald and all the churches of British Columbia, however, when his other debts were added to his very large legal fees, the judgement also added to his financial woes.[45]

Throughout his battle, MacDonald had tried to solicit the help of others, especially richer dioceses and advised the Vatican to demand such a reform. However, in 1922 he was highly critical of the Holy See when it reformed canon law to increase the financial accountability of bishops by requiring them to gain its permission before spending any amount over $5,000. Complaining to the apostolic delegate in Ottawa, MacDonald declared: "My imagination refuses to picture Our Lord and Savior Jesus Christ doling out dispensations and faculties as is done today in Rome." In view of the authoritarian environment in the Vatican at the time, it was certainly an imprudent statement, and given his own vulnerability after his protracted financial problems, it seemed career suicide. As a result, in spring 1923 he was summoned to Rome, accused of "modernism," a spurious charge that was later dropped, but not before he was forced to resign the see. Thus, after Orth, MacDonald became the second bishop of Victoria to leave under a cloud.[46]

Alexander MacDonald remained a very bitter, angry and defiant man. Without doubt, MacDonald's legal victory ultimately benefited the churches of British Columbia. Still, despite the single tax, the real estate market collapse and city hall's negative attitudes towards him as a major land speculator, most, if not all of his financial problems, which had triggered his court battles, were due solely to his own deplorable mismanagement of diocesan funds. He would continue to publicly insist until his death in 1938 that he was still the bishop of Victoria, blaming everyone but himself, especially Rome and the pope, for all his problems.[47]

✤ The Oblates and the Church on the Mainland

WHEN PAUL DURIEU SUCCEEDED D'HERBOMEZ in 1890 and became the first bishop of the newly established diocese of New Westminster, one of his initial acts was to order each Oblate to answer a list of questions on the state of the European Catholic church on the mainland. Among his questions were: where did priests celebrate Mass; how frequently; did children receive catechism instruction; how many adults received communion and confessed; what of general attendance figures and financial support. He even asked if they thought that dancing should be forbidden. The returns to the last question drew a universal negative, though the rest of the responses indicated that church attendance and general participation among European Catholics throughout the mainland were not encouraging. Actually total attendance was less than ten percent of the official census figure, and below four percent of the total that D'Herbomez had estimated in 1889.[48]

The earliest European parish to survive outside New Westminster was Sacred Heart in Kamloops, which was then a major railroad hub and distribution centre for the farmers and ranchers of the region. The parish was officially erected in 1887 and the church blessed by Durieu in 1890. Julien-Augustin Bedard (1887–92) was the first pastor, and in 1892 Frédéric Guertin followed him, to be replaced in 1898 by André Michels (1898–1909). By then Michels was reporting rather grim statistics with regard to church attendance, stating that out of 250 registered parishioners fewer than 100 attended with any regularity. He believed that without the choir that he had begun, far fewer would come; an interesting conclusion, indicating that entertainment was a major reason for church going. There was also a small parish school for girls run by the Sisters of St. Ann. By 1885 it had classes up to the tenth grade, with a total enrollment of about 36. Sacred Heart had the usual parish organizations. An Altar Society, run by several ladies, looked after the cleaning of the church and maintenance of the vestments and linens. A Men's Club maintained and repaired parish buildings, and a branch of the Young Men's Institute, which helped members meet "good" Catholic women, showed some promise. As for clerical salaries in the parish, they reflected the annual regional Oblate average of $300, whereas the Anglican clergy in British Columbia then received over $2,500. Celibacy certainly had a lot to do with such an extreme disparity, but even without a family, the difference is quite startling. Certainly this fact goes a long way in explaining why Catholic institutions throughout the far west, such as schools and hospitals, given their extremely cheap labour force, were thus far more numerous than Protestant ones.[49]

While Catholic personnel were far less expensive than their Protestant counterparts, reflecting the general lack of interest in the far west of all forms of organized religion, even cheaper staff did not translate into higher church attendance rates, This was certainly the case in the huge area surrounding Kamloops. LeJeune covered the territory east of the city along the CPR line as far as Field. In his attempt to minister to Europeans in this region, he calculated that annually he had Mass in 31 homes, which he visited no more than twice annually. He estimated that probably less than half the Catholics ever came to Mass, though in reality, he felt, the actual figure was surely far less, and probably as low as ten percent, and most of these were women. Protestants, Native and European dominated the area north of Kamloops, and no Oblates ever visit there. After he left Sacred Heart in 1892, Bedard regularly visited towns along the CPR from Golden to Nelson where he said Mass in local homes. The first secular priest in the area, Joseph Accorsini, from the archdiocese of New York, arrived in 1893, and worked for a short time in Revelstoke and Donald, where he built tiny chapels. Nevertheless, given Oblate dominance and control, Accorsini felt terribly isolated. He left the region and British Columbia in 1894 to be replaced by an Oblate, Peytavin. By then two other secular priests, Albert Lemay and James Poitras, were also working in the area, the former had taken charge of the parish in the mining towns of Rossland and Nelson and the latter was ministering in Slocan. Golden received a small church in 1895, where LeJeune was pastor. From their residence at the Oblate Missions in Kamloops and the Kootenays, James Walsh and Pierre Richard traveled extensively throughout the Okanagan. In Vernon, Walsh tried to encourage his congregation to construct a church, but he was too ill and died in 1897 at the age of 34 before he accomplished it. Oliver Cornellier, who had begun coming there in 1894, saw a very small one realized in 1896. Beginning in 1892 Bedard worked in and around Nelson, which was becoming an important mining and administrative centre. He was succeeded by Peytavin, whose major accomplishment was to lower the parish debts in both Nelson and Revelstoke. The famous Archduke Francis Ferdinand of Austria, whose assassination in 1914 triggered the First World War, made an official tour of Canada in 1885, and was reportedly prevailed upon by a lady from the Revelstoke parish to make a "generous donation." From 1895 onwards Peytavin appears to have limited his work to the towns along the mainline of the CPR. In 1899 the Oblate and second bishop of New Westminster, Augustin Dontenwill (1899–1908) laid the cornerstone for the church of the Immaculate Conception in Nelson. However, all the Oblates in the area complained of poor attendance figures, frequently less than ten percent, and those who did come to church were very poor givers. Charles Marchal (1868–1906), when he was superior of St. Louis Mission (1899–1905), lamented that, as far as European Catholics in the entire Okanagan and Kooteneys were concerned, their church was "the last thing on their minds."[50]

By 1899 the Williams Lake region had almost no European Catholics. Peytavin, in a review of his work there noted that his ministry among Europeans was so minor that there was nothing to report. Although, apparently intended as a touch of dark humour, he did believe, given his long experience, that the local Europeans were at least a "bit more positive" towards St. Joseph's Mission and its thriving Oblate farm. Clearly, local European settlers, even including Catholics, often resented Oblate success, especially in farming. While general indifference to organized religion was a central reason, no doubt jealousy lessened local church attendance, especially if Oblates were officiating.[51]

During the 1890s, and despite a downturn due to a general depression, the Kootenays still showed dramatic economic growth, especially in mining, though it usually depended on outside financial forces, particularly American. Early prospectors arrived from Montana, Idaho, Colorado and Washington, and with a sharp rise in international silver prices, by 1895 experts from all over the world were pouring into the region. By 1898, Nelson, still very much a frontier town in 1887, had become as famous as the general area, which now rivaled the Rand. By then British and Canadian capital was taking the place of American investments.[52]

As a major sign of this growth, the region received its first Catholic hospitals—Mater Misericordia in Rossland and St. Eugene's in Cranbrook. The Sisters of Providence founded St. Eugene's, drawing upon some of their staff and funding from St. Paul's in Vancouver. Mater Misericordia became a reality due to the generosity of the Sisters of St. Joseph of Peace who then had their headquarters in Bellingham, Washington. In 1896 they opened a temporary 30-bed unit, but in less than a year they had completed a facility over twice that size. When a miners' strike threatened to close the hospital, its head, Sister Teresa Kiernan convinced the provincial government, since Mater was then the only hospital in the region, to provide an annual grant. It thus became the first denominational hospital in British Columbia to receive public assistance.[53]

During this boom period in the Kootenays, the Oblates and a few, though slowly growing number of secular clergy were attending to the needs of its still very scattered Catholic population. John Welch, an English-born secular who would later become an Oblate, traveled regularly from Fernie to Fort Steele and Moyie. He built tiny chapels in these locations, but admitted that because of the cost of building them, the people could give very little in the regular collections. Coccola complained that it was hard to keep track of the little towns that were mushrooming everywhere. Often the Europeans attended the Native chapel on the nearest reserve and gave when they could, which was infrequently. However, Coccola spoke of his hopes for Kimberley and Windermere. Indicating his lack of influence over the European laity, Coccola said that often he only learned of marriages between Catholics and Protestants when they were announced in the local press. He believed this growing trend was due to a preference that Catholics had for ministers over priests in order to avoid any church restrictions on their mixed marriages. For his part, Norbert Ouellette hoped that the poor givers in Cranbrook would be more generous once they had their own church. However, the state of the church throughout the interior and south-east was not an especially promising one.[54]

By 1900, circumstances in the Lower Fraser Valley were not much better. At Hope, Catholics numbered no more than 20, mostly Métis who, when a priest could not visit them, conducted a Sunday rosary and a young woman regularly taught catechism to the children. On Nicomen Island, which a priest visited very irregularly, there were about 20 Catholics, who, for an unexplained reason, did not get along with each other and there seemed little hope of reconciliation. A few of the twelve Catholics in Yale attended Mass at the Native church. At Agassiz, where there was also a small church, few of the 32 Catholics came and among those who did, almost none ever went to confession. At Mission City about 25 to 30 Catholics struggled to build a parish, but they were so scattered there seemed little likelihood of that ever happening. At Port Haney the church was attended irregularly by at most 20 Catholics. At Ladner there was a small chapel dedicated to the Sacred Heart where Camille Desrochers (1890–92) and William Morgan (1892–94) worked. By 1899 an influx of over a hundred Italians had arrived there, who, however, except for a handful of women, rarely came to Mass. Chilliwack was one of the very few bright spots in the area; there the tiny church appeared to have a fairly good, and even regular, attendance rate.[55]

By the end of the century, as the terminus of the CPR, Vancouver had supplanted New Westminster as the mainland's leading city, yet the Royal City remained the centre of the mainland church until Vancouver became an archdiocese in 1908. Holy Rosary Parish would eventually become its cathedral. Until then St. Peter's continued in that role. There Ouellette (1892–96) and William Morgan (1896–1901) tried to conduct High Mass with a reasonably good choir, though apparently infrequent practice some-times produced less than satisfactory results. Still, such performances were a major factor in keeping up attendance rates. Outside summer months, the choir also sang solemn vespers on most Sunday evenings followed by Benediction of the Blessed Sacrament. In the parish hall fairly frequent sec-ular amusements, such as amateur music and theatrics, were provided by the St. Joseph's Society as well as the Young Men's Institute.[56]

There had been a boom economy throughout most of the far west in the 1880s, especially after the arrival of the CPR, however, in 1893, due largely to the collapse of silver stock speculations in the United States, a depression soon spread throughout North America. All of British Columbia suffered, however, New Westminster, which was already feeling the effects of Vancouver's rising influence, was especially hard hit. Yet both cities experi-enced "starvation and misery" that all the churches tried to alleviate with emergency shelters and volunteer soup kitchens. St. Louis College had been very badly affected by the depression. Even in the best of times, competition from the local public high school had always posed a threat to its existence. However, in 1897, because of a serious drop in students due to a continued poor economy, the high school division was closed. The two St. Ann's Academies, in Victoria and New Westminster, felt the effects of the financial crash after the student body in both dramatically declined. In the Royal City it more than halved from a high of 75. The Sisters of St. Ann seriously consid-ered closing it and concentrating on their school in the capital. However, they decided to stay, since, because of the depressed real estate market, they could not find a buyer for the building. Their fortunes, and that of the city's, were finally reversed in 1898 when the Klondike gold rush signaled a regional rebirth, though much of the local growth, though influenced, was independ-ent of what was happening in the Klondike. By 1911, its fortunes had improved to such a degree that the Sisters had added a new wing to the school to pro-vide for an increase in the student population to well over a hundred.[57]

The depression also ended the publication of *The Month*. Durieu had started the monthly magazine in January 1892. It was intended to provide local Catholic readers with news of church happenings in the western world, including Canada, the United States and Europe, though it particu-larly emphasized events in the local church. From funerals to weddings, to church construction and the movements of the clergy, despite the highly secular society of British Columbia, *The Month* tried to provide its readers with a sense that there was indeed a Catholic reality in the far west and beyond. Supported by both annual subscriptions of one dollar or ten cents an issue and local business advertising, the decline of the latter, mainly because of the hard economic times, forced *The Month* to cease publication in October 1896.[58]

While the depression had a negative influence upon many undertakings and institutions in the diocese, it did not seem to have an impact on a major decision by Durieu to start the first seminary in British Columbia. In announcing his decision in a special pastoral letter in November 1894, Durieu remarked how much harder it had become to obtain clergy from outside the diocese, and the numbers attracted were by no means sufficient, especially given the needs, he wrote, of "our vast diocese." He therefore decided to turn to local Catholic families with the hope that they would encourage their sons, who showed "more favorable dispositions and qualities of character" to consider a vocation to the priesthood. He described the types of candidates he was looking for: the best would be both holy and brilliant, but since this was rare, the second, though not "so highly gifted" in brains, would be "seriously pious." Finally, there were those who, though they had "great acuteness of intellect and soundness of judgement," were still possessed of a "certain amount of levity" and "impetuosity," however, if these qualities could be "overcome," then they too would make "valued servants of God in the sacred ministry."[59]

By the summer of 1895 Nazareth Seminary was under construction. Built to house 25 students, Euro-Canadian as well as Native labor, mainly from the Squamish and Sechelt tribes was used in its construction. The building was quite up-to-date, for, besides central heating, it also had electric lights. Perhaps such modern conveniences helped in the recruiting, although literature insisted that while "material comfort" was "most important," "spiritual direction," was "more essential." Whatever, when the institution finally opened on 9 March 1896 it had twelve "young boys" as seminarians. It was hardly a success, due mainly to a lack of interest among local Europeans in seeing their sons become priests, an attitude greatly influenced by the strong secular environment of British Columbia. By the time it finally closed in 1909, after 13 years of existence, Nazareth Seminary had produced only two priests![60]

Until 1886, Vancouver did not exist. Before then several logging camps and a sawmill on the shore of the Burrard Inlet supported a European population of about 500. With the coming of the railroad the area's development was spectacular. By the turn of the century Vancouver was the undisputed metropolitan center of British Columbia. Reflecting the city, within barely 25 years of the CPR's arrival, Vancouver was the archdiocese or metropolitan see of the ecclesiastical province, with its only suffragan sees, the diocese of Victoria and vicariate apostolic of the Yukon.[61]

The uniqueness of Vancouver is best reflected in the fact that its first priest was not an Oblate, but a secular priest, an indication of things to come. Patrick Fay was a Scot and personified the slow but growing increase in secular clergy and a subsequent decline of Oblate dominance of the mainland church. While Nicolas Coccola also ministered to CPR construction workers, it was only as an adjunct to his general work, especially among the local Natives and Europeans. However, Fay had traveled across Canada as a Catholic chaplain solely to the employees of the CPR, and he represented the dramatic impact of the railroad on everything in far western Canada. Given his initial parishioners, it is not surprising that when he opened his first "church" in the spring of 1885, it was located in a back room of Billy Blair's Terminus Saloon on Water Street in Gastown. Yet, within a year he had a parish of almost 70 Catholic families, which convinced him to begin construction of the first church. Selecting a highpoint in what was still a forest, Holy Rosary Church was soon a reality. However, on 13 June 1886 a clearing fire that blew out of control destroyed it along with the surrounding town. By 1888 Fay had secured a $5,000 loan towards a new wooden edifice and additional land, all of which was secured in Durieu's name as corporation sole. By 1892 urban and parish growth required yet another expansion to both the land and the building.[62]

Parish institutions, especially girls' schools, could be important in attracting and retaining the laity in a parish, even though they always had to depend on non-Catholic students to survive. Reflecting its steady growth, Holy Rosary saw its first school for girls open in 1888 when the Sisters of St. Ann founded Sacred Heart Academy on Dunsmuir Street. The Sisters had only been able to undertake this new venture after the closure of their Williams Lake School in the same year. The Williams Lake School for girls had been founded in 1876. The drastic decline of the local economy, especially the gold mining industry, certainly did not helped. The School had really never been able to attract a large enough student body to justify its existence, since "finishing" schools for young ladies, while popular in urban areas, were still considered a great luxury in the interior. Therefore it seemed a prudent and sound investment to borrow the almost twelve thousand dollars to erect their new school in Vancouver. By 1891, with well over 100 girls in attendance, Sacred Heart Academy was second only to St. Ann's Academy in Victoria. However, by then, due to unpaid principle and interest, made far worse by parents who frequently were not able to pay tuition, with interest on their loan, the Sisters had increased their original financial burden to well over fifteen thousand dollars. Soon the school was being dubbed "Job's House," reflecting the perennial problem of making Catholic education in Canada a going concern without government assistance, but especially in British Columbia.[63]

Holy Rosary provided lay societies for both men and women. Women were encouraged to join an Apostleship of Prayer and a Ladies Social Club, which drew women together for socializing and for volunteer charity work. Probably the most important early society was the Young Men's Institute, which within a few months of its founding in 1892 had over 140 members, mostly Irish. Its first president, James Byrne noted its central purpose, namely, that since women, except for prostitutes, were then in very short supply in Vancouver, young men needed the "moral guidance" of a good wife, in order to follow "the path of rectitude." Originally founded in San Francisco in 1883, the YMI was ostensibly intended to encourage loyalty to church and nation, since it only admitted "practicing Catholics," and took as its motto a popular Irish nationalist rallying cry, *"Pro Deo, Pro Patria."* It also provided its full members with modest sick and funeral benefits. Nevertheless, its most practical and significant objective was helping its younger and not so young members find, through its socials and dances, a "good Catholic woman" and vice versa. Its importance in the lives of Catholic men, as well as women, reflected the continued unsettled, though rapidly developing state of both the Northwest Territories and British Columbia, the only areas covered by the Institute in Canada. By 1892 there were YMIs in Vancouver, as well as in the interior at Williams Lake, Kamloops and Revelstoke, while on Vancouver Island there were branches in Victoria, Nanaimo, and, not far north of Nanaimo, Wellington, a major mining center on the Island.[64]

After six years in Vancouver, in October 1892 Fay left Holy Rosary to return to his native Scotland, though his departure was largely precipitated by some of his financial dealings and other irregularities. As a pioneer priest, Fay was used to the rough and tumble of life, although in his case this also extended to speculation and profit, especially through the use of other people's money. Chief among them was his vision, by local standards, of a massive new Holy Rosary, foreseeing the likelihood that it might someday be a cathedral. Late in the 1880s he had a local architect, Charles Sorby draw up elaborate plans for the first large stone Catholic church on the mainland. By 1891 the accumulated and unpaid debt from this and other unauthorized projects that Fay had undertaken resulted in irate parishioners and creditors clamoring for both accountability and their money. Furious, Durieu asked for Fay's resignation. Among others, Sorby demanded payment of $3,000 for his architectural services. When Durieu only offered him $300, Sorby took his case to the Holy See. When Rome asked for an explanation, Durieu replied that Fay had plans for a church that would have cost the then incredible sum of over $150,000. Such a church, declared Durieu, would "never" be built in Vancouver, and since they had not authorized the idea, neither the bishop nor the parishioners were prepared to fully compensate Sorby. Sorby sued Durieu in a local court, but, in July 1895, unable to prove that Fay had permission from Durieu, Sorby's case was thrown out of court. The Fay incident was another example of some of the frequently "volunteered," independent minded, sometimes troublesome and problematic European clergy who worked in British Columbia.[65]

The parishioners of Holy Rosary, despite their problems with Fay, were determined to have a secular priest whose first language was English and who, unlike the Oblates, would give his undivided attention to the parish. It took about six months to find such a replacement, during which two Oblates from New Westminster, Jean-Marie Fayard (1889–98) and Irenée Jacob (1892–93) looked after Holy Rosary, until finally in April 1893 Henry Eummelen, a priest of the diocese of Leavenworth, Kansas arrived. Since the parishioners insisted upon having an anglophone and secular priest, Durieu decided that they should also be required to cover his expenses. Therefore, the bishop made a contract with Eummelen by which he would receive a monthly salary of $200, and, if he should become permanently disabled, a lifetime pension of $600. The salary was similar to that received by most of the local Protestant clergy, and it reflected both Eummelen's persuasiveness as well as his business acumen, part of the reason for his appointment. He was the type of priest that the parishioners of Holy Rosary were looking for, someone who was capable of both running a parish, but also was able to raise the funds necessary to cover his own expenses. The guarantors of his contract did not include the bishop, but only the parishioners. Except for the parish's payment to Durieu of an annual cathedraticum of $60, Holy Rosary was on its own with regard to the support of its new pastor.[66]

All of this was reflected in Eummelen's abilities as an organizer par excellence, clearly an important consideration in his appointment, high salary, contract and financial independence from Durieu. Soon he had established new societies to look after the needs of the parish and even divided it into seven districts, each with a committee from the Ladies Guild who were expected to visit the poor and sick and seek out lapsed Catholics and encourage their return. Within weeks of his arrival he began raising money for a new rectory through door-to-door solicitation. He soon completed a large facility that served that purpose for its priests and later two archbishops. This addition also meant that the original rectory, which was attached to the post-fire church, once the dividing wall was removed, would now accommodate almost 300 more people. Reflecting his independence from Bishop Durieu, and perhaps the growing strain between the Oblates and secular clergy, in January 1895 Eummelen invited the secular bishop of Victoria, John Lemmens (1888–97) to celebrate the inaugural Mass and preach in the "(practically) new church." No Oblate clergy took part in what was the first pontifical High Mass to take place in the city of Vancouver.[67]

Eummelen was also deeply involved in the development of St. Paul's Hospital, Vancouver, which opened in 1894 under the care of the Sisters of Providence. Eummelen was the person most responsible for raising the necessary funds for the new 25-bed facility, though the Sisters also contributed to its $27,000 construction cost by selling a form of early health insurance, then a common practice in most hospitals in British Columbia. In this case, the nuns sold tickets that entitled the bearer to a limited amount of medical care, but which did not cover any treatment for alcoholism. Again, in 1896 Eummelen single-handedly raised enough money for an ambulance, which had the most up-to-date equipment for the "painless moving" of patients, making St. Paul's one of the best equipped hospitals in the province.[68]

Perhaps reflecting his apparent independent ways, it is not surprising that, for his times, Eummelen was rather ecumenical. In 1894 he acted as treasurer of a grand concert sponsored by most of the clergy of the city as well as many businesses to raise money for the benefit of the city's large number of unemployed. Local merchants and everyone connected with the endeavor refused a salary. The event raised a considerable amount of money, all of which, after minimum expenses, was contributed to the city with the sole proviso that it could only be used as an unemployment fund.[69]

While appearances may have suggested otherwise, Eummelen and Durieu were on very good terms, and the latter was certainly impressed with Eummelen's abilities as a businessman and administrator, though their relationship would eventually end in disaster. While Eummelen was always sickly, his request to leave Vancouver in July 1898 for Rossland, B.C., was not purely for health reasons. In fact the three-year leave of absence appears to have been connected to a get-rich scheme that he convinced Durieu to join. Durieu constantly needed cash, since the support of the many and various diocesan undertakings, such as Nazareth Seminary, was never possible either through special collections or events, such as parish fairs. Thus the priest's desire to move to Rossland was to facilitate his involvement in the great mining boom in the Kootenays in 1896. While there were then dozens of firms operating in the Kootenays, Eummelen chose to invest in one of the largest, the Maple Leaf Mining and Development Company which owned a major share of 18 lead, silver and gold mining operations. Its one million one dollar shares were divided between the initial investors, who received one-third, Henry Eummelen, who represented Durieu, the largest single stock holder, who also held one-third, and the rest were to be offered to outside investors. To finance his share of such a massive outlay, in 1896 Durieu had sold the very valuable Oblate farm at the Okanagan Mission. Both Eummelan and Durieu also advertised and promoted the company among the clergy and laity throughout North America. In 1899, the year of Durieu's death, Eummelen, due to poor health, left Rossland for the sunnier climes of southern California. Over the next few years, Eummelen continued to capitalize the scheme, encouraging Dontenwill, Durieu's successor, to support him.[70]

However, even before Durieu's death and for some years thereafter, reports began to appear in the press questioning the solvency of the whole enterprise. On 20 April 1898, in the midst of the Spanish-American War, the *Los Angeles Daily Times* described Eummelen in very unflattering terms. Then visiting the area in order to raise funds for the mining enterprise, the paper described the priest, who was dark, as a Spanish spy, and that he was really there to inspect American naval defenses in order to facilitate a Spanish invasion of California. However, by 1902 reports were far more to the point, for in San Francisco, *The Monitor* declared that the whole mining scheme in British Columbia was a "gigantic swindle." While, after complaints from Eummelen, it later withdrew the accusation, it was too late to prevent a public panic.[71]

Anxious investors began to write, especially to Dontenwill, asking for reassurances. Some wondered if the bishop had any knowledge of the whole business. Others, in both Canada and the United States, complained that they had invested their entire life's savings in the venture because it was under the sponsorship of the church, and thus they assumed it must be safe. Undoubtedly exaggerating, one irate correspondent noted that the money forfeited in the scheme could have paid off the debts of many, if not most dioceses in North America. There is no indication of the actual sum that was lost, but it appears to have been considerable, and certainly the fault must be shared by many, but particularly Durieu and Eummelen. Clearly the most disastrous result for the Oblates was Durieu's foolish decision in 1896 to sell the valuable Oblate farm at the Okanagan Mission, an asset that they could ill afford to lose. Durieu was warned by his Oblate advisers not to do so, however, as a corporation sole, he could and did ignore their council. Even so, as late as 1911 Eummelen complained to Archbishop Sbarretti, the Apostolic Delegate in Ottawa that his letters both to Dontenwill, who was now the Oblate Superior General and Neil McNeil, then the archbishop of Vancouver, were being ignored. Eummelen insisted that both he and Durieu had only the best interests of the church at heart, though Eummelen implies he acted under directions from Durieu, who, being dead, was not there to defend himself. Certainly Eummelen appears to have been the main architect of the scheme. Without Durieu's help he could never have succeeded. Therefore, while both deserve a balanced share of the blame for helping to create the whole disaster, as the local bishop and leader, Durieu, who, no doubt, was often headstrong, authoritarian and a poor administrator, must assume the major responsibility.[72]

✤ The Beginning of the End of Oblate Dominance

EUMMELEN AND FAY demonstrated that with the dramatic rise of the mainly English speaking Euro-Canadian population in the province, the French-speaking Oblates, were becoming, at least for anglophone parishioners, a less desirable resource. Durieu tried to address this by assigning Oblates to Holy Rosary who spoke English as their mother tongue. Henry

Thayer and John Whelan, who had been recently ordained, spent time ministering in Vancouver. Although Whelan devoted eight (1894–1902) years to Holy Rosary Parish, and Thayer 14 (1913–27), they were often absent due to Oblate needs and commitments in other parts of the vicariate. Their place was usually taken temporarily by Oblate fill-ins who may or may not have spoken good English. By 1898 Durieu was conscious of the frustration felt by many Vancouver parishioners due to these frequent absences and rotations, but he insisted that he had no secular priest or anglophone Oblate whom he could assign there as a steady pastor.[73]

The Oblate personnel problem in Holy Rosary Parish reflected the general situation through the vicariate, and which were further compounded by events in France where, by 1880, growing government anticlericalism was making Oblate life there increasingly difficult. The demographic shift in British Columbia meant that the Native people no longer dominated the region's population, for over 25 years the ostensible Oblate raison d'être on the mainland. The most graphic result was the very rapid growth of urban centres on the lower mainland where most Europeans, mainly anglophones, settled. Unless the Oblates were able to provide large numbers of English-speaking clergy to meet these immediate needs, this new reality meant that they were certain to be passed over. In time, this would put pressure on Rome to appoint a secular bishop to lead the diocese, and the Oblates would again find themselves back under a secular ordinary with all the potential problems that such an arrangement usually entailed. In France, the church continued to support the return of the old order, and though Napoleon III and the Second Empire (1852–70) seemed to fulfil that dream, at least for some, the Franco-Prussian War (1870–71) ended it. With the founding of the Third Republic (1870–1940), it seemed that France had rejected monarchy and the old order. Since their foundation, the Oblates, like most French regulars or religious clergy, had not only supported a return to the old order, but also the growth of extreme ultramontanism. Due to their popularity in conservative circles, by 1878 regulars in France had increased to levels not seen in over a hundred years, and by then their numbers were three-times that of the secular clergy. Suspicions against regulars even under the old order had been strong, largely due to their international character, however, nineteenth century French nationalism further increased these attitudes. Hoping to undermine this predominance, in 1879 the French government passed a law that restricted their activities, especially in education, the major

Father Adrien-Gabriel Morice, 1896 (AD)

source of both their livelihood and social influence. However, far more ominous, it called for the expulsion of all unregistered male communities or those who had not gained government approval. Beginning with the Jesuits, then the largest French community, and perceived by many as the most anti-republican and ultramontane, by November 1880 all "other non-authorized male congregations" were ordered to leave the country. This directive included the Oblates who were "violently expelled from 17 of their [French] houses." Like most extreme solutions, by 1886 normality had more or less returned, however, it was clear that in France the regulars, including the Oblates, would never again regain their former prominence.[74]

One immediate effect of the crisis of 1880 was that it brought three Oblates to British Columbia, Nicolas di Coccola (1880–1943), Jean-Dominique Chiappini (1880–1912) and Adrien-Gabriel Morice (1880–1908), the largest number to arrive in the far west since 1847. Morice was by far the best known, mainly because he was the most contentious, and was certainly the most celebrated Oblate ever to work in British Columbia. During his years (1880–1908) there he would engage and enrage Oblates authorities both locally and in Europe, and in fact more than any other before or since.

After completing his theology under Alphonse Carion at St. Mary's Mission, Morice was ordained in 1882 and began a stormy career that taxed the patience of almost everyone. The Oblates would probably have expelled a less brilliant member, in fact the eccentricities of his fellow Frenchman and ethnologist, Émile Petitot (1838–1917), who worked in eastern Canada, finally lead to that extreme in 1886. Yet Morice far eclipsed Petitot, publishing numerous books and articles, mainly based upon his years among the Carrier at Stuart Lake (1885–1906), and which made him famous in intellectual circles. Impossible to live with, his superiors finally allowed him to retire to a private residence in Winnipeg, Manitoba where he continued to publish and remained an Oblate, though in name only, until his death on 21 April 1938.[75]

Morice was, without doubt, the most famous and, for many contemporary Oblates, infamous member of their Congregation to have ever worked in British Columbia. He deserves to be remembered as a scholar who was definitely a "misfit" as a missionary. He has been compared to his fellow missionary in British Columbia, the Anglican William Duncan. Duncan, like Morice, was also extremely out of place in the "white" world, and both men hungered for the isolation and control that a remote Native Mission could provide. However, unlike Morice, Duncan was a serious proselytizer, although Duncan did not share Morice's ability either in exploration or scholarship. Morice was quite talented, for, as his many writings testify, he was a very capable linguist, ethnologist and historian. His general history of the Catholic Church in Western Canada, a relatively small part of which deals with the far west, remains, to date, the only published work on the region. The Oblates, to their credit, recognizing his abilities, did try to compromise, and in the end, no doubt also fearing public scandal, allowed him to be himself. Perhaps one of the most telling and accurate judgements of the man was made by another Oblate, Pierre Dommeau (1892–98), who wisely noted regarding people such as Morice, that, while "brilliant," they too often were "consumed with pride, and then they become more foolish than the ignorant."[76]

While the crisis in France of 1880 brought three Oblates to British Columbia, that of 1901 provided the church there with twelve priests and one brother, the highest number in its history, although there were no "Morices" among them. Certainly the Dreyfus Affair (1894–98), one of those very dark pages in Catholic church history, fed French anticlericalism. As for liberal republicans, regulars headed their enemy list because of their international character as well as their strong involvement in private and often very exclusive secondary schools. For it was there that the liberals believed the regulars were making their most disruptive social contributions, especially in "negatively" influencing the children of the "upper echelons" of society.[77]

Under the Laws Concerning Associations of 1901, French religious congregations, especially male ones, were given three months to apply for official government recognition or face confiscation of their property and expulsion from France. Some refused to even bother, but chose to leave France or disperse, others, like the Oblates did seek authorization, but, like most, the government would ultimately reject their request. During 1903 and 1904 about twenty-thousand regulars were expelled. While the Oblates legally resisted, from March through June 1904 21 Oblate communities were dispersed and their property confiscated by the state. While the law allowed disbanded communities to regroup as "civil societies" with the right to "buy back confiscated property" from their new owners, by November 1905 the Oblates had made the definitive decision to move their central headquarters to Rome.[78]

Because many regulars had been chaplains in World War I, there was, after 1918, a great lessening of official hostility towards religious congregations in France. In response some Oblate houses were either re-established in the same or new locations. Yet, a decline in vocations as well as financial restraints, when coupled to the fear that similar, or even worse, state interference could well happen again, all these factors prevented and discouraged complete restoration. Thus, not only would the Oblates never again regain their former prominence in France, but Italy and Rome now replaced it as their European center and world headquarters.[79]

Because of the Laws Concerning Associations of 1901, for years French Oblates were, in effect, denied the right of French citizenship. Thus, fleeing this oppression, between 1901 and 1908 13 Oblates arrived in the diocese of New Westminster. Like a flame that flares the brightest just before it begins to die, this marked the beginning of the end of the French Oblate presence in far-western Canada. For of the 13, only two, one priest and one brother, were to die in British Columbia. Of the remaining eleven, two quit the Congregation to join the secular clergy, one died in Alberta, and eight, or almost two-thirds returned to France. Actually, out of a total of 61 Oblates who came to British Columbia between 1880 and 1908, 30 were from France, and of these four quit the Congregation, two died in the United States, ten in Canada (seven in B.C.), and almost half were to die in France. Of the fourteen who returned to France, all had left Canada well before the outbreak of World War II. For the French Oblates, who had founded the church on the mainland of British Columbia, it, indeed, marked the end of an era.[80]

By 1908, Rome finally recognized Vancouver, because of its dominant size, as the logical metropolitan, and so Victoria, demoted again to being a diocese, became one of its two suffragan sees, the other being the apostolic prefecture of the Yukon; whereas the diocese of New Westminster was suppressed. An Oblate, Augustin Dontenwill, the second bishop of New Westminster (1899–1908), became the first archbishop of Vancouver. The event appeared to mark a new beginning for the Oblates, who now had one of their own as

The Oblates at a retreat at New Westminster, 1908

(l–r) sitting: J. Welch, É. Grouard, A. Dontenwill, É. Bunoz, L. Lewis;

first row: A. Michaels, F.-M. Thomas, L. Choisel, A. Madden, E. Peytavin, J. Bédard,

E. Chirouse, J. Wagner, J. Rocher, L. Manceau, V. Rohr;

second row: V. Fazzolare, F. Beck, D. McCullough, J. Wagner,

J. Duplanil, P. Lepage, E. Lambot (AD)

the most important ordinary in the ecclesiastical province. Still, it was a distinction that was to be very short lived. For within a few months Dontenwill was elected the superior general of the Oblates, and soon afterwards resigned the archbishopric, and it would be 84 years (1992) before another Oblate, Archbishop Adam Exner would again head the archdiocese of Vancouver.

Had Dontenwill remained, and he lived until 1931, the Oblates might have continued to dominate the church in British Columbia, however, due to the steady decline in French Oblates, this was very unlikely. The great increase in anglophone settlers to the region further hastened it. By 1911, the Native people, once dominant, were barely five percent of the population. While Catholic Church development was naturally strongest in the southern half of the mainland of the British Columbia, where most of the new population and economic boom was taking place, other regions were also showing signs of

The Years After the Railroad

growth and change. Around the turn of the century it appeared that, outside Vancouver, Prince Rupert would be the next major city on the mainland, a belief that was further strengthened when it become the northern terminus of the Grand Trunk Pacific Railway (GTPR). Because of its location and ice-free harbor, its promoters were convinced, with what they envisioned as a guarantee of huge population shifts north, that Prince Rupert would soon surpass even Vancouver. Yet economic power was still concentrated in eastern Canada, and Prince Rupert was just too far west. Before the railway was even completed in 1914, the expected economic dream had collapsed and the federal government finally had to take over the bankrupt GTPR. Unlike the CPR, which had given birth to Vancouver, the folly of the GTPR doomed Prince Rupert. In fact, Stephen Leacock, a professor of economics at McGill University and perhaps Canada's best known humorist, dubbed the GTPR a railroad "from nowhere to nowhere, passing nowhere," and so by the 1950s the regional center had moved to Prince George. However, in 1908, when the boom in Prince Rupert still seemed certain, Rome added a third ecclesiastical district to the far west, the apostolic prefecture of the Yukon. In 1917 it was raised to the next ecclesiastical grade of apostolic vicariate of the Yukon and Prince Rupert. Both the prefecture and vicariate had their first centre at Prince Rupert, although, reflecting economic shifts, it would eventually be moved to Prince George. Geographically it covered the northern half of the province and the Yukon Territory, and had an Oblate, Émile Bunoz (1908–44) as its first bishop.[81]

✤ New Oblate Policies and Lay Demands

DONTENWILL WAS NOT DURIEU. Perhaps it had to do with his background; Dontenwill had spent most of his career as an educator. Immediately after ordination, he became a professor at the University of Ottawa (1885–89), and then was the director (1889–97) of both St. Louis College and Nazareth Seminary in New Westminster. What is more important, Dontenwill loved the world of formal learning, and he appears to have had few real interests outside of it.[82]

When Dontenwill became an ordinary in 1899, chief among his objectives was to shift directions away from the more traditional types of Oblate ministry to the Native people. The central point that influenced this change was the enormous growth in the local Euro-Canadian population. He also viewed it as good missiology for all concerned. The past experience of the Oblates had shown that most Euro-Canadians who came to British Columbia were not interested in taking part in organized religion. He apparently hoped that the latest arrivals would act differently. By the end of his first five years as the local ordinary and vicariate superior, Dontenwill appears to have convinced most of his Oblate colleagues that they could best continue their ministry among the Native people by shifting their emphasis to the larger society. In so doing, he believed they would help the aboriginals follow their example. By 1904, the Oblates, with the vital assistance of several orders of religious women, had begun to spend far more time working among the European population, both in parishes and other ministries.[83]

During the 1880s and 1890s the railroad had produced mines, sawmills and towns in the interior where only a few years before there had been nothing but forests. French Oblates were active in many of these regions. In Revelstoke, a young Rémi Pécoul (1906–08) served a community of approximately 60 families made up of English and Italians who, under his guidance, were able to build a new church. Pécoul also noted the presence of at least another two to three hundred or so, at best nominal, Catholic families in the surrounding area whom he hoped would eventually join the local congregation. However, in 1909 Pécoul decided to become a secular priest. To do so on the mainland church would have meant a priest would still have been in a very distinct minority, for at the time there were no more than five secular or diocesan clergy working anywhere in what was the archdiocese of Vancouver. Therefore, after spending two years (1908–09) in Vernon, Pécoul left the Oblates and Canada and became a secular priest in the diocese of Boise, Idaho where he ministered until his death in 1950. In Kamloops, André Michels (1899–1909), who replaced Charles Marchal in 1905 as Mission superior, concentrated on his work as pastor of the local parish of the Sacred Heart. There he enlarged the church, added stained glass windows, new pews and installed a rebuilt furnace.[84]

Immigration continued to influence the church's growth in the area. In Cranbrook, St. Eugene's Hospital, still under the Sisters of Providence, witnessed a sizable addition. Again, in 1901 population expansion and the need for health care prompted the Sisters of St. Joseph of Peace to open Sacred Heart Hospital in the mining town of Greenwood. The veteran, city-loving Oblate, Norbert Ouellette had been in Cranbrook since 1896, where he had not only built the first church, but by 1904 he was forced to enlarge it. He was soon replaced by another young French Oblate, Louis Choisnel, who spent many years (1904–37) in parish work throughout the interior and the lower mainland. Since 1903 Coccola, then in residence at St. Eugene's Mission in the Kootenay, spent his summers establishing parishes in Michel, Morrissey and Fernie. At Michel he reported that there were upwards of two to three thousand Catholics. Among these there were some anglophones from the British Isles as well as Canada. Most were immigrants from Eastern Europe, including Russians, Poles, Czechs, Slovaks, and Hungarians, although Italians were also among them, and some of whom could even speak a little English. Coccola mused, among the non-English speakers who showed any interest in Catholicism, most demanded the impossible, namely a church dedicated to their culture and a priest who was fluent in their mother tongue. François-Régis Lardon (1902–37), who had just arrived from France in 1902, and who initially spoke little English, was then (1904) trying to cope with the non-French speaking influx of immigrants, again mainly from Eastern Europe, around the railway divisional point of Revelstoke. Another recently (1899) arrived French Oblate, Jacques Wagner was then ministering in Wardner and Moyie, and like Choisnel, he too would devote much of his life (1901–31) working in "white" parishes throughout the region. Such was the steady growth in large areas of the interior that some Catholic newcomers called for Catholic schools as well as parishes. Their desire arose from their initial discomfort of sending their offspring to public institutions where they would soon become not only Canadianised, but far worse, lose their cultural heritage. Thus their parents' desire for parochial schools was prompted not by religion, but ethnicity. In response to this concern, by 1908, Choisnel was making plans to open a parish school in Cranbrook.[85]

Unfortunately, many of the new communities had a very unstable economic base that depended on such factors as the constantly fluctuating price of metals. These economic problems affected the health of the local church. In Greenwood, the collapse of copper prices after World War I reduced it to a ghost town and thus ended the short life (1901–18) of its Sacred Heart Hospital. In the Williams Lake region, ranching had replaced the mining boom of the 1860s as the area's economic foundation. There François Thomas complained that, while there was indeed a solid European population base, most Euro-Canadians, due to the rapidly shifting labor environment, never seemed to stay put in one place for very long. Thus by 1904 he reported that the population had declined by at least a thousand, but that probably only 3000 "whites" and about 700 Chinese still remained there. He estimated that of these, about five to six hundred were Catholic, but while many were friendly towards him, they had little or no interest in practicing their faith, or for that matter any religion, though, much to his distress, a handful had become "heretics," that is Protestants. Somewhat naively, Thomas was certain that if Catholic schools were established in the region, their graduates would soon form a core of solid believers who, with their children similarly educated, would then ensure the future of the local church.[86]

This lack of interest among Catholics was also reflected in the Fraser Valley. By 1905, six Oblates: Victor Rohr (1898–39), Pierre Plamondon (1913–26), Peytavin, Chirouse, Fouquet, and Jean-Marie Tavernier (1899–1915) were visiting Euro-Canadian settlements in Lytton, Ashcroft, Lillooet, Yale, Hope, Agassiz, Harrison and Mission. However, like Thomas, Chirouse ruefully noted that, while there were "white" Catholics throughout the Fraser region, and in some areas in fairly large numbers, they did not seem to feel any need or desire either to come to church, and worse, to support it or its clergy. In an attempt to address the issue, Chirouse concluded in a letter to his superior, that if Dontenwill wrote a pastoral on this subject, and presumably published it in the local press, it might have the desired results of increasing both attendance and support. At Mission, Tavernier, rejecting the evidence of his colleagues and in a definite pollyannaish mood, was certain that the church had a very bright future, since, with the notable except of the Métis, according to Tavernier, all of the "white" Catholics were eager to learn about their faith.[87]

This, at the very best, lukewarm condition in other areas of the mainland church was not necessarily reflected in 1904 in New Westminster were at least the Euro-Canadian population was growing. The continued expansion of a handful of Catholic institutions there—St. Ann's Academy, St. Mary's Hospital, St. Louis College, the Providence Orphanage and Nazareth Seminary, though by no means all—reflected the growth. Moreover, the Royal City was the location of two important public establishments, the federal Penitentiary and the provincial Insane Asylum. At the Penitentiary, according to Peytanin, the superior at St. Charles, there were about 40 Catholics inmates in 1904 and one Protestant under instruction, all of whom attended Sunday Mass when a chaplain was available. This was also the case with the Asylum, and though Peytavin does not indicate the number of its Catholic patients, one of its early superintendents, Dr. James Doherty was a Catholic. St. Ann's Academy, with well over 80 boarders, was in Peytavin's view the only bright spot in the local Catholic education scene. St. Louis College, Peytavin noted that, though not necessarily near death, was barely holding its own, and he hoped that Oblates throughout the diocese would redouble their efforts in encouraging parents to send their sons there. However, Peytavin believed that a miracle would be necessary to rescue the Nazareth Seminary, since by 1904 it had only five students, and, it would close in 1909. In 1900 the Sisters of Providence had also reestablished a orphanage, Providence St. Genevieve, on a new site after a 1899 fire had destroyed a previous one located in Sapperton. In their new facility the nuns cared for about 60 children, either because they were orphans or because their parents could no longer support them. Finally, St. Mary's Hospital, since it drew on the general population for its survival, seemed quite healthy in 1904.[88]

St. Peter's Cathedral parish in New Westminster in 1904, appeared in reasonably good condition, though there were also difficulties. There, over 700 mainly anglophone Canadians were being looked after by an Oblate Irishmen, John O'Neill (1900–1928). Certainly its finances appeared buoyant, especially since the parish had recently burned the mortgage on the church. However, there were also indications of problems as well. The mortgage on St. Patrick's Hall continued to drain parish finances, since, except for parish activities, there was little public demand for the facility and an opportunity to raise the funds needed to clear its mortgage. There was a continuing interest in lay associations such as the Young Men's Institute, as well as others, which implied that things were at least stable, if not growing.[89]

However, nowhere was the new reality that Dontenwill was trying to instill in his fellow Oblates more obvious than in Holy Rosary, Vancouver, still its only parish. By 1904 it was without question the most flourishing one on the mainland. During this period (1899–1914), James McGuckin, John Whelan, Pierre Plamondon (1898–1955) and Pierre-Louis LeChesne (1899–1914) worked there to meet its many needs. In response to its steady growth, one of the first acts of the indefatigable McGuckin was to build the present church, which would eventually become Holy Rosary Cathedral.

Given the new vision that he was promoting, it was certainly a decision that Dontenwill fully supported. For only a few years before almost everyone, including the laity, would have agreed with Durieu, who, in 1894, predicted that the number of Catholics in Vancouver would never justify such a large edifice. However, a firm supporter of Dontenwill's outlook for the future, McGuckin set about building a new Holy Rosary, which probably remains the largest church on the mainland, and certainly was and remains the most significant stone church in

Father John J. Whelan (AD)

the archdiocese. Its construction also symbolized a new optimism among local Catholics, apparently, and not surprisingly, sparked by McGuckin who was convinced that there would be no end to Vancouver's growth. Therefore, in order to bring his dream to fruition, and with Dontenwill's enthusiastic blessing, in 1899 he hired the architectural firm of T.E. Julian and H.J. Williams. The position of general builder and contractor was given to R.P. Forshaw and Company. Similar to St. Andrew's Cathedral in Victoria, although it is built in red brick, the architects also selected a neo-Gothic, asymmetric design. As to size, it also imaged St. Andrew's, with its tallest tower rising to 246 feet, its transept measuring 104 feet, and its overall length being 160 feet. Reflecting New Westminster's suffragan connection, its corner stone was laid on the 16 July 1899 by the Oblate archbishop of St. Boniface, Adélard Langevin (1895–1915) who, on the same day, had installed Dontenwill as the second (1899–1908) bishop of New Westminster at St. Peter's Cathedral. Celebrating its completion and Vancouver's growing national status, on the 21 October 1900, a peal of seven bells, which had been cast in Savoy, France, was "christened" by the apostolic delegate to Canada, Diomede Falconio. The bells were eventually hung and change rung, that peculiarly English method of ringing bells. Today Holy Rosary has one of only three such peals in British Columbia, the other two being at the Anglican Cathedral of Christ Church in Victoria, and Westminster Abbey, Mission. Finally, perhaps as a sign of Oblate goodwill, on the 9 December 1900, Alexander Christie, the sixth and former bishop of Victoria (1898–99), now the fourth (1899–1925) archbishop of Portland, Oregon was invited to bless the church.[90]

The Years After the Railroad

While such events seemed to confirm McGuckin's optimism, Durieu's earlier and far less sanguine view was not unjustified. For by the standards of British Columbia, where organized religion remained a very low priority for most of its citizens, the new church would eventually prove to be an albatross around the diocesan neck. As graphic proof of the enormity of such an undertaking for the still struggling Catholic congregation, for years Holy Rosary was referred to as "McGuckin's Folly." In 1917 the Ontario born Oblate and Pastor, William P. O'Boyle (1913–27), of what by then was the pro-cathedral, noted sarcastically in *The Monthly Bulletin*, that, while Holy Rosary might be "a thing of beauty," it was not necessarily "a joy forever." The situation was made far worse by the single tax system. For decades the annual upkeep and debt repayment on the cathedral proved to be a terrible drain on diocesan finances. Even in the best of times, local church donations were never in ready supply, reflecting the lack of interest in church attendance among most of the area's largely nominal Catholics, and, when they did, the often miserliness of their contributions. There were few leading Catholics in the city who might have contributed and encouraged others to give, for while in 1891 11.5 per cent of the population was Catholic, none of these qualified as "business leaders." By 1911, the Catholic population had fallen to 10.2 per cent and overall only 6.4 per cent of Catholics were commercially significant. In fact, Protestants were not only the largest religious group in Vancouver, their members dominated the most "respectable" classes, whereas Catholics as a whole were in the working class. This was particularly the case among Italian labourers, who were "concentrated in the east end of Strathcona," and who not only shared the lowest rung of that ladder with non-Christian Asians, but their part of town was the only one that had "any claim to being an 'ethnic' neighborhood." Also, the hard economic times that lay ahead, due to local land speculation, the single tax system and the Great Depression that followed, made the diocesan financial situation far worse. It is no surprise that for many years, the wisdom of McGuckin's original decision was called into question.[91]

During the early years of the new century, most indications were that things were, indeed, going fairly well, especially in Vancouver. A strong indication of the more settled nature of the local society came in 1906 when Holy Rosary inaugurated the first Canadian Council of the Knights of Columbus west of Winnipeg. The Knights had been initially established in the United States in 1882, with the first Canadian council being founded in

Montreal in 1897. Reflecting it working class roots, the K of C started as a small philanthropic organization that principally contributed modest burial benefits to the families of deceased knights. And this was the major purpose of the Holy Rosary Council. Among the 64 charter members at Holy Rosary were the Oblates: Ambrose Madden, Ernest Connolly and John Welch. Its first grand knight was William Hickey. James D. Byrne, who had been instrumental in founding the local branch of the Young Men's Institute, and was then a prominent real estate agent and the first administrator and county assessor for the city, became its territorial deputy and, in 1910, its first provincial deputy. In 1907, a second Council was begun in St. Peter's Cathedral Parish, New Westminster. As well as the pastor, William P. O'Boyle, it had 35 charter members, with Peter Byrne as its grand knight. One the signs of change was the YMI, which had been inaugurated in 1892 to help its members meet suitable marriage partners. Yet, by 1906, because of the great swell in immigration both in Vancouver and the province, especially of women, the YMI had begun to outlive its main raison d'être. Therefore, its members, who chose to join another Catholic body, would obviously have gravitated towards the K of C.[92]

Another sign of Vancouver's growth had came in 1905, when Dontenwill opened its second parish, Sacred Heart, on the east side of the city, a strong working class area, which contained a large Italian immigrant population. He dedicated the first church on the 3 September 1905. When its founding pastor and Oblate, Norbert Ouellette died in 1907, he was replaced by another Oblate, François-Régis Lardon (1907–11) who was assisted by a colleague, Jeannes-Marius Duplanil (1908–11), who had just arrived from France. Sacred Heart would become the foundation of other parishes in that part of Vancouver and it was also there that several new lay organizations were founded. The first was the Catholic Order of Foresters, which always had a strong non-Irish, especially Italian membership, since its beginnings in Chicago in 1883. While it was involved in parish charitable and social activities, its major purpose, like the Irish-dominated Knights of Columbus, was to supply funeral insurance for the families of its members, though, unlike the Knights, it also had a branch for women. However, it reflected a society in which, for most people, voluntarism was still, outside their immediate families, the only source of support in times of social need. Except for public education, most citizens still believed that the larger community should not be taxed in order that the state might provide what would become a far more equitable and adequate method of providing such necessities, especially health care and old-age insurance. Therefore, in voluntarism's well-meaning, but always deficient attempt to address public suffering, to complement the Foresters, in 1911 a similar volunteer body, the Ladies' Benevolent Society was inaugurated at Sacred Heart.[93]

Certainly women formed the core of most voluntarist organizations, whether Catholic or not, since they were far more aware than men of the social shortcomings of their society, not only its disregard of women, but also its harsh treatment of its most vulnerable members, its children. Like women, both religious and lay, children, until this century, have been the forgotten members of most western societies, and this was true in British Columbia. Children were traditionally viewed as potential adults, thus, like adults, they began to work as soon as possible, especially if they were members of the poor or working classes. In time, in line with the gradual public recognition of women's rights, especially in the suffragette movement, the rights of children also began to be viewed as important, and deserving of legal protection.[94]

In 1901, in line with this crucial challenge, which was spear-headed by the local Women's Christian Temperance Union, a Protestant organization, British Columbia enacted the first Child Protection Act, which was intended to assist in looking after "neglected and dependent" children. Because of racism, it was limited to "neglected and dependent" Euro-Canadian children. However, except for children who would be placed with volunteer organizations, either nonsectarian or denominational, through court intervention, until 1910 no public money was available for such work. Therefore, the local Catholic Church, like other churches, set up bodies such as the Catholic Children's Aid Society, which had branches in both the dioceses of Vancouver and Victoria, and where clergy assigned children to Catholic volunteer foster families. As an expected reward for their role in caring for such children, if they were not already baptized members, most denominations, including the Catholic Church, usually set out to proselytize their new dependents, with the hope that ultimately they would gain more "converts."[95]

In Vancouver, the Catholic Children's Aid Society was headed by the Ottawa born Oblate, Ambrose Madden, who was then (1902–12) a priest at Holy Rosary Parish. Assisting Madden were his English-born Oblate colleague, John Welch, who was also stationed (1904–21) at Holy Rosary, and where they were joined by five lay collaborators: James Foran, James Byrne,

Azilda Martin, Catherine Tierney, and Lewis G. McPhillips, a prominent barrister. On the 25 August 1905 Victoria chartered the Catholic Children's Aid Society of Vancouver, with Byrne as its first president and Madden its secretary. Its first act was to assume responsibility for 15 children who until then were under the care of the non-sectarian Children's Aid Society of Vancouver, which was also finding it increasingly difficult to meet the growing demand.[96]

Within a year similar church communities throughout the diocese were attempting to duplicate their activities. As in Vancouver, pastors usually acted as agents, who accepted children committed to their care by the courts and who placed such children in foster homes or in church-run orphanages. Since there was no provincial financial assistance, the volunteer bodies also had to raise their own funds to cover operating expenses. The clergy who acted as agents in the interior included Michels, Tavernier, Althoff, Choisnel, Heynan, and McKinner. Orphanages were then the overwhelming caretakers, whereas foster families were a very secondary alternative, unless the child was to be legally adopted. Thus, in the case of Catholics, the children were usually were placed with the Sisters of Our Lady of Charity of Refuge at Good Shepherd Monastery in Vancouver, who also had established a school there for delinquent girls. In addition, they were also sent to the Sisters of Providence at Providence St. Genevieve Orphanage in New Westminster.[97]

Because of the great need, such voluntarism was soon overwhelmed, and by end of 1907 and early 1908, Holy Rosary Children's Aid Society was petitioning the equally hard-pressed and nonsectarian Children's Aid Societies of both New Westminster and Vancouver to assume responsibility for most their charges. It was not until 1914 that the province began to provide the bulk of the financial support for homeless or abandoned children. Then it would usually be in the form of grants to orphanages, for they were the cheapest solution. In 1920 the Legislative Assembly of British Columbia passed the "Mothers' Pension Act" that allowed women, who also had income from employment, to withdraw their children from orphanages. Nevertheless, in the 1930s, as the tax base almost disappeared, this support ended and it would not be until the 1950s and 1960s before other, more adequate and successful alternatives, such as provincially funded adoption schemes, would be considered.[98]

Although voluntarism, Catholic and otherwise, attempted, though largely unsuccessfully to address the very serious problems of neglected and needy children in British Columbia, it had proven itself far more capable in other, more traditional areas, especially education and healthcare. Certainly, voluntarism greatly influenced the expansion of Catholic education and health care in Vancouver, as elsewhere in the province. The work of religious women remained the essential backbone of such ministries. Clearly education and nursing were the core ministries of most nuns, and this was certainly true of the Sisters of St. Ann who in 1888 founded Sacred Heart Academy for girls near Holy Rosary. To complement it, in 1901 the nuns opened St. Mary's School for boys on Richards Street. Private "finishing" schools for girls were always in much greater public demand than private schools for boys. Given this attitude, it is no surprise that in 1903 the Sisters of St. Ann were able to open a second boarding school for girls, named after their historic foundation in Victoria, St. Ann's Academy, and which was located on Homer Street.[99]

Another example of the vital importance of religious communities was St. Paul's Hospital, Vancouver, founded by the Sisters of Providence in 1899. Yet they would not have been able to expand their work in 1903 without the fundraising and other efforts of the Ladies of Charity of St. Paul's, which was made up of lay women volunteers. With the aim of better preparing the ladies for their duties, in 1908, the Sisters opened a training program for full-time and volunteer nurses, which would eventually become its School of Nursing. Like its counterpart at St. Joseph's Hospital in Victoria, the School reflected the increasing professionalism of Catholic nursing, although student nurses, who were unpaid, also provided hospitals with a cheap labour force.[100]

By 1908 Catholic religious community supported hospitals and orphanages, especially those led by women, when combined with lay voluntarism, provided an important, thought still very inadequate social safety net in British Columbia. This was certainly due in part to the fact that their focus tended to be narrowly denominational in character. Despite this, such services had and would continue to contribute some of the only "works of mercy." "Works of justice" would have to wait for many more years until British Columbian society was prepared to take responsibilities, especially through taxation, of providing more inclusive and equitable answers for such important social needs.

14

The Oblates and the
First Secular Archbishops

✤ *New Leadership in Vancouver*

WHEN ARCHBISHOP DONTENWILL resigned in 1908 to become the
Oblate superior general, his place was immediately taken by another
Oblate, the English-born, John Welch. Welch became the apostolic adminis-
trator (1908–10) of Vancouver as well as the Oblate vicar of Missions. In 1910
Rome appointed a new metropolitan, a Nova Scotian secular or diocesan
cleric, Neil McNeil (1910–12).

The numbers of secular or diocesan clergy, though still a very definite
minority on the mainland, were increasing. While the Oblates continued to
dominate the clerical scene up to this period, Dontenwill had realized that
English-speaking clergy, who reflected the cultural realities of the region,
were essential to the future of the diocese. As the French Oblate recruits
continued to decline, Dontenwill knew that they would have to curtail their
ministry in far-western Canada. Patrick Fay had been the only secular to
work under D'Herbomez, although Durieu welcomed five more: Arthur
Lemay, Henry Eummelen, Joseph Accorsini, John Welch and Henry Thayer.

Demonstrating their continued and very strong influence in the region, and the historic tensions between the secular and regular clergy, of the five only Welch (1903–44) and Thayer (1909–43) remained, and both eventually became Oblates. During his tenure (1899–1908), Dontenwill added five more secular priests to the diocese. John Althoff, a Belgian, had worked for years in the diocese of Victoria, and, under Seghers, had become a founding pastor in Alaska where he spent 14 (1878–84; 1886–94), largely fruitless and frustrating years trying to establish a parish in Wrangell. Unhappy with Bishop Orth (1900–1903), in 1902 Althoff decided to leave (excardinate from) Victoria and join (incardinate to) the diocese of New Westminster. There he spend ten (1902–12) years ministering in Nelson before becoming the vicar general of the archdiocese of Vancouver and pastor of Sacred Heart, Vancouver, holding both offices until his death in 1926. Little is known of the other four, except where and when they ministered. Charles Pelletier worked first in Lumby (1908–11), then Maillardville, which had a significant francophone community, at last moving to Grand Forks (1914–17), where he died. Another diocesan priest, Désiré Jeannotte ministered at Sandon (1908–12) and then Lumby (1913) before his death. Emmanuel Garon served in Vernon (1907–12) and later, until his death, in Maillardville (1912–15). Kelowna had Francis Verbeke (1908–17) as their pastor, the last of the five seculars.[1]

Since the Oblates remained the major clerical force in the archdiocese in 1908, there was still an expectation that an Oblate would succeed Dontenwill; Welch was mentioned as a possible replacement. The major problem was that, although the Oblates remained very prominent in 1908, most were Frenchmen who did not reflect the anglophone dominance in British Columbia. Even if an English speaking Oblate such as Welch were appointed archbishop, he would also be the head of the Oblate vicariate, which remained largely French. He would be expected to lead two clerical groups, the slowly growing secular clergy, mainly anglophone, and the francophone Oblates, which would have added linguistic divisions and tensions to the traditional clerical ones between regulars and seculars. It was a situation that few would have relished.

Certainly Welch appreciated these serious barriers. Given what he believed would be a temporary position and also because of the limited canonical authority of an apostolic administrator, he did little during this short period. Yet he did begin to plan for a third parish in Vancouver, which

Most Reverend Neil McNeil, D.D., Archbishop of Vancouver (AD)

would eventually become St. Patrick's. One of the first acts of the new arch-bishop was to inaugurate St. Patrick's and to assign Welch (1911–21) to be its first pastor. Sometime in 1909, Welch also initiated the publication of the *B.C. Western Catholic*, which, even more than *The Month* (1892–96), tried on a regular basis to provide its readers with news from around the "Catholic world," but especially local church news. After two years as apostolic administrator, Welch finally turned over his responsibilities to the second archbishop of Vancouver, Neil McNeil (1910–12).[2]

McNeil, the first of three Maritimers who would head Vancouver between 1910 and 1964, was a priest of the diocese of Antigonish, Nova Scotia. After completing his studies in Rome and his ordination there in 1879, McNeil became rector of St. Francis Xavier College in Antigonish as well as the founding editor in 1881 of a local Catholic news organ, *The Aurora*. Among its principal readership were the fishermen of Nova Scotia. Under McNeil the paper's major editorial theme centered upon Catholic concepts of labor justice, which were also the focus of *The Casket*, which he bought in 1890 and turned into what remains the diocesan newspaper for Antigonish.[3]

His Catholic journalistic-based "activism" and his continued Roman contacts fostered McNeil's career advancement. His promotion of labor unions that were effectively under company and/or clerical control reflected the principles that would eventually be advocated by the Confederation of Canadian Catholic Labourers (CCCL) founded in 1921. The labor philosophy of McNeil and the CCCL was based on *Rerum Novarum* (1891), the pro labor encyclical of Leo XIII (1878–1903), which was in effect a call to rein in extreme or laissez-faire capitalism in favor of what might be called Catholic "corporate paternalism." By looking after their workers' basic needs, Leo believed managers and/or capitalists would make worker-controlled labor unions unnecessary, especially their implicit threat of socialism, which Rome believed totally undermined the "natural law," particularly in the area of private property ownership. While this was a traditional Catholic position, since the Holy See was still smarting over its loss of the Papal States to Italy in 1870, Leo was even more prepared to defend the status quo against the supposed "moral evils" of all forms of socialism. In championing such an approach to unions, McNeil endeared himself to Rome, which ultimately appointed him to be the first vicar apostolic (1895–1904) and then bishop (1904–10) of the diocese of St. George, Newfoundland. There he would continue his Catholic form of labor advocacy through *The Western Star,* which he purchased in 1901. As archbishop of Vancouver and then Toronto (1912–34), he was the first Canadian bishop to strongly promote the "humanization" of capitalism as outlined in *Rerum Novarum*.[4]

The only example McNeil provided in Vancouver of his classist view of labor was a Labour Day pastoral or circular letter he published in August 1912, shortly before he left for Toronto. In it he strongly advocated Leo XIII's "paternalistic" approach to the labor question as a guarantee of both equitable profits and wages, that, more importantly, would prevent employees from being "tempted" to join worker-controlled unions, or, far worse, be "damned" into becoming "godless" socialists. Mimicking Pope Leo, McNeil noted that the first "social question" for Vancouver's Catholic clergy was "how to assure normal domestic life to the poor." The great danger for both owners and workers were the "false ideas and false theories issuing in hostile relations between labor and capital," that is, traditional unionism and, its major "horrid" bedfellow, socialism. Instead, McNeil advised his clergy to encourage their "Catholic workmen" to have an "active interest" only in unions that encouraged cooperation "between labour and capital," and that ideally should be under clerical control. Such reactionary solutions would never be adopted in British Columbia, where labor was then far more radical than in either Atlantic Canada or Quebec.[5]

McNeil had similar classist attitudes towards education, which he also imported from his eastern experience and that he hoped to establish in British Columbia. The strong economic growth there seemed to encourage such an approach. Vancouver, the center of the archdiocese, was going through another one of its early boom phases. By 1910, the city contained almost 50 percent of the province's "white" population. Because the extraordinary speed of its development was based on male-dominated industries, notably mining and lumber, there were one and a half times as many men as women in British Columbia. Since organized religion has always been a largely female-supported phenomenon, this reality further compounded the area's already marked indifference to churches and public worship. These circumstances therefore would make McNeil's plans, especially prompting Catholic parochial education, impossible to implement.[6]

As in the labor question, McNeil was convinced that he could apply another eastern solution in British Columbia, this time in education, namely, that the parochial school built the parish church. He immediately began putting his scheme into practice, theorizing that by building schools that could double as churches, he would soon be able to add a parish church, assuming that such parish schools would have wide support among the laity. Initially he even planned, in order to save money, one large, centrally located convent where all of the nuns would live who were to teach in the proposed schools, and from which they would travel by tram to the parish school to which they would be assigned. By 1912, with this master plan in mind, McNeil had opened five new parishes in greater Vancouver: St. Patrick's (1910), St. Augustine's (1911), St. Andrew's (1911), St. Joseph's (1911) and St. Helen's (1912). Thus, with Holy Rosary (1880) and Sacred Heart (1905), to seven parishes had been created since the city had been founded only 26 years before. Greater New Westminster had, after 50 years, only one parish, and in greater Victoria, after 66 years, the church still had only two parishes, St. Andrew's Cathedral and St. Joseph's in Esquimalt.

Still, such rapid additions did seem logical, since Vancouver contained half the province's Euro-Canadian population, whereas, Victoria and New Westminster combined contained only 25 percent of the local "white" people. Nevertheless, this rapid expansion was postulated on a principle that had never been tested in British Columbia, namely, that the parishes would prosper because of lay support for parochial day schools.[7]

This educational philosophy worked well in the east, especially since tax money there had long supported separate school systems. But this idea could not be transferred to British Columbia, which had long rejected the idea of public financial support for denominational schools. The Sisters of St. Ann had established three schools in Vancouver: Sacred Heart (1888) and St. Ann's (1904), both of which were boarding schools for girls, and in 1901, they founded a similar one (St. Mary's) for boys. While all of these schools had day students, boarders, who paid at least twice as much, were considered essential to their economic survival, and a significant number of their pupils were also non-Catholic. Now, McNeil wanted the Sisters to abandon a successful format that they had been following for over 50 years. Instead, he expected them to adopt one that local history showed would fail since most parents preferred, whether Catholic or not, to use free, tax supported public schools.[8]

McNeil supported the idea of boarding schools, but again they were based on a definite class bias. This is clear in his decision to invite the Madames of the Sacred Heart, known for their exclusive eastern schools for the daughters of upper-class Catholics, to establish a similar boarding school for girls in Vancouver. In a 1912 article in the *B.C. Western Catholic*, McNeil advocated that the daughters of the Catholic upper or upper middle classes should now be entrusted to the "greatest teaching order in the old country, the Dames of the Sacred Heart." If his advice were followed, McNeil continued, "no wealthy man needs to entrust his daughters to eastern, old country, or foreign convents for the completion of their education, for right in Vancouver, in the Convent of the Sacred Heart Dames, may be secured an education and a finish rarely equaled in any other institution." McNeil also believed that an industrial-domestic education was the best one for lower or lower-middle class Catholic girls, such as in the day schools that he hoped would soon be in operation under the "good nuns of St. Ann." McNeil's idea was certainly "foreign" when it came to understanding British Columbia, and therefore it would not work. The region, already disinterested in organized religion, was cool, if not cold to rigid eastern class-consciousness. For though class certainly played an important role in British Columbian society, it was assumed that anyone who could pay was free to send their daughter to a girls' boarding school, and that such an education was not to be ostensibly restricted to the "wealthy."[9]

McNeil tried to follow a similar classist scheme in boy's education, with even worse results. Some middle-class Catholics and non-Catholic parents were willing to send their daughters to what were viewed as "finishing" schools, such as the academies conducted by the Sisters of St. Ann. However, far fewer saw any need to send their sons to male equivalents, especially when public schools were available and, far more importantly, free. With little awareness of, or, if so, with apparent disregard of this local reality, McNeil invited the English Benedictines to come to Vancouver. Like the Madames, they too were known for operating upper-class Catholic prep schools. When he was unable to convince the Benedictines to establish a new school, McNeil asked the Oblates at St. Louis College, New Westminster, if they would accept some Benedictines on their staff, with the clear implication that they would eventually take over that institution. In reply, the Oblate head (1906–13) of the school, William O'Boyle (1906–49) informed McNeil that even in the best of times, due mainly to a lack of enrolment, St. Louis could barely survive. In a clear criticism of the strong classism contained in McNeil's educational philosophy, who was, by then, the archbishop of Toronto, O'Boyle retorted: "we are a little short of what the Torontonians call 'Culchaw.'"[10]

All this potential growth in church infrastructure also meant that it was necessary for McNeil to purchase land at a period when property prices were extremely high throughout the province. In 1912 in Victoria and Vancouver land values began to collapse virtually bankrupting both dioceses. In line with his expansion plans, by 1911, McNeil, and the investors he convinced to join him, had become major land speculators purchasing a total of over 7000 acres in Pitt Meadows, Shannon Park, New Westminster, Burnaby and West Vancouver. McNeil's investments were possible since as a corporation sole, under secular law he owned all of the real assets of the archdiocese. Reflecting again his strong class bias, he advertised the lots in these various locations for "high-class buildings." Clearly his target was the well-to-do, if not wealthy Catholic, who at the time would have been a very tiny minority in the area.[11]

By the time he left Vancouver in August 1912 to become the archbishop of Toronto, McNeil and his fellow land speculating partners, all lay people, had acquired holdings, at boom prices, which were then worth a staggering $250,000. However, when the property market began to collapse, McNeil's dream of making a handsome profit for the archdiocese and his fellow business partners rapidly turned into a nightmare, especially for the hundreds of investors who had joined them. For the very few who had actually built homes, especially those who, at McNeil's assurance, were convinced that they would soon have many "good Catholic" neighbors, they quickly discovered that they had no neighbors at all. Far worse, however, they had no roads, schools, or other vital amenities that McNeil had also promised, and so felt badly used by the archbishop.[12]

Throughout his short time in Vancouver, McNeil also graphically revealed what the arrival of a secular archbishop meant for the Oblates. The Oblate efforts to establish St. Augustine's Parish, Vancouver, well demonstrated a situation that would have been unheard of before 1910. As part of his determination to build as many parishes with schools and as quickly as possible, in 1910 McNeil requested that the Oblates establish a new parish, St. Augustine, in the CPR's new "better class" and expanding Kitsilano area of Vancouver. By 1911, McNeil and the Oblates had agreed to the appointment of Jean-Marie Tavernier (1899–1915) as the first pastor. So rife was land speculation that when, in February, Tavernier attempted to purchase five lots on the northeast corner of Eighth and Maple Streets, the asking price of $32,400 rose within a few days to $38,000. Since the Oblates were investing their own capital, they asked and received a promise from McNeil that the parish should be assigned to them *in perpetuum*. However, demonstrating their new predicament, within weeks McNeil toyed with the idea of founding another parish nearby and thus circumscribe St. Augustine's "to such a point," the Oblates privately complained that they would "be reduced to starvation." Reflecting similar regular-secular tensions in the Pacific Northwest, the Oblates feared that they might finally be "obliged to give up [their] parish [of St. Augustine's] as the Benedictine Fathers had to do in Seattle." Although McNeil dropped his plans to found a neighboring parish, and, finally laid the cornerstone on 23 July 1911, the incident was a sign that their troubles with him and his secular successors were just beginning.[13]

Building costs for St. Augustine's rose almost as rapidly as land prices. McNeil had originally offered to invest $15,000 towards the construction of the parish plant, a sum which would have only covered a quarter of the final estimate of over $60,000. When the Oblates inquired into a promised bequest which they hoped to use to defray their costs, they learned that McNeil, apparently through some rather secret maneuverings, had been named its sole beneficiary. To make matters worse, McNeil began to dictate the precise location of the buildings, even though he would eventually contribute nothing to their construction. In the end, the Oblates were obliged to assume a far greater financial burden than they had originally anticipated. While the church and school, which had been accepted by the Sisters of St. Ann, were both in full operation by 1913, the onset of a depression that year caused a major decline in land prices and corresponding rise in unemployment. As a consequence, for many years there was no major settlement in the area. While the Oblates had a huge mortgage of $62,461, for over a decade the annual parish contributions were never higher than a $1000, with the result that the Oblates had to assume most of the financial burden. And not until after 1945 would the Kitsilano area be well established and flourishing.[14]

✤ The McNeil Legacy and the Fight to Maintain an Oblate Presence

TIMOTHY CASEY (1912–31), McNeil's successor, would inherit the latter's fiscal mess. Initially, McNeil did compensate some of those who had lost fortunes in his many speculative land transactions. By 1921, property sold for no more than ten percent of its 1910–12 value. In the meantime the banks were demanding both principal and interest on their loans on the now almost worthless land. W.R. Austin, a major investor in Shannon Park did receive a loan from McNeil of about half of what he owed. However, a Mr. Donnelly, one of the largest stockholders in Pitt Meadows, demanded compensation for all of his loses, although he received less than half. Even so, there were still some who continued to try to sell their Pitt Meadows investments at pre-1913 prices, and one naively predicted in 1914 that the ultimate sale of the entire property was still possible and would soon realise a grand total of $600,000.[15]

In 1913 the pastor of St. Joseph's in Port Moody and a secular priest, Felix Kientz, informed McNeil of the dismal conditions at Pitt Meadows, which was a Mission parish to St. Joseph's. He wrote that the few Catholic families who had settled there were thinking of leaving. In 1915 Kientz announced

Most Reverend Timothy Casey, D.D., Archbishop of Vancouver (AD)

that there were only a handful of "good families" left. By then, most of Pitt
Meadows was up for sale for unpaid taxes. What in 1914 one speculator
thought would bring in $600,000 could now be acquired for back taxes, or
the comparatively paltry sum of $1,803.04. Casey saw the logic of purchas-
ing so much for so very little, yet by 1917 his meagre cash flow did not seem
able to cover even this relatively small amount. By 1921, most of the land
had been sold to ranchers who used it to graze cattle. The little chapel
which McNeil had erected until a larger parish church could be built to
serve the enclave of "wealthy" Catholic families he envisioned, was being
used as a cattle shed. Reacting to this latest insult, one potential parishioner, Frank Cahill, complained angrily to McNeil: "Very black it is [;] a
disgrace to the Catholics of Van."[16]

The McNeil years in Vancouver, though very few, had certainly left their scars. By 1916 the archdiocese owed a staggering debt of $169,994.52, and of this, the enormous amount of $103,684.44 was in arrears. In trying to make some compensation for his wild land speculations, McNeil did offer "loans" to Casey at 6% interest, or two percentage points below the market rate. However, the $17,000 that McNeil could extend to Casey seemed almost an insult considering the overall gravity of the situation. Given such financial burdens that had been largely created by McNeil's poor judgement, the diocese appeared unprepared to meet any new challenges. Certainly the problems of the period would demand more sober, careful, and circumspect leadership.[17]

At first Archbishop Casey seemed to inspire hope among the Oblates and others that he would be more cooperative. He was described as more "temperamentally approachable" than McNeil, but in the end, they were to be even more disappointed. Dealing with the terrible financial state of the diocese bequeathed to him by his predecessor, made far worse by the depression of 1913, constituted the central problem of Casey's tenure. He was also someone who, at least at first, displayed some of the marks of an authoritarian, for within weeks of his arrival, Casey complained that he had no "palace," pulpit, nor even a cathedral to reflect his "high status" as an archbishop. Though he never realized his "palace," he began to eye the most financially important parish in his see, Holy Rosary, as the primary candidate for his cathedral.[18]

The Oblates were determined to retain Holy Rosary. Although the new church continued to drain parish resources, its sizable congregation meant that it was the only parish in the archdiocese that could pay not only its own expenses, but could also provide a surplus for other needs. So resolved were the Oblates on this point, that in 1913 they suggested to Casey that he use St. Patrick's Parish church as a pro-cathedral while he was waiting to build a new cathedral. To achieve their ends, the Oblates tried to "bribe" Casey with a "gift" of $25,000 towards the purchase of a four-acre property and building, then owned by the Sisters of St. Ann, in the prestigious Shaughnessy Heights area of the city. They envisioned that Casey could reside there and build his cathedral nearby. They expected that the Sisters of St. Ann would found another school for girls on an adjacent six-acre site also owned by the Sisters. Developing their argument still further, the Oblates reasoned that a downtown church such as Holy Rosary, with its "confessionals and ser-

Cathedral of the Holy Rosary, Vancouver (AD)

mons," was better "conducted by religious." The Oblates also reported to Casey that the "influential members" of the laity at Holy Rosary wanted them to remain. Yet the central factor behind their desire was that Holy Rosary was "an asset" that not only provided financial security, but was "admirably suited" to be their regional "headquarters," and, given its central location, also symbolized their continued prominence in British Columbia. For the Oblates were certain that, "in the event of [their] eviction" by Casey from Holy Rosary, their "prestige not only in B.C., but in all of Canada would suffer a serious blow."[19]

Clearly, when compared to McNeil, Casey was very lacking in leadership abilities, which when coupled to his poor health, meant that the church on most of the mainland would have to wait until the appointment of his coadjutor-successor, William Mark Duke (1928–64). As for Timothy Casey, Vancouver was definitely not blessed. Since he had apparently made little impact on his former diocese of St. John, New Brunswick, where he had been bishop for eleven (1901–12) years, it is perhaps no surprise that the 50-year old, now an archbishop, was not likely to change.[20]

The financial morass that McNeil left behind was not encouraging, still a more creative and energetic person would have viewed the crisis as an opportunity to assert his leadership in trying at least to lessen its terribly negative impact. If anything, problems seemed only to further debilitate Casey, who already needed no further excuses to procrastinate. Albert Mostyn, one of the secular priests whom McNeil had brought with him from Nova Scotia, complained that no one knew Casey, since few ever saw him. Writing to McNeil in August 1913, Mostyn noted: "I don't know what he does do." During his first year in the diocese, Casey did not visit a single parish. The Ontario born Oblate, William O'Boyle, who had been appointed the pastor (1913–27) at Holy Rosary, concluded that Casey seemed incapable of being a leader. Although the full weight of the woes of McNeil's financial investments had not yet had their full impact in 1913, O'Boyle lamented losing McNeil. He believed that, at the time of his transfer to Toronto, McNeil was just beginning to realize that the far west was not Atlantic Canada, and McNeil had begun to develop a "comprehensive sympathy" for the "peculiar conditions" of British Columbia. In support of such judgements, in March 1912, McNeil noted that for the first time since his ordination in 1879 he was "unable...to earn a living" by employing the methods he had learned in the Maritimes. McNeil had started to grasp the fact that, unlike the east, where tax supported separate schools were then the norm, in British Columbia the school did *not* build the church. Therefore it was impossible, as McNeil was apparently recognizing, to impose a parochial school on every parish, unless the intention was to ultimately bankrupt it. Clearly, if he had remained, McNeil, unlike Casey, would probably have risen to the new challenges of the west coast, even to the financial disaster that he had helped to create. Unlike Casey, McNeil would certainly not have hidden or run from his responsibilities.[21]

Both O'Boyle and Mostyn would have found a sympathetic ear in Mother Wenceslaus, a Sister of Providence who had headed St. Paul's Hospital during Casey's initial years. She saw few hopeful signs in the new archbishop. From her new assignment in California, she reflected on her experiences with McNeil. His term had coincided with her work (1910–15) in completing an addition to St. Paul's during which she found McNeil to be very supportive, especially when she began to experience health problems due to the added strain of that undertaking. As for Casey, she got no such encouragement, instead she saw him as a hopeless, even incompetent leader. "Poor man!" she remarked, and believed Rome should never have appointed him, for he had neither "the courage nor will to grasp" what was needed in the "new country" of British Columbia, which, she said, demanded "tact and enterprise," skills, she concluded, Casey totally lacked.[22]

The Oblates and the First Secular Archbishops

Father John Althoff's "farewell gesture to the pioneer clergy residence" in Victoria.
This was the first bishop's residence, erected 1851,
converted into clergy quarters 1887 (ASSA)

Others tried to compensate for Casey's serious shortcomings. John Althoff eventually became (1903–26) pastor of Nelson and vicar general to Casey. As the most important secular priest in the interior and one of the leading clerics in the diocese, other diocesan priests looked up to him as a sort of father figure, which, due to Casey's weak leadership, further increased. Using Nelson as his home base, Althoff traveled by motorcycle throughout the southern interior where he assisted overworked clergy while he tried to attract new secular clergy to work in the region and added his moral support to their ministries.[23]

Like Althoff, the Oblate vicar of Missions, John Welch also tried to make up for Casey's serious lack of leadership. With Casey's permission, Welch offered to publicize their great financial plight to eastern Canadian bishops, particularly on the need to save Catholic schools in British Columbia. Naturally Casey agreed.[24]

In approving the plan, Casey also revealed his own feelings about the state of parochial education and other issues in the diocese. Casey complained of Catholics in British Columbia being forced to pay for both their own schools and the public ones. With regard to the single tax, until Bishop MacDonald of Victoria won his historic case in 1921 which extended to all church property, Casey complained that the single tax assumed that Catholic institutions were "business establishments bringing in a large income." As an easterner, he found it hard to imagine a parish without its school, but this, he said, seemed the "sad prospect for the future of our children" in British Columbia. He also noted that one parish in Vancouver would soon lose its school due to back taxes and other debts amounting to over $12,000. He hoped Welch's appeal would gain the needed financial support, for, he said, "I know of no such unjust conditions in any other province of Canada, or, indeed, of the British Empire!" As for the type of Catholics he found in his diocese, he longed for those he had left back east, who were "so much better than" those in British Columbia. Again like McNeil, Casey misread the attitudes of most Catholics in British Columbia, who saw little reason to invest in parochial schools when public ones were readily available. This did not necessarily mean that eastern Catholics were "much better" than their counterparts in the far west, but rather that their taxes were being spent to support a separate schools system. In point of fact, though Welch tried to raise thousands, he appears to have received only a $1,000 from the archbishop of Quebec, Cardinal Bégin. It seems clear that while eastern Catholics had tax supported separate school systems, they were apparently no more generous in their private donations to their church than their counterparts in British Columbia.[25]

Unlike Althoff and Welch, others were eager to take advantage of the Casey's poor leadership abilities for their own benefit. Certainly, J.D. Kearns, a Catholic layman, fit such a description, and the opportunity was the faltering diocesan newspaper, the *B.C. Western Catholic*. Although O'Boyle was its initial founder, McNeil hoped it would prosper as had his other publishing enterprises back east. O'Boyle's original plan limited it to mostly local church news, but McNeil expanded the *B.C. Western Catholic* into covering mainly global "Catholic" issues. As he had on the education question, he failed to comprehend that in British Columbia there was no strong interest among most Catholics for purely "Catholic" world news. Running at a deficit since its inauguration in 1909, by 1914 it was just one more financial drain on the fading resources of the diocese. For while it was estimated that there were approximately 5000 potential Catholic readers, fewer than 500 subscribed to it, and by 1914, "many of these" were "behind in their payments." It was at this point that Kearns entered the picture. The CEO of the British Columbia Financial and Investment Company, Ltd.,

Kearns was in effect one of Casey's many creditors. He offered to purchase the paper at a considerable lose to its owner, Western Press, which was the archdiocese. In August 1915 Kearns bought Western Press for a paltry $1,000, which included all of its plant and equipment, while he refused to assume its old debts, though, for a commission, he agreed to collect monies that were still outstanding. As for the *B.C. Western Catholic*, he paid $1.00, but assured Casey it would continue to be a "Catholic paper," with "absolutely no political affiliations." In addition, Kearns promised Casey that it would "combat socialism," by promoting "proper...social reform work," or that approved of by the Vatican as outlined in *"Rerum Novarum."* Kearns, as the new publisher, also agreed to "encourage" Catholic education. He would do this by: "plugging" the establishment of a Catholic boy's secondary school; fostering "all Catholic Charities and [related] institutions;" providing "all Catholic news of interest;" and obtaining "recognition in every respect of the rights of Catholics as regards taxes and government aid." The last point was crucial, given the single tax system, and was a central factor in the archdiocese's continued financial problems. However, Casey did nothing to address the single tax system and its taxation of church lands, leaving it up to others, in this case Bishop MacDonald of Victoria. The *B.C. Western Catholic*, was never a success, and Kearns clearly allowed it to die soon after acquiring it.[26]

While some tried to help and others hinder the situation, it was Timothy Casey who was the real problem. Casey used the deepening financial difficulties that were so much a part of the archdiocese as just one more, though a major excuse, to retreat from reality, leaving others, both lay people and clergy to shoulder that increasing burden. Casey's inability to lead meant that, except for applying very temporary Band-Aid solutions to local problems, there were no diocesan-wide answers, so in time such a circumstance only further exacerbated matters. By March 1916, the corporation sole of the diocese, or Timothy Casey, had liabilities past due of $23,035.75, and a further $127,724.83 would be added during that year. By 1917 an additional $83,736.42 in debts would accrue. In all a staggering total of over $235,000 would be owed, mostly because of McNeil's direct land purchases or his investments in other land projects. A loan of $100,000 had been taken out in 1913 using St. Peter's Church, New Westminster and Good Shepherd Monastery as collateral. By 1916, due to the diocese's inability to maintain payments, the annual interest alone had risen to over $8,000.[27]

To add even further to his problems, Casey considered indebting himself an additional $53,000 by purchasing four acres and a building in Shaughnessy Heights, which he intended to use as a "palace," and which was partly owned by the Sisters of St. Ann. In an apparent attempt to ingratiate themselves with Casey, with the hope that he would allow them to remain at Holy Rosary, the Oblates had also offered him $25,000 towards its purchase as a future site for his "cathedral," though there is no evidence that he ever accepted their gift. On the other hand, laymen, such as Patrick Donnelly, Dominic and Patrick Burns, "Messrs. Foley, Welch and Stewart," the last three having also promoted the ill-fated Pacific Great Eastern Railway, had all "invested" in this property, easily convincing Casey that it would make an excellent *"domaine"* for his intended episcopal "palace." Yet by 1916, when land prices continued to plummet, they found it "very hard," Donnelly told McNeil, "to carry out their good intentions," and left Casey and the diocese with the responsibility for most of the debt. The Sisters of St. Ann ultimately came to the rescue by reassuming the entire loan and, due to the single tax system, paying the ever-rising property taxes on the site, which included even minor costs, such as a new boiler. Thus, within in a few years of his arrival, Casey was living in a house that was almost totally subsidized by the Sisters of St. Ann, since he paid little rent. He remained there until 1927, when he moved to the rectory of Holy Rosary Cathedral.[28]

What made this initial affair doubly frustrating for the Sisters of St. Ann was the fact that they had originally purchased the Shaughnessy property in 1910 with the intention of building a girls' boarding school to complement the ones they were already operating in Victoria, Vancouver, New Westminster and Kamloops. When times improved, it would (1927) become Little Flower Academy. Since the area constituted a new prestigious subdivision, the Sisters intended to found a "finishing" school for the daughters of the elite. Perhaps, it was meant to challenge McNeil's initial "grand vision" of trying to relegate the Sisters of St. Ann to operating parochial day schools while inviting the Madames of the Sacred Heart to open a "proper" boarding school for the daughters of "upper class" Catholics. Yet as part of the agreement in purchasing it, the CPR, who owned the Shaughnessy area, made a stipulation with all new owners. Namely, that any building had to have a minimum value of $10,000 and must be comparable in architecture to other structures in the area. When Casey agreed to occupy the building, the nuns hoped that they could at least gain enough in rent from the archbishop in order to pay the ever-increasing property tax burden. Although a small rent was paid, it was at best sporadic, and certainly well below the basic upkeep on the property.[29]

The Sisters of St. Ann had provided Casey with what was virtually a free residence, and in assuming the debt on the property, had saved him an additional outlay of $53,000. Casey continued his dithering with regard to other loans, which only added to his financial woes. He apparently based his behavior on a belief that procrastination would solve the problem. Reflecting this mentality, he was a very poor record keeper, and as the Vancouver archdiocesan archives reveal, he threw away most of his correspondence. By the end of 1916, with principle and interest, the archdiocese owed over $186,000, of which $120,000 was overdue. Patrick Donnelly tried to intervene, but he was part of the problem, since, as a principal executive of the Canadian Trust Company, his advice had helped to create the land speculation mess in the first place. Now hoping at least to lessen the crisis, and relieve his own investment woes, Donnelly tried to convince Casey to at least pay the taxes on the Pitt Meadows property before the municipality sold it for a mere $1,803.04 in back taxes. Worse, according to Donnelly, Casey had recently collected $2,500 in taxes on the property from which he could now easily pay his liability to the city, but having made no attempt to do so, now faced losing land for a fraction of its original cost of over $35,000. Though in his inability to make important decisions, he compounded his dire situation, Casey had no hand in creating the problem, whereas, McNeil and Donnelly were two of the principal architects of the diocese's property debacle. This reality must elicit some sympathy for Casey's situation. Still, this did not change the fact that Casey was a very poor leader and administrator, and that his failure to act only worsened matters. In fact, in 1917 the diocese lost the Pitt Meadows property because of Casey's failure to pay the back taxes.[30]

Despite the grave consequences of the financial situation for the archdiocese, other significant issues, in which Casey had little or no involvement, still helped to shape events in the local church. Surely one of these was the development by an Oblate, William O'Boyle of *The Monthly Bulletin* and *The Bulletin*. As pastor of Holy Rosary (1913–27), he was arguably the most important regular parish priest in the archdiocese. Despite his responsibilities there, he started and edited (1917) *The Monthly Bulletin,* which he later (1924) enlarged into a weekly called *The Bulletin.*

Unlike the *B.C. Western Catholic*, O'Boyle's paper made "no pretension to exalted journalistic standards," but rather, much like Durieu's *The Month* (1892–96), tried, with apparent success, to address local parish issues. But he also reported other topics as well, such as independent labor unions and socialism, which, as a supporter of papal teachings on the issue, he naturally condemned. In addition *The Monthly Bulletin* and *The Bulletin* covered other pertinent contemporary issues, which even included the theory of relativity. O'Boyle speculated on this and other topics, always judging them in the light of "Catholic teachings," which he hoped would strengthen laypeople's loyalty to their church.[31]

Indeed, these times witnessed rapid change throughout the far west, but rather than heralding a new groundswell of support for organized religion, as O'Boyle and others hoped, they ushered in a period of "outright rebellion against religion and flight from the churches" throughout Canada. This was in part due to the "uncritical patriotic" stance of the vast majority of the clergy during World War I. As Bishop MacDonald demonstrated, this was definitely the attitude of the Catholic clergy in British Columbia, and where affiliation figures reported in the 1921 census (12.2%) indicated that the Catholic Church had reached an all-time low which had barely changed (12.7%) by 1931.[32]

Besides clerical chauvinism that further fueled traditional indifference to organized religion in British Columbia, this latest fact also probably reflected lay hostility over the introduction of prohibition in the province in 1917. Prohibition was very short lived, having been mainly introduced as a wartime measure and was repealed after a 1920 referendum. Promoted by Christian evangelicals, the Catholic Church in the far west also supported it. The increasing lack of interest in supporting the Catholic Church in British Columbia could be partly attributed to their stance on prohibition. For although earlier issues of both *The Monthly Bulletin* and *The Bulletin* excluded liquor ads, by 1928, perhaps in an attempt to address lay Catholic rejection of total sobriety, that policy had changed and in fact *The Bulletin* began to carry prominent ads which even championed "Beer as a Food!"[33]

The Monthly Bulletin also trumpeted the essential value of Catholic education for parents, Catholic or not, who wished to see that their children received a truly "moral" education, which, claimed the *Bulletin*, public schools could never supply. For among Christian denominations, it was asserted, only the Catholic Church saw "religion" as a vital element in education. Quoting from the conclusions of an article in the *New England Journal of Education*, its author, a former public school advocate who had been converted to parochial education, wrote that only Catholics had gotten the issue right. Unless, that is, the author noted, you do not believe that "a man [is]...worth more than a dog, or the human soul—with eternity for duration—is of more value than the span of animal existence for a day." He concluded, "If they [Catholics] are right, then we [public education advocates] are wrong."[34]

With ultramontanism then in full flood, Catholics everywhere were encouraged to believe that, to be "right," education must be "Catholic" at all levels, including the university. When the University of British Columbia had its first commencement in 1917, *The Monthly Bulletin* carried the news, but without comment. However, in 1920, in suggesting that "Protestant" and "secular" education was in essence the same, especially at the university level, it implied that institutions such as UBC could never truly serve the needs of Roman Catholics. The aims of UBC, which excluded the centrality of religion in its curriculum, were, *The Monthly Bulletin* declared, "not consistent with the requirements of the Catholic religion and of Catholic doctrine respecting the education of youth. Therefore, it is our business to look to our own universities."[35]

Though Catholic universities were then a reality in the east, such a "dream" in British Columbia was heady stuff, and indeed, for the same reasons that dissuaded Catholics from supporting parochial schools, "higher education" never became a reality during this period with one exception. The Seminary of Christ the King was founded by Archbishop Duke in Ladner in 1931 under a secular priest and Englishman, Francis Chaloner. It was then no more than a high school with an enrollment that never exceeded 31. In 1940 the seminary was expanded to include a college and school of theology when it was taken over by a group of Benedictines from Mount Angel Abbey in Oregon, who moved it to Burnaby in that year. It still operates as part of Westminster Abbey.[36]

In the first issue of *The Bulletin* in June 1924, O'Boyle indicated that, besides the fact that the renamed paper would appear more frequently and have a larger format, its appearance also heralded a new era for the Catholic Church and Catholic education in the region. Actually, it did signal an improvement in the fortunes of the Catholic Church in British Columbia which was by then beginning to climb out from under the terrible financial burden of the previous decade. The inaugural issue also spoke of the "dream" of seeing a new cathedral on "the noblest site in the city," near Vancouver College, which the Irish Christian Brothers had recently founded, and which O'Boyle implied would eventually be transformed into the first Catholic university of British Columbia. Although this would never happen, Vancouver College, which opened in 1922 with a hundred students in a wooden structure on Richards Street, finally moved into new quarters in Shaughnessy Heights in September 1925 where it soon admitted 200 boys, from grade three through senior matriculation. Archbishop Casey also hoped that it would eventually provide a university education, senior matriculation, which was equivalent to first year university, was the closest it ever came to achieving that objective.[37]

Seeing the need to address more global Catholic questions, O'Boyle eventually used the American National Catholic Welfare Council News Service as a ready source of international Catholic news, including many very important and timely topics such as female suffrage. The Catholic Church in Canada, lead by the bishops in Quebec, initially rejected the right of women to have the vote, as this, it concluded, would "undermine" the natural law that dictated that men alone were the "God-ordained" heads of both society and the family. This was not true of other churches; the evangelical-based, Woman's Christian Temperance Union was one of the earliest to campaign for women's suffrage which was finally won provincially in 1917 and federally in 1918. As a legal fact, the Catholic Church in British Columbia now had to deal with the reality. *The Monthly Bulletin* revealed the Catholic position when it reported on the Catholic Women's Union, which was founded to "assist" Catholic women in making the best or proper use of their new voting rights. Reflecting upon their "Catholic" responsibilities, an article by Hanna More entitled "Young Ladies' Education" noted that "Catholic women" must be trained to be good "daughters, wives, mothers and mistresses of families." Thus a "good" Catholic woman would be a man's best friend, there to both "comfort and counsel him" and "assist him in his affairs, lighten his cares, soothe his sorrow, purify his joy, strength his ideas and properly educate his children." In short, "good Catholic women," though they might now have the vote, were reminded that men were still in charge of society, including the home.[38]

While the Oblates would continue to be deeply involved in promoting the general interests of the Catholic Church, 1926 brought the "serious blow" from Casey that they had long feared: he took Holy Rosary Parish from them. Due to the enormous financial burden he had inherited from McNeil, for years, Casey left the parish in Oblate hands since Holy Rosary had its own very serious debts, especially its huge mortgage. However, in 1916 he certainly made his ultimate intentions clear when he selected Holy Rosary as his cathedral. Yet it was obvious that, in order to have total control over them, as a secular ordinary, Casey would ultimately put secular clergy in charge there. Due largely to Oblate leadership, in January 1925 Holy Rosary burned its mortgage, which for Casey, who also now had sufficient seculars to staff the parish, was the signal to act. As for the Oblates, faced with a growing manpower shortage, occasioned by both the continued departure of French members and a lack of anglophone vocations to replace them, it represented another serious setback. Apparently the move was so psychologically painful, that it took almost two years before the Oblates finally vacated Holy Rosary. Actually, so great was the seeming strain on O'Boyle, who was the last Oblate pastor there, that he quit the Congregation in 1927, and spent the rest of his career as a chaplain in the Royal Canadian Navy until his death in 1949. However, by 1928, not only had the secular clergy taken over Holy Rosary, by then the Oblates had also erected a new province for English-speaking members; it was a decision that would eventually prove to be a major solution to their personnel problems.[39]

15

The Church During and Between the Wars

✤ *Finally an Oblate Province*

WHILE THE OBLATES had been in the far west for 79 (1847–1926) years, reflecting its remoteness and its inability to supply native clergy, they had designated it a vicariate of Missions rather than a province. As such, in canon law it was directly under the authority of the superior general in Rome. In 1926, it gained greater independence when it became the national province of St. Peter's with its headquarters in Ottawa. Its central justification and modus operandi was that it was to include only English-speaking Oblates. To create it, the other, predominantly French-speaking provinces across Canada transferred to it a number of English-speaking parishes. Over the next 18 years, it added parishes throughout British Columbia, as well as in Lethbridge, Edmonton, and Ottawa. In 1944, it reached its ultimate extent when the vicariate apostolic of Prince Rupert was joined to it. By then it comprised 13 parishes and a number of Native residential schools stretching from British Columbia and the Yukon Territory to Ontario.[1]

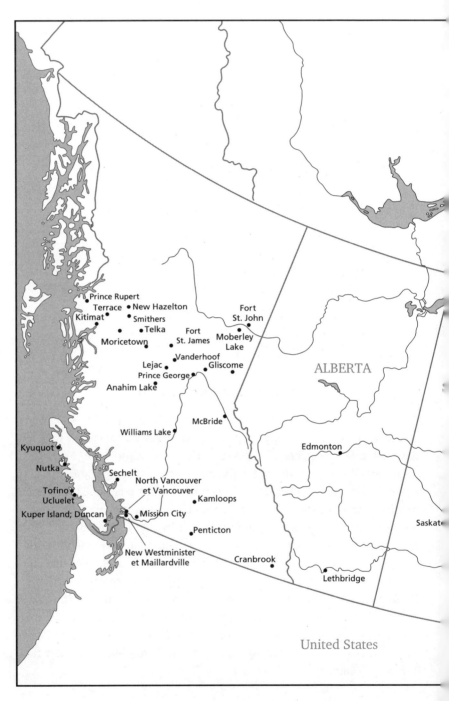

St. Peter's Province

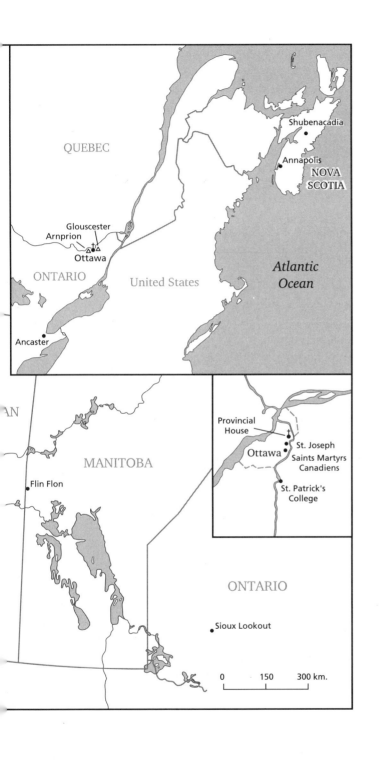

QUEBEC

Shubenacadia

Annapolis
NOVA
SCOTIA

Glouscester
Arnprion
Ottawa

ONTARIO

United States

Atlantic
Ocean

Ancaster

AN

MANITOBA

Flin Flon

Provincial
House

Ottawa

St. Joseph
Saints Martyrs
Canadiens

St. Patrick's
College

ONTARIO

Sioux Lookout

0   150   300 km.

It took many years of planning and soul-searching, however, before this reality was finally achieved. Since at least 1910, with the steady decline in French-speaking members, it had become increasingly clear to the Oblates in the far west that they would have to reconfigure their organization if they hoped to survive. Durieu had tried to attract local vocations by establishing Nazareth Seminary in 1894. However, Dontenwill, the second bishop of New Westminster (1899–1908) and the first archbishop of Vancouver (1908), who had headed that institution for six years (1894–99), realized that Nazareth Seminary would never supply sufficient vocations to meet their needs in the region, and so it was closed in 1909. By 1910, Dontenwill, now superior general, encouraged his colleagues in the far west to explore alternatives. For several years, it was thought that British Columbia could establish an English-speaking novitiate linked to the Oblate province of Alberta. However, most Oblates in the far west feared that a "thorough English-speaking education suited...[to] the needs of the church in the west" would not be possible in Alberta, where francophones continued to dominate the formation program.²

Many Oblates still hoped to see a viable novitiate established in British Columbia and looked for ways to achieve that objective. In 1914 the provincial government gave the archdiocese of Vancouver and, the major Protestant denominations property near what, in the 1920s would become the main campus of the new University of British Columbia. While, apart from the small land grant, it gave them no financial assistance, Victoria encouraged them to build colleges or residences to educate their future clergy and take advantage of the facilities that would be provided by the nearby university. As the major male religious congregation in the diocese, the Oblates hoped that Archbishop Casey would designate them as the founding order of such a college, which they could then also use as a local novitiate. Some Oblates, however, were concerned that if their prospective seminarians associated too closely with divinity students from other denominations, and even attended classes at the university, they might lose both their "souls" and their "vocations." Yet others believed the arrangement would allow them to attract potential vocations from the wider university community. Within months, however, of the government's offer in 1914, Casey, clearly revealing his negative feelings towards the Oblates, offered the use of the land to the Benedictines who he hoped would eventually found a Catholic college or university there. With the closing of that door, a few Oblates again looked to

St. Louis College in New Westminster as a possible solution. But by 1914 Dontenwill had directed them to close it, since in his view, which was shared by most others, St. Louis would never be more than an unacceptable drain, both financial and human, on their increasingly limited resources. The closure of the college, which took place in 1917, ended forever the possibility of establishing a local noviciate.[3]

By then it was clear that Timothy Casey was not prepared to be a supporter, much less an Oblate patron. The earliest Oblate recognition of this came in 1916 when John Welch, the vicar of Missions (1910–26) and the first head (1926–29) of St. Peter's Province moved his residence from Holy Rosary, Vancouver to St. Peter's, New Westminster. In 1929, William Grant-Byrne (1929–33) succeeded Welch as provincial, and in 1932 he transferred his headquarters from New Westminster to St. Joseph's Parish, Ottawa. In 1930, he had opened St. Patrick's College and Holy Rosary Scholasticate in nearby Orleans. Within a few years these two facilities became the major training ground for Oblates preparing to minister in the far west, and which drew almost all of its candidates from eastern Canada, especially Ontario.[4]

By 1948, St. Peter's Province was served by 132 priests, 31 brothers and 20 scholastics, almost all of whom had English as their first language. In total, the province then had 19 Missions, including the vicariate apostolic of Prince Rupert in British Columbia.[5]

Although the Oblates continued to work with Native people, by then Euro-Canadians had also become a major focus of their ministry. In New Westminster they had St. Peter's Parish, which they had been granted in perpetuity, and which was not only their major local ministry, but also their most important financial base in the Royal City. Until they closed them, they also taught at St. Louis College (1917) and Nazareth (1909) Novitiate and Minor Seminary. In Vancouver, besides Holy Rosary (1897–1927), the Oblates worked for a short time at Sacred Heart (1905–11) and St. Patrick's (1910–11). In North Vancouver, the Oblates had also founded St. Edmund's (1911) Parish, although, due to apparent staffing shortages, they did not remain there for very long. Their most important parish in the area would eventually be St. Augustine's (1909–), which, like St. Peter's, they also held in perpetuity.[6]

As British Columbia grew, the archdiocese asked the Oblates to establish parishes in Cranbrook, Fernie, Kimberley, Nelson, Vernon, Kamloops, Lillooet, Okanagan Falls and Penticton. By 1948, indicating the growth of the secular

The hospital and church in Dawson City, the first mission in the Yukon (AD)

clergy as well as other religious communities, only two of these—Okanagan Falls and Penticton—remained in Oblate hands. By 1936 the diocese of Nelson was established and the diocese of Kamloops was added in 1945. While the Oblates remained the dominant religious congregation working in these dioceses, from the outset the secular clergy constituted an absolute majority, and which would continue to increase.[7]

In 1908, in anticipation of the coming of the Grand Trunk Pacific Railway (GPTR), the northern half of British Columbia and the Yukon Territory had been entrusted by Rome to the Oblates, first as a prefecture (1908) and finally as a vicariate (1916–44) under Émile Bunoz (1908–45), and which had its center at Prince Rupert. This huge region extended in the south to the fifty-fourth parallel, and then north to the Arctic Ocean, with its eastern boundary being the Rocky Mountains and its western limits Alaska and the Pacific Ocean. The Oblates had first arrived in the region in 1873 when, at Fort St. James, they began what would eventually become Our Lady of Good Hope Mission. Bunoz had begun his ministry in Dawson City, Yukon Territory in 1902, drawn there by the Klondike gold rush of 1898. He left in 1908 for Prince Rupert when it seemed likely to become a settlement that some hoped would eventually overshadow even Vancouver. In 1916 he was made the prefect apostolic and the vicar of Missions of the Yukon and Prince Rupert. By 1936, after slow but steady settlement by Euro-Canadians, in northern British Columbia Jean-Louis Coudert (1936–44), another Oblate, had been named Bunoz's coadjutor. Residing at Smithers, Coudert was given responsibility for the most northerly Missions, while Bunoz continued to concentrate on the southern area.[8]

With Prince Rupert as its center in 1910, a small band of missionaries, which never numbered more than seven, began pressing north. However, not only was progress difficult, by 1920, with the collapse of the gold rush economy in 1903, most had concluded that the region had no future, and the depression of the 1930s seemed to further support such a judgement. Yet in the wake of World War II, conditions began to improve.[9]

Over the years the Oblates founded a number of Missions in this immense region. Besides continuing their central work with the Native peoples, Missions to Euro-Canadians were founded in Prince George (1914), Smithers (1915), Terrace (1920) and Lejac (1922). By 1920 the boom and bust economy had reduced the combined population of these settlements and the surrounding area from a high of 55,000 to a low of only two to three thousand. As such, in 1920 the Sisters of St. Ann abandoned their school and hospital in Dawson, and it was reported that there were no more than 300 Catholics throughout this immense region. As for the Native Missions, they were in a far worse state, since by then there were only a few dozen adherents.[10]

In the midst of the Great Depression of the 1930s, which also brought an increase in vocations, with the essential support of outside funding, the Oblates undertook new obligations by establishing or reopening Missions. Each had a resident priest and they were located in McLeod (1936), Telegraph Creek Babine (1936), Lower Post (1937), Mayo (1938), Teslin (1938), Stony Creek (1939), Moricetown (1939), and Vanderhoof (1939).[11]

By 1939 the vicariate of the Yukon had developed into an Oblate dominated ministry. Only two secular clergy assisted the 30 Oblates stationed there. Of these, 18 worked in ten parishes and 13 Mission stations along the Canadian National Railway from Jasper Park to Prince Rupert. Another 16 priests ministered in eleven Mission posts located as much as 1500 kilometers from the nearest railway station. World War II greatly increased the population, and finally resulted in the Alaska Highway. Nevertheless, while the residents of Whitehorse rose during the war to over 22,000, by 1949 the city had again dropped to only 3500.[12]

Father Nicolas Coccola, 1958 (AD)

Missionary life in such remote areas could be trying, especially for those ill-suited to it, and judgements against them by other Oblates were often harsh. In 1913, a Frenchman, Joseph Hartmann (1905–37), who worked in Dawson (1913–14) and Anyox (1914–19), was criticized by Bunoz for spending, without approval, $2,000 on a central heating system for the church and rectory at Dawson. His superiors concluded that the priest was "too far gone from the spirit of his vocation to benefit by any censure from anybody." Accused of "inefficiency," or in a word, laziness, Hartmann left the north in 1920. Succeeding years found him in Cranbrook (1920–21), New Westminster (1921–25), Saskatoon (1932–33) and finally back in Cranbrook (1933–37) before he returned (1937–49) to France.[13]

Personality conflicts were also part of the problem, which the climate could further compound, frequently producing illnesses, both physical and psychological. Thus the French-born Charles Wolf (1910–32) found it difficult working (1911–15) at Stuart Lake with the sometimes eccentric Corsican, Nicolas Coccola (1881–1943). After making "repeated" demands, he left there for Whitehorse (1915–17), from whence he moved to Prince George (1917–21) where he and Joseph Hartmann (1919–20) fought continuously. Wolf then went to Fraser Lake (1921–23), returning to Stuart Lake (1923–28), which Coccola had left in 1921. After a second brief (1928–31) term in Prince George and Anyox (1931–32), he spent the rest of his Oblate career (1932–52) in Africa. Joseph Schuster (1909–17), a German, was seriously sick much of the time, and though by 1915 he expressed the wish to return to his homeland, after leaving the region he spent the remainder of his ministry (1917–45) in the United States.[14]

Reflecting the very special qualities needed to work in this remote region, many Oblates who succeeded in the far north spent a very large part of their lives there. For example, the German-born Gottfried Eichelsbacker

Fathers Émile Leray and Gottfried Eichelsbacher (AD)

lived for an incredible 69 (1901–70) years in the area, building churches in Bonanza Creek (1902), Whitehorse (1905–07) and Dawson (1901–05; 1907–10). He also built chapels along the GTPR, as well as churches at Moricetown and Smithers. His longest ministry was as the hospital chaplain (1941–69) at Smithers. Joseph-François Allard (1903–41), from Quebec, founded churches in Sulpher and Greenville. In 1922, he became the principal of the Lejac Residential School at Fraser Lake, after which he spent his remaining (1925–41) years in Whitehorse, Smithers, Atlin, and Teslin. His brother, Jean-Baptiste-Barnabé-*Elphège* Allard (1918–35), 20 years his junior, worked at the Lejac (1922–23) School and Terrace (1923–27), where he built a church. He also visited many of the mining camps from Stewart to Hyder. From 1925 to 1935 he was in charge of the Missions at Telegraph Creek, McDame, Lower Liard Post and Stuart Lake. He was one of the first Oblates to pilot a plane. Tragically, he drowned on 13 July 1935 in the Stikine River during one of his many plane trips, and was buried in Whitehorse.

Father Joseph-François Allard with a group of Tlinkit Natives in Atlin (AD)

Father Jean-Baptiste-Barnabé-Elphège Allard,
August 1919 (AD)

The colourful Corsican missionary to the Native peoples, Nicolas Coccola (1905–43) spent most of his career in the region working at Stuart Lake (1905–21) and at the nearby Lejac School (1922–34), where he was also principal. He devoted his last years to being chaplain (1934–43) at the hospital in Smithers. Another Quebecois, Honorius Rivet (1904–39) ministered at Dawson (1904–06) and then at Hunker, Last Chance, Eldorado, Sulpher and Bonanza (1906–09), as well as Prince Rupert, Prince George, Moricetown, Hagwilget, Smithers, Terrace, Ocean Falls, and Anyox (1910–32), which was an important copper mining and smelting town. He was also on the staff of the Lejac Residential School. He lived his final years in the vicariate apostolic of Mackenzie, where he died suddenly

Church in Terrace, founded by Father Elphège Allard (AD)

and under mysterious circumstances, sometime between the 30th or 31st of May 1939, and was buried at Goldfields, Saskatchewan.

Philéas Gagné, also from Quebec, ministered in the Yukon for 36 (1919–56) years spending his time in Dawson (1919–50) and Whitehorse (1950–56). Bernard Edmund Burley Anderson, for years the only religious brother in the region, devoted over thirty (1923–64) years teaching at the Lejac Residential School.[15]

This environment, given its huge distances and remoteness, was bound to demand and develop men who did not always reflect the Oblate "ideal," especially "strict" observance of the "holy rule," although in other ways they acted similarly to their colleagues in the south. This was the impression of a canonical visitation of the Yukon and Prince Rupert Vicariate conducted by Joseph Rousseau in June-October 1942. In his report, Rousseau complained that "religious poverty" was practiced more in the breach, especially since such luxuries as personal "cameras," "worldly amusements," including "public games and the movies," were, according to Rousseau, common activities among Oblate missionaries in the region. In reaction, Rousseau posed the question: "what authority shall we have to thunder in the pulpit against the dangers of so many immoral representations, if we ourselves are seen assisting at them?" Rather the laity, he declared, would "rightly" reply:

"*medice, cura teipsum.*" He also noted problems that were common among all the Oblates working in the far west, particularly the widespread "ignorance of Indian tongues," which Rousseau said was "almost complete and universal" throughout the entire region.[16]

With the division by Rome of the apostolic vicariate of the Yukon in 1944, the northern part became the apostolic vicariate of Whitehorse, while the southern was named the vicariate of Prince Rupert (1944) and eventually (1968) the diocese of Prince George. Jean-Louis Coudert (1944–65) became the first vicar apostolic of Whitehorse, which was directly under St. Peter's Province. By 1947 Whitehorse had about 2500 Catholics, most of whom (1600) were Euro-Canadians, although this was out of a total population of around 10,000. To serve it, there were then two parishes, nine Missions, and 13 Mission Stations. The overwhelmingly Oblate personnel included one bishop, 20 priests, and three brothers. During the same period, the vicariate of Prince Rupert had 4000 Catholics, most of whom were Natives and mainly nominal, out of a total population of 8000. As for financial support, all of the Missions in the far north depended almost totally upon outside support, especially the funds supplied by the Catholic Church Extension Society of Toronto. It had eleven Missions each with a resident priest and about 50 Mission Stations. As well as a bishop, it had a mainly Oblate staff of 21 priests and one brother.[17]

✤ Ministering to Asians

RACISM, ever since the coming of Europeans, had been a central feature of life in the far west. Native peoples were the first to feel its pain, and Asians were soon added to the list. Viewed as a cheap and ready supply of labor, the Fraser River gold rush in 1858 and later the building of the CPR gradually brought large Asian populations to the region. For almost a century Asians supplied simplistic explanations for "white" unemployment. The Chinese, since they were the most numerous, were the major target, though by the 1890s, the Japanese were also beginning to experience public prejudice and hostility. Finally, bowing to this historic disgrace, in 1923 the federal government passed a Chinese immigration law that would totally prohibit their entry into Canada until 1947.[18]

Racism had long been implicitly fostered by the Catholic Church, and this sin of omission was clear in the centuries-long pro-western approach it

Chinese Mission in Vancouver (AD)

had taken in trying to proselytize in foreign lands. In the far west, with a few exceptions, this attitude is evident in the church's essential dismissal of Native culture, which always implied an attitude of Native inferiority. It is hardly surprising that there were no attempts to challenge such bigotry against Asians, especially when it came from Catholics. Instead, it was either accepted in silence or even encouraged as part of the status quo. In Vancouver, articles in *The Monthly Bulletin* as well as *The Bulletin* reflected this. While Native people might have been implied, in most cases it was Asians who were the most obvious targets, especially the more numerous Chinese, who by the 1920s had become the most popular scapegoats in explaining most social problems, particularly Euro-Canadian unemployment. From its inception in 1917, *The Monthly Bulletin* and its successor, *The Bulletin* carried a prominently displayed and explicitly racist advertisement sponsored by *The Coast Lumber and Fuel Company,* which assured its customers that "*White* Drivers Only Deliver Our Coal and Wood."[19]

It is hardly surprising that, except for the establishment of several small Missions in Vancouver and Victoria, there was never a significant effort by the Catholic Church to evangelize Asians in British Columbia. Protestant denominations made some attempt to proselytise among Asians in the late nineteenth century, but, except for the Methodists who were a bit more tolerant, the rest were as racist as the general population. Racism was very strong among Catholics, though much like other churches, cultural ignorance on the part of both Asians and Euro-Canadian Catholics must not be excluded. As there were far fewer Japanese, perhaps making them much less a threat to the Euro-Canadian job market, it was towards them that the initial approach was made when in 1912 the archdiocese of Vancouver opened its first Asian Mission. As a further indication of its relatively minor importance, especially when compared to "white" ministries, the Mission was initially put in the sole care of religious women, and it was a policy that would be continued with regard to other Asians. The first director, a member of the Sisters of the Franciscan Tertiary, was Sister Mary of the Angels, who was assisted by Sister Jeanne Marie. Together they opened the Japanese Catholic Mission, first in a rented room and then a building on Cordova Street East. For several years, until his death in 1916, the secular pastor of Sacred Heart, J.F. McNeil conducted Mass for the nuns, and afterwards this duty was assumed by an Ontario-born Oblate, Julien-Augustin Bédard (1887–1932). The major education undertaken at the Mission was the teaching of English. No doubt this was the central reason why most Japanese attended it, for after eight years the two sisters had produced only seven converts: six men and one woman, all of whom were of school age, averaging from 16 to 24. Financial support was also a problem, since local "white" racism, which some would cloak under the term "indifference," meant few Euro-Canadian Catholics were prepared to support a school which taught skills that many were certain would ultimately threatened their livelihoods.[20]

It was not until 1921 that a Catholic Chinese Mission was opened in Vancouver. Again, reflecting its inferior status in a male dominated church, religious women were also placed in charge. Its staff consisted of four Missionary Sisters of the Immaculate Conception, a Quebec order that specialized in Asian Missions. The first company included Sisters Marie de Saint Georges, Aimée de Jésus, Marie du Saint Rédempteur and Marie du Sacré Coeur. While they also opened a school that concentrated on teaching English, since French was their first language, and the only one that the nuns had mastered, they had a serious problem attracting Chinese students. By 1923 they had turned their attention from education to "death-bed conversions" as the far easier means of "gaining Chinese souls," and started a small Catholic Chinese Hospital to care for the elderly poor and dying. By 1928, it had grown from a 32 to a 85 bed unit facility, which forced it to move from Pender Street to a much larger building on the corner of Cordova and

Campbell. Most of its financial support came from the local Chinese community, which apparently appreciated the nuns' willingness to care for the Chinese who were sick and dying and had no other family. Though it was officially known as the Catholic Chinese Hospital, locals, both Chinese and Euro-Canadians called it the "The Oriental Home," reflecting the fact that it was in effect a hospice.[21]

In Victoria there was no Mission to Asians until 1940, and then only to the Chinese. Again, as in Vancouver, religious women were in charge, and here the staff comprised three Sisters of Our Lady of the Angels of Sherbrooke, Quebec: Mother Mary of the Sacred Heart, and Sisters Margaret Mary and St. Rita. Together they established the Chinese Catholic Mission on the corner of North Park and Quadra Streets. However, the nuns were soon joined by William Matte, a priest of the Scarboro Foreign Mission Society, a recently established Canadian order whose sole purpose was to work among Asians both in Canada and the far east. In 1942, another Scarboro missionary priest, Lawrence Hart joined the Mission. Like its counterparts in Vancouver, the Mission also concentrated on the teaching of English in the hope of gaining Catholic converts; as usual there seemed to be little interest in that regard among most of their students. To obtain Asian "souls," the Victoria Mission also opened a very tiny Chinese Hospital on Herald Street, where most of the patients consisted of the poor and old who, as in Vancouver, had no other family to care for them. As members of a "captive audience" nearing death, they formed the bulk of the Chinese "converts" in Victoria, whose "souls" the "white" Catholics believed would thus be "wafted to Heaven...after [they received] the saving grace of Baptism." Therefore, although it was never realized, the hope was expressed in Victoria that a much larger Catholic Chinese hospital, similar to the one in Vancouver, might soon be established "where the cure of souls" could accompany the "cure of bodies." Continued financial problems, however, made such an expectation quite unrealistic.[22]

✣ The Years Before 1945

IN THE DIOCESE OF VICTORIA, the generation following the MacDonald period (1909–1923), like that of the province, were marked by faltering growth and deep depression, and only after 1945 would there be any true economic stability. Lay contributions, even in the best of times, were always

St. Andrew's Cathedral, Victoria, 1897 (ASSD)

sporadic, and, as noted, even today, but then far more so, the diocese was heavily dependent upon the generosity of the Catholic Church Extension Society of Toronto. However, the Great Depression forced the Extension Society to impose cutbacks, and thus this period was far worse, making physical expansion very difficult. Besides the economy, another major reason was the short tenure of MacDonald's immediate successors: Thomas O'Donnell (1924–29), Gerald Murray (1930–33), and John MacDonald (1934–36), all of whom were quickly and respectively promoted to the archdioceses of Halifax, Winnipeg and Edmonton. It seemed that Victoria was becoming a "school for bishops" where a person acquired some basic skills as an ordinary, and, if apparently mastered, moved on to bigger, and thus

Church festival in Fort St. James (AD)

more responsible assignments. Anselm Wood, an Englishman and a convert from Anglicanism, and rector of St. Andrew's Cathedral noted in 1923 that Victoria appeared to be a place where a bishop learned to "sacrifice" himself in what Wood called "this outpost of civilization," and then, if "successful," graduated to a more promising diocese. The dearth of a Catholic population in greater Victoria, still, in effect, the diocese, which during the period hovered around 6.3 percent, the lowest in Canada, was not a very encouraging reality.[23]

Even so, there was very modest growth. During this time a few small, garage-sized chapels of ease were built, mainly by the local laity, on the outskirts of Victoria in Strawberry Vale, Lakehill, Metchosin, and Langford, and served by clergy from Victoria. The most noteworthy event occurred on 16 May 1931 with the opening of the new St. Louis College building on Pandora Street. Outside Victoria, Holy Family parish was founded in Port Alberni (1925) with John Bradley as it first pastor, and Courtney also gained that distinction in 1937 with the construction of Canadian Martyrs where Carl Albury became pastor. Due to the work of the Sisters of St. Ann, St. Joseph's Hospital in Victoria was expanded, and the nuns took over the small hospital in Campbell River, originally founded in 1914 by the Sisters of St. Joseph of Toronto.[24]

John C. Cody, the twelfth bishop of Victoria (1937–46) provided the diocese with a bit more stability. During his time a Memorial Chapel was built under St. Andrew's Cathedral commemorating Demers, Seghers, and John Jonckau, a pioneer priest, and where their mortal remains were buried. Chapels of ease were also constructed in a number of locations, including Port Alice and Alert Bay, which were served by John Bradley. The Sisters of St. Ann opened Mount Saint Mary's Nursing Home in Victoria, and the city also witnessed the establishment of the "Veritas" Library at 222 Menzies Street that contained, as the name implied, over 2000 volumes on Catholic themes, especially apologetics. In 1938 the Oblates returned to Vancouver Island to replace the Benedictines at the Kakawis Residential School. The Catholic Youth Organization (CYO) began in September 1937 in St. Andrew's and was inaugurated in Vancouver in 1939. Reflecting the times, Cody also popularized Eucharistic devotions, and before leaving to become the bishop of London, Ontario, and as part of the centenary celebration of the diocese in July 1946, he held the first public *Corpus Christi* procession through the streets of Victoria. The event sparked a Protestant protest lead by a Baptist minister, J.B. Rowell, a veteran critic of Catholicism, who complained that it should be stopped since it was "repugnant" to local Protestants. However, the majority of Victoria residents ignored the controversy as many did organized religion.[25]

This period saw the continued growth of Catholic triumphalism, ultramontanism and clericalism. Marian devotions were still central in reinforcing this type of ahistoric ecclesiology. Such views are well exemplified in a retreat that Cody conducted in September 1939 at the Oblate English-speaking Scholasticate of the Holy Rosary near Ottawa. Reflecting on confession, Cody noted that no matter how long a Catholic might have to spend in Purgatory, if he confessed well, "his soul is saved. On the other hand," he noted, "the non-catholic has to wait until he dies to find out if he is forgiven." Moving on to a Marian theme, Cody, referring to the naval victory of Lepanto of 7 October 1571 when the western Europeans defeated the Ottoman Empire, he maintained that the date was "the only feast of the Church which commemorates a battle...[as a result of which] Europe was saved from the Turks by means of the Rosary." As for Mary, his audience was assured that, to save sinners, she "would have been willing...to have nailed Christ to the Cross...with Her own hands." Given his audience, Cody stressed the priesthood. Applauding the attitude of the "old Irish people," he declared that "if a priest happened to have a failing for drink, for instance, they would hide him away and endeavour to keep it [liquor?] from him but not one word of criticism would pass their lips. Unfortunately," he concluded, "we of today criticize the priest far too freely." As for the sacrament of penance, Cody insisted that it "never has been known, even for a fallen-away priest, for one to dare break the sacred seal of Confession." If, he concluded, "Judas had only waited a few days before hanging himself he could have gone to one of the Apostles (one of the priests of the new law) and had his sins forgiven in the Sacrament of Penance!"[26]

During this period, in both Vancouver and Victoria, disinterest, reflected in continued poor contributions, dominated the thinking of most Catholics where lay giving remained a serious problem even after 1945, although it showed a marked increase beginning in the 1950s. In the years leading up to the Second World War, there were lay Catholics who tried to redouble their efforts to retire parish liabilities throughout the mainland and on Vancouver Island. But when it came to raising the necessary funds, it was always an uphill battle. With the coming of the Great Depression, it was almost impossible. Before 1929 phrases such as "a decided lack of co-operation," to an "absolute selfish indifference" reflected the problem and the various attempts to solve it. In March 1920, the suspected backsliders, as well as those who refused to help, were warned that soon they would have no church to attend. Such threats, however, if they had any impact, probably only hardened attitudes that were already indifferent, and they most likely made others even more hostile. It would require years of further fund-raising and sacrifice by the minority of church goers that did give until at least some progress was finally achieved. It was not until April 1927 that the most prosperous parish in the entire archdiocese, Holy Rosary finally announced it was "in excellent financial condition." Within three years, the Great Depression would bring not only further financial woes to Holy Rosary, but, except for the money that was needed for the barest essentials, until at least the mid 1940s, fundraising was extremely difficult throughout the far west.[27]

Despite continued setbacks, due at least in part to Casey's (1912–31) lack of ability, because of the lead taken by the local clergy, there were also signs of growth in parishes and clerical personnel in the archdiocese. In 1912 St. Joseph's church in Port Moody was opened, and in the following year, St. Anthony of Padua in Agassiz and Our Lady of Good Hope in Hope became realities. In Vancouver, St. Andrew's Parish was begun in 1912 and formally established in the following year. In 1912, the Servites of Mary began Our Lady of Sorrows Parish, and in the following year they also opened Corpus Christi.28

However, all was far from rosy. In 1912 Our Lady of Lourdes in Maillardville, which was the center of a French Canadian community, was destroyed by fire. In the following year Désiré Jeannotte, a secular priest, who was pastor in Sandon and Lumby, suddenly died. The Oblates, John Welch and Jean-Baptiste Salles (1908-26) were both ill, the former from a weak heart and latter from an illness that required frequent hospitalization, and another Oblate, Joannes-Marius Duplanil (1908-38) was then suffering from consumption. An Oblate, Victor Rohr (1898-1939) complained to Neil McNeil in 1913 of the continued priest shortage in British Columbia, and lamented that the new archbishop of Toronto had not stayed "a few more years" in order to supply "a few more good priests and to help us organize." Frequent transfers during Casey's tenure seemed to indicate morale problems. Priests were assigned and then just disappeared. There were at least a few instances of "substance abuse," probably alcoholism, and in such cases men were simply sent packing with little or no regard for where they might go or to whom they might seek help. As in the secular realm, so in the church, it was an age of denial, in which "problem" people, especially priests, brothers and nuns, simply did not exist.29

During the worst years (1913-27) that followed the land speculation crisis, while few new parishes were opened, there was a steady, though, given certain "problem" personnel, an often halting increase in secular clergy. From the time of Casey's arrival in 1912 until his death in 1931, the number of diocesan clergy had risen from 17 to 38, most of whom had arrived already ordained and from outside the archdiocese. For, like the Oblates, most secular clergy came mainly from the east and south, especially Ontario and the United States.30

For years the archdiocese of Vancouver had been in need of sound leadership, which it finally obtained in 1928 when William Mark Duke (1931-64), another Maritimer from St. John, New Brunswick, was named coadjutor to Casey with right of succession. Soon known both affectionately and otherwise as the "Iron" Duke, the much more effective head of the archdiocese inaugurated major administrative changes, chief among them being the subdivision of the huge territory into districts, the largest of which eventually become the dioceses of Nelson (1936) and Kamloops (1946). During his lengthy term in office, Duke also established 32 parishes and 24 parochial schools, and raised the number of secular priests from 23 to 72. Regular clergy had also increased during the same period from 43 to 86, most of whom were Oblates, who by 1964 had 38 priests and 18 brothers working in the archdiocese. In fact, the Oblates, despite their setbacks, remained the most important clerical body in the Catholic Church both on the mainland of British Columbia as well as in the Yukon.[31]

Statistics, however important, hardly tell the human story, for while the Oblates remained the largest male religious community in the archdiocese, like McNeil and Casey, the "Iron" Duke was no Oblate patron. Since their arrival in the far west in 1847, the Oblates had been forced to contend with secular ordinaries who, though they wished to retain their services, often resented their independence and numerical strength. The Oblates had been able to escape this predicament for 45 (1863–1908) years through the appointment of three Oblate bishops. Since the advent of the first secular archbishop, Neil McNeil, the Oblates saw their influence gradually wane, although he and his successor, Casey, while not friends, neither is there any evidence of their overt hostility towards the Oblates. Yet this was not the case with Duke who by June 1933 was complaining that both the Oblates and the Sisters of St. Ann were far too free in giving or withholding their services, implying that the archdiocese would perhaps be better off without them. In November 1936, he indicated that there were "too many" Oblates and Sisters of St. Ann in the archdiocese, and by December, as a "practical" solution, he suggested that all of the French Oblates should be recalled. By the early 1940s, Duke was insisting that he had a right to have financial statements from all of the Oblate residential schools in order that he could "tax" them. In July 1948, according to the Oblates, he expressed a "most senseless" notion of creating a diocesan superintendent of Native Oblate Missions and of appointing a secular priest to fill such an office. While there appear to have been no serious repercussions on either side from such incidents, and certainly Duke remained far too dependent upon the Oblates and Sister of St. Ann to take any concrete steps against them, his behavior was a powerful sign that, while the Oblates remained the largest clerical body on the mainland of British Columbia, by 1945 they had ceased being the dominant clerical power in the archdiocese of Vancouver.[32]

✦ Challenging the Status Quo

REFLECTING ON THE EVENTS of the 1930s and 1940s in British Columbia
reveals how the Catholic Church there did little to challenge the status quo.
Rather, again stressing a form of Gnostic-dualism or other worldly theology,
it largely avoided dealing with the systemic problems of class, race and gender that had fed societal separation and also fostered and helped to bring
about the Great Depression. Through the experiences of those years, it was
"secular" society, in recognizing its responsibility to promote democratic
socialization, that began the process of making life better for all. The
Catholic Church had little or nothing to do in helping to bring about this
new understanding, but instead, especially in its determined opposition to
all forms of socialism, it implicitly and at times explicitly helped to perpetuate racial, class and gender discrimination.

The vast majority of the Catholic laity in British Columbia were working
class and were terribly affected by the Great Depression. The financial crisis
would not be fully alleviated until 1939 and the beginning of the war, the
results of which, after 1945, would slowly transform life throughout the
region. The Kidd Report was the initial reaction of the Conservative government in Victoria to the financial crisis. The Report was essentially a
laissez-faire, élitist reaction that revealed the "fundamental dichotomy"
within far western society, particularly in the areas of race, class and gender.
Due to the general public's rejection of this formerly perennial approach and
the Conservative party that represented it, the Liberals were the immediate
beneficiaries of the Great Depression. Nevertheless, the strength of the Cooperative Commonwealth Federation (CCF) also demonstrated that many
citizens desired far more extreme solutions—ranging from the social gospel
to female activism to radical socialism. By 1933, though the Liberals were the
government of British Columbia, the left, represented by the CCF, had
become the official opposition, a regional situation unheard of before then.[33]

By 1935 the economy showed some signs of recovery. This was especially
true in forestry and fisheries; however, mining, except for gold, reflected the
major industrial downturn. Agriculture, traditionally a very small share of
the local market, fared even worse. Agricultural co-ops, particularly in the
fruit industries made some progress, but viewed by many, especially those
in power, as another version of feared industrial unionism, at first they had
to face federal legal injunctions. By then the work camps that the provincial

and federal governments had established to control, for they did not solve the growing unemployment, had produced strong working class frustration and unity. In December 1934 over a thousand men descended on Vancouver protesting camp conditions. For those in power, the central anxiety was that such unrest would soon lead to a "revolution," or, worse, a "communist government in Canada."[34]

Though Ottawa tried to introduce unemployment insurance in 1935, it was not declared constitutional until 1940, for it was only with the advent of war, and the enormous economic boast it provided, that the "problem" of the depression was finally "solved." By then the airplane and radio had reduced isolation in the far west. Canada had already begun the process of moving from an agricultural to an industrial nation during the First World War, a process that World War Two completed. The Second World War also meant a boom for all sectors of the economy in the far west, and America's entry into the conflict in 1941, which resulted in the construction of the Alaska Highway, further opened up northern and central British Columbia as well as the Yukon Territory. After 1945, labor unions too became "an integral part of public policy," especially in the forest industry.[35]

The only regional group who suffered as a direct result of the war was the Japanese, whether native born or not, especially after the attack on Pearl Harbor. There had always been a "smoldering hatred of Orientals," in the region, and war events gave full vent to it. Since most of the Japanese internment camps were located in the Nelson area, the bishop of Nelson, Martin Johnson (1936–54) asked and received help in dealing with this new reality. Three religious communities of women responded, all from Quebec: the Sisters of the Assumption, the Sisters of Our Lady of the Angels and the Missionary Sisters of Christ the King. While the provincial school curriculum was taught in the camps, the federal Department of Labour, which administered the schools, only provided elementary education. Thus, the Christian churches, since the Anglican and United Churches also conducted such schools, saw an opportunity and offered kindergarten and high school classes. As English was at best the nuns' second language, and most spoke it poorly, if at all, they had to depend upon Japanese internees to translate for them. The hope of the Sisters was to gain "conversions," though given the "captive" nature of their students and families, largely a result of Western racism, such an expectation was even less likely in the internment camps. In fact, Japanese Canadians were stripped of everything, including their citizenship, and were compelled to abandon their property for which most gained little or no compensation. Not until 1988 would the federal government officially apologize and grant some financial reparations. It would take another decade before Ottawa made a similar admission to the Native people. Class, race and gender, and the terrible anomalies they represented, would begin to gain public recognition after 1945, and slowly change the "way things were" in the far west to the way things "ought to be."[36]

Nowhere in the events that dominated the period before 1945, especially in challenging the evils of classism, racism and sexism was the Catholic Church a leader, locally, nationally or internationally. Greatly influenced by its Gnostic and dualistic theology, the Catholic Church, defending the status quo, essentially stood on the "theoretical sidelines." This remained its stance, despite the fact that most of its members, as working class Euro-Canadians, were among those who suffered most as a result of the hard economic times. The ultramontane focus of the church's constitution, obstinately defended by its hierarchy, sometimes out of fear of Vatican displeasure, meant that all "wisdom" emanated from Rome. In 1931, Pius XI "answered" the global crisis with his encyclical *Quadragesimo anno,* which marked the fortieth anniversary of *"Rerum Novarum"* (1891) by Leo XIII, the first serious papal reflection on the modern world. Like Leo, Pius condemned individual human greed as the central cause of the latest international disaster, but he did not do so collectively, especially as that greed was expressed in laissez-faire capitalism. Further, since Rome had seen its own historical territory seized by Italian nationalists in the nineteenth century, and because "natural law" supposedly defended it, Pius insisted that "private property," including extreme personal wealth, must not be questioned. Instead, he offered as his major solution to the international problem the re-Christianization of Western Europe, which, for him, effectively equated into a return to pre-French Revolutionary society that, if ever realized, would have re-instated Catholicism to its supposed feudal prominence.[37]

Not only did capitalism get off quite lightly in the pope's critique, by comparison socialism, in any form, was roundly condemned. For, wrote Pius, "if, like all error, socialism contains a certain element of truth, it is nevertheless founded upon a doctrine of human society peculiarly its own, which is opposed to true Christianity." Pius believed either "religious socialism" or "Christian socialism" to be oxymorons. Pius stated that "no one can be at the same time a sincere Catholic and a true socialist." Church leaders, with the pope at the forefront, viewed the economic status quo, which for centuries had been expressed in some form of capitalism, as essentially acceptable; just as the church had doggedly defended feudalism as "natural," since it reflected the then "reality" of secular power. In effect, ever since the time of the Emperor Constantine I (d. 337) and Augustine's (d. 430) *City of God*, unless, like Soviet communism, it was overtly atheistic, Roman Catholicism has usually blessed the status quo as part of some "divine" plan. Thus the church kept to its almost studied role of being the caboose and was rarely counter-cultural or the engine of social change. By 1945 there was a half-hearted willingness on the part of some bishops outside Quebec to allow Catholics to support the CCF. Most bishops, however, remained staunch ultramontane reactionaries, who, after all, owed their positions as ordinaries to the Vatican. Bishops throughout Canada, but especially in Quebec where the church was strongest, continued to condemn all forms of democratic "socialization."[38]

This was certainly the case with regard to the Catholic Church in British Columbia. There, throughout these years of social, economic and political turmoil, the church did nothing more radical than to support voluntarism, a traditional Christian answer to such problems and the only acceptable alternative to any form of democratic socialism. As for its overall numerical position, at least nominally, not until 1951 would the church see a tiny rise in its share of denominational affiliation in British Columbia to 14.4%, whereas both the Anglican (27.1%) and United (29.3%) churches were then almost or more than twice as large. Yet in Vancouver, Victoria and Nelson, the seven bishops who lead the church during this period made no attempt to adopt any new methods that might have challenged the societal status quo. Instead they merely promoted local branches of the National Catholic Welfare Bureau, a national organization which was essentially a voluntarist body that supported the relief of the poor through direct charity and "spiritual renewal." Carefully keeping with papal teaching, the bishops in the region refused to back any form of socialism. Especially that promoted by the CCF which then represented varying shades of socialism from the very far left to "Christian socialists," such as that espoused by many clergy in the United Church of Canada. In the eyes of the Catholic bishops of British Columbia, however, and following Rome's lead, any form of socialism implicitly promoted class warfare, attacked private property, and was always overtly "materialistic."[39]

Native Missions booth, Vancouver Missionary Exhibition, 1945 (AD)

16

Years of Reaction, Reform and Reflection

✤ The Europeans and the Catholic Church After 1945[1]

THE SECOND WORLD WAR influenced extraordinary changes in British Columbia, especially in its move away from the "racist and patriarchal assumptions of an earlier age." Building on the expectations of a pre-war socialist philosophy of such groups as the CCF, in a society that now had the money to fund such hopes, British Columbia began providing for all of its citizens, especially for those who would otherwise have been unable to fulfill such needs.

In 1936, the province was the first in Canada to propose publicly funded health care. Though a referendum supported it, the medical profession then had sufficient political clout to frighten Victoria into abandoning the idea. Later, following the lead of a CCF government in Saskatchewan, Victoria introduced hospital insurance in 1948. Public dissatisfaction with the inefficiency of hospital insurance ultimately contributed to Social Credit's first victory in 1952. With necessary federal assistance, full medical insurance became a reality in 1965.

By 1966, due to a gradual rise in life expectancy from 61 in 1931 to 73 by 1971, the federal government established the contributory Canada Pension Plan, and in 1970 the retirement age was lowered from 70 to 65.

In 1960 a provincial study recommended that all students should finish high school. By then the province's school districts had become more manageable and equitable, having been reduced from a high of 650 to under 100. In line with this, studies showed that at least 20 percent of high school graduates would benefit from higher education which, in the 1960s, lead to the establishment of three new universities and a system of community colleges throughout the province.

Trade unions also became more user-friendly, especially for employers, since they were gradually stripped of radical, even revolutionary elements. Owners were less frightened of the unions and improved working conditions for employees—a central aim even in pure Marxism.

Women were also affected, since while most left their wartime jobs in 1945 as they had done in 1918, by the 1950s there was a growing feminist movement that had made modest gains in the province. With the highest childless marriage rate in Canada, by 1970 British Columbia had the highest percentage of women in the workforce. Progress was very slow in childless families in encouraging husbands to share responsibility in the home. Studies at the time showed that under such conditions married men with working wives contributed only six minutes a week to household chores. Where there were children, the husband's total weekly contribution skyrocketed to an entire hour. While progress was being made in the workforce, outside the professions, by the 1990s females doing the same job were still only being paid two-third's the male rate.[2]

In trying to meet the marked increase in the Euro-Canadian population in British Columbia, between 1936 and 1968 four new dioceses were created: Nelson (1936), Kamloops (1945), Whitehorse (1967) and Prince George (1968). By 1910, Vancouver and Victoria, with their urban infrastructure reflected in such things as electric street cars, were as "sophisticated" as any cities in North America. Nelson, while "a pale reflection," due to mining and the arrival of the CPR, was then the only other city in the province that apparently merited that description. Highway construction under the Social Credit Party in the 1950s made the final links. Mining was why first the Americans and after them the British and Canadians saw great potential in the region. Once the population base reached a high enough level, a diocese was created. Like other dioceses, Nelson had its share of diocesan organizations such as the CWL, K of C and others. Similar to the Church throughout the mainland, its roots were Oblate, with Fouquet and Richard being followed by the secular Althoff. They were initially assisted by the Sisters of St. Joseph of Peace. Beginning with twelve priests and eleven parishes in 1936, today Nelson is served by 44 clergy, including nine communities of nuns, who work in 30 parishes. While Nelson, like all dioceses, remains essentially strongly hierarchic, since Vatican II lay participation in decision making is more visible, if not always effectual.[3]

Until after 1945 Kamloops remained "a sunny healthful town of some five thousand people who mixed trout fishing with cattle ranching," but, due to regional economic growth, that in British Columbia has always been centered in urban areas, by the 1960s it began "to look dangerously like a city," and today it has a population of over seventy thousand. The early roots of church activity there were Oblate: Grandidier, Martin, Le Jacq, Le Jeune, and Coccola are among the earliest to work in the Kamloops area. In 1941, Archbishop Duke established Kamloops as the administrative headquarters for the interior of B.C. Soon he had removed the Oblates from Sacred Heart Parish, where they had ministered for over 50 years, replacing them with seculars, lead by Duke's first auxiliary bishop, Quentin Jennings, who eventually became the first bishop of Kamloops (1946–52). In 1880 the Sisters of St. Ann became the initial community of nuns to assist the Oblates there by establishing St. Ann's Academy at Mission Flats near Kamloops. By the time of its foundation in 1946, the diocese had nine parishes, 21 priest, 13 of whom were religious and three communities of women religious. Today there are 29 parishes, 21 priests, eleven of whom are religious, mostly Oblates, and 22 nuns from seven communities. Statistically, over the last 50 years the general population of the region has increased almost ten-fold, whereas its Catholic population is four times its pre-World War II size.[4]

The diocese of Whitehorse (1967), though a suffragan of the archdiocese of Grouard-McLennan, and while its focus is the Yukon Territory, also covers part of far northern British Columbia. Since the Catholic Church's permanent beginnings in the Yukon in 1896, the Oblates have continued to dominate ministry in this huge region, which is served by the Oblate Province of Grandin, Edmonton. A Quebecois, Camille Lefebvre (1898–1906) was the first, though others were to follow such as Edmond Gendreau (1898–1902), Alphonse Desmarais (1897–1901), Augustin Dumas (1898–1901), Émile

Bunoz (1902–36), Jean-Louis Coudert (1936–65), James Mulvihill (1967–71) Hubert O'Connor (1971–86) and many more. In 1967, the diocese had 16 parishes served by 22 priests, all but one being Oblate, three Oblate brothers, and 22 religious women divided between five communities. Today there are 14 Oblates, two of whom are brothers, and four secular priests minister, all of whom work in twelve parishes. There are five religious congregations of women in the region with a total of eight members. Although the general population has remained fairly constant over this period, averaging about thirty-four thousand, the number of Catholics, at least statistically, has reportedly more than tripled from four to over twelve thousand.[5]

Before becoming a diocese in 1968, Prince George had been the prefecture of the Yukon (1908) the vicariate of the Yukon and Prince Rupert (1916), and the vicariate of Prince Rupert (1944). Local economic considerations determined its history. In 1908 some believed the GTPR would soon make Prince Rupert more important than Vancouver, and while this never materialized, a few thousand settlers remained in the region. Due to the Alaska Highway, which gradually promoted northern interior growth, by 1971 Prince George was twice the size of Prince Rupert, and today is over four times larger with a population of over seventy thousand, making it the fifth largest city in the province after Vancouver, Victoria, Nanaimo, and Kelowna. Such was its success, that in 1989 Prince George convinced Victoria to make it the site the province's latest autonomous University of Northern British Columbia. It is against this backdrop that the diocese also grew, again from Oblate roots, which continue to dominate its clerical base. In 1908 it had 21 Oblate priests and 16 brother who were assisted by two communities of women religious, which included ten Sisters of St. Ann and 18 Grey Nuns of Montreal. Today there are 13 Oblate priests, two brothers and eight secular priests. Thirty religious women from ten congregations presently work there. During the same period the Catholic population in the region has statistically gone from twelve thousand to almost sixty thousand, although the general population is twenty times what it was in 1908.[6]

Fergus O'Grady, an Oblate and the first bishop of Prince George (1956–86) is probably best remembered for founding the Frontier Apostolate, a volunteer organization that drew people, mostly in their twenties, and mainly from Canada, the United States and the British Isles to dedicate at least a year of their lives to various needs in the diocese. Often referred to as "Bishop O'Grady's Peace Corps," it started in 1956. Further inspiration came from Vatican II (1962–65) and its emphasis upon lay involvement in church ministry. By 1976, it had attracted almost two thousand people who worked in a wide variety of occupations including cooks, teachers, secretaries, houseparents, religious educators, bus drivers, maintenance and general construction. The last occupation was perhaps the most important during its early years, which saw the building and ultimately the operation of twelve grade schools and one high school (Prince George College) in the diocese. To supply their construction needs, the volunteers also operated a glass and brick factory. Although there were still a dozen or so volunteers in the early 1990s, the advent of provincial funding of private schools in 1978 gradually made such volunteerism unnecessary, so much so that the Frontier Apostolate was finally phased out in 1996.[7]

Education remained one of the central concerns for the Catholic Church in British Columbia before Vatican II, along with Marian and Eucharistic devotions. In encouraging vocations and the education of seminarians, Bishop James Hill of Victoria (1946–62) stressed the need for "docile" candidates, a condition that Catholic education hoped to engender in all of its graduates, and so make them "loyal" members of mother church. For example, in 1956, while Carlow College in Ireland indicated its willingness to prepare a few Native Irish candidates for Victoria, Hill suspected that they would only select "difficult ones" who had no sense of "proper discipline," and thus, Hill believed, the diocese would be better off without such men.

It was also during this decade that Marian devotions reached a level of popularity formerly unheard of in the Catholic Church in North America, so much so that throughout the region Mary often appeared far more important than Jesus Christ, and British Columbia was no exception. As it had for over a century, the papacy was behind the movement, seeing it as a central means of increasing its universal influence, especially over women who were the most involved, not only in Marian devotions, but who remained the backbone in sustaining lay interest in all organized religion. The initiating moment of the latest version of Marianism came on 1 November 1950 when Pius XII, in the only use of papal infallibility since it had been defined at Vatican I in 1870, solemnly declared *ex cathedra* the Roman Catholic doctrine of the Assumption, or that Mary had been bodily assumed into heaven. While 1954 was declared the International Marian Year, annual public celebrations during the decade, especially in October and May, were held throughout the far west, growing in size and intensity. That is until Vatican II which discouraged such religious observances, with the result that strong papal promotions of Marianism rapidly declined and, outside of international shrines such as Lourdes, have essentially become part of private devotionalism. Though certainly secondary, the other major public religious event during this period was the Eucharistic Congress. These consisted of large public displays, usually held once in a decade, centering on Benediction of the Blessed Sacrament, and because of infrequency, which doubtless heightened their popularity, they were often conducted in sports stadiums, since no local church building could have held the numbers. Like Marian devotions, they too rapidly declined after Vatican II which, in its liturgical reforms, stressed lay participation in public worship, something that Eucharistic congresses, which remain a largely clerical activity, do not encourage.[8]

Education, especially the separate schools issue, continued to dominate public reports on the Catholic Church in British Columbia. On 20 November 1947, in the course of dedicating a new school in Vancouver, Archbishop Duke declared that, like the rest of Canada, the Catholics of British Columbia had a right to separate schools, including a Catholic university. To achieve this, Duke believed that Catholics had to be "noisier" than, what he called, certain "small groups." He was referring to the evangelical Protestants in the Lower Fraser Valley, whose demands, he declared, while they were "not nearly so reasonable" as those of Catholics, used methods that were calculated to always achieve the desired objective. A few days later the regional edition of the *CCF News* responded to Duke's challenge. It praised British Columbia as the only province in Canada that had studiously avoided mixing "organized religion and public affairs." The clearest example of this was its refusal to fund separate schools, which the *News* insisted "proved so disastrous" in the rest of the country. The *News* also asserted that the province's nonsectarian public school system had the great benefit of developing a "democratic attitude to life," especially by "wielding together people of diverse backgrounds." Duke, in a mildly worded letter to the *News*, naturally took exception to such a conclusion. However, his diocesan controlled newspaper, the *B.C. Catholic* went much further, asserting on December 4th that the CCF editorial contained "shades of Nazism," something that a "shouting Goebbels" would have applauded. In reply, the *News* dubbed the *B.C. Catholic* piece "arrant nonsense," and that its "intolerant tone" only served to prove the point of their objection, for the *News* was convinced that a separate provincial school system would only "place walls of intolerance between young people." Nor, it believed, could such schools provide the "objective and unbiased education possible in non-secular schools," which it concluded were "sorely needed in a democratic society."[9]

In 1953 and 1954 the separate schools question was again raised. As before, some Catholics in British Columbia, especially bishops such as the "Iron" Duke, initiated the debate and publicly condemned the refusal of Victoria to support Catholic schools as "manifestly unjust." In March 1953 in a published letter to the premier, W.A.C. Bennett, the CWL repeated a long held belief among a minority of local Catholics that the provincial public schools system would never be acceptable to "good" Catholics since they were manifestly "Godless," and thus implicitly immoral. Opponents of a separate schools system in British Columbia were equally adamant, calling Roman Catholic desires "outrageous demands," and in 1953 one critic insisted that if they "had the power," Roman Catholics would "dominate the world more ruthlessly than the Russians." In 1954, J.B. Rowell, the pastor of the Central Baptist Church in Victoria and veteran critic of Catholicism, published a pamphlet entitled: *Separate Schools: A Vital Question.* He noted that some Catholic bishops used as a threat the fear of hell and even excommunication to intimidate Catholic parents into sending their children to parochial schools. He also observed that in both Ireland and Spain, where the church had considerable public support, Protestants were still referred to in school textbooks as "heretics." He also cited a church history book published in the late nineteenth century but still in use in the state funded Catholic schools in Ireland. In it, Rowell reported, the priest author, T. Gilmartin suggested that the state had a duty "in suppressing heretics" even to the point of imposing the "death penalty." Though a less jaded observer might have cited textbooks then in use in Ontario's separate system that were not overtly abusive of Protestantism, the isolated nature of organized religion in British Columbia tended to bring out the very worst in everyone concerned. Thus, as in the past, the separate schools controversy generated far more heat than light, and in the end, only demonstrated the inherent divisiveness of all extreme denominationalism. With their hopes for a separate system again defeated, Catholics in British Columbia, particularly their bishops, once again retreated, though not, they hoped, in final defeat.[10]

Although not as a separate schools system, in 1978, the Legislative Assembly of British Columbia finally did agree to begin funding nonpublic schools. This change was mainly influenced by a steady increase of conservative Christian immigration to the Lower Fraser Valley which had begun after 1945, especially Dutch Calvinists and other strongly traditionalist/conservative evangelical Protestant denominations. Recent statistics indicate these churches have more than doubled since 1981. With over half a million, British Columbia, the most unchurched province in Canada also contains, paradoxically, one of the nation's most significant "Bible belts." Beginning at 30 percent, within a decade Victoria was covering over 70 percent of private education costs. So much so that pupils in private schools in British Columbia have now doubled to over eight percent.

There are several other ironies here, chief among them being that between 1965 and 1978 Catholic education in British Columbia very noticeably declined because of a lack of inexpensive teachers from religious orders. Now, because of provincial funding, student numbers in Catholic schools are about twice what they were during their previous high levels in the 1950s. Their earlier inability to grow was partly the result of the growth of social liberalism after 1945, witnessed especially in public welfare such as in health care as well as other areas. However, another important factor in this regard was the historic lack of Catholic unity or lay interest, mainly because most of the laity had always preferred to send their offspring to free public schools rather than to pay tuition for any Catholic alternative. Yet, as Duke noted in 1947, it is now the fundamentalist Protestants of British Columbia that are providing the political clout to achieve something for the Catholic Church that it had never been able to achieve on its own, due to the fact that the bishops did not enjoy the strong and vital support of most of the laity on the issue. This situation is now being repeated in Quebec and Newfoundland, where a growing lack of public support for separate schools has recently lead to the abandonment of the concept. Even so, contemporary studies show that most parents who send their children to religious schools in British Columbia, as elsewhere, especially Catholic ones, do so mainly for nonreligious reasons. Smaller classes, more discipline, less fear of drugs, pre-marital sex, and even classism are often cited. However, religious instruction is a quite secondary consideration in their decision, whereas before 1965, religion had been a central factor in that decision. Reflecting this reality, well over 50 percent of parents who send their children to Catholic schools in the province are not Catholic and apparently have little or no interest in converting.[11]

The first and still the only Catholic college in British Columbia is the Seminary of Christ the King, which was founded in 1940 and operates as part of Westminster Abbey in Burnaby. St. Mark's College, on the UBC campus, was for years the hoped-for site of an independent Catholic liberal arts college that the local hierarchy hoped could gain university status and provincial support and funding. While St. Mark's was viewed by UBC authorities as a potential school of theology, Catholic leaders, especially Duke saw no need for another seminary, since Christ the King was already fulfilling that role. Although in 1950 the Basilians began to teach at UBC, Duke's insistence that he must have an independent institution meant that St. Mark's remained unincorporated until 1956, when Henry Carr, CSB, became its first principal. However, like its neighboring denominational colleges, it could only grant degrees in theology. Since very few lay Catholics were interested in majoring in theology, and the archdiocese was bound to protect the interests of Christ the King as the diocesan seminary, St. Mark's remained in an educational limbo. While it was used as a residence hall, given the unwillingness of UBC to make an exception for St. Mark's that it was not prepared to extend to its denominational neighbors, the desire to found such a Catholic liberal arts college in British Columbia failed.[12]

Things seemed more hopeful when Notre Dame University of Nelson began in 1950. Martin Johnson, the first bishop of Nelson (1936–56) and later Duke's coadjutor (1956–64) and successor (1964–69), was its founder. Johnson wanted to provide a local alternative for Catholics in the Kootenays so that they would not have to go to the nearby Jesuit (Gonzaga University) institution in Spokane, Washington, since most Canadians who went there remained, many becoming American citizens after graduation. Notre Dame continued to struggle to gain provincial recognition until 1963 when it was granted a provincial charter along with the Universities of Simon Fraser and Victoria. Most local Catholics who could afford to do so did not wish to attend a small, purely "Catholic" institution, but rather preferred the nonsectarian alternatives where there were larger faculties and better equipment. Good faculty were also hard to obtain or retain given Nelson's relative remoteness, and worse, its city fathers took little interest in a "Catholic" University, which meant operating money, essential to its survival, was very hard to obtain. All of these problems finally lead to its closure in 1983.[13]

Although Duke would never budge in his determination to have a separate Catholic university, the hopelessness of such an undertaking seemed already clear in the early 1950s. At a meeting set up to review a provincial government offer to fund St. Mark's, but only as a theological college, an intractable Duke insisted that he only "wanted a Catholic university." One of the three Catholic lay members of the committee, Angelo Branca, a well-known provincial judge and alumnus of UBC, angrily retorted: "where the hell are you going to get the money?" When Duke refused to discuss the matter further, Branca "stamped out" of the meeting, and as a result, the Catholic college project went nowhere. Certainly against a backdrop of recent public funding of primary and secondary private education, a small Catholic minority in British Columbia persist in their determination that a tax supported Catholic liberal arts college must ultimately become a reality there—St. Mark's continuing as the major candidate. Because many formerly church controlled institutions of higher education elsewhere in Canada have been taken over by provincial governments, this possibility seems most unlikely.[14]

In contrast to the essentially small Catholic minority in British Columbia, the Catholic electorate in Quebec and Newfoundland now appear to see little value in separate schools. In Quebec, language and not denomination is now the determining factor in defining its separate boards. In Newfoundland, in a September 1997 referendum the public, of which over 30 percent are Catholic, voted by a resounding majority of over 70 percent to end publicly funded denominational schools. In responding to the results, Premier Brian Tobin, a Catholic, noted that if the churches still wished to educate their children in their religious traditions, it must henceforth be their duty and not that of the taxpayer to fund such institutions. In addressing the results Tobin noted: "parents, not the churches, will have the ultimate right and responsibility to direct their children's education." "We will hire our teachers because they are competent, caring and committed, not because of any religious consideration." From this time forward, he said, parents and elected legislators would be accountable, and not "non-elected and unaccountable church representatives," who would "have no special role and no special place in the new school system."[15]

Since the 1860s such a nonsectarian public view has dominated and continues to do so in British Columbian society. It is true that for the last 20 years provincial funds have been available for nonpublic schools, however, the overwhelming majority of Catholics who sent their children to such private schools do so for nonreligious reasons. It is very possible that such funding could end as quickly as it began, especially if there is a perceived improvement in public schools in the province. Or again, given the long tradition in the province against tax supported separate schools, there is a public reaction against what many must even now consider special treatment for private, mainly denominational schools.

As Premier Tobin noted, if church leaders in Newfoundland wish to have such schools, in the future they will have to obtain funding directly from their laity. To do so Catholic bishops there as elsewhere must convince them that a religion-based education is better than a public alternative. For certainly at present most of the Catholic laity, the core of the *sensus fidelium*, especially in Quebec and Newfoundland, and certainly this would include British Columbia, do not believe so. As John Robson, the liberal editor of the *British Columbian* and a future premier noted in 1865, it behooves Christian denominations to stop "pretending" that they are uniquely suited to contribute to the moral improvement of society. But rather, as history and the present show, by their frequent encouragement of religious bigotry, particularly in their often negative thinking in such areas as gender, race, class and sexual orientation, they have often produced just the opposite effect. Church history then as now would seem to support Robson's conclusion. For far from improving general morality, especially in the recognition and support of a pluralistic society that respects and encourages diversity and even ambiguity, religious education has many times promoted quite opposite attitudes. Frequently, it has fostered religious and other forms of narrowness and intolerance. Perhaps the churches can reform themselves and through serious ecumenism rid themselves of these negative elements. They can strive to become truly counter-cultural in encouraging ever greater social tolerance and acceptance of others, and so challenge their all-too-frequent historic support of the status quo.[16]

However, history does not bode well for Christianity, either in Canada or elsewhere. In two of its major past crises, its split from its Jewish roots and the divisions occasioned by the Reformation, its reactions to both showed a frightening inability to appreciate and even learn from differences as Jesus taught. Instead, usually with state support, the churches accepted and even celebrated bigotry and hate, or, sadly, instead of defending the radical inclusiveness of the gospel, they have too often fostered the all-too-human easy-way-out, or the status quo.

✤ The Church of Vatican II and Beyond

PERHAPS THE MOST CONTROVERSIAL CATHOLIC ISSUE in Canada to indirectly touch the Catholic Church in British Columbia during the years just before Vatican II was the case of Archbishop Joseph Charbonneau of Montreal, who would "retire" to Victoria in 1949 under an ecclesiastical shadow.

Quebec was long used to church-controlled trade unions such as the Confederation of Canadian Catholic Labourers (CCCL). Beginning in the 1920s and especially after 1945, lay members in the CCCL had begun to challenge clerical influence and interference. This was possible because the war years had encouraged a professionalisation of the CCCL, which took on full-time lay leadership that was prepared to challenge the status quo. Reflecting these changes, in 1949, over 5,000 asbestos workers in Quebec, ignoring clerical and management opposition, struck for both higher wages and stricter health precautions.

Identifying himself with the strikers, and the changing labor environment in Quebec, Charbonneau declared in a famous sermon that the working class in the province was a "victim of a conspiracy," the sole aim of which was "to crush it." Until then, in one of the extremely rare instances in Canadian Catholic church history in which a church leader challenged the status quo, Charbonneau continued: "when there is a conspiracy to crush the working class, the Church has a duty to intervene." Responding to this new trend, in 1943 Charbonneau had been instrumental in giving Quebec Catholics the "green light" to vote for the progressive CCF. In 1949, Maurice Duplessis, the Union Nationale premier of Quebec, who owed his political position to the powerful, mainly anglophone business community in the province, and his popular support to Quebecois nationalists, began to intensify his efforts to remove his opposition. Beginning with the liberal Dominican, Georges-Henri Lévesque, Duplessis complained to Rome and the Holy See soon responded by beginning to "investigate" the priest. Even Charbonneau had felt forced to bend, removing Jean D'Auteuil Richard, the editor of the liberal *Relations* after the paper was threatened with a libel suit by Duplessis and a number of powerful local businessmen. In 1949, given Rome's long tradition of almost always supporting state power, no matter the religious affiliation, Charbonneau was forced "into exile" in Victoria. Until his death on 19 November 1959, Charbonneau served as a chaplain at St. Joseph's Hospital, Victoria. In reporting his death, the Victoria press raised obvious questions about his "sudden and mysterious resignation" a decade before. His funeral oration, which took place in St. Andrew's Cathedral, was preached by Bishop Laurent Morin (1959–83) of Prince Albert, Saskatchewan, who only noted that in 1949 Charbonneau had "submitted his resignation" to the Vatican and was given a "papal honour in return."[17]

The incident marked an important turning point for the Catholic Church in Canada, including even British Columbia. In Quebec, the Charbonneau affair heralded the first signs of what came to be called the "quiet revolution" which by the 1980s had effectively ended the powerful official social influence of the church in that province. Most church leaders in Quebec seemed eager to relinquish such influence. For the Charbonneau affair also demonstrated that the clergy, no matter how highly placed, were not really in charge. For if they attempted to assert themselves, like Charbonneau, they soon learned where the real power resided, namely with the secular state which Rome, through its concordats, both formal and informal, has often been happy to oblige. The ostensible reason normally given by the Roman curia in removing a "troublesome" cleric, such as a Charbonneau, was that the "good of religion" demanded it.

It was also for the "good of religion" that Pope John XXIII decided to convene the Second Vatican Council (1962–65) in 1959, the same year as Charonneau's death, in order to achieve an *aggiornamento,* literally a "shaking-up" or up-dating of the church to meet the challenges of the contemporary world. Not since the French Revolution had the Catholic Church officially questioned where it was going. The French Revolution, with its radical rejection of the "old order," was the watershed that ultramontanism tried to answer, and it became its raison d'être and the basis for the foundation of the Oblates and most other religious communities of men and women throughout the nineteenth and most of the twentieth centuries. In a real sense, Vatican II was the Catholic Church's French Revolution, for it effectively marked the beginning of the end of its "old order." In line with the future Council, in 1961 John XXIII issued his encyclical *Mater et Magistra* signaling the church's final acceptance of the modern world and defending political, social and economic "socialization" as important facts of modern life. By then, democratic "socialization," such as health care, social welfare and other government programs were beginning to become an accepted and very valued part of Canadian society, especially in British Columbia.

Nowhere has the "old order" in the Catholic Church in Canada more dramatically ended than in Quebec. There, as the result of a Liberal government's advent, within a decade the "quiet revolution" effectively terminated the church's former dominance in the province, which had been part of Quebec society since the failed rebellion of 1837 and the union of Upper and Lower Canada in 1841. The Dumont commission in 1971 called for the democratization of the Catholic Church in Quebec where attendance has plummeted from a high of 88 percent in 1957 to less than ten percent today. However, unlike France, secularization and a growing respect for pluralism in Quebec has been achieved with very little official anticlericalism. While the church in Quebec is struggling to find its way, one direction appears to be its desire to become the countercultural social conscience of the province. It is a movement reflected on the national level by many in the Canadian Conference of Catholic Bishops. Their recently published works include *Ethical Reflects on the Economic Crisis* (1983), *Will the Poor Have the Most to Fear from Social Security Reform?* (1994), and, on the rights of the Native people, *Let Justice Flow Like a Mighty River* (1993).[18]

What of the Catholic Church in British Columbia where organized religion has always had a difficult time? There the latest Canada census indicates that over 30 percent now report "no religion," whereas nationally, in 1991 that figure was 20 percent, the highest in Canadian history. Experts who study the future of Christianity throughout Canada expect that any real change within the churches will be very unlikely since most remain "largely aloof from Canadian society," operating rather as "isolated and insulated religious clubs." This prediction seems already reflected in the fact that for the first time an overwhelming majority (approximately 80%) of Canadians no longer or very infrequently attend church, and this includes women and the middle class who were long the backbone of those who continued to go. It appears that the rest of Canada has joined British Columbia in expressing something that seems irrevocable, namely that Canada is no longer a Christian country, and an ever growing pluralism appears to indicate that such a reality is permanent.[19]

Just as in the past relationship of the Oblates and the Catholic Church with the Native people, again there is "no future" to the present system of rigid denominationalism, especially as reflected in its narrow and mutually exclusionist theology that still predominates in Euro-Canadian society, since religion is increasingly "irrelevant" to the lives of most Canadians. Much of the problem centers upon the Gnostic-dualism that continues to bedevil Christian theology. Instead, what is needed is the cohesion of the natural and supernatural. With such an understanding, commitment to social justice is also a spiritual event, not just "activism," for "it includes faith and the transformation of consciousness" into "a single history." While organized Christianity continues to insist that it is much more than any culture, it rarely practices what it preaches. For instead of affirming hope, unity and compassion and interpersonal connections between God and individuals both locally and globally, by its need to cling to denominational "truth" it consequently intensifies societal divisions. The historic and present evidence on this point, especially in the on-going ethnic-religious civil wars in many parts of the world, such as Northern Ireland or Rwanda, that have a "Catholic" or "Christian" basis, is sadly too voluminous and too obvious. That is except for those, who, preferring "fantasy," choose not to see, insisting instead that "religion," and the bigotry and divisiveness that have long been fostered by all types of rigid denominationalism, have absolutely nothing to do with such horrors. Thus, rather than being countercultural as the gospel demands, Christianity often continues to be just one more reflection and reinforcement of cultural prejudice, distrust and dysfunctionalism.[20]

Perhaps the most important conclusion is that there is an enormous spiritual hunger in Canada as in the rest of the world, a hunger that Christianity, properly reformed, could well help to address. The question is when might this happen. Certainly, as reflected in the hoped-for Oblate relationship with the Native peoples, it must be rooted in the desire to form "a renewed convenant of solidarity," which must be grounded in interdenominational and ultimately interfaith. Yet, as their influence declines, many Canadian Christians who see no need for change on their part, have instead adopted a "victimy" approach, implying that the larger society, in its increasing view of the irrelevance of all organized religion, is somehow "persecuting" all Christians. This has recently lead to such public displays in Vancouver and other cities as the "March for Jesus" which is backed by the major, Toronto based religious right organization in Canada, *100 Huntley Street,* and which stress the need to "protect [the]...dwindling rights" of Christians in Canadian society. It would appear that few Canadians, especially in British Columbia, are probably prepared to accept such "fantasy" versions of reality, especially given the recent public funding of private, mainly denominational schools in the province. Actually, such displays may well backfire on the churches, and, as in Newfoundland, instead prompt the majority of the electorate to demand that public funds only be spent on nonsectarian, public education.[21]

Reflecting on the irrelevance that most Canadians now feel towards all organized Christianity, in the fall of 1995, the bishop of Victoria, Remi De Roo (1962–99) noted a growing desire among people for ecumenical communities that are not connected to a parish or any institution. "Most promising Catholics," in De Roo's view, "are no longer in the churches." What saddens him most is that "at the very moment when church institutions are on the eve of collapse, they seem bent on reaffirming their power and bringing everything under control and convincing themselves that they can weather the storm." In a sobering conclusion, he noted: "we are into a very heavy session of Good Friday, and Easter is a long way around the corner."[22] In an even more chilling conclusion for those who still believe that God and the church are joined immortally, Scott Peck, the popular and bestselling author on spirituality, believes that God has "possibly largely left the church."[23]

Yet it is the gospel and not the institutional church that is central to the Christian message and faith. The gospel's demands have never been easy, perhaps explaining why they have usually been ignored by the churches. Certainly one of the central requirements of that gospel, and a basic root of Jesus Christ's message, is the command that his followers must be inclusive. Thus, they are called to reject all narrow-minded bigotry and triumphalism, and truly accept others, especially societal "out groups," such as other religions, women and Native people, as they accept God and themselves, and all of which is so well exemplified in the parable of the Good Samaritan. In addressing that challenge, Pope John Paul II noted that, as the Christian churches enter the third millennium, they must become increasingly aware of all those times in their past that they have departed from that gospel, and instead indulged in "forms of counterwitness and scandal." To achieve this, John Paul II believes that it is necessary for all Christians not only to remember those many past shadows, but also in some explicit way to learn to "make amends" for them. For ultimately, he writes, the truth of the gospel "cannot impose itself except by virtue of its own truth." That "truth" totally rejects "intolerance," or the "use of violence" of any kind, but, instead, demands the "power" of "gentleness," the power of love. Perhaps for many Canadian Christians, this is *the* important lesson and challenge that church history has to teach us all both in *The Lord's Distant Vineyard* as well as throughout Canada.[24]

Historic Oblate Cemetery, Mission City, British Columbia (AD)

Appendices

APPENDIX I

Ecclesiastical Jurisdictions

1843	Vicariate Apostolic of the Oregon Territory
1846	Ecclesiastical Province of Oregon City (Portland)
1846	Archdiocese of Oregon City (Portland)
1846	Diocese of Walla Walla (Suppressed 1853)
1846	Diocese of Vancouver Island (Later (1908) Victoria)
1850	Diocese of Nesqually (1850) (Later (1907) Seattle)
1847	Oblate Religious Vicariate of Oregon (under Rome)
1857	Oblate Religious Vicariate of British Columbia (under Rome)
1863	Vicariate Apostolic of British Columbia (under Rome)
1871	Vicariate of British Columbia (under Archdiocese of St. Boniface)
	became
1890	Diocese of New Westminster
1903	Archdiocese of Victoria (Reverted 1908)
1903	Diocese of New Westminster(Suppressed 1908)
1908	Archdiocese of Vancouver
1908	Diocese of Victoria
1936	Diocese of Nelson
1945	Diocese of Kamloops
1968	Diocese of Prince George
1944	Archdiocese of Grouard-McLennan
1944	Vicariate Apostolic of Whitehouse
1967	Diocese of Whitehorse
1926	St. Peter's Oblate Province (New Westminster-Ottawa)
1968	St. Paul's Vice Province (Vancouver)
1973	St. Paul's Province (Vancouver)

Oblate Vicars-Mission Superiors

Pascal Ricard (1847–1857)
Louis D'Herbomez (1857–1890)
Paul Durieu (1890–1899)
Augustine Dontenwill (1899–1908)
John Welch (1908–1926)

Oblate (St. Peter's) Provincials

John Welch (1926–1929)
William Byrne-Grant (1929–1932)
Denis Finnegan (1932–1935)
Joseph Scannell (1935–1947)
Joseph R. Birch (1947–1953)
Fergus O'Grady (1953–1956)
Lawrence K. Poupore (1956–1962)
Gerald E. Cousineau (1962–1968)
J. Lorne MacDonald (1968–1973)

Oblate (St. Paul's) Vice-Provincials

John Hennessy (1968–1973)

Oblate (St. Paul's) Provincials

John Hennessy (1973–1974)
John Massel (1974–1979)
Allan Noonan (1979–1985)
Thomas Lobsinger (1986–1987)
Larry MacLennan (1987–1993)
Raymond L'Henaff (1993–)

Ordinaries

Vicariate Apostolic of British Columbia
(1863–1890)
Diocese of New Westminster
(1890–1908)
Archdiocese of Vancouver (1908)

Louis-Joseph D'Herbomez, OMI
(1864–1890)
Paul Durieu, OMI (1890–1899)
Augustine Dontenwill, OMI (1899–1908)
Neil McNeil (1910–1912)
Timothy Casey (1912–1931)
William Mark Duke (1931–1964)
Martin Johnson (1964–1969)
James Carney (1969–1990)
Adam Exner, OMI (1991–)

Diocese of Victoria (1846)

Modeste Demers (1847–1871)
Charles John Seghers (1873–1878)
Jean Baptiste Brondel (1879–1883)
Charles John Seghers (1885–1886)
John N. Lemmens (1888–1897)
Alexander Christie (1898–1899)
Bertram Orth (1900–1908)
Alexander MacDonald (1909–1923)
Thomas O'Donnell (1924–1929)
Gerald Murray, C.Ss.R. (1930–1936)
John Cody (1937–1946)
James Hill (1946–1962)
Remi J. De Roo (1962–1999)
Raymond Roussin, SM (1999–)

Diocese of Nelson (1936)

Martin Johnson (1936–1954)
Thomas McCarthy (1955–1958)
Wilfred Emmet Doyle (1958–1989)
Peter Mallon (1990–)

Diocese of Kamloops (1946)

Edward Jennings (1946–1952)
Michael Harrington (1952–1973)
Adam Exner, OMI (1974–1982)
Lawrence Sabatini (1982–)

Vicariate (1908) and Diocese
of Prince George (1968)

Émile Bunoz, OMI (1908–1945)
Anthony Jordan, OMI (1945–1955)
Fergus O'Grady, OMI (1956–1986)
H. P. O'Connor, OMI (1986–1991)
Gerald Wiesner, OMI (1992–)

Archdiocese of Grouard-McLennan

Vicariate (1944) and Diocese
of Whitehorse (1967)

Jean-Louis Coubert, OMI (1936–1965)
James Mulvihill, OMI (1967–1971)
Hubert O'Connor, OMI (1971–1986)
Thomas J. Lobsinger OMI (1987–2000)

Table 1: Select Populations

Year	Canada	Natives		British Columbia	Yukon
1871	3,689,257	n.a.		36,247 (0.9%)	n.a.
1881	4,324,810	108,547 (0.025%)	105,690 (0.024%)	49,459 (1.1%)	n.a.
1891	4,833,239	n.a.		98,173 (2.0%)	n.a.
1901	5,371,315	127,941 (0.028%)		178,657 (3.3%)	27,219 (0.00506%)
1911	7,206,643	105,611 (0.014%)	105,492 (0.014%)	392,480 (5.4%)	8,512 (0.00118%)
1921	8,787,949	113,728 (0.012%)	110,814 (0.012%)	524,582 (5.9%)	4,157 (0.00047%)
1931	10,376,786	128,890 (0.012%)		694,263 (6.6%)	4,230 (0.00040%)
1941	11,506,655	125,521 (0.010%)		817,861 (7.1%)	4,914 (0.00042%)
1951	14,009,429	165,607 (0.011%)		1,165,210 (8.3%)	9,096 (0.00064%)
1961	18,238,247	220,121 (0.012%)		1,629,082 (8.9%)	14,628 (0.00080%)
1971	21,568,311	312,760 (0.014%)		2,184,621 (10.1%)	18,388 (0.00085%)
1981	24,343,181	491,460 (0.020%)		2,744,500 (11.2%)	23,070 (0.00094%)
1991	26,994,045	532,060 (0.019%)		3,247,505 (12.0%)	27,655 (0.00102%)

SOURCE: Lascelles, *Roman Catholic Residential Schools*, p. 93. Second set of numbers are variants; *Statistics Canada*, 1991, 93–315, p. 12.

Table 2: Native People in British Columbia and the Yukon

Year	British Columbia		Yukon	
1871	25,661		n.a.	
1881	25,661		n.a.	
	35,052			
1891	35,202		n.a.	
1901	28,949		3,322	(11.4%)
	25,488		2,600	(10.2%)
1911	20,174		3,500	(17.3%)
	1,489	(07.3%)		
1921	22,377		1,390	(06.2%)
1931	24,599		1,628	(06.6%)
	1,543	(06.2%)		
1941	24,882		1,508	(06.0%)
1951	28,504		1,563	(05.4%)
1961	38,814		2,207	(05.6%)
1971	54,425		2,590	(04.7%)
1981	82,645		4,045	(04.8%)
1991	94,615		3,775	(03.9%)

SOURCE: Lascelles, *Roman Catholic Residential Schools*, p. 94. Second set of numbers are variants; *Statistics Canada*, 1991, 93–315, p. 93.

Table 3: Roman Catholics

Year	Canada		British Columbia		Yukon	
	Natives	Total	Natives	Total	Natives	Total
1871		1,532,471				
		1,536,733				
1881		1,791,982		10,043 (.0056%)		
		1,814,055		14,141 (.0077%)		
1891		1,992,017		20,843 (.0104%)		
		2,009,201		21,350 (.0106%)		
1901	39,350 (.0017%)	2,229,600	11,627 (.0052%)	33,639 (.015%)		4,453 (.0019%)
		2,238,955		34,020 (.015%)		6,594 (.0029%)
1911	44,031 (.0015%)	2,833,041	11,726 (.0041%)	58,397 (.020%)		1,849 (.0006%)
		2,841,881	58,760 (.020%)	1,902 (.0006%)		
1921	43,986 (.012%)	3,389,626	12,389 (.0036%)	64,180 (.018%)	100	739 (.0002%)
		3,399,011	1,528 (.0004%)			
1931	67,201 (.016%)	4,102,960	14,289 (.0034%)	91,641 (.022%)	64	668 (.0001%)
	64,898 (.015%)	4,289,839				
1941	63,268 (.013%)	4,806,431	14,503 (.0030%)	113,282 (.023%)	93	742 (.0001%)
1951	88,508 (.014%)	6,069,496	16,479 (.0027%)	168,016 (.027%)	266	1,845 (.0003%)
1961	121,148 (.014%)	8,342,826	22,258 (.0026%)	285,184 (.034%)	693	3,981 (.0004%)

1971	174,050 (.017%)	9,974,895	28,180 (.0028%)	408,335 (.040%)	845	4,675 (.0004%)
1981	271,625 (.024%)	11,210,390	526,335 (.046%)			5,465 (.0004%)
1991	470,615 (.038%)	12,335,255	603,080 (.044%)			5,580 (.0004%)

SOURCE: Lascelles, *Roman Catholic Residential Schools*, p. 95. Second set of numbers are variants.

Table 4: Day and Residential Schools

Year	Roman Catholic		Anglican		Presbyterian		Methodist-United		Salvation Army		Total			
	Day	Res.	Day	Res.	Day	Res.	Day	Res.	Day	Res.	Day BC	Day CA	Res. BC	Res. CA
1890												213	6	29
1895												245	10	45
1900	100		94		14		41				28	226	14	61
1905	74	33	55	17	7	9	39	8	1		33	232	17	71
1910	73	39	70	17	6	9	40	7	2		42	241	16	74
1915	90	39	71	21	5	8	40	8	2		46	257	18	78
1920	83	40	68	19	4	7	41	7	1		39	247	17	74
1925	78	39	72	20	5	7	39	7	1		42	247	16	73
1930		43		20		2		13			46	264	16	78
1935		44		20		2		13			48	262	16	79
1940		45		20		2		12			65	288	15	79
1945		45		19		2		10			55	255	13	76
1950		43		17		2		7			65	329	12	69
1955		46		15		2		6			65	368	13	69

1960	43	15	2	6	67	379	12	66
1965	42	15	2	6	66	342	12	66
1970	37				37	228	12	52

SOURCE: Lascelles, *Roman Catholic Residential Schools*, p. 96.

Appendices

Table 5: Native Students

Year	British Columbia			Canada		
	Day	Residential	Total	Day	Residential	Total
1890			491	5,649	1,022	6,671
1895			1,029			8,349
1900	893	675	1,568	6,349	3,285	9,634
1905	974	833	1,807	6,500	3,631	10,131
1910	1,149	836	1,985	6,784	3,841	10,625
1915	1,428	941	2,369	8,065	4,403	12,468
1920	1,197	1,115	2,312	7,477	4,719	12,196
1925	1,297	1,403	2,736	7,997	6,031	14,222
1930	1,437	1,846	3,291	8,299	7,302	15,743
1935	1,518	2,198	3,726	8,638	8,709	17,560
1940	2,035	2,025	4,067	9,140	9,027	18,396
1945	1,636	2,014	3,650	7,480	8,865	16,438
1950	2,704	2,182	5,463	13,986	9,316	25,054
1955	2,809	2,605	7,575	16,172	10,501	32,525
1960	3,194	2,107	8,898	19,174	9,109	40,637

1965	5,773	11,657	21,764	10,294	57,265
1970				27,870	66,707
1975				37,614	76,364
1980				34,083	89,967
1997				1,842	112,060

SOURCE: Lascelles, *Roman Catholic Residential Schools*, p. 97. Numbers often include Natives in non-Native schools, especially after 1945.

Table 6: Government Funding of Native Education

Year	Canada	British Columbia			Yukon		
		Day	Residential	Total	Day	Residential	Total
1890				40,496.15			
1895				53,200.00			
1900		8,400.00	59,050.00	67,450.00			
1905		12,350.00	78,550.00	90,900.00	5,000.00		
1910	402,542.82	13,822.13	71,517.93	85,340.06	2,399.41		2,399.41
1915	984,030.58	29,119.53	167,798.02	199,943.20	2,520.80	11,417.64	14,168.45
1920	1,057,662.00	43,225.12	127,314.39	176,346.64	3,472.50	11,474.80	15,017.58
1925	1,854,608.00	44,092.84	366,757.47	422,151.43	1,999.76	16,556.72	18,693.48
1930	2,330,438.00	60,509.33	462,517.45	532,578,97	2,502.70	13,493.64	16,422.86
1935	1,655,829.00	53,134.16	300,284.53	367,222.52	3,162.80	15,297.66	18,663.32
1940	2,331,553.00	85,695.94	338,445.20	424,141.14	3,045.00	18,629.18	21,674.18
1945	2,156,882.00	89,311.92	370,929.37	460,241.29	2,464.04	9,167.91	11,631.95
1950	6,221,792.00	470,700.09	722,062.39	1,192,762.48	30,525.86	29,555.95	60,081.81
1955	10,464,532.00	624,234.57	1,047,661.26	1,671,895.83	35,101.11	137,180.18	172,281.40
1960	24,908,023.00	1,783,881.69	2,532,433.04	4,316,314.73	14,129.24	1,277,753.78	1,291,883.00

1965	35,692,976.00	7,046,600.34	655,348.67
1970	100,000,000.00		
1975	164,500,000.00		
1980	224,426,000.00		
1986	234,888,970.00		
1991	762,333,671.00		
1993	893,448,050.00		
1997	770,362,000.00		

SOURCE: Lascelles, *Roman Catholic Residential Schools*, p. 98. *Public Accounts of Canada: Details of Expenditures and Revenues*, 1986, 1991, 1993, 1997.

Appendices

Table 7: British Columbia Population by Ethnic Origin

Year	British		Continental European		Asian		Native		Total
1871	8,576	(23.7%)	1,548	(4.3%),	25,661	(70.8%)	36,247		
1881	14,403	(29.6%)	2,490	(5.0%)	4,350	(8.8%)	25,661	(51.9%)	49,459
1891	n.a.		n.a.		n.a.		est. 27,305	(27.8%)	98,173
1901	106,403	(60.0%)	21,784	(12.2%)	19,524	(10.9%)	28,949	(16.2%)	178,657
1911	266,295	(67.8%)	69,799	(17.8%)	30,864	(7.9%)	20,174	(5.1%)	392,480
1921	387,513	(73.9%)	72,743	(13.9%)	39,739	(7.6%)	22,377	(4.3%)	524,582
1931	489,923	(70.7%)	127,246	(18.3%)	50,951	(7.3%)	24,599	(3.5%)	694,263
1941	571,336	(69.9%)	175,512	(21.5%)	42,472	(5.2%)	24,882	(3.0%)	817,861
1951	766,189	(65.8%)	319,056	(27.4%)	25,644	(2.2%)	25,504	(2.4%)	1,165,210
1961	966,881	(59.4%)	554,712	(34.1%)	40,299	(2.5%)	38,814	(2.4%)	1,629,082
1971	1,265,455	(57.9%)	767,808	(35.2%)	76,695	(3.5%)	52,430	(2.4%)	2,184,625
1981	1,505,467	(55.5%)	874,269	(32.2%)	204,856	(7.5%)	73,670	(2.7%)	2,713,615
1991	812,470	(25.0%)	539,565		739,835		74,415		3,247,505

SOURCE: Barman, *The West Beyond the West*, p. 363; Statistics Canada, 1991, 93–315.

Table 8: British Columbia Population by Religious Affiliation

Year	Anglic.	Unitd	Presby.	Luth. Prot.*	Cons. Cath.	Rom.	Jews	Confuc. Buddhi.	Other & None	Total
1881	10,913 (22.1%)	5,042 (10.2%)	5,753 (11.6%)	632 (1.3%)	621 (1.3%)	14,141 (28.6%)	104 (0.2%)	n.a.	12,252 (24.7%)	49,459
1891	24,196 (24.7%)	15,440 (15.7%)	15,655 (16.0%)	2,129 (2.2%)	3,648 (3.7%)	21,350 (21.8%)	277 (0.3%)	n.a.	15,478 (15.6%)	98,173
1901	41,457 (23.2%)	26,541 (14.9%)	34,478 (19.3%)	5,398 (3.0%)	7,555 (4.2%)	34,020 (19.0%)	554 (0.3%)	15,050 (8.4%)	13,607 (15.6%)	178,657
1911	101,582 (25.9%)	55,308 (14.1%)	82,735 (21.1%)	19,483 (5.0%)	20,533 (5.2%)	58,760 (15.0%)	1,384 (0.4%)	22,435 (5.7%)	30,260 (7.6%)	392,480
1921	161,494 (30.8%)	67,590 (12.9%)	123,419 (23.5%)	17,709 (3.4%)	24,451 (4.7%)	64,180 (12.2%)	1,654 (0.3%)	30,317 (5.8%)	33,768 (6.4%)	524,582
1931	206,867 (29.8%)	166,233 (23.9%)	84,941 (12.2%)	36,938 (5.3%)	32,025 (4.6%)	88,106 (12.7%)	2,666 (0.4%)	32,917 (4.7%)	43,570 (6.3%)	694,263
1941	246,191 (30.1%)	201,357 (24.6%)	94,554 (11.6%)	41,884 (5.1%)	49,323 (6.0%)	109,929 (13.4%)	3,244 (0.4%)	29,215 (3.6%)	42,167 (5.2%)	817,861
1951	315,469 (27.1%)	341,914 (29.3%)	97,151 (8.3%)	60,641 (5.2%)	81,712 (7.0%)	168,016 (14.4%)	5,969 (0.5%)	6,969 (0.6%)	87,410 (7.6%)	1,165,210
1961	367,096 (22.5%)	504,317 (31.0%)	90,093 (5.5%)	100,393 (6.2%)	113,141 (7.0%)	285,184 (17.5%)	7,816 (0.5%)	7,893 (0.5%)	153,143 (9.3%)	1,629,082

1971	386,670 (17.7%)	537,565 (24.6%)	100,940 (4.6%)	120,335 (5.5%)	172,552 (7.9%)	408,330 (18.7%)	9,715 (0.4%)	7,080 (0.3%)	441,438 (20.3%)	2,184,625
1981	374,055 (13.4%)	548,360 (20.2%)	89,810 (3.3%)	122,395 (4.5%)	233,635 (8.6%)	526,355 (19.5%)	14,680 (0.5%)	11,820 (0.4%)	782,499 (29.6%)	2,713,615
1991	328,580	420,760	63,985	108,190	552,000	595,320	16,565	36,430	987,985	3,247,505

SOURCE: Barman, *The West Beyond the West*, p. 367; *Statistics Canada*, 1991, 93–319.

*Barman, *The West Beyond the West*, p. 368. Conservative Protestants include "Baptists, Pentecostals, Mennonites, Church of God, Church of the Nazarene, Evangelicals, Free Methodists, Salvation Army, Christian and Missionary Alliance, Evangelical Free, Plymouth Brethren, Church of Christ, Disciples of Christ and any other comparable body."

Appendices

Table 9: British Columbia Non-Native Population by Sex

Year	Males		Females		Total
1870	5,477	(72.9%)	2,035	(27.1%)	7,512
1881	13,431	(74.4%)	4,613	(25.6%)	18,044
1891	41,354	(74.6%)	14,081	(25.4%)	55,435
1901	81,946	(70.9%)	33,687	(29.1%)	115,633
1911	198,783	(70.0%)	89,528	(30.0%)	288,311
1921	211,029	(58.5%)	149,781	(41.5%)	360,800
1931	290,727	(57.3%)	216,614	(42.7%)	507,341
1941	338,492	(54.0%)	288,492	(46.0%)	626,984
1951	432,830	(51.4%)	409,751	(48.6%)	842,581
1961	553,621	(50.7%)	538,478	(49.3%)	1,092,099
1971	773,277	(50.2%)	768,277	(49.8%)	1,541,504
1981	1,040,206	(49.3%)	1,068,811	(50.7%)	2,109,017
1991	1,625,975	(49.5%)	1,656,085	(50.5%)	3,282,060

SOURCE: Barman, *The West Beyond the West*, p. 369; *Statistics Canada*, 1991, 93–310.

Table 10: Population in British Columbia's Southwestern Corner

Year	Victoria City	Greater Victoria	Saanich Peninsula	New Westminster	Vancouver City	Greater Vancouver	Lower Fraser Valley
1881	5,925	c.600	488	1,500	n.a.	n.a.	n.a.
1891	16,841	c.750	610	6,678	13,709	n.a	n.a.
1901	20,919	c.1,250	n.a.	6,499	27,010	6,069	12,521
1911	31,660	5,919	6,026	13,199	100,401	35,890	29,138
1921	38,727	7,617	10,534	14,495	117,217	76,747	43,616
1931	39,082	9,166	12,968	17,524	246,593	52,405	57,480
1941	44,068	12,977	18,173	21,967	275,353	63,848	79,744
1951	51,331	22,113	30,550	28,639	344,833	123,828	139,157
1961	54,941	28,983	53,386	33,654	384,522	209,379	243,184
1971	61,761	31,348	78,645	42,835	426,256	286,421	385,660
1981	64,379	32,896	103,500	38,550	414,281	377,497	573,453
1991	71,228	40,246	105,600	43,585	471,844	489,471	689,766

SOURCE: Barman, *The West Beyond the West*, p. 374; *Statistics Canada*, 1991, 93–304.

Table 11: Population of Regional Urban Centres in British Columbia

Year	Nanaimo	Port Alberni	Prince Rupert	Prince George	Kamloops	Vernon	Kelowna	Nelson	Trial
1901	6,130	—	—	—	1,594	802	261	5,273	1,360
1911	8,306	—	4,184	—	3,722	2,671	1,663	4,476	1,460
1921	6,304	1,056	6,393	2,053	4,501	3,685	2,520	5,230	3,020
1931	6,745	2,356	6,350	2,479	6,167	3,937	4,655	5,992	7,573
1941	6,635	4,584	6,714	2,027	5,959	5,209	5,118	5,912	9,392
1951	7,196	7,845	8,546	4,703	8,099	7,822	8,517	6,772	11,430
1961	14,135	11,560	11,967	13,877	10,076	10,250	13,188	7,074	11,580
1971	34,029	20,063	15,747	33,101	26,168	13,283	19,412	9,400	11,149
1981	47,069	19,892	16,197	67,559	64,048	19,987	59,196	9,143	9,599
1991	101,736	18,403	16,620	69,653	67,057	23,514	75,950	8,760	3,558

SOURCE: Barman, *The West Beyond the West*, p. 375; *Statistics Canada*, 1991, 93–304.

Notes

ABBREVIATIONS

ACLA	American College Louvain Archives
AD	Archives Deschâtelets
AHA	All Hallows Archives, Dublin
ASSA	Archives of the Sisters of St Ann, Victoria
BCDA	British Columbia (Anglican) Diocesan Archives, Victoria
BCARS	British Columbia Archives and Records Service
HBCA	Hudson Bay Company Archives
JDA	Juneau Diocesan Archives
JPAS	Jesuit Provincial Archives, Spokane
Les Oblats	*Les Oblats de Marie Immaculée en Oregon*
Missions	*Missions de la Congrégation Des Missionnaires Oblats De Marie Immaculée*
MAA	Montreal Archdiocesan Archives
MAAO	Mount Angel Archives, Oregon
NAC	National Archives of Canada
NAP	National Archives, Paris
PAA	Portland Archdiocesan Archives
PFAR	Propaganda Fide Archives, Rome
QAA	Quebec Archdiocesan Archive
ROA	Rome, Oblate Archives
Rapport	*Rapport sur les Missions de Diocese du Quebec quo sont secourues par l'association de la Propagation de la foi*
Report	*Report of the Columbia [Anglican] Missions*
SFXUA	St Francis Xavior University Archives
SOCG AC	Scritture Originali...Congregazione Generali, Americano Centrale, Rome
TAA	Toronto Archdiocesan Archives
VAA	Vancouver Archdiocesan Archives
VanCA	Vancouver City Archives
VCA	Victoria City Archives
VDA	Victoria Diocesan Archives
VOA	Vancouver Oblate [Provincial] Archives

Notes

✤ Preface

1. The name of the province, British Columbia came into being on 19 November 1858, and until 19 November 1866 it only referred to the mainland, since until then Vancouver Island remained a separate colony.
2. A.G. Morice, *History of the Catholic Church in Western Canada: From Lake Superior to the Pacific, 1659-1895*, 2 vols. (Toronto: Musson, 1910); A.G. Morice, *Histoire de l'Église Catholique dans l'Ouest canadien, du Lac Supérior au Pacifique* (1659-1915), éd. Définitive (quatrième), 4 vols. (Winnipeg: chez l'auteur, 1928). Both works deal mainly with the church east of the Rocky Mountains. The first, out of 800 pages, devotes less than 100 pages to the far west, and though the second work spends almost 200 pages on British Columbia, this is out of a total of almost 2000 pages. As noted in the bibliography, Morice republished these works several times.
3. Reginald W. Bibby, *Fragmented Gods: The Poverty and Potential of Religion in Canada* (Toronto: Irwin Publishing, 1987), p. 271.
4. John Paul II, *Apostolic Letter: Tertio Millennio Adveniente* (New York: St. Paul Books & Media, 1994), pp. 39-40.
5. Doug Crosby, "Canadian Oblates' Statement: An Apology to Native Peoples," *Origin* 15 (August 1991): 183-84.
6. *Report* (London: Rivington 1882-1883), pp. 18-20.
7. Jean Barman, *The West Beyond the West: A History of British Columbia* (Toronto: University of Toronto Press, 1991), pp. 58-59, 69, 88-89, 91-92, 115, 142, 156-58, 163, 169, 209-11, 226, 265, 273-74, 300, 312, 335, 367-68.
8. Vincent J. McNally, "Victoria: An American Diocese in Canada," *Historical Studies* of the Canadian Catholic Historical Association 57 (1990): 25.

✤ Prologue

1. Jean Leflon, *Eugene de Mazenod, Bishop of Marseilles and Founder of the Oblates of Mary Immaculate*, Vol. I (New York: Fordham University Press, 1961), pp. 54, 256, 288-89; ROA, Eugene to his Father, Charles-Antoine de Mazenod, 7 December 1814.
2. Eugene de Mazenod to Charles de Forbin-Jansen, 9 October 1816, *Oblate Writings*, Vol. VI (Rome: General Postulation OMI, 1981), p. 24
3. AD, Méjanes Library, Aix-en-Provence, Ms B 69, Eugene to Charles-Antione de Mazenod, 28 August and 6 September 1817.
4. Leflon, *Eugene de Mazenod*, Vol. I, p. 288-89; T. Rambert, OMI, *Vie de Monseigneur Charles-Joseph-Eugene de Mazenod, éveque de Marseilles, fondateur de la Congrégation des Oblats de Marie Immaculée*, Vol. I (Tours: Romber, 1883), p. 250; Achille Rey, OMI, *Histoire de Monseigneur Charles-Joseph-Eugene de Mazenod, éveque de Marseilles, fondateur de la Congregation des Oblats de Marie Immaculée*, Vol. I (Rome: General Postulation, 1928), p. 319.

5. Hubert Jedin, ed., *History of the Church*, Vol. VII (New York: Crossroad Press, 1989), pp. 50–82, 84, 86, 115–25, 133, 148.

6. Hans Küng, *On Being a Christian* (New York: Doubleday & Co., 1968), pp. 460–62.

7. *Oblate Writings*, Vol. VII (Rome: General Postulations: OMI, 1984), p. 63. Mazenod to Tempier, 20 March 1826.

8. Jedin, *History of the Church,* Vol. VIII, pp. 23–24, 98–99, 106, 122, 133, 153, 211, 219, 222.

9. Achille Rey, *Histoire de Monseigneur Charles-Joseph-Eugène de Mazenod*, Vol. I (Rome, Oblate Generalate, 1928), pp. 237, 240, 295; *Missions* 35 (1897), pp. 188, 190, 199; Rambert, *Vie*, Vol. I, p. 205; Leflon, *Mazenod*, Vol. II, pp. 145–52.

10. Terrence Murphy and Roberto Perin, *A Concise History of Christianity in Canada* (Toronto: Oxford University Press, 1996), pp. 104–6, 223–28; Jedin, *History of the Church*, Vol. VII, p. 179; Vincent J. McNally, *Reform, Revolution and Reaction: Archbishop John Thomas Troy and the Catholic Church in Ireland 1787-1817* (Lanham, New York, London: University Press of America, 1995), pp. 27–35, 222–25.

11. A. Perbal, "Eugène de Mazenod sa vocation missionnaire," *Études Oblates* XIX (1950): 57-58; MAA, Relation du voyage de l'évêque de Montréal Ignace Bourget en Europe, 3 May to 23 September 1841. Bourget Letters, Vol. 9, pp. 312, 330, 399–400.

12. Gaston Carrière, *Dictionnaire Biographique des Oblats de Marie Immaculée au Canada*, Vol. I (Ottawa: Éditions de l'Université d'Ottawa, 1976–1987), pp. 34–35; Unless noted otherwise, most of the dates as well as other information regarding individual Oblates throughout the book will be drawn from this invaluable work; Ibid., Vol. III, pp. 210–11; Gaston Carrière, OMI, "Mgr Provencher à la recherche d'un coadjuteur," *Rapport de la Société canadienne d'Histoire de l'Église catholique* 37 (1970): 71-93; Gaston Carrière, OMI, "L'élévation du père Vital Grandin, OMI, à l'épiscopat, *Études oblates* 32 (1973): 100-134.

✣ 1 The First Europeans

1. Reuben Gold Thwaites, ed., *The Jesuit Relations and Allied Documents: Travels and Explorations of the Jesuit Missionaries in New France, 1610-1791,* Vol. 68 (Cleveland: Janis Press, 1896–1901), p. 334; Zephyrin Englehardt, *The Missions and Missionaries of California*, Vol. 2 (San Francisco: The James Barry Co., 1912), p. 146-47. On 17 July 1774 Fathers Juan Crespi and Thomas de la Perra made the first recorded sighting by Europeans of the Queen Charlotte Islands.

2. E.O.S. Scholefield and F.W. Howay, *British Columbia from the Earliest Times to the Present*, Vol. 1 (Vancouver: S.J. Clarke, 1914), p. 142.

3. Walter N. Sage, "Sir James Douglas and British Columbia," *University of Toronto Studies* 6, no. 1 (1941): 140.

4. Robert C. Johnson, *John McLoughlin: Father of Oregon* (Portland: Smith & Company Publishers, 1935), p. 26; Edwin V. O'Hara, *Pioneer History of Oregon* (Portland: Glass & Prudhomme, 1911), pp. 7, 13–14.

5. Daniel Lee and J.M. Frost, *Ten Years in Oregon* (Fairfield, WA: Ye Galleon Press, 1968), pp. 110, 125–28; F.G. Young, ed., *The Correspondence and Journals of Captain Nathaniel J. Wyeth, 1831-1836* (Eugene: University of Oregon Press, 1988), pp. 66–80; "Diary of Jason Lee," *Oregon Historical Quarterly* 17 (June 1916): 142, 247, 261–65.

6. Oregon State Historical Society, Manuscript Division, "Petition of [sixteen] Williamette [Catholic] Settlers [for a priest] to the Bishop of Juliopolis," i.e., Joseph Provencher, 8 March 1837.

7. E.E. Rich, ed., *The Letters of John McLoughlin*, Vol. II (Toronto: The Champlain Society, 1941–44), p. 202; Ibid., Vol. IV, pp. 239–40.

8. Francis Norbert Blanchet, *Historical Sketches of the Catholic Church in Oregon During the First Forty Years* (Portland: Catholic Sentinel Press, 1878), pp. 45–46, 72.

9. Jedin, *History of the Church*, Vol. VII, pp. 177–79; BCARA, F/B/D39D Demers to his family, 17 March 1839. Laments their giving up practising their religion; he believes, though he may be wrong, they did it in reaction to his decision to become a missionary.

10. Blanchet, *Historical Sketches,* pp. 18–20.

11. Etienne Theodore Packet, *Fragments de L'Historie Religieuse et Civilie et la Paroise de Sant-Nicolas* (Quebec: Paroise de Sant Nicolas, 1984), pp. 95–105; Blanchet, *Historical Sketches*, pp. 38–52; Alice Esther Oksness, "Reverend Modeste Demers: Missionary in the Northwest" (M.A. thesis: University of Washington, Seattle, WA., 1934), pp. 2–7.

12. Blanchet, *Historical Sketches*, pp. 61–65, 76–79; Robert Gatke, ed., "A Document of Mission History 1833–1843," *Oregon Historical Quarterly* 36 (March 1935): 87.

13. H.K. Hines, *Missionary History of the Pacific Northwest* (Chicago: The Lewis Publishing Company, 1899), p. 258.

14. *Rapport sur les Missions de Diocèse de Québec qui sont secourues part L'Association de las Propagation de la Foi* (Quebec: I.'Association de las Propagation de la Foi, 1847–1871), p. 47; Leslie M. Scott, "First Taxes in Oregon," *Oregon Historical Quarterly* 3 (March 1930): 7-12. In 1844 McLoughlin was by far the wealthiest ($12,212) individual with Hamilton Campbell second ($5,969), the Methodist Mission was third ($5,950), and Blanchet was fourth ($4,297).

15. Blanchet, *Historical Sketches*, pp. 148–50.

16. PFAR, Acta vol. 209, fols. 148-188, 24 May 1846. Blanchet states (f.149) that if a province is created, it will "be easy to convert a least 140,000 of the 200,000 savages in the region"; Carl Landholm, ed., *Notices and Voyages of the Famed Quebec Missions to the Pacific Northwest* (Portland: Oregon Historical Society, Champoeg Press, Reed College, 1956), p. 212ff. Contains extracts of the most interesting parts of Blanchet's enormous *Memoriale* to Propaganda Fide in Rome; Gilbert J. Garraghen, *The Jesuits of the Middle United States*, Vol. II (New York: American Press, 1939), p. 287. States that the huge new ecclesiastical province contained "a mere handful of Catholics."

17. PFAR, Acta, vol. 209, ff. 144–88, Blanchet *Memoriale,* 24 May 1846.

18. Quebec Archdiocesan Archives (hereafter QAA), Bishop Francis Kenrick of Philadelphia, 29 May 1843; Philadelphia Archdiocese Archives, Eccleston to Kenrick, 18 August 1846; Baltimore Archdiocesan Archives, Blanchet to Eccleston, Oregon City, 16 September 1846.

19. Blanchet, *Historical Sketches*, p. 144.

20. Ibid., p. 144; *Rapport* (1839): 56–58, 73; Ibid. (1841), p. 71–76; Ibid. (1842–1844), p. 78; Ibid. (1843), p. 81; Lee and Frost, *Ten Years in Oregon*, p. 283; Blanchet, *Historical Sketches*, pp. 102–4.

21. Lee and Frost, *Ten Years in Oregon*, p. 283; Blanchet, *Historical Sketches*, pp. 102–4.

22. QAA, Demers to Cazeau, Secretary to Archbishop Signay, Oregon City, 10 October 1845. Speaks of his growing regard for many Americans and their ways; Ibid., Demers to Cazeau, St. Paul, Oregon, 22 September 1847; *Rapport* (1849): 96–97.

✤ 2 The First Oblates

1. ROA, Mazenod to Pierre Aubert, 3 February 1847.

2. MDA, Bourget Letters, Mazenod to Bourget, 20 January 1847; E. Lamirande, "L'Implanation de l'Église catholique en Columbia Brittanique 1838–1848," *Revue de l'Universitè d'Ottawa* XXVIII (1958): 482. Contains letter of Provencher to Bishop Turgeon of Quebec, 14 June 1847 with his criticisms of Blanchet.

3. Alfred Yenveux, OMI, *Les Saintes Règles de la Congrégation des Missionaires Oblats de Marie Immaculée*, Vol. VII (Paris: Oblats de Marie Immaculée, 1903), pp. 37, Mazenod to Guigues, 5 December 1844; Ibid., pp. 120–21, Mazenod to Guigues, 24 March 1845; ROA, Mazenod to Pierre Aubert, 3 February 1847.

4. Ibid., Mazenod to Aubert, 3 February 1847; Yenveux, *Saint Règles*, Vol. IX, p. 187

5. Ibid., Mazenod to Aubert, 3 February 1847; Yenveux, *Saint Règles*, Vol. IX, p. 187

6. Rt. Rev. A.M.A. Blanchet, *Journal of a Catholic Bishop on the Oregon Trail...from Montreal to Oregon Territory, March 23, 1847 to January 13, 1851*, Edward Kowrach, ed. (Fairfield, WA: Ye Galleon Press, 1978), pp. 24–50; MDA, Oblate File, Mazenod to Bourget, 12 February 1848.

7. *Les Oblats*, Vol. I (Ottawa: Archives Deschâtelets, 1992), p. 1–14, Ricard to A. Blanchet, 4 November 1847.

8. *Les Oblats*, Vol. I, pp. 15–17, Ricard to Oregon Provincial Bishops, 3 February 1848; Ibid., pp. 18–19, Oregon Provincial Bishops to Ricard, 12 February 1848; Ibid., pp. 19–20, Ricard to A. Blanchet, 16 February 1848; Ibid., pp. 21–23, A. Blanchet to Ricard, 18 February 1848; Ibid., pp. 23–24, Ricard to A. Blanchet and Demers, 18 February 1848; Ibid., pp. 25–26, N. Blanchet and Demers to Ricard, 3 March 1848.

9. Clarence B. Bagley, ed., *Early Catholic Missions in Old Oregon* (Seattle: Lowman & Hanford Co., 1932). Vol. I, p. 188; Edward J. Kowrach, *Historical Sketches of the Catholic Church in Oregon by the Most Reverend Francis Norbert Blanchet* (Fairfield WA: Ye Galleon Press, 1983), p. 132.

Notes

10. PFAR, SOCG, AC, vol. 14, fol. 670, Blanchets to Propaganda Fide, St. Paul, Oregon, 15 March 1848.

11. John P. Marschall, "Diocesan and Religious Clergy: The History of a Relationship," in *The Catholic Priest in the United States,* John Tracy Ellis, ed. (Collegeville, MN: Liturgical Press, 1974), p. 401.

12. *Decreta Concili Provincialis Oregoniensis in Santi Pauli Habiti Diebus 28–29 Februarii et 1 Martii 1848 Necnon et Kalendarius Romanum cum Officiis Proviniciae Oregonensis et Sancta Sede Concessis* (Portland: McCormick Press, 1855), p. 3; Blanchet, *Historical Sketches*, p. 163; PFAR, Acta, vol. 212, fol. 256v, Rome approved the synod decrees on 22 April 1850.

13. PFAR, SOCG, AC, vol. 14, fol. 730, Pellegrini to Propaganda Fide, 2 September 1848, Ibid., f. 750, Mazenod to Canon Lowenbrük, 26 October 1848; *Les Oblats*, pp. 35–37, Mazenod to Propaganda Fide, 23 November 1848.

14. PFAR, Acta vol. 211, fol. 235, Propaganda decision made on 23 November 1848; Garraghan, *The Jesuits in the Middle United States*, Vol. 2, pp. 279–80; Letitia Mary Lyons, *Francis Norbert Blanchet and the Founding of the Oregon Missions, 1848–1948* (Washington, D.C.: Catholic University of America Press, 1940), p. 146.

15. Carrière, *Dictionnaire Biographique*, Vol. II, pp. 171–72; *Les Oblats*, Vol. 1, pp. 45–46, N. Blanchet to Ricard, Oregon City, 4 May 1849; PFAR, SOCG, AC, vol. 212, fols. 253–259, General Congregation, 22 April 1850.

16. MAA, Ignace Bourget to N. Blanchet, 24 October 1849; PFAR, Acta, vol. 212, fol. 259, General Congregation, 22 April 1850.

17. PFAR, Acta, vol. 212, fol. 283, Mazenod to Propaganda (Bishop Barnabo), 29 December 1829; Ibid., SOCG, Anglia, vol. 12, fol. 545, Mazenod to Propaganda (Cardinal Fransoni), 25 July 1850; Ibid., SOCG, AC, vol. 15, fols. 817–818, Mazenod to Propaganda (Bishop Barnabo); Ibid., vol. 15, fols. 929–930, Mazenod to Propaganda (Cardinal Fransoni), 8 December 1851.

18. PFAR, SOCG, AC, vol. 212, fols. 771–773, Father Cenas to Propaganda Fide, 15 May 1851.

19. PFAR, SOCG, AC, vol. 212, fols. 779–781, Jesuit Superior General Roothaan to Propaganda Fide (Cardinal Fransoni), 14 September 1850; Ibid., Acta, vol. 215, fol. 207, Suppression of Walla Walla, 29 July 1853.

20. *Les Oblats*, Vol. II, pp. 490–95, Louis D'Herbomez to Mazenod, 19 October 1854.

21. Kowrach, *Historical Sketches*, pp. 140–41.

22. *Les Oblats*, Vol. II, pp. 599–601, Demers to Ricard, 28 December 1855; Ibid., pp. 601–2, Chirouse to Mesplie, 15 January 1856.

23. Ibid., Vol. II, pp. 604–5, Mazenod to Propagation of the Faith, Lyon, 25 February 1856.

24. Ibid., Vol. II, pp. 674–79, D'Herbomez to Mazenod, 26 February 1857; Ibid., Vol. 2, pp. 1040–46, D'Herbomez to Mazenod, 20 July 1860.

25. QAA, Demers to Cazeau, Secretary to Archbishop Signay, 22 September 1847; ACLA, Charles John Seghers to Rector De Neve, 16 December 1863 BCARS, ADD. Mss 505, vol. 1, folder 8/1, Rev. Louis Lootens to Dr. John S. Helmcken, 19 January 1859; *Les Oblats*, Vol. II, pp. 846–48, Lootens to D'Herbomez, 20 March 1859.

26. Mary Margaret Down, *A Century of Service: A History of the Sisters of St. Ann and Their Contribution to Education in British Columbia and Alaska* (Victoria: Morriss Press, 1966), pp. 23–26; QAA, Demers to Archbishop Turgeon, 26 October 1852; A.G. Morice, *History of the Catholic Church in Western Canada*, pp. 297–98. Morice is the only authority claiming that Lempfrit conducted "thousands" of marriages.

27. Pamela Amoss, *Coast Salish Spirit Dancing: The Survival of An Ancestral Religion* (Seattle: University of Washington Press, 1978), p. 22; Alan D. McMillan, *Native Peoples and Cultures of Canada: An Anthropological Overview* (Vancouver: Douglas and McIntyre, 1988), pp. 204–5.

28. Patricia Meyer, ed., *Honoré-Timothée Lempfrit, His Oregon Trail Journal and Letters from the Pacific Northwest, 1848–1853* (Fairfield, WA: Ye Galleon Press, 1985), pp. 21–27, 38–39. Indicates that he was never defrocked nor censured, but retired to France and died in 1862 as the parish priest of Morville-Les Vic in the Moselle District; Emilien Lamirande, "Le Pere Honoré-Timothée Lempfrit et son Ministere aupres des autochtones de l'Ile de Vancouver 1849–1852," in *Western Oblate Studies 1/ l'Études Oblates de l'Ouest 1*, ed. by Raymond Huel (Edmonton: Western Canadian Publishers, 1990): 53–70; BCARS, Holy Rosary, reel 707, Frame 4149, Demers to Lempfrit, 26 May 1852; Eugene de Mazenod, *Collection: Oblate Writings II: Letters to North America: 1851–1860,* Vol. 2 (Rome: General OMI Postulation, 1979), pp. 67–68, Mazenod to Lempfrit, Marseille, 17 December 1853. Lempfrit was expelled from the Oblates on 20 September 1853 for "scandalous conduct in the diocese of Vancouver Island."

29. *Les Oblats*, Vol. II, pp. 436–38, Demers to Ricard, 20 June 1854; Ibid., pp. 438–41, Lootens to Ricard, 23 June 1854.

30. Ibid., Vol. II, pp. 433–35, Demers to Ricard, 11 June 1854.

31. PFAR, Lettere, vol. 346, fol. 529, Propaganda Fide to Mazenod, 23 July 1855; Ibid., fol. 594, Propaganda Fide to Mazenod, 3 September 1855; Ibid., vol. 347, fol. 390, Propaganda to Mazenod, 26 July 1856; *Les Oblats,* Vol. II, pp. 530–32, Demers to Ricard, 29 December 1854; Ibid., pp. 566–68, Demers to Ricard, 11 May 1855; PFAR, SOCG, AC, vol. 16, fol. 800, Demers to Propaganda Fide, 10 November 1855.

32. *Les Oblats,* Vol. II, pp. 606–7, Demers to Ricard, 28 April 1856; Ibid., pp. 621–22, Demers to Ricard, 7 July 1856; AHA, Demers to Woodlock, 5 January 1857.

33. *Les Oblats*, Vol. II, pp. 674–79, D'Herbomez to Mazenod, St. Joseph's Mission, Olympia, 26 February 1857; Ibid., pp. 792–96, Act of Visitation by F.X. Bermond, St. Joseph's Mission, Olympia, 15 September 1858.

34. Ibid., Vol. III, pp. 927–28; N. Blanchet to Propaganda Fide, 5 November 1859; PFAR, SOCG, AC, vol. 18, fol. 288, Demers to Propaganda, 12 July 1858; *Les Oblats*, Vol. III, pp. 806–8, Arrangements between Demers and Bermond re: the Oblates, Victoria, 6 October 1858.

35. Mazenod, *Letters to North America,* 1851–1860, Vol. 2 (Rome: General Postulation OMI, 1979), pp. 203–7, Mazenod to Bermond, 20 December 1858.

1. Walter M. Abbott, Gen. Ed., *The Documents of Vatican II, With Notes and Comments by Catholic, Protestant and Orthodox Authorities* (New York: The American Press, 1966), p. 662.

2. Ibid., pp. 661, 668, 663. Italics added; R.T.B., ed., *The Oxford Dictionary of Quotations*, Third Edition (Oxford: Oxford University Press, 1980), p. 414.

3. Ibid., p. 148.

4. Jennifer Reid, *Myth, Symbol and Colonial Encounter* (Ottawa: University of Ottawa Press, 1995), passim; Jaroslav Pelikan, *The Christian Tradition: A History of the Development of Doctrine: Volume 1: The Emergence of the Catholic Tradition (100–600)* (Chicago: University of Chicago Press, 1971), passim; Charles S. Bryant and Abel Much, *A History of the Great Massacre by the Sioux Indians in Minnesota* (Cincinnati: Rickey and Carroll, 1864), p. 134.

5. R. Cole Harris, ed., *Historical Atlas of Canada,* Vol. 1 (Toronto: University of Toronto Press, 1987), plates 1–2.

6. Ralph Maud, *A Guide to B.C. Indian Myth and Legend: A Short History of Myth-Collecting and a Survey of Published Texts* (Vancouver: Talonbooks, 1982), pp. 10–15.

7. "The Aboriginal Peoples have developed over the centuries rich traditions founded on experiences relating to ecology, education, economics, political structures, as well as expressing different social and spiritual values. The wisdom contained in them could enrich our own culture. Their loss would mean our own impoverishment. Why go searching abroad for that which native citizens are willing to share with us here at home?" *Island Catholic News*, April 1991, "Church Leaders' Statement of Pastoral Concern." Signed by Bishop Ronald Shephard of the Anglican Diocese of British Columbia, The Rev. William Howie, Moderator of the United Church of Canada and Bishop Remi J. De Roo of the Roman Catholic Diocese of Victoria.

8. Matthew Fox, *A Spirituality Named Compassion* (Minneapolis: Winston Press, 1979), pp. 164–65.

9. Maud, *A Guide*, passim.

10. Ibid., 9-28; John J. Cove and George F. MacDonald, eds., *Tsimshian Narratives I collected by Marius Barbeau and William Beynon* (Ottawa: Canadian Museum of Civilization, 1987), pp. vi–xii; Mircea Eliade, *A History of Religious Ideas*, Vol. 2 (Chicago: University of Chicago, 1982), p. 277–81; George Clutesi, *Son of Raven, Son of Deer* (Sidney, B.C.: Gray's Publishing Ltd., 1967), pp. 9–14, 113–24; Marius Barbeau, *Totem Poles According to Crests and Topics* (Ottawa: National Museum of Canada, 1950), pp. 1–12.

11. Franz Boas, *Material for the Study of the Inheritance in Man* (New York: Columbia University Press, 1928), pp. 202, 235.

Notes

1. Sage, "Sir James Douglas," p. 140.
2. Landholm, *Notices and Voyages*, pp. 193–94, 198.
3. Sage, "Sir James Douglas," p. 140; Blanchet, *Historical Sketches*, pp. 133–34; Landholm, *Notices and Voyages,* pp. 193–94, 198.
4. Blanchet, *Historical Sketches*, pp. 61–65, 76–79; Robert Gatke, ed., "A Document of Mission History 1833–1843," *Oregon Historical Quarterly* 36 (March 1935): 87.
5. Blanchet, *Historical Sketches*, p. 26.
6. Ibid., pp. 26, 65. The mission lasted from 24 November 1838 until 15 April 1839.
7. Ibid., p. 58. Demers was referring to the Chinook Tribe who were the closest Native settlement to Fort Vancouver, and thus they became the first victims of the disease.
8. Robin Fisher, *Contact and Conflict: Indian-European Relations in British Columbia, 1774–1890* (Vancouver: University of British Columbia Press, 1977), p. 141.
9. Blanchet, *Historical Sketches*, pp. 26, 130, 134–35.
10. Blanchet, *Historical Sketches*, pp. 26, 130, 134–35; *Rapport*, pp. 14, 17, 23–24; *United States Magazine* (Baltimore: Catholic Press, 1843), pp. 741–43. Demers relates his experiences; Lee and Frost, *Ten Years in Oregon*, p. 283. Gives reasons for Protestant lack of success; Adrian G. Morice, *The History of the Northern Interior of British Columbia Formerly New Caledonia 1660–1880* (Toronto: William Briggs, 1904), p. 234; Margaret A. Ormsby, *British Columbia: A History* (Toronto: Macmillans, 1958), p. 168; Morice, *History of the Catholic Church in Western Canada,* Vol. 2, p. 298.
11. Blanchet, *Historical Sketches*, pp. 144, 148–50; *Rapport* (1839), pp. 56–58, 73; Ibid. (1841), p. 71–76; Ibid. (1842–1844), p. 78; Ibid. (1843), p. 81; Lee and Frost, *Ten Years in Oregon*, p. 283.
12. Blanchet, *Historical Sketches*, pp. 102–4; QAA, Demers to Cazeau, St. Paul, Oregon, 22 September 1847; *Rapport* (1849), pp. 96–97; PFAR, SOCG, AC, vol. 15, fols. 771–73, Father Cenas to Propaganda Fide, 15 May 1851.
13. Jean Barman, *The West Beyond the West,* p. 363; AD P 2210–2239, Report of 1861 to General Chapter by Louis D'Herbomez
14. J.R. Miller*, Skyscrapers Hide the Heavens: A History of Indian-White Relations in Canada* (Toronto: University of Toronto Press, 1989), p. 142. AD, P 2210–2239, Report of 1861 to General Chapter by Louis D'Herbomez; Hugh J.M. Johnston, *The Pacific Province: A History of British Columbia* (Vancouver: Douglas & McIntyre, 1996), pp. 32–34. By 1775 the six languages were "Salish or Salishan, Athapascan or Dene, Waskashan, Haida, Tsimshian and Kootenay"; Barman, *The West Beyond the West*, pp. 169–70.
15. AD, P 2210–2239, Report of 1861 to General Chapter by Louis D'Herbomez.
16. VDA, D'Herbomez to Mazenod, Esquimalt, 26 January 1860; Ibid., D'Herbomez to J. Fabre, Esquimalt, 25 August 1863; *Canada Sessional Papers* (Ottawa: J.B. Taylor 1872), no. 10, Appendix BB, pp. 159–60. Opinion of D'Herbomez to H.L. Langevin, Federal Minister of Public Works, New Westminster, 29 September 1871; John

Webster Grant, *Moon of Wintertime: Missionaries and The Indians of Canada in Encounter since 1534* (Toronto: University of Toronto Press, 1984), p. 125; The first residential school in the Diocese of Victoria was the Kuper Island Residential School which was founded in 1890; Blanchet, *Historical Sketches*, pp. 26, 65; Margaret Whitehead, "Now You Are My Brother: Missionaries in British Columbia," *Sound Heritage Series* 34 (1981): 33–34. Reports on interview with Oblate priest, John Hennessy recorded in the 1970s in which he speaks of the folly of preaching missions in Chinook; Jacqueline Gresko, "Creating Little Dominions within the Dominion: Early Catholic Indian Schools in Saskatchewan and British Columbia," in Jean Barman, Yvonne Hèbert, and Don McCaskill, eds., *Indian Education in Canada: Volume 1: The Legacy* (Vancouver: University of British Columbia Press, 1986), p. 97.

17. Richard C. Mayne, *Four Years in British Columbia and Vancouver Island* (London: John Murray, 1862), p. 176; BCARS, Hills Correspondence Books, Hills to Secretary of Society for the Propagation of the Gospel, Victoria, 8 May 1860; Ibid., Hills to same, Victoria, 12 December 1861.

18. Whitehead, "Now You are My Brother," pp. 27–39.

19. John McGloin, "John Nobili, S.J., Founder of California's Santa Clara College: The New Caledonia Years, 1845–1848" *British Columbia Historical Quarterly* 17 (1953): 253 et seq.; AD, P 6413–6415, Charles Pandozy to D'Herbomez, L'Anse au Sable, 9 October 1859.

20. Ibid., P 1368–1375, "A Descriptive Letter taken from the Manuscript 'Western Missions and Missionaries in the United States,'" by P.J. De Smet and made by John Nobili, University of St. Louis, 18 January 1858; Edward J. Kowrach, *Mie. Charles Pandosy, OMI: A Missionary of the Northwest* (Fairfield, Washington: Ye Galleon Press, 1992), passim.

21. Gaston Carrière, "The Yakima War: The Oblates Falsely Accused," *Vie Oblate-Oblate Life* (June 1975): 147–73; Ibid. (December 1975): 261–94; AD 6360–6408, Documents relating to Oblate attempts to gain compensation from the U.S. federal government for the financial loses in the Yakima Wars of 1855–56. Contains itemised lists of their loses and correspondence between 1860–69 addressed to various U.S. federal government authorities.

22. AD P 6783–6787, Richard to D'Herbomez, 25 September 1859; Ibid., Richard to D'Herbomez, 15 October 1859; BCARS, Cox Papers, F375-19, "Returns of Pre-empted Land Recorded with William George Cox, Esq., Magistrate, Rock Creek," Richard Enclosure in Cox to Young, 14 April 1861; AD, P 6434–6440, Richard to D'Herbomez, 30 November 1860; Ibid., Richard to D'Herbomez, 15 April 1860; Duncan Duane Thomson, "A History of the Okanagan: Indians and Whites in the Settlement Era, 1860–1920" (Ph.D. thesis, University of British Columbia, 1985), pp. 37–110.

23. BCARS, CC, F 453, Demers to William Young, Acting Colonial Secretary, 1 August 1860. Demers requests lots in Hope, Yale, Nanaimo, Douglas and New Westminster on which to build churches; Ibid., F 533, Demers to Young, 11 August 1860. Again requests lots as above; Ibid., F 723/3, 21 September 1860, F 923/5, F923/36,

3 November 1860. Gives title to Demers of lots in Hope, Yale, New Westminster and Douglas. The Church of England was also requesting and receiving similar parcels of land from the provincial government. AD P 2599–2620, Léon Fouquet to D'Herbomez, St. Charles, n.d., probably 1862. Report on State of St. Charles Mission.

24. ROA, Léon Fouquet to François Tempier, New Westminster, 8 June 1863.

25. AD P 2599–2620, Fouquet to D'Herbomez, St. Charles, n.d., probably 1862. Report on the State of St. Charles Mission.

26. F.W. Howay, "The Introduction of Intoxicating Liquors amongst the Indians of the Northwest Coast," *British Columbia Historical Quarterly* 6 (July 1942): 157; *The British Columbian*, 23 May 1863; Ibid., 2 December 1863; *Missions* 1 (1862): 149. Fouquet letter dated: 15 February 1861; Ibid., 12 (1874): 326; Ibid., 24 (1886): 486. Notes unwillingness of Natives to give up "old customs," although there is no understanding on the part of the writer of why except because of Native "stupidity"; Wilson Duff, *The Upper Stalo Indians of the Fraser Valley, British Columbia, Memoir No. 1. Provincial Museum of British Columbia* (Victoria: Provincial Museum of British Columbia, 1952), p. 92.

27. AD, PC 101.V21C.5, Manuscript remarks from Sisters of St. Ann, no date. Covers years 1858–68; Ibid., P 1643–1646, D'Herbomez to Demers, Esquimalt, 10 December 1862; Ibid., P 1647–1648, D'Herbomez to Demers, Esquimalt, 18 November 1863; Ibid., P 1336–1337, Demers to D'Herbomez, Victoria, 21 November 1863; Ibid., P 1478–1479, D'Herbomez to Demers, Esquimalt, 24 November 1863; Ibid., P 1338–1339, Demers to D'Herbomez, 5 December 1863.

28. Gerard G. Steckler, *Charles John Seghers: Priest and Bishop in the Pacific Northwest 1839–1886: A Biography* (Fairfield, WA: Ye Galleon Press, 1986), pp. 15–36; ACL, Seghers to "Friends," Louvain, 13 May 1863; Ibid., Seghers to Rector De Neve, Victoria, 16 December 1863; Ibid., Seghers to De Neve, n.d., probably 1864; PFAR, SOCG, AC, vol. 20, fol. 1394, N.F. Blanchet to Propaganda, Portland, 15 December 1864; *The Colonist*, 12 December 1864; VDA, Cardinal Barnabo, Prefect of Propaganda Fide, Rome, 1 February 1870; Ibid., same to same, March 1870.

✤ 5 Trying to Transform a People

1. Jacqueline Gresko, "Roman Catholic Missionary Effort and Indian Acculturation in the Fraser Valley, BC" (BA essay, University of British Columbia, 1969), p. 3; Martin E. Marty, *Pilgrims in Their Own Land: 500 Years of Religion in America* (Boston: Little, Brown and Company, 1984), pp. 86–88; Melville Herskovits, *Acculturation: The Study of Cultural Contact* (Gloucester, MA: Peter Smith, 1958), p. 10; Edward Spicer, ed., *Perspectives in American Indian Culture Change* (Chicago: The University of Chicago Press, 1956), p. 519; Paul Tennant, *Aboriginal People and Politics: The Indian Land Question in British Columbia* (Vancouver, B.C: The University of British Columbia Press, 1990), pp. 39–52.

2. Duff, *The Upper Stalo Indians*, pp. 11–12; Barman, *The West Beyond the West*, p. 16; Barnett, Homer G., "Applied Anthropology in 1860" *Applied Anthropology*, 1, no. 3 (April-June 1942): 19–25.

3. Duff, *The Upper Stalo Indians,* pp. 80–81, 84–87, 121–22; Barman, *The West Beyond the West*, pp. 15–16.

4. Gresko, "Indian [Stó:lô] Acculturation," passim, contains an excellent examination of issues; Ralph Maud, *The Salish People: The Local Contribution of Charles Hill-Tout, Volume IV: The Sechelt and South-Eastern Tribes of Vancouver Island* (Vancouver: Talonbooks, 1978), p. 104; Duff, *The Upper Stalo Indians*, pp. 25–27, 77–82.

5. Ibid., p. 78–79.

6. W.K. Lamb, ed., *The Letters and Journals of Simon Fraser* (Toronto: Macmillan, 1960), pp. 101–2; Maud, *The Salish People*, pp. 95–96.

7. Duff, *The Upper Stalo Indians*, pp. 79–88; Maud, *The Salish People*, pp. 99–100, 107–8; Maud, *A Guide to B.C. Indian Myth and Legend*, pp. 59–60.

8. Maud, *The Salish People*, pp. 99–100; B.L. Verma, "The Squamish: A Study of Changing Political Organisation" (M.A. thesis, University of British Columbia, 1954), pp. 12, 15–18.

9. Duff, *The Upper Stalo Indians*, pp. 94–95; Maud, *The Salish People*, p. 100.

10. Wilson Duff, *Indian History of British Columbia, Anthropology in British Columbia Memoir No 5* (Victoria: Provincial Museum of British Columbia, 1964), p. 38; Pelikan, *The Christian Tradition: Volume 1*, pp. 11–67; Lamb, *The Letters and Journals of Simon Fraser,* pp. 101–2; Duff, *The Upper Stalo Indians*, pp. 121–23.

11. Ibid., pp. 94; Jean Barman, Yvonne Hèbert, and Don McCaskill, "The Legacy of the Past: An Overview," from Jean Barman, Yvonne Hèbert, and Don McCaskill, eds., *Indian Education in Canada. Volume 1: The Legacy* (Vancouver: University of British Columbia Press, 1986), p. 2; J.R. Miller, *Shingwauk's Vision: A History of Native Residential Schools* (Toronto: University of Toronto Press, 1996), pp. 15–17.

12. Duff, *The Upper Stalo Indians*, pp. 23–25, 40–41, 128–30; Fisher, *Contact and Conflict*, p. 30; Barman, *The West Beyond the West*, pp. 41–42, 61, 65–71, passim.

13. Blanchet, *Historical Sketches*, pp. 40–42.

14. Jedin, *History of the Church*, Vol. V, pp. 585–87; Ibid., Vol. VI, p. 570.

15. Frances E. Herring, *Among the People of British Columbia: Red, White, Yellow and Brown* (London: T. Fisher Unwin, 1903), pp. 184–89; Keith Thor Carlson, ed., *You Are Asked to Witness: The Stó:lô in Canada's Pacific Coast History* (Winnipeg: Hignell Printing Limited, 1997), p. 100.

16. Philip M. Hanley, *History of the Catholic Ladder* (Fairfield, WA: Ye Galleon Press, 1993), passim; Blanchet, *Historical Sketches*, p. 83; Nellie B. Pipes, "The Protestant Ladder," *Oregon Historical Review* XXXVII (1936): 237–40; Margaret Whitehead, "Christianity, a Matter of Choice: The Historic Role of Indian Catechists in Oregon and British Columbia," *Pacific Northwest Quarterly* 72, no. 3 (July 1981): 98–106.

17. Blanchet, *Historical Sketches*, pp. 31–32, 41–42, 49; Denys Nelson, *Fort Langley 1827–1927* (Vancouver: Vancouver Art Historical and Scientific Association, 1927), pp. 19–20.

Notes

18.	*Missions* 1 (1862), pp. 93–111, D'Herbomez Report, 1861, pp. 101, 183–84.

19.	AD, PB 179 P47 R. 1, Regulations for the operation of Missions (1864), no place indicated, but probably New Westminster; Whitehead, "Now Your Are My Brother," p. 34. Jacqueline Gresko, "Missionary Acculturation Programs in British Columbia," *Études Oblates,* 32 (1973): 145–58.

20.	Jedin, *History of the Church,* Vol. V, pp. 577–78; *Les Oblats,* Vol. III, pp. 796–802; François-Xavier Bermond, Report on Missions, 17 September 1858.

21.	*Les Oblats,* Vol. III, pp. 796–802; Bermond, Report on the Missions, 17 September 1858; Herring, *Among the People of British Columbia,* p. 163; *Rapport,* no. 6 (July 1845): 34. Speaks of the first temperance society founded by Blanchet and Demers in the Willamette River Mission in a letter: Blanchet to Signay, 4 March 1843.

22.	*Les Oblats,* Vol. III, pp. 796–802, Bermond, Report on the Missions, 17 September 1858. Spells out the need to appoint "chiefs" to be the watchmen so as to keep up "religious living" during a priest's absence as well as the use of trial, public confession and payment of fines which could then be used to help support the Mission; *Missions* 1 (1862): 121–29. Durieu to Mazenod, 1 September 1860. Reports on his use of watchmen to also guard against "sorcerers."

23.	*Les Oblats,* Vol. III, pp. 796–802; François-Xavier Bermond, Report on Missions, 17 September 1858; *Missions* 1 (1862): 101; *Missions* 3 (1864): 207; *Missions* 9 (1870): 133; *Missions* 12 (1874): 318; *Missions* 28 (1890); *Missions* 50 (1912): 168, 173.

24.	*Missions* 4 (1865): 265–69, 326–30; Grant, *Moon of Wintertime,* pp. 119–42.

25.	ASSA, Mary Lumena ms.: "A Sketch of Mission City" (c1869–72), Ff. 20–26.

26.	*Missions* 4 (1865): 265–75. D'Herbomez reflections, 16 February 1863; Carlson, *You Are Asked to Witness,* pp. 30, 75–77, 96–97, 100–101.

27.	*Missions* 4 (1865): 290–95; Gresko, "Creating Little Dominions," pp. 94–95; Carlson, *You Are Asked to Witness,* p. 102; ROA, D'Herbomez to Fabre, New Westminster, 12 October 1864; Carrière, *Dictionnaire,* Vol. II, pp. 242–43.

28.	ASSA, D'Herbomez to M. Providence, 16 August 1864; Ibid., D'Herbomez to M. Providence, 4 January 1865; Ibid., D'Herbomez to M. Providence, 10 June 1865; Ibid., M. de la Providence to D'Herbomez, 12 June 1865; Ibid., M. des Sept-Douleurs, "Fondation de N. Westminster," ff. 104–6, Ms, the reminiscences of her years in British Columbia before her death in Victoria in 1876; Jacqueline Gresko, "The 'Serfs of the System?' Oblate Brothers and the Sisters of St. Ann in British Columbia Schools, 1858–1920," *Western Oblate Studies 4/Études Oblates de l'Ouest 4* (Edmonton: Western Canadian Publishers, 1996): 119–41.

29.	ASSA, M. Jeanne de Chantal to D'Herbomez, 29 June 1866; AD, G, LPP, 1399. D'Herbomez to Fabre, 29 March 1865. Speaks of racism in Victoria and how he had to force the principal of St. Louis College, Julien Baudre to accept African American students and talks of the continued problems of racism in the province; ASSA, M. des Sept-Douleurs, "Fondation de N. Westminster," ff. 109–12, 217.

30. ASSA, Sister M. Theodore, "St. Mary's Indian School Mission, Mission City on the Fraser," 1869–1891, passim; Based on information supplied by Sister M. Luména, ff. 7–24.

31. Ibid.

32. Ibid.

33. Ibid.

34. Robert Berkhofer, "Model Zions for the American Indian," *American Quarterly* 15, no. 2 (1963): 184; *Missions* 31 (1893): 140–44. Discusses how students will bring this Catholic world about; "French Education in the Nineteenth Century," in *A Cyclopedia of Education*, edited by Paul Monroe, Vol. 2 (New York: The Macmillan Company, 1911), pp. 656–74.

35. *Missions* 31 (1893): 141–43, 129–61; Gerald C. Treacy, *Five Great Encyclicals* (New York: The Paulist Press,1939), pp. 35–68. "On the Christian Education of Youth," Pius XI, 1939.

36. *Missions* 12 (1874): 352–53. Eugène-Casimir Chirouse to D'Herbomez, Tulalip, 24 November 1872. How the future will be so different when the present students have helped the rest of their Native family to abandon their old ways; Ibid., 19 (1881): 211–14. This aim is spelled out by James McGuckin (27 November 1878) in talking about St. Joseph's Mission, Williams Lake; Raymond Huel, *Proclaiming the Gospel to the Indians and the Métis* (Edmonton: The University of Alberta Press and Western Canadian Publishers, 1996), p. 8.

✦ 6 Early Influences

1. QAA, Demers to Turgeon, Victoria, 30 July 1853; Ibid., Demers to Cazeau (Turgeon's Secretary), Victoria, 11 December 1853; *Rapport* (1855), pp. 107–17; Ibid. (1857), pp. 79–80; QAA, Demers to Turgeon, 26 October 1852.

2. QAA, Demers to Turgeon, Victoria, 30 July 1853; Ibid., Demers to Cazeau, 11 December 1853; *Rapport* (1855), pp. 107–17; Ibid. (1857), pp. 79, 90; Fisher, *Indian-European Relations*, p. 143; *Rapport* (1864), pp. 85–93; *The Colonist*, 8–12 May 1863.

3. ACL, Seghers to De Neve, Victoria, 16 December 1863; Ibid., Seghers to De Neve, Victoria, 31 January 1869.

4. M. Theodore, "Historical Sketches of the Diocese of Victoria from the Year 1847 to 1913," *The British Orphan's Friend: Historical Number* (December 1914), pp. 47, 27–33.

5. ASSA, Kenneth Duncan, "History of the Cowichan," unpublished manuscript. f. 2.

6. M.M. Roden, "The Cowichan, Saanich and Kuper Island Missions," *The British Columbia Orphans' Friend: Historical Number* (December 1914), p. 47; Francis Boshauwers, "Early Cowichan History," *The British Columbia Orphans' Friend* (October 1928): 3; BCARS, B/1857, Indian Affairs, RG 10, vol. 6037, F/152/8B/1, J. Stewart, Assistant Secretary, Memorandum, 30 December 1903; ASSA, Sister Mary Theodore Pineault, "North Pacific Shores," unpublished manuscript, p. 33.

7. Maud, *The Salish People*, p. 100; Miller, *Shingwauk's Vision*, pp. 34–35.

8. Cole Harris, *The Resettlement of British Columbia* (Vancouver: University of British Columbia Press, 1997), p. 147. Estimate of a third of the population died; Duff, *Indian History of B.C.*, p. 43 repeats this; Philip Drucker, *Cultures of the North Pacific Coast* (San Francisco: Chandler Publishing Company, 1965), p. 198; Fisher, *Contact and Conflict*, p. 116.

9. *Daily Press*, Victoria, 26 March 1862; *The Colonist*, 1 and 14 May 1862; *British Columbian*, 12 May 1854, 24 December 1864; BCARS, CC, file 214, C.L. Brown to Douglas, 18 February 1863; Harris, *The Resettlement of British Columbia*, p. 147. Estimate of a third; Duff, *Indian History of B.C.*, p. 43 repeats this; Philip Drucker, *Cultures of the North Pacific Coast* (San Francisco: Chandler Publishing Company, 1965), p. 198; Fisher, *Contact and Conflict*, p. 116. Clearly more research needs to be done on this important issue.

10. Numbers vaccinated in brackets: *The Colonist*, 26 April 1862 (200); *British Columbian*, 14 May 1862 (3,000); *Daily Press*, Victoria, 27 March and 27 April 1862 (30 and 500).

11. *Rapport* (1863), pp. 81–83. Report written by Demers at Victoria, 17 July 1862.

12. AD, P 2218, D'Herbomez, Report on the state of the Oblate Missions in Oregon and B.C., 1861; *Missions* 3 (1864): 198. *British Columbian*, 14 May 1862 reported the highest figure in the entire province of 3000.

13. AD, P 1497–1498, D'Herbomez to Fabre, 17 October 1870; Ibid., P 2437–2440, Fabre to D'Herbomez, 6 November 1870; Ibid., P 2441–2444, Fabre to D'Herbomez, 10 December 1870; Ibid., P 2445–2447, Fabre to D'Herbomez, 2 March 1871.

14. Donat Levasseur, *A History of the Missionary Oblates of Mary Immaculate: Towards a Synthesis: Volume 1, 1815–1898* (Rome: General House, 1985), passim; Donat Levasseur, *A History of the Missionary Oblates of Mary Immaculate: Towards a Synthesis: Volume 2, 1898–1985* (Rome: General House, 1989), passim.

15. Kowrach, *Charles Pandosy,* passim; François Lardon, Rev. Charles Pandozy, *The Monthly Bulletin* 1 August 1917, pp. 11–21; Carrière, *Dictionnaire Biographique*, passim.

16. Paul Durieu (1860–64) and François Jayol (1864–66) each spent a few years there. Florimond Gendre ministered at the Mission for the last ten (1863–73) years of his life. Julien Baudre (1869–78), Charles Grandidier (1872–80), and Louis-Napoléon Grégoire (1881–82) served for a time there. In addition, James Walsh (1893–97), Charles Marchal (1872–80), Julien-Augustin Bedard (1887–92), Olivier Cornellier (1894–97), Alphonse Carion (1893–1916) and Brothers Joseph Buchman (1863–68) and Félix Guillet (1875–79) all worked at St. Louis. Carrière, *Dictionnaire Biographique*, passim.

17. AD, P 3745–3748, Jayol to D'Herbomez, 10 March 1865. Complains of problems with staff and Europeans; Ibid., P 3772–3779. Jayol to D'Herbomez, 3 November 1865. Senses that he is unable to cope with problems, and asks to be discharged; Ibid., P 17–18, Boudre to D'Herbomez, 7 September 1866. Asks to be able to stay in his room and say Mass; Ibid., P 3029–3034. Gendre to D'Herbomez, 5 February 1867. Troubled

with lay brothers and terrible alcoholism among Europeans and Natives; Ibid., P 3041–3044, Gendre to D'Herbomez, 26 May 1867. Speaks of problems with others; Ibid., P 6828–6835, Richard to D'Herbomez, 16 March 1868. Asks for advice on how to resolve differences; Ibid., P 6836–6839, Richard to D'Herbomez, 25 May 1868. Pain from resulting differences and divisions in community; Ibid., P 3094–3097, Gendre to D'Herbomez, 17 September 1868. Difficulties, trying to take responsibility; Ibid., P 574–575, Brother Joseph Buchman to D'Herbomez, 11 October 1868. Complains of Gendre; Ibid., D'Herbomez to Pandosy, 11 October 1868. Stresses need for harmony with Gendre; Ibid., P 572–573, Buchman and Brother Guilllet to D'Herbomez, 24 March 1869. "Your most obedient child," instead of "servant," was a frequent usage among the Oblates when addressing superiors, especially bishops.

18. AD, P 6471–6435, Pandosy to D'Herbomez, 5 August 1868; Ibid., P 6977–6980, Richard to D'Herbomez, 15 November 1880; Ibid., P 570–572, Buchman to D'Herbomez, 24 March 1868, Ibid., P 573–576 Buchman to D'Herbomez, 11 October 1868. Buchman complains of Gendre's lack of co-operation. Carrière in his *Dictionnaire Biographique* does not mention Buchman, who apparently was dismissed or perhaps left the Oblates sometime around 1868. Raymond Huel, "Western Oblate History: The Need for Reinterpretation," *Western Oblate Studies 3/Études Oblates de l'Ouest 3,* ed. by R. Huel (Edmonton: Western Canadian Publishers, 1994), p. 30; Lamirande, "Le Pere Honoré-Timothée Lempfrit," pp. 53–70. Lempfrit was dismissed for reasons that certainly contained personality issues.

19. Carrière, *Dictionnaire Biographique*, passim; AD, P 6432; Ibid., 6436–6437, D'Herbomez to Pandosy, 11 October 1868. Tells him to learn Okanagan as Gendre has learned Shuswap.

20. Ibid., P 3761–3767, Jayol to D'Herbomez, 11 September 1865; Ibid., P 3757–3760, Jayol to D'Herbomez, 12 August 1865; Ibid., P 932–935, Chiappini to D'Herbomez, 3 November 1881.

✦ 7 *Founding More Missions*

1. VAA, D'Herbomez Register, ff. 120–21; *Missions* 6 (1867): 24–30; AD, P 3745–48, Jayol to D'Herbomez, 10 March 1865; *Missions* 12 (1874): 334–35.
2. AD, P 3749–52, Jayol to D'Herbomez, 27 April 1865.
3. F.M. Buckland, *Ogopago's Vigil* (Kelowna, B.C.: Okanagan Historical Society, 1979), p. 27; AD, HPK, 5102 B86C2, Okanagan Mission Financial Records, 1859–88.
4. *Études Oblates* 1 (1942): 193–95; AD, P 3735–744, Jayol to D'Herbomez, 1–18 January 1865; Ibid., P 1763–64, D'Herbomez to Gendre, 5 February 1868; Ibid., P 3745–48, Jayol to D'Herbomez, 10 March 1865; Ibid., P 89–92, Baudre to D'Herbomez, 24 April 1873; Ibid., P 168–71, Baudre to D'Herbomez, 30 September 1874; Ibid., P 6454, Pandosy to D'Herbomez, 26 May 1874; Ibid., P 6496–97, Pandosy to D'Herbomez, 24 November 1876.

Notes

---

5. AD, P 3343–45, Grandidier to D'Herbomez, 10 September 1867; Ibid., P 3045–52, Gendre to D'Herbomez, 19 June 1867; Ibid., P 3081–84, Gendre to D'Herbomez, 4 March 1868.

6. *Études Oblates* 1 (1942): 193–95

7. AD, P 3772–79, Jayol to D'Herbomez, 10 December 1865; Ibid., P 6872–74, Richard to D'Herbomez, 31 March 1879.

8. AD, P 172–81, Baudre to D'Herbomez, 18 January 1875; Ibid., P 6482, Pandosy to D'Herbomez, 26 May 1867; Ibid., P 205–12, Baudre to D'Herbomez, 24 January 1876;

9. Ibid., P 6482, Pandosy to D'Herbomez, 26 May 1867; Ibid., P 205–212, Baudre to D'Herbomez, 24 January 1876; Ibid., P 6503, Pandosy to D'Herbomez, 27 August 1877; Ibid., P 6505–8, Pandosy to D'Herbomez, 5 November 1877.

10. AD, P 61–67, Baudre to D'Herbomez, 9 December 1872, Ibid., P 205–12, Baudre to D'Herbomez, 24 January 1876.

11. Fisher, *Contact and Conflict*, pp. 144–45; Harold Cardinal, *The Unjust Society: The Tragedy of Canada's Indians* (Edmonton: M.G. Hurtig Ltd. Publishers, 1969), pp. 162–71.

12. Ibid., P 3735–44, Jayol to D'Herbomez, 1 and 18 January 1865; Ibid., P 3177–80, Grandidier to D'Herbomez, 18 December 1866; Ibid., P 3796–3800, Jayol to D'Herbomez, 25 December 1866; Ibid., P 3081–84, Gendre to D'Herbomez, 4 March 1868; Ibid., P 3085–88, Gendre to D'Herbomez, 27 April 1868.

13. Ibid., P 6840–41, Richard to D'Herbomez, 3 June 1868; Ibid., Richard to D'Herbomez, 13 June 1868.

14. McGuckin was President of St. Louis College, New Westminster (1882–89), a delegate to the General Chapter of 1887, Rector of the University of Ottawa (1889–98) and Rector of Holy Rosary Parish, Vancouver (1898–1903), then the most important parish in the Oblate province where he died in 1903. Carrière, *Dictionnaire Biographique*, Vol. II, pp. 342–43.

15. *Cariboo Sentinel*, 11 June 1868. Speaks of one minister at Barkerville who went out to other communities on alternate Sundays; Frank A. Peake, *The Anglican Church in British Columbia* (Vancouver: Mitchell Press, 1959), pp. 38–45.

16. AD P 5011–5013, McGuckin to D'Herbomez, 15 May 1867.

17. Ibid., P 5017–5018, McGuckin to D'Herbomez, 8 July 1867. Deeds signed in August 1867.

18. AD, P 5065–5070, McGuckin to Horris, 27 August 1869; Ibid., P 5071–73, McGuckin to Durieu, 28 August 1869; Ibid., P 5094–99, McGuckin to Durieu, 2 October 1870; Ibid., P 5147–5150, McGuckin to D'Herbomez, 24 June 1871; Ibid., P 5724–31, McGuckin to D'Herbomez, 6 August 1881; Ibid., PA 401.W43C.44, Augustin Dontenwill to Welch, 6 June 1915. Speaks of the sale of cattle from Williams Lake bringing in $25,000 for the Vicariate.

19. AD, P 5028–31, McGuckin to D'Herbomez, 9 July 1867; Fisher, *Contact and Conflict*, pp. 35, 107–10, 157, 159, 169–70, 184–85.

20. AD, McGuckin to D'Herbomez, 8 July 1867; Ibid., P 5029–31, McGuckin to D'Herbomez, 9 July 1867.

21. Ibid., P 3155, Grandidier to Fouquet, 20 June 1866; Ibid., 5079–82, McGuckin to Edward Horris, Vicariate Bursur, 3 January 1870.

22. These were St. Patrick's, Richfield; St. Michael's, Quesnel; St. James', Fort Alexandria; St. Ann's, Soda Creek; St. Peter's, Alkali Lake; St. Paul's, Dog Creek; St. Gabriel's, Canoe Creek; St. Laurence's, Til-te-Naïten; St. Mary's Refuge of Sinners, Pavillion, and Assumption, Clinton.

23. *Missions* 9 (1870): 106; VAA, D'Herbomez Register, Ff. 42–43; *Missions* 17 (1879): 410–27; Ibid., 18 (1880): 58–72; 273–81.

24. AD, P 5032–35, McGuckin to D'Herbomez, 20 August 1867; Ibid., P 5051–56, McGuckin to D'Herbomez, 4 December 1867

25. Ibid., P 5032–35, McGuckin to D'Herbomez, 20 August 1867; Ibid., P 5051–56, McGuckin to D'Herbomez, 4 December 1867; Fisher, *Contact and Conflict*, p. 136.

26. Peake, *The Anglican Church*, p. 70. AD, P 5032–35, McGuckin to D'Herbomez, 20 August 1867; Ibid., P 5051–56, McGuckin to D'Herbomez, 4 December 1867.

27. Margaret Whitehead, *The Cariboo Mission: A History of the Oblates* (Victoria: Sono Nis Press, 1981), p. 50.

28. *Missions* 33 (1896): 23. Letter of LeJacq to Superior General, Williams Lake, 21 October 1895.

29. AD, P 5061–63, McGuckin to D'Herbomez, 23 June 1869.

30. Ibid., P 5061–63, McGuckin to D'Herbomez, 23 June 1869; Ibid., P 4248–51. LeJacq to Durieu, 28 August 1896, Ibid., P 4275–78, LeJacq to Durieu, 1870 March 22; Ibid., P 4808–11, LeJacq, 28 March 1871; Ibid., P 4312–15, LeJacq to Durieu, 18 April 1871. LeJacq's letters almost always deal with what tribe he has just visited and where he is going next.

31. AD, P 5021–31, McGuckin to D'Herbomez, 9 July 1867; Ibid., P 4259–60, LeJacq to D'Herbomez, 19 September 1869; *Missions* 9 (1870): 134–40; Ibid., 11 (1872): 68 et seq.; Ibid., 12 (1874): 348–50.

32. Diamond Jenness, *The Carrier Indians of the Bulkley River: Their Social and Religious Life. Anthropological Papers*, No. 25, pp. 546, 549; Diamond Jenness, "The Ancient Education of a Carrier Indian," *Bulletin of the Canadian Department of Mines* 62 (1947): 22–27; Deward E. Walker, Jr. "New Light on the Prophet Dance Controversy," *Ethnohistory* 16 (1969): 245–51; Robin Ridington, *Swan People: A Study of the Dunne-za Prophet Dance*, National Museum of Man, Canadian Ethnology Service Paper 38 (1978): 4–5, 27–29; Kenelm Burridge, *New Heaven, New Earth: A Study of Millenarian Activities* (New York: Schocken Books, 1969), p. 22; Reid, *Myth, Symbol and Colonial Encounter*, passim.

33. AD, P 475–78, Blanchet to D'Herbomez, 9 January 1875; Carrière, *Dictionnaire Biographique*, Vol. I, pp. 102–3; Ibid., Vol. II, p. 305.

34. HBCA, B226/b/47, Graham to Hamilton, 21 July 1873; Ibid., B188/b/14, MacFarlone to McIntosh, 19 January 1889.

Notes

35. *Les Oblats*, Vol. III, pp. 792–96, François-Xavier Bermond, Act of Visitation, 15 September 1858; *Missions* 12 (1874): 221–22, 226, 230–32, LeJacq to D'Herbomez, 29 November 1872.

36. *Missions* 17 (1880): 70–72.

37. AD, P 479–482, Blanchet to D'Herbomez, 18 January 1876; *Missions* 12 (1874): 346–48.

38. AD, P 5021–31, McGuckin to D'Herbomez, 9 July 1867; Ibid., P 479–82, Blanchet to D'Herbomez, 18 January 1876; Ibid., P 4426–29, LeJacq to D'Herbomez, 25 April 1880.

39. Ibid., P 5021–31, McGuckin to D'Herbomez, 9 July 1867; Ibid., P 479–82, Blanchet to D'Herbomez, 18 January 1876; Ibid., P 4426–29, LeJacq to D'Herbomez, 25 April 1880; A.G. Morice, *The Déné Syllabary and Its Advantages: A First Collection of Minor Essays, Mostly Anthropological* (Stuart Lake Mission: By the Author, 1902), p. 67; AD, P 505–8, Blanchet to D'Herbomez, 15 March 1880.

40. Fisher, *Contact and Conflict*, pp. 82–84. For a comprehensive treatment of Kootenay ethnography see: Harry Holbert Turney-High "Ethnography of the Kutenai," *Memoirs of the American Anthropological Association* 56 (1941): 1–202; Duff, *Indian History of B.C.*, Vol. 1, p. 14.

41. Duff, *Indian History of B.C.*, Vol. 1, p. 39; Department of Indian Affairs, "Annual Report...1885," *Sessional Papers* (Ottawa: Queen's Printer, 1886), no. 4, part 1, pp. 29, 48–49, 199; Turney-High, "Ethnography of the Kutenai": 33–55, 69–74; Pierre De Smet, *New Indian Sketches*, Edward J. Kowrach, ed. (Washington: Ye Galleon Press, 1985), p. 101; AD P 2686–98, Fouquet to D'Herbomez, 9 February 1875; *Census of Canada 1880–1881* (Ottawa: Maclean, Roger & Co., 1883), Vol. 3, pp. 112–13, table XXII; *Census of Canada 1890–91* (Ottawa: S.E. Dawson, 1893), Vol. 1, pp. 8, 10, table II; G.W. Taylor, *Builders of British Columbia, An Industrial History* (Victoria: Morriss Publishing Company, 1982), pp. 12, 144–45.

42. De Smet, *New Indian Sketches*, pp. 99–106.

43. A.F. Chamberlain, "Report on the Kootenay Indians of South-Eastern British Columbia," *Report of the British Association for the Advancement of Science 1892* (London: Murray, 1893), pp. 559–60; Jenness, *Indians of Canada,* pp. 359–61; Turney-High, "Ethnography of the Kutenai": 170–88; *Kootenay*, British Columbia Heritage Series. Series 1, Vol. 8 (Victoria: Provincial Archives of British Columbia,1952), pp. 28–30; De Smet, *New Indian Sketches,* pp. 99–106; Wilfred Schoenberg, *Paths to the Northwest: A Jesuit History of the Oregon Province* (Chicago: Loyola Press, 1982), pp. 2–3; Paul E. Baker, *The Forgotten Kutenai* (Boise: Mountain State Press, 1955), p. 64; Claude E. Schaeffer, "Early Christian Missions of the Kutenai Indians," *Oregon Historical Quarterly* 71 (1970): 325–48; Philip Goldring, "Religion, Missions and Native Culture," *Journal of Canadian Church Historical Society* XXVI (1984): 48.

44. AD, HPK 5102, B80c, 18a, "Mission St Michel chez les Kakwals." Manuscript appears to be in Durieu's hand; *Daily British Colonist*, 25 August 1875 "Kootenay Correspondence."

Notes

---

45. AD, P 2971-74, Peytavin to Fouquet, July 1879; Ibid., HPK 5102, B86C, p. 4, A.
Martinet, "Act de la Visite de la Mission de St Eugène de Kootenays," 8 July 1882;
Grant, *Moon of Wintertime,* pp. 58-63, 109; AD, P 2686-89, Fouquet to D'Herbomez,
9 February 1875; Canada, Department of Indian Affairs, "Annual Report...1887,"
Canada, *Sessional Papers,* 6th Parliament, 2nd Session, 1888, vol. 15, part 1, pp.
cxii-cxiii; Jacqueline Gresko, "Roman Catholic Missions to the Indians of British
Columbia: A Reappraisal of the Lemert Thesis," *Journal of the Canadian Church
Historical Society* XXIV (1982): 53; NAC, RG 10, vol. 3627, file 6176, D'Herbomez to
J. Cauchon, 4 February 1876; Ibid., RG 10, vol. 3738, file 28-13-3, p. 21. W. Powell
Report to the Superintendent General of Indian Affairs, 18 November 1886.

46. Franz Boas, "First General Report on the Indians of British Columbia*," Report of the
British Association for the Advancement of Science, 1889* (London: Murray, 1890),
p. 807; AD, PC 101, C89, "Codex Historicus Cranbrook 1884-1948," pp. 41, 43, 46,
48, 51 (1884-87), and pp. 1, 2, 3, 11-13, 15, 17, 19-21, 23, 25 (1887-90); Chamberlain,
"Report on the Kootenay Indians of South-Eastern British Columbia," p. 561; Jenness,
Indians of Canada, p. 359; Horatio Hale, "Remarks on the Ethnology of British
Columbia: Introductory to the Second General Report of Dr. Franz Boas on the
Indians of that Province," *British Association for the Advancement of Science 1890*
(London: Murray 1891), p. 561; S.B. Steele, *Forty Years in Canada* (Toronto:
McLelland and Stewart, 1914), p. 250; Sylvia L. Thrupp, "A History of the Cranbrook
District in East Kootenay" (M.A. thesis, University of British Columbia, 1929),
pp. 43-45, 57-59; AD, P 2709-10, Fouquet to D'Herbomez, 30 May 1875; Schoenberg,
Paths to the Northwest, pp. 94-95, 112, 120-21; *Missions* 3 (1864): 165-66, 175, 178-82,
187, 196-97, 201, 205; Ibid., 18 (1880): 274, 279; AD, P 2690-93, Fouquet
to D'Herbomez, 29 March 1875; *Missions* 18 (1880): 277-78.

47. VOA, Baptismal Register, St. Eugene's Mission, Cranbrook, B.C., 1877-1899 and
Marriage Register, St. Eugene's Mission, Cranbrook, B.C. 1877-1909. AD, P
2669-2673, Fouquet to D'Herbomez, 18 January 1875; *Missions* 15 (1877): 81; AD,
P 2694-97, Fouquet to D'Herbomez, 6 April 1875; Ibid., P 2971-74, Peytavin to
Fouquet, July 1879; Ibid., P 2648, Fouquet to D'Herbomez, 24 November 1875; Ibid.,
P 3583-84, Grégoire to D'Herbomez, 30 July 1876; Ibid., P 3596-99, Grégoire to
D'Herbomez, 2 April 1877; Ibid., P 3607-10, Grégoire to D'Herbomez, 28 September
1877; Ibid., P 3617-19, Grégoire to D'Herbomez, 15 January 1878; Ibid., P 3622-24,
Grégoire to D'Herbomez, 28 July 1878; Ibid., P 3627-28, Grégoire to Fouquet, 2
October 1878; Ibid., P 2852-54, Fouquet to D'Herbomez, 2 October 1878. Ibid.,
P 3630, Fouquet to D'Herbomez, 3 October 1878.

48. Théodore Ortolan, *Les Oblats de Marie Immaculée durant le Premier Siècle de leur
Existence* (Paris: Librairie Saint-Paul, 1914), Vol. 1, p. 310, 323, 376; Yvon Beaudoin,
"Le Scolasticat de Montolivet," *Études Oblates* 27 (1968): 133-75, 238-70; Carrière,
Dictionnaire Biographique, Vol. I, pp. 211-12; Vol. II, pp. 42-43; AD, P 2674-85,
Fouquet to D'Herbomez, 8 February 1875; Ibid., P 2772-79, Fouquet to D'Herbomez,
10 October 1876; Ibid., 2786-87, Fouquet to D'Herbomez, 1 May 1877; Ibid., HPK 5242

Notes

381

D96L13, ex. 1 and 2, D'Herbomez to Fouquet, 30 June 1877; Ibid., P 2845–47, Fouquet to D'Herbomez, 26 November 1877; Ibid., P 2865–68, Fouquet to D'Herbomez, 30 June 1879; *Missions* 18 (1880): 280; AD, P 2906–15, Fouquet to D'Herbomez, 20 March 1881; Ibid., P 2936–39, Fouquet to D'Herbomez, 2 December 1881; F. Henry Johnson, *A History of Public Education in British Columbia* (Vancouver: University of British Columbia Press, 1964), pp. 48–49.

49. AD, P 2657–60, Fouquet to D'Herbomez, 25 October 1874; Ibid., P 2663–2666, Fouquet to D'Herbomez, 20 November 1874; Ibid., P 2711–26, Fouquet to D'Herbomez, 10 July 1875; Ibid., P 2788–95, Fouquet to D'Herbomez, 24 November 1876; Ibid., P 3596–99, Grégoire to D'Herbomez, 2 April 1877; Ibid., P 2830–33, Fouquet to D'Herbomez, 25 May 1877; Ibid., P 3627–28, Grégoire to Fouquet, 2 October 1878; Ibid., P 2897–98, Fouquet to D'Herbomez, 1 July 1880; Ibid., HPK 5102, B86c 8, pp. 3–7, Aimé Martinet, "Acte de Visitation de la Mission de St. Eugène des Kootenays, Colombie Brittanique, du 1 au 8 Juillet, 1882."

50. AD, P 2674–85, Fouquet to D'Herbomez, 8 February 1875; Ibid., P 3529–32, Grégoire to Fouquet, 21 July 1875; Ibid., P 3583–84, Grégoire to D'Herbomez, 30 July 1876; Ibid., P 2780–85, Fouquet to D'Herbomez, 24–29 September 1876; Ibid., P 3589–92, Grégoire to D'Herbomez, 23 November 1876; Ibid., P 3596–99, Grégoire to D'Herbomez, 2 April 1877; Ibid., P 2852–54, Fouquet to D'Herbomez, 2 October 1878; Carrière, *Dictionnaire Biographique*, Vol. I, p. 150; Vol. II, pp. 42–43; 111–12, 371; Vol. III, pp. 71–72, 126–127; AD, P 609–11, Burns to D'Herbomez, 18 March 1882; Ibid., P 6627–30, Peytavin to D'Herbomez, 30 June 1880; Ibid., P 2893–96, Fouquet to D'Herbomez, 24 August 1880; Ibid., P 2901–4, Fouquet to D'Herbomez, 15 December 1880; Ibid., P 6646–49, Peytavin to D'Herbomez, 11 March 1881; Ibid., P 2926–39, Fouquet to D'Herbomez, 2 December 1881.

51. AD, P 5900–5903, Martin to D'Herbomez, 14 December 1880; Ibid., P 5914–27, Martin to D'Herbomez, 18 March 1882, Ibid., P 6685–86, Peytavin to D'Herbomez, 26 March 1882; Ibid., P 2540–43, Joseph Fabre, Superior General to D'Herbomez, 19 November 1883; Ibid., Fouquet to Fabre, 3 July 1883; Ibid., P 2571–75, Fabre to D'Herbomez, 5 January 1888, Ibid., Fouquet to Fabre, 1 September 1887; Carrière, *Dictionnaire Biographique*, Vol. II, pp. 42–43.

52. Jean Usher, *William Duncan of Metlakatla: A Victorian Missionary in British Columbia*. National Museum of Man Publications in History No. 5 (Ottawa: National Museum of Canada, 1974), pp. 94–95; David Mulhall, *Will to Power: The Missionary Career of Father Morice* (Vancouver: University of British Columbia Press, 1986), pp. 33–35, 180–81.

Notes

✢ 8 The Native People and the Diocese of Victoria

1. Grant, *Moon of Wintertime*, p. 125; ACL, Seghers to De Neve, Victoria, 11 May 1866; Ibid., same to same, Victoria, 31 January 1869.

2. ACL, Seghers to De Neve, Victoria, 17 May 1869; Ibid., Seghers to Benoit and Joseph Van Loo, Victoria, 6 April 1874.

3. Engelhardt, *Missions and Missionaries of California*, Vol. II, p. 441; Fisher, *Contact and Conflict*, p. 121; Philip Drucker, "The Northern and Central Nootkan Tribes," *Smithsonian Institution Bureau of American Ethnology: Bulletin* 14 (Washington, D.C.: Government Printing Office, 1951): 13; ACL, Seghers to Van Loo, Victoria, 17 May 1869; Ibid., Seghers to Benoit and Joseph Van Loo, Victoria, 6 April 1874; Archives of Society for the Advancement of the Faith, Paris, Seghers's File, Seghers to Verdiere, Victoria, 21 May 1874; Helena, Montana Diocesan Archives, Seghers to Brondel, Victoria, 20 May 1874; *The Colonist*, 21 October 1874; ASSA, C.J. Seghers, "Indian Missions," ms. copy of sermon preached at the Third Plenary Council of Baltimore, 1884; Joseph Van Der Heyden, *Life and Letters of Father Brabant: A Flemish Missionary Hero* (Louvain: J. Wouter-Ick Printers, 1920), p. 37.

4. Charles Lillard, *Mission to Nootka*, 1874–1900 (Sidney, B.C.: Gray's Publishing Ltd., 1977), pp. 38–48; *The Colonist*, 6 November 1875.

5. Lillard, *Mission to Nootka*, pp. 38–48; *The Colonist*, 23 March 1876.

6. Lillard, *Mission to Nootka*, pp. 38–48; *The Colonist*, 6 November 1875; ACL, Seghers to Acting Rector Sebastian Goens, St. Ann's Mission, Cowichan, 10 January 1876; *The Colonist*, 23 March 1876; Ibid., 21 May 1886; BCARS, GR 443/U22 Lt. Governor Joseph W. Trutch to Captain R. Harris, R.N. Victoria, 5 November 1875. Harris was called upon to "rescue" Brabant, though initially, apparently reacting negatively to Brabant's role in having spread smallpox, he refused, though he did comply on 2 December 1875.

7. Lillard, *Mission to Nootka*, pp. 38–48; Whitehead, *Now You Are My Brother*, p. 34.

8. Ibid., pp. 68–74, 79, 86–88, 93, 100–101, 103, 109, 112–18; Columbia Mission Reports (1870), p. 21; Charles Moser, *Reminiscences of the West Coast of Vancouver Island* (Victoria: Acme Press Ltd., 1926), pp. 3–131; MAAO, Christie Residential School File, passim.

9. Moser, *Reminiscences of the West Coast*, pp. 9–131.

10. ASSA, Lemmens File, "Haps and Mishaps," 1 August 1883 to 2 February 1886, no foliation.

11. Ibid.

12. Ibid.

13. Ibid.

14. Ibid.

15. Ibid., Lemmens File, "Sermons"—"On Eternal Life," no foliation. Others sermons are entitled: "On the End of Man," "On Grace," and all are dated 1875. They were apparently written before he left Belgium. Volume also contains theological notes in Latin: Ibid., Lemmens File, "Haps and Mishaps..."; McMillan, *Native Peoples and Cultures of Canada*, pp. 200–201.

16. PFAR, Acta, vol. 258, fols. 167–68, Appointment of Lemmens, 9 April 1888. Brabant and Althoff, both missionaries to the Native people, were also recommended; ACLA, Seghers to Acting Rector, Sebastian Goens, St. Ann's Cowichan, 10 January 1876; *The Colonist*, 10, 13 May 1888; Ibid., 14 August 1888.

17. Vincent A. Yzermans, *Saint Rose of Wrangell: The [Catholic] Church's Beginning in Southeast Alaska* (St. Paul, Minnesota: North Central Publishing Company, 1979), pp. 1–14.

18. *The Colonist*, 6 January 1868. Reports a letter from a Mr. Thomas G. Murphy of Sitka to Demers asking him to send a priest there; ACL, Seghers to De Neve, Victoria, 16 December 1863. Hopes to go there; Ibid., Seghers to "Lawyer," Cowichan, St. Ann's, 5 May 1885; Ibid., Seghers to De Neve, Juneau, 21 September 1885; Ibid., Seghers to De Neve, Victoria, 26 October 1885. Sheldon Jackson, *Facts About Alaska: Its People, Villages, Missions, Schools* (New York: Women's Board of Home Missions of the Presbyterian Church, 1910), pp. 3–27, 34–35; Fisher, *Contact and Conflict*, pp. 119–45; U.S. Census Office, *Report on Population and Resources of Alaska...1890* (Washington, D.C.: Government Printing Office, 1893), pp. 182–88; Margaret Cantwell, *North To Share: The Sisters of Saint Ann in Alaska and the Yukon Territory* (Victoria, B.C.: Sisters of St. Ann, 1992), p. 175.

19. ACLA, Seghers to "My Friend," Victoria, 9 December 1885; JPAS, "Kootenay Kopy," n.d.; Ibid., "*Residentia Wrangellensis S. Rosae et St. Joannis*," ms.; Ibid., "Juneau and Sitka, Althoff and Heyman," ms.; JDA, "Some Incidents in the Life of Very Reverend J.A. Althoff, V.G., Archdiocese of Vancouver [Island]," Ms.;. Sheldon Jackson, *Facts About Alaska: Its People, Villages, Missions, Schools* (New York: Women's Board of Home Missions of the Presbyterian Church, 1910), pp. 3–27, 34–35; Fisher, *Contact and Conflict*, pp. 119–45; U.S. Census Office, *Report on Population and Resources of Alaska...1890*, pp. 182–88; Cantwell, *North To Share*, p. 175.

20. JPAS, Seghers to Louis Palladino, 12 February 1886; Ibid., Joseph Cataldo to Pascal Tosi, 21 February 1886.

21. JPAS, "Diary of Sacred Heart Mission, 1878–1939," see entries: 26 January 1883, 5 March 1883, 16 August 1883, 5 January 1884, 14, 17, 22 June 1884, 6, 29 September 1884, 20 October 1884; Ibid., Francis Monroe, S.J., "Story of the Assassination of Bishop Seghers," ms. (hereafter "Seghers"); Ibid., "Diary of St. Francis Regis Mission, Colville," see entries: 22 December 1884, 4 June 1885, 21 November 1885, 2 December 1885; "Agreement," signed by Fuller at St. Michael's Mission, 23 December 1885; Ibid., Cataldo to Tosi, Spokane, 17 March 1886; Ibid., Jette, "Comments on Fr. Frank Barnum's Account of Death of Archbishop Seghers," ms.; PAA, Seghers to Cataldo, Portland, 20 July 1883; *The Colonist*, 19 July 1887.

22. JPAS, Tosi to Cataldo, Juneau, 19 July 1886; Ibid., Robaut to Cataldo, Mouth of the Stewart River, 28 November 1886; Ibid., Robaut to Jonckau, Anvik, 31 July 1887; ACLA, Seghers to Jonckau, Mouth of the Salmon River, 31 August 1886; *The Colonist,* 22 July 1887.

23. JPAS, Robaut to Jonchau, Anvik, 31 July 1887; *The Colonist,* 19, 22 July 1887; Ibid., 24 September 1887; PAA, Seghers, "Diary of 1886," ms., see entries: September-November 1886; Alaska State Archives, Juneau, Alaska, Commission's Docket, Case No. 160, U.S.A. versus Frank Fuller.

24. Federal Records Center, Seattle, WA, "U.S.A. versus Frank Fuller," Case no. 54554-1; *The Alaskan,* 19 September 1887; Ibid., 12 November 1887; *The Colonist,* 24 September 1887; Ibid., 9 December 1887; Ibid., 12 May 1888*; Seattle Post-Intelligencer,* 1 January 1888; Ibid., 15 May 1888; Alfred P. Swineford*, Report of the Governor of Alaska for the Year* 1887 (Washington, D.C.: Government Printing Office, 1887), pp. 43–45; Portland, Oregon, *Catholic Sentinel,* 16 February 1886.

25. Steckler, *Charles John Seghers,* pp. 1–56; 229–77; Cantwell, *North to Share,* pp. 21, 55.

26. Ibid., ACLA, Seghers to De Neve, n.d., c. 1864; Ibid., same to same, "Ancon Steamer," 16 July 1886.

27. VDA, Seghers Miscellaneous File. Anonymous report of his funeral, n.d.

28. Ibid., Sister of St. Ann (JM) view of Seghers, May 1973.

✤ 9 *Oblate Approaches to the Native People*

1. VOA, *An Apology to Native Peoples,* Lac Ste. Anne, Alberta, 24 July 1991. File also contains reactions from a number of Oblates of St. Paul's Province, almost all of them quite negative; Ibid., "Our Story: Extracts of Interviews by Oblates on Residential Schools, December 1991."

2. *Études Oblates* 1 (1942): 193.

3. VAA, D'Herbomez to Begbie, n.d., 1876.

4. Ibid., Begbie to D'Herbomez, 21 August 1876.

5. Barman, *The West Beyond the West,* pp. 17, 152–55, 158–59, 163–64, 168, 173.

6. Ibid., pp. 17, 152–55, 158–59, 163–64, 168, 173; Tennant, *Aboriginal Peoples and Politics,* pp. 3–87.

7. Thomas A. Lascelles, *Mission on the Inlet: St. Paul's Indian Catholic Church, North Vancouver, B.C., 1863–1984* (Vancouver: Schuman/Harte Ltd., 1984), pp. 10–13.

8. VAA, D'Herbomez to Howe, 5 July 1871.

9. Ibid., D'Herbomez to Langevin, 29 September 1871.

10. Ibid., Petitions of Natives from Lower Fraser Valley to I.W. Powell, Superintendent of Indian Affairs in British Columbia, 13 April 1873 and 24 May 1873; *Mainland Guardian,* 6 June 1875; Ibid., 16 June 1875. Continuing attempts by Durieu to resolve the land problem; VAA, Grandidier to Superintendent General of Indian Affairs, 12 June 1879; Barman, *The West Beyond the West,* p. 173.

11. ASSA, M. Theodore, "St. Mary's Indian Mission, Mission City on the Fraser," Ms., passim; VAA, D'Herbomez to Hector Langevin, Victoria, 22 September 1871.

12. VAA, Langevin to D'Herbomez, Victoria, 22 September 1871; Ibid., D'Herbomez to Powell, n.d. Refers to a letter from Powell on 13 May 1874; Ibid., D'Herbomez to Powell, 27 April 1875

13. George S. Tomkins, *A Common Countenance: Stability and Change in Canadian Curriculum* (Scarborough, Ont: Prentice Hall, 1986), pp. 37–40.

14. Miller, *Shingwauk's Vision*, pp. 154–55.

15. J.R. Miller, "Denominational Rivalry in Indian Residential Education," *Études Oblates de l'Ouest/Western Oblate Studies* 2 (1992): 139–55.

16. Peake, *The Anglican Church in British Columbia*, pp. 66–71, 99; NAC, RG 10, vol. 3694, file 14676, Sillitoe to Powell, 8 November 1883; Ibid., Sillitoe to Macdonald, 30 July 1884, Ibid., Powell to Macdonald, 10 November 1884; Ibid., Sillitoe to J.A.R. Homer, MP, 16 February 1885; Ibid., H. Lomas to Powell, 27 December 1884, Ibid., Vankoughnet to Macdonald, 18 March 1885; Ibid., Powell to Macdonald, 7 April 1885; Ibid., Sillitoe to Vankoughnet, 22 June 1885; J.R. Miller, "Denominational Rivalry in Indian Residential Education": 139–55.

17. Ormsby, *British Columbia: A History*, p. 227. Miller, *Shingwauk's Vision*, pp. 101–3, 219, 456, n. 39.

18. Ibid.

19. VAA, D'Herbomez notes on interview with Vankoughnet in Ottawa, n.d. Likely sometime in the spring of 1887; Ibid., Vankoughnet to D'Herbomez, 4 October 1887, Ibid., D'Herbomez to Vankoughnet, 17 October 1887; Ibid., Vankoughnet to D'Herbomez, 31 October 1888; Ibid., D'Herbomez to Vankoughnet, 27 November 1888.

20. Bunoz "Bishop Durieu's System," pp. 193–209. Although written in 1942 by Bunoz, then the apostolic vicar of Prince Rupert, the article is important as an accurate description of the Durieu System since Bunoz knew Durieu personally. Since Durieu never published a detailed description of his "System," although it is described in many of his letters to Oblate missionaries, the Bunoz article can be considered a "primary" source.

21. Betty C. Keller and Rosella M. Leslie, *Bright Seas, Pioneer Spirits: The Sunshine Coast* (Victoria, B.C.: Horsdal & Schubart, 1996), pp. 28–31.

22. Bunoz, "Bishop Durieu's System," pp. 193–96.

23. Ibid., pp. 193–96.

24. Ibid., pp. 196–200.

25. Ibid., pp. 196–200.

26. Ibid., pp. 196–200; Barman, *The West Beyond the West*, pp. 15–16; Grant, *Moon of Wintertime*, pp. 17–20; Johnston, *The Pacific Province*, p. 48; Maud, *The Salish People*, p. 69.

27. Bunoz, "Bishop Durieu's System," pp. 200–201.

28. Whitehead, *The Cariboo Mission*, pp. 117–19; Bunoz, "Bishop Durieu's System," pp. 201–2.

29. Ibid., pp. 202–4; VAA, Contains a large array of begging letters and letters of thanks to European mission societies from D'Herbomez and Durieu from the 1860s to the 1890s.

30. Bunoz, "Bishop Durieu's System," pp. 204–6.

31. Ibid., pp. 206–8.

32. Ibid., pp. 206–8.

33. *The Month* (June 1892), p. 125–33. Contains the entire case as well as the various editorials from the local press.

34. Ibid., pp. 131–32.

35. AD, P 2377–2379, Durieu to "Father," 30 November 1893.

36. *Missions* 43 (1905): 274–76.

37. Whitehead, *Now You Are My Brother*, pp. 34–35.

38. AD, PC 101, V22A.7, Dontenwill to Oblate Priests and Brothers, 28 September 1898.

✣ 10 The Residential Schools

1. Johnston, *The Pacific Province*, pp. 175–76; NAC, RG 10, vol. 3656, file 9059, Powell to Superintendent General of Indian Affairs, 15 April 1914; Grant Willis, "Second Lower Similkameen School," *Okanagan Historical Studies* 37 (1973): 115–19; NAC, RG 10, col. 3965, file 150,000–150,013. Contains a large correspondence on this subject.

2. NAC, RG 10, vol. 3698, file 15,924, Sproat to Superintendent General of Indian Affairs, 3 September 1879; AD, P 3334–3337, Grandidier to D'Herbomez, 29 June 1876; Ibid., P 912–922, Caron to D'Herbomez, September 1880.

3. AD, [Jean-Marie Le Jeune] *Okanagan Manuel*, printed, n.d., probably 1893; [Jean-Marie LeJeune] *English Manual or Prayers and Catechism in English Typography with the Approbation of Right Rev. P. Durien [sic] Bishop of New Westminster* (Kamloops: By Author, 1896).

4. Department of Indian Affairs, *Annual Report* (Ottawa: Queen's Printer 1880), p. 210; Barman, *The West Beyond the West*, p. 363; NAC, RG 10, vol. 3752, file 30614, Report on Schools, MacKay to Powell, 22 August 1886.

5. NAC, RG 10, vol. 3752, file 30614, Le Jeune to MacKay to Powell, 22 August 1886; Ibid., vol. 3799, file 48,431–2. Contains further correspondence on subject; VAA, Durieu to Dewdney, 18 March 1890; Ibid., Vankoughnet to Durieu, 26 December 1890; Ibid., Durieu to Superintendent General, 16 July 1892; Ibid., Vowell to Durieu, 21 January 1893; Ibid., Vowell to Durieu, 26 January 1893; Ibid., Vowell to Durieu, 15 February 1893; Carrière, *Dictionnaire Biographique*, vol. I, pp. 68, 162–63; Thomas Lascelles, *Roman Catholic Indian Residential Schools in British Columbia* (Vancouver: Oblates of Mary Immaculate, 1990), pp. 69–70.

6. NAC, RG 10, vol. 3799, file 48,432–1, Vankoughnet to Dewdney, 18 June 1890; Ibid., vol. 3964, file 149,874, "Kamloops School Attendance"; Ibid., vol. 3799, file 48,432–1, MacKay to Vowell, 14 January 1892; Ibid., vol. 3694, file 14676, Bishop Sillitoe to Homer, MP, February 1885; Ibid., vol. 3964, file 149,874, Morrow to Vowell, 16 December 1904.

7. NAC, RG 10, vol. 3753, file 30614, MacKay to Powell, 22 August 1886; Johnston, *The Pacific Province*, pp. 297–98; Department of Indian Affairs, *Annual Report, 1896–1897* (Ottawa: Queen's Printer, 1898), p. 288.

8. Department of Indian Affairs, *Annual Report 1899–1900* (Ottawa: Queen's Printer, 1901), p. xxix; NAC, RG 10, vol. 3964, file 149,874; AD P 895–897, Carion to D'Herbomez, 13 September 1893.

9. Department of Indian Affairs, *Annual Report 1909–1910* (Ottawa: King's Printer, 1911), p. 500; NAC, RG 10, vol. 3656, file 9059, McDougall Report of Residential Schools in British Columbia, 1910.

10. Ibid., vol. 4043, file 343,016, Reverend John McDougall, Inspector for Department of Indian Affairs for British Columbia, "Report," 1910.

11. Ibid., vol. 4043, file 343,016, Reverend John McDougall, Inspector for Department of Indian Affairs for British Columbia, "Report," 1910; Ibid., vol., 4043, file 343,016, Megraw to McLean, 4 April 1914.

12. VOA, Patrick McGuire to A.F. McKenzie, 24 September 1927; Lascelles, *Indian Residential Schools*, pp. 58, 70–71.

13. Barman, *The West Beyond the West*, pp. 190, 195.

14. Margaret Whitehead, ed., *They Call Me Father: Memoirs of Father Nicolas Coccola* (Vancouver: University of British Columbia Press, 1988), pp. 33–43.

15. AD, P 1128–1133, Coccola Description of Kootenay troubles, March 1887; Whitehead, *They Call Me Father*, pp. 43–45, 112–13.

16. VVA, Durieu to Jean de la Croix, 5 May 1890; Ibid., M. Godefrey to Durieu, 24 May 1890.

17. VVA, Durieu to Vankoughnet, 28 May 1890; Ibid., Vankoughnet to Durieu, 9 June 1890; Ibid., Durieu to J. Dewdney, Assistant to Vankoughnet, 30 June 1890; Ibid., Durieu to Coccola, 5 August 1890.

18. VAA, Durieu to Coccola, 5 August 1890; Ibid., Coccola to Superintendent General of Indian Affairs, 1 July 1892.

19. VAA, Coccola to Superintendent General of Indian Affairs, 1 July 1892; Lascelles, *Indian Residential Schools*, p. 72.

20. Whitehead, *They Call Me Father*, pp. 119–20.

21. NAC, RG 10, vol. 3694, file 14676, Memorial of Chief of the Lower Fraser to Dewdney, n.d.; VAA, same to Vowell, 1891; NAC, RG 10, vol. 3694, file 14696, Vankoughnet to Dewdney, 13 May 1891; Ibid., D.C. Scott, memorandum, 2 October 1891; Ibid., Durieu to Daly, 24 January 1893; Ibid., McGuckin to Daly, 25 January 1893; Ibid., Vankoughnet to McGuckin, 27 January 1893; Ibid., P.M.O. Corneiller, OMI, Principal of St. Mary's to Daly, 23 December 1893; Ibid., McGuckin to Daly, 31 January 1894;

Ibid., Vankoughnet to Cornellier, 1 February 1894; Ibid., Vankoughnet to Vowell, 30 July 1894; Carrière, *Dictionnaire Biographique*, Vol. II, pp. 342–43.

22. VAA, Pacifique to Durieu, 15 October 1891; Whitehead, *They Call Me Father*, pp. 120–23; NAC, RG 10, vol. 3964, folder 149,874, Schedule of Statistics of Pupils Discharged from Industrial Schools to 30 June 1897; VAA, School reports and letters from various people dealing with the school during the years: 1891–1894; see also NAC, RG 10, vol. 1022, 216–18, 260–62.

23. VOA, Codex Historicus, Cranbrook, 1884–1948, p. 128; Lascelles, *Indian Residential Schools*, pp. 59, 72.

24. Ibid., pp. 72–73.

25. VAA, Durieu Register, pp. 207–8, Durieu to Bernard, 18 March 1890; Ibid., McGuckin to Durieu, 8 March 1890 encouraging Durieu to write to Bernard.

26. NAC, RG 10, vol. 6436, file 878–1, Part 1, Durieu to Meason, 24 February 1891; ASSA, Marie Anne of Jesus, Superior to D'Herbomez, 23 May 1888; VAA, Durieu to Providence Sisters, 23 February 1891; Ibid., Durieu to Providence Sisters, 26 May 1891; Ibid., Providence Sisters to Durieu, 27 February 1891; Ibid., Providence Sisters to Durieu, 22 May 1891; Ibid., Providence Sisters to Durieu, 11 June 1891; Ibid., Pierre d'Alcantara to Durieu, 25 May 1891; Ibid., Superior General of Sisters of Providence to Durieu, 14 July 1891.

27. Whitehead, *The Cariboo Mission*, pp. 118–19.

28. Ibid.

29. Levasseur, *A History of the Missionary Oblates*, Vol. 1, p. 264; A.G. Morice, *Histoire de l'Église catholique dans l'Ouest, du Lac Supérior au Pacifique 1659–1905*, Vol. IV (Montreal: Murrow, 1922), p. 336; NAC, RG 10, vol. 6436, file 878–1, part 1, Vankoughnet to Dewdney, 6 May 1891; Ibid., Vankoughnet to Chief Clerk, 11 May 1891; Whitehead, *The Cariboo Mission*, p. 112.

30. NAC, RG 10, vol. 6436, file 878–1, part 1, Dewdney to Sinclair, 13 October 1891; Ibid., Sinclair to Dewdney, 14 October 1891; Ibid., Sinclair to Deputy Superintendent, 30 June 1893; VAA, Durieu Register, f. 208, Vowell to Durieu, 18 May 1891; NAC, RG 10, vol. 6436, file 878–1, Part 1, LeJacq to Vowell, 15 June 1893; VAA, Vowell to LeJacq, 14 August 1894; Ibid., Durieu Register, ff. 210–212. Durieu to Daly, 28 November 1893; Ibid., Daly to Durieu, 24 December 1893; Ibid., Durieu to Daly, 18 January 1894; Ibid., Durieu to Daly, 21 December 1894; NAC, RG 10, vol. 3894, file 97063. Contains federal expenditures for years 1875 through 1894. Ibid., vol. 6436, file 878–1, part 1, Acting Deputy to LeJacq, 29 August 1895; Carrière, *Dictionnaire Biographique*, vol. II, p. 305; Lascelles, *Indian Residential Schools*, pp. 72–73.

31. Whitehead, *The Cariboo Mission*, pp. 120–21.

32. Ibid., pp. 114, 122–25.

33. Ibid., pp. 126–28.

34. Lascelles, *Indian Residential Schools*, pp. 72–73.

35. Ibid., p. 70.

36. Alexander MacDonald, ed., *The British Columbia Orphans' Friend: Historical Number, 1847–1914* (Victoria, B.C.: Diocese of Victoria, 1914), p. 64.

37. BCARS, Add. Ms 1267, vols. 1, 602, Donckele to A.W. Vowell, 1 June 1895; Ibid., vol. 3, 507, Donckele to A.E. Green, 23 March 1905; Ibid., vol. 4, 323, Lemmens to Agent, Cowichan Agency, 25 July 1914; Ibid., vol. 4, 324, Lemmens to W.R. Robertson, 30 July 1914.

38. BCARS, Add. Ms 1267, vols. 1–5, 38–39, 40. Kuper Island Progress Reports, 1890–1914; NAC, RG 10, vol. 1333. Kuper Island School Administrative Reports, 1890–1914.

39. MacDonald, *The...Orphans' Friend*, pp. 64–65; *The Colonist*, 5 August 1897.

40. Lascelles, *Indian Residential Schools*, p. 70.

41. Miriam Margaret O'Donnell, "In Faith and Kindness: The Life of the Most Reverend Alexander Christie" (M.A. thesis, University of Portland 1945), pp. 16–25; BCARS, B/1872/RG 10/1333, Sr. Mary Celestine, SSA to H.W. Lomas, St. Ann's Convent, Cowichan Lake, 6 June 1889; Ibid., Add. ms. 1267/vols. 1–5, 38–40, Kuper Island Progress Reports, 1890–1914.

42. Indian Affairs Educational Division Members, ed., *The Education of Indian Children in Canada* (Toronto: Ryerson Press 1965), p. 17; James Redford, "Attendance at Indian Residential Schools in British Columbia, 1890–1920," *BC Studies* 44 (Winter 1979–1980): 41–43; Lillard, *Mission to Nootka*, pp. 112–16; Gresko, "Creating Little Dominions," pp. 94–97.

43. *The Education of Indian Children*, p. 17; Redford, "Attendance at Indian Residential Schools in British Columbia": 41–43; Lillard, *Mission to Nootka*, pp. 112–16; Fisher, *Contact and Conflict*, p. 141; BCARS, Indian Affairs, B 1857, RG 10, vol. 6037, F/152 - *B-1, pt 1/253854, B. Orth to C. Sifton, 15 December 1903. Complains that the Methodists in Cowichan Valley were trying to "pervert" the "Catholic Indians"; Ibid., Indian Affairs, B 1873, vol. 1370, pp. 167–69, 242–43, 319–24. Letters from W.H. Lomas, Indian Agent, Cowichan District, 1891, 1895, 1896 and 1897; Ibid., Indian Affairs, B 1357, RG 10, vol. 6039, F\159\42\1, Rev. J. Campbell to A.W. Vowell, Victoria, 15 July 1901.

44. Anonymous, *Golden Jubilee of Christie Indian Residential School 1900–1950* (Victoria, B.C.: Acme Press, 1950), no pagination.

45. MAAO, Brabant to St. M. Placide, Hesquiat, 18 July 1902; Ibid., Maurus Schneider to unidentified person, Mowichat, 23 December 1904; Ibid., E. Sobry to Schneider, 30 May 1906; Ibid., same to same, 13 January 1907; Miller, *Shingwauk's Vision*, pp. 45–46, 50, 130–34, 179, 256, 301–5, 349–50, 366, 461 n.42; Gresko, "Early Catholic Schools in...British Columbia," p. 98; VOA, Christie Residential School Files; Department of Indian Affairs, *Annual Report* (Ottawa: King's Printer, 1906), p. 249.

46. MAAO, Stern to Schneider, Nootka, 22 June 1907; Ibid., Stern to Schneider, Nootka, 24 February 1908; Ibid., Stern to "My Dear Boys and Girls," Nootka, 27 December 1908; Ibid., Joseph Schindler to Schneider, Kakawis, 3 January 1913; Ibid., Christie Residential School File, "*Codex Historica*."

47. Dorothy Haegert, *Children of the First People* (Vancouver, B.C.: Tillicum Library, 1983), pp. 120–21; MAAO, August Murphy to Schneider, Friendly Cove, Nootka, B.C., 17 June 1952; Gresko, "Early Catholic Indian Schools in...British Columbia," pp. 97–102; *Golden Jubilee of Christie Indian Residential School*, no pagination; Greg Brian Shoop, "The Participation of the Ohiaht Indians in the Commercial Fisheries of the Bamfield-Barkley Sound Area of British Columbia" (M.A. thesis, University of Victoria, 1972), pp. 45–58; E.Y. Arima, *The West Coast People: The Nootka of Vancouver Island and Cape Flattery: British Columbia Provincial Museum, Special Publication No. 6* (Victoria: British Columbia Provincial Museum, 1983), pp. 140–45.

48. Lascelles, *Indian Residential Schools*, p. 71.

49. VAA, D'Herbomez to Langevin, 28 December 1888; Ibid., D'Herbomez to Langevin, 12 March 1889; NAC, RG 10, vol. 3694, file 14676, Langevin to D'Herbomez, 3 January 1889; Ibid., D'Herbomez to Dewdney, 11 March 1889; Ibid., Langevin to D'Herbomez, 9 April 1889; Ibid., Vankoughnet to Durieu, 10 July 1890; VVA, Durieu to J.E. Corbauld, MP, 10 September 1890; NAC, RG 10, vol. 3694, file 97,063. 1875–1878: $350; 1879–1881: $262.50; 1882–1884: $350; 1885–1886: $500; 1886–1887: $625; 1887–1888: $500; 1888–1890:$625; 1889–1891: $500; 1891–1892: $750.

50. NAC, RG 10, vol. 3694, file 14676, Elders' Memorial to Dewdney, n.d.; VAA, Copy of Memorial, 1891; NAC, RG 10, vol. 3694, file 14696, Vankoughnet to Dewdney, 13 May 1891; Ibid., D.C. Scott, memorandum, 2 October 1891; Ibid., Durieu to Daly, 24 January 1893; Ibid., McGuckin to Daly, 25 January 1893; Ibid., Vankoughnet to McGuckin, 27 January 1893; Ibid., P.M.O. Corneiller, OMI, Principal of St. Mary's to Daly, 23 December 1893; Ibid., McGuckin to Daly, 31 January 1894; Ibid., Vankoughnet to Cornellier, 1 February 1894; Ibid., Vankoughnet to Vowell, 30 July 1894; Carrière, *Dictionnaire Biographique*, Vol. II, pp. 342–43.

51. VVA, Vowell to Durieu, 30 December 1896; Ibid., Durieu to Vowell, 5 January 1897; Ibid., Charts dealing with statistics, 1896–97; Ibid., Durieu and Dontenwill to Sifton, 5 November 1897; Department of Indian Affairs, *Annual Report* 1897 (Ottawa: Queen's Printer, 1898), pp. 405–9; 430–33.

52. Department of Indian Affairs, *Annual Report* 1917 (Ottawa: King's Printer, 1918), pp. 175–94.

53. VOA, Prince George Papers, Box 1, File 23, 1915–1916 correspondence, Coccola Petition; Cronin, *Cross in the Wilderness*, pp. 211–15; Whitehead, *They Call Me Father*, p. 148; Lascelles, *Indian Residential Schools*, p. 69.

54. Ibid., pp. 69–73.

55. Ibid., p. 73.

56. Keller, *Bright Seas, Pioneer Spirits*, pp. 29–31; Lascelles, *Indian Residential Schools*, pp. 71–72.

57. Ibid., p. 72.

58. Ibid., p. 73.

59. Ibid., p. 73.

60. *The Oxford Dictionary of Quotations* (Oxford: Oxford University Press, 1979), p. 148.

61. Miller, *Shingwauk's Vision*, pp. 134–35.

62. Jean Friesen, "Commentary on Jean Barman's 'All Hallows School' and Ken Coates' 'Betwixt and Between'" *BC Studies Conference*, Vancouver, BC, 6 February 1984, p. 2; Bunoz, "Bishop Durieu's System," pp. 200–201.

✤ 11 *The Native People and the Catholic Church*

1. Albert Dréan, "En avant! Vive Marie!," *L'Apostolat* 12 (1941), pp. 54–55.

2. Kenneth Coates, "Best Left as Indians: Native-White Relations in the Yukon Territory, 1840–1950" (Ph.D. thesis: University of British Columbia, 1984), pp. 202–32; Huel, *Proclaiming the Gospel to the Indians and the Métis,* pp. 269–89; Martha McCarthy, *From the Great River to the Ends of the Earth: Oblate Missions to the Dene, 1847–1921* (Edmonton: University of Alberta Press and Western Canadian Publishers, 1995), pp. 179–91.

3. AD, P 2218, D'Herbomez Report on the State of the Oblate Missions in Oregon and British Columbia, 1861; Durieu, *Missions* 24 (1886): 121–22; Bunoz, "Bishop Durieu's System," p. 208; Joseph Scannell, "General Chapter Report from St. Peter's Province, Canada, 1947" *Missions* 74 (1947): 488–520.

4. George Forbes, "Province Saint-Pierre," *Missions* 73 (1939): 41.

5. Welch, "Report," *Missions* 55 (1921): 17–21; Maurice Gilbert, *Dictionnaire Biographique*, Vol. IV, p. 37; John Boekenfoehr, *General Act of the Canonical Visitation of St. Peter's Province, September 1943-March 1944* (Rome: Oblate Generalate, 1944), pp. 44–47; Whitehead, *Now You Are My Brother*, pp. 34–35.

6. Doug Crosby, "Canadian Oblates' Statement: An Apology to Native Peoples," *Origins*, August 15, 1991, pp. 183–84. In his homily celebrating the "Day of Pardon" on 12 March 2000, Pope John Paul II was highly critical of the "violence" that so many Roman Catholics have so long "used in the service of the truth" of Christianity, as well as "for the distrustful and hostile attitudes" that Catholics have and continue to harbour "towards the followers of other religions." In conclusion, he declared that today must be a "time of reconciliation, a time of salvation for all believers and for everyone who is searching for God!" (www.vatican.va/holy-father/john-pa...ents/hf-jp-ii.hom.20000312_pardon_en.html (March 2000)).

7. John DeMont, "Ottawa says it is Sorry," *Maclean's,* January 19, 1998, p. 32; Miller, *Shingwauk's Vision*, p. 328; The Fort Alexander Industrial School was opened in 1897; Father Charles Arthur Cahill (1897–1903) was its founding principal. See Levasseur, *A History of the Missionary Oblates*, Vol. 1, p. 239.

8. Barman, *The West Beyond the West*, pp. 305–11.

9. James Mulvihill, "The Dilemma in Indian Education," *Oblate News*, January 1963, p 11; Sister Margaret Denis, SOS, *Report Submitted to the Canadian Catholic Conference of Bishops, National Office of Religious Education on the Religious Education of the Indian and Métis Peoples* (Ottawa: CCCB, 1972), pp. 37–38.

10. St. Paul's Province in British Columbia had became a Vice Province in 1968 when it was separated from St. Peter's, and a Province in 1973.

11. VOA, "Our Story: Extracts of Interviews by Oblates on Residential Schools," December 1991, pp. 1–15.

12. Jerry A. Prazma, OMI, "The North American Indians and the Missionaries: From the Lessons of the Past, a Hope for the Future" (Master of Spirituality thesis: Gonzaga University, 1989), pp. 24–33; Achiel Peelman, "A Native Church for Today and Tomorrow," *Native Ministry Seminar-St. Peter's Province, Galilee Community, Arnprior, Ontario* (Ottawa: Saint Paul's University, 1988), p. 5.

13. Holst, "Revisiting Our Past": 194–201.

14. Elizabeth Furniss, *Victims of Benevolence: Discipline and Death at The Williams Lake Indian Residential School, 1891–1920* (Williams Lake, B.C.: Cariboo Tribal Council, 1992), pp. 46–47.

15. Doug Crosby, "Canadian Oblates' Statement: An Apology to Native Peoples," *Origins*, August 15, 1991, pp. 183–84.

16. VOA, File on 1991 *Apology*. The overwhelming majority of correspondence contained in it totally rejects the *Apology* as unnecessary and hurtful, especially to the Oblates. Thus, it is essentially a denial of the past. That, in effect, while mistakes were made, the past should now be forgotten. Such a stand, though hardly unusual in the church, does not bode well for the future. In the *Declaration on the Relationship of the Church to Non-Christian Religions* it is noted that while mistakes happened in the past, it encourages "all to forget the past and to strive sincerely for mutual under-standing." See Walter M. Abbott, General Editor, *The Documents of Vatican II* (New York: Guild Press 1966), p. 663. It is this forgetting of the past that also seems to continue to dominate most Oblate attitudes in St. Paul's Province regarding the Native peoples of the far-west; Wayne Holst, "Revisiting Our Past: Revisioning Our Future. Reflections on the Next 150 Years of Missionary Activity in Canada," *Western Oblate Studies 4/Études Oblates de l'Ouest 4* (1996): 189–204: John Paul II, *Tertio Millennio Adveniente*, p. 42.

✤ 12 The Years Before the Railroad

1. PRAR, Scritture Originale, vol. 209, fols. 147–51, 4 May 1846; Ibid., Lettere, vol. 334, fol. 780, Propaganda to Demers, 17 July 1846. Established the diocese and informed Demers of his appointment to Vancouver Island (Victoria). It is an historic fact that also graphically demonstrates the folly of the creation of the ecclesiastical province of Oregon City, it was done not by one pope, but by two, since Gregory XVI had approved its erection just before his death in 1846 and his successor, Pius IX upheld that decision. Harvey J. McKay, *St. Paul, Oregon 1830–1890* (Portland: Binford & Mort, 1980), pp. 14–15; Blanchet, *Historical Sketches*, p. 122; QAA, Demers to Cazeau, 5 March 1846.

Notes

2. QAA, Demers to Cazeau, St. Paul's, Oregon, 22 September 1847; ROA, Mazenod to Pierre Aubert, 3 February 1847; *Rapport* (1849): 96–97; QAA, Demers to Cazeau, Lachine, October 1848; Ibid., Demers to Turgeon, St. Louis, 23 November 1848; Ibid., Demers to Cazeau, Montreal, 27 October 1849; Ibid., Demers to Turgeon, Montreal, 30 October 1849; Jedin, *History of the Church*, vol. VIII, p. 139.

3. Jedin, *History of the Church*, vol. VIII, pp. 285–87; QAA, Demers to Cazeau, Paris, 6 July 1850; Ibid., Demers to Cazeau, Paris, 31 December 1850; AHA, J. Painchaud [Demers's agent] to Dr. Woodlock, Rector, Paris, 30 January 1851.

4. Jedin, *History of the Church*, vol. VIII, pp. 262–67; QAA, Demers to Turgeon, Paris, 14 May 1851. There were five originally, they were La Roche, Le Lamer, Lootens, Deyaert and Haerden. La Roche apparently never arrived, and by 1855 the rest had all left the diocese. See St. Andrew's Cathedral Archives, Victoria, B.C., "Register of Births, Marriages and Deaths (1849–1871)," passim.

5. *Les Oblats*, Vol. III, pp. 846–48, Rev. Louis Lootens to D'Herbomez, 20 March 1859; Ibid.; AHA, Demers to Rector, 9 March 1855; Ibid., Demers to Woodlock, Victoria, 18 June 1855; PFAR, SOCG, AC, Demers to Propaganda Fide, 11 May 1855; QAA, Demers to Turgeon, 18 June 1854.

6. Jedin, *History of the Church*, Vol. VIII, pp. 126–30.

7. *Les Oblats*, Vol. II, pp. 436–38, Demers to Ricard, 20 June 1854; Ibid., Vol. II, pp. 438–41, Lootens to Ricard, 23 June 1854; Ibid., Vol. II, pp. 606–7, Demers to Ricard, 28 April 1856; Ibid., vol. II, pp. 621–22, Demers to Ricard, 7 July 1856; AHA, Demers to Woodlock, 5 January 1857.

8. QAA, Demers to Turgeon, Victoria, 26 October 1852; Ibid., Demers to Cazeau, Victoria, 18 May 1853; Ibid., Demers to Turgeon, Victoria, 30 July 1853; Ibid., Demers to Cazeau, Victoria, 11 December 1853; Ibid., Demers to Cazeau, Victoria, 13 June 1854; Ibid., Demers to Turgeon, Victoria, 18 June 1854; PFAR, SOCG, AC, vol. 17, fol. 305, Demers to Propaganda, Victoria, 11 May 1855; Ibid., vol. 17, fol. 358, Demers to Propaganda, Victoria, 23 June 1855; AHA, Demers to Woodlock, Victoria, 18 December 1855; VAA, Demers to Presidents of the Propagation of the Faith, Paris, July 1858; PFAR, SOCG, CA, vol. 18, fol. 288, Demers to Propaganda, Victoria, 12 July 1858; QAA, Demers to Cazeau, Victoria, 5 July 1858; BCARS, ADD ms. 505/1/8, Rev. Louis Lootens to Dr. John S. Helmcken, Sonora, California, 19 January 1859. This letter summarises early clergy problems in Victoria and is very critical of Demers.

9. John S. Moir, *The Church in the British Era: From the British Conquest to Confederation* (Toronto: McGraw-Hill/Ryerson, 1972), pp. 36, 62, 115, 180–81; Frank A. Peake, "From the Red River to the Arctic," *Journal of the Canadian Church Historical Association* 31, no. 2 (October 1989): 9; Thomas E. Jessett, ed. *Reports and Letters of Herbert Beaver 1836–1838* (Portland & San Francisco: Champoeg Press, 1959), pp. xix–xxi; G. Hollis Slater, "Rev. Robert John Staines: Pioneer Priest, Pedagogue and Political Agitator," *British Columbia Historical Quarterly* 14 (October 1950): 212ff.

10. BCARS, CC, E/B/D39C, Demers to Benjamin Howe, Colonial Office, London, 16 August 1850 QQA, Demers to Cazeau, Fort Vancouver, 10 October 1845. Expresses his appreciation of the American spirit of being open to what is new and different; BCARS, CC, E/B/D39C, Demers to Benjamin Howe, Colonial Office, London, 16 August 1850; AHA, Demers to Woodlock, Victoria, 18 June 1855.

11. *Report of the Columbia Mission* (London: Rivington 1860) (hereafter *Report*), pp. 14, 27–32; Roberta L. Bagshaw, ed., *No Better Land: The 1860 Diaries of the Anglican Colonial Bishop, George Hills* (Victoria: Sono Nis Press, 1996), p. 81.

12. *The Colonist*, 13 October 1830. Amor De Cosmos (1825–1897) was born William Smith in Nova Scotia, but before coming to Victoria in 1858 and founding *The British Colonist*, he had had a very successful career as a photographer in California where he legally changed his name. See Walter N. Sage, "Amor De Cosmos, Journalist and Politician," *British Columbia Historical Quarterly* 8 (1944): 189–212; Also H. Robert McKendrick, "Amor De Cosmos and Confederation," in W. George Shelton, ed., *British Columbia and Confederation* (Victoria: Morriss Press, 1967), pp. 67–96.

13. George Hills, *Occasional Paper* (Victoria: Colonist Press, 1860), pp. 3–6.

14. Willard E. Ireland, "British Columbia's American Heritage," *Canadian Historical Association Annual Report* (1948), p. 67; Kenneth McNaught, *The Pelican History of Canada* (New York: Penguin Books, 1982), p. 145; McNally, "Victoria: An American Diocese in Canada," p. 8. The equivalent of Great Britain's Britannia, Columbia graces the dome of the U.S. Capital Building in Washington, D.C.

15. Hills, *Occasional Paper*, passim; Bagshaw, *No Better Land*, pp. 66, 81.

16. *The Colonist*, 13 October 1860.

17. BCRS, CC, F/4534, Demers to Douglas, Victoria, 8 November 1860; Ibid., F/340/3a, Hills to Douglas, Victoria, 24 November 1860; Ibid., Demers to Douglas, Victoria, 20 December 1860. Demers expresses "shock" that Douglas is so strong in his defence of the Anglican claim; Ibid., F/340/4, Hills to Douglas, 4 March 1861. Hills's plan for settling the issue out of court; BCDA, J.H. Hinton, "Account of the History of the Church Trust 1854–1937," unpublished manuscript.

18. *The Colonist*, 3–11, May 1861. Contains full report of the "The Church Reserve Case"; *Rapport* (1863), p. 76–78; *The Colonist*, 11 May 1861.

19. Peake, "The Anglican Church in British Columbia": 48–49. Peake does not examine the church reserves issue. BCDA, Hinton, "Account of the History of the Christ Church Trust 1854–1937," unpublished manuscript.

20. *The Colonist*, 14 October 1861.

21. BCARS, CC, F/62/2b, George Cary, Attorney General to Early Gray, British Colonist Secretary, Victoria, 18 May 1863. Cary, who had supported Hills's claim in 1861 (see ibid., F/49/22, Cary to Grey, December 1861), now advised against it; BCDA, "Christ Church Trust Deed," 6 May 1864; Hinton, "Account of the History of Christ Church Trust 1854–1937." Relates that in 1914 the local Anglican Synod became the sole trustee, however, by 1937, due to mismanagement and financial defaults, the actual value of the Trust had fallen to less than forty-three thousand dollars; Ormsby,

British Columbia: A History, pp. 168–69. Ormsby, still a major survey history of the province, incorrectly states that Demers, in her only reference to him, played no role in affecting the outcome of the church reserve/established church controversy, and gives most of the credit for defeating it to Amor De Cosmos and *The Colonist*.

22. Jedin, *History of the Church*, Vol. VIII, pp. 262–64; ACL, Seghers to Benoit Van Look, Victoria, 29 January 1874.

23. V. Pineault, "Historical Sketches of the Diocese of Victoria," *The British Columbia Orphan's Friend: Historical Number* (December 1914): 18.

24. Robert O'Driscoll and Lorna Reynolds, eds., *The Untold Story: The Irish in Canada*, Vol. I (Toronto: Celtic Arts of Canada, 1988), p. 439–40, 449; PFAR, Scritture Originale, vol. 18, fol. 1005, Demers to Propaganda, Victoria, 22 October 1859.

25. Jedin, *History of the Church*, Vol. VIII, pp. 126–30.

26. AHA, Demers to Woodlock, Victoria, 24 November 1860; Ibid., Demers to Bennett, Victoria, 4 June 1863; Ibid., Demers to Bennett, Victoria, 5 April 1865; Ibid., Demers to Bennett, Victoria, 9 November 1865; Ibid., Demers to Bennett, Victoria, 12 December 1865; ACL, Seghers to De Neve, Victoria, 11 May 1866; AHA, Demers to Rector Fortune, Halifax, 5 June 1867; PFAR, Acta, vol. 996, fol. 974, Demers to Propaganda, Paris, 2 August 1867; *The Colonist*, 1 August 1871.

27. Down, *A Century of Service*, pp. 23–27, 34; see Part 2 for an explanation of Lempfrit's problems.

28. Ibid., pp. 23–27, 34; Jean Barman, "Transfer, Imposition or Consensus?: The Emergence of Educational Structure in Nineteenth Century British Columbia," in Nancy M. Sheehan, ed., *Schools in the West: Essays in Canadian Educational History* (Calgary: Detselig Enterprise, 1988), pp. 242–48; D.L. MacLaurin, "The History of Education in The Crown Colonies of Vancouver Island and British Columbia" (Ph.D. thesis, University of Washington, 1936), pp. 22–29; D.L. MacLaurin, "Education before the [Fraser River] Gold Rush," *British Columbia Historical Quarterly* (October 1958): 251; AHA, Demers to Woodlock, Victoria, 8 March 1853; Whitehead, *The Cariboo Mission*, p. 21; BCARS, CC, F/395/1, Cridge to Douglas, Victoria, 20 November 1856. This is the earliest evidence of Demers's school for boys.

29. AD, P 2210–2239, D'Herbomez to Father General Émile Fabre, Report to Superior General, 1861; Ibid., PC 101. V58C, 2, 3, 10, no author. Manuscript history of St. Louis College, Victoria;

30. AD, PC 101.V58c, 2, *Prospectus of St. Louis College...Victoria, VI*, n.d. (note indicates "1863"); Derek Reimer, ed., "A Victoria Tapestry: Impressions of Life in Victoria, B.C., 1880–1914," *Sound Heritage Series* VII, No. 3 (1978): 25.

31. AD, P 1346–1347, Demers to Léon Fouquet, San Francisco, 29 January 1865; Ibid., P 1350a, Demers to Reverend Father, 29 August 1865; Ibid., P 1348–1350, Demers to D'Herbomez, Victoria, 27 November 1865; VOA, Demers to D'Herbomez, 19 March 1866; AD, P 1361–65, Final Financial Agreement, signed by Demers and Fouquet for D'Herbomez, 16 April 1866; Ibid., P 1366–67, James Mondart, vicar general to Demers to Reverend Father, Victoria, 31 May 1866. Complains that the Oblates have

asked and received more than they deserve in compensation for St. Louis College; AHA, Demers to Bedford, 14 April 1866. Complains like Mondart.

32. Down, *A Century of Service*, pp. 32–41; ASSA, Mary Pineault, "North Pacific Shores," ff. 72–74.

33. AD, P 1399–1402, D'Herbomez to Fabre, 29 March 1865; ASSA, "Rules and Regulations for Pupils 1860"; Down, *A Century of Service*, pp. 32–41; Barman, *The West Beyond the West*, pp. 66, 76, 85, 89, 100; ASSA, Mary Pineault, "North Pacific Shores," ff. 72–74.

34. Peake, *The Anglican Church in British Columbia*, p. 72; Report (186), p. 14; BCDA, Hills to Secretary of the Society for the Propagation of the Gospel, Victoria, 8 May 1860.

35. Barman, "Transfer, Imposition or Consensus?" pp. 242–48.

36. Ibid., pp. 242–48; *The Colonist*, 11 April 1864. American authorities were the only ones cited at the meeting; *The Colonist*, 4, 13 April 1864.

37. Barman, "Transfer, Imposition or Consensus?" pp. 242–48; *The Colonist*, 25 November 1864.

38. Jedin, *History of the Church*, Vol. VIII, p. 16 et seq.

39. AD, P 5017–5018, McGuckin to D'Herbomez, 8 July 1867; Ibid., P 5032–5054, McGuckin to D'Herbomez, 20 August 1867; Ibid., P 5036–5037, McGuckin to Frederick Lima, Esq., Richfield, 22 August 1867.

40. ACLA, Seghers to Rector John De Neve, Victoria, n.d. (probably late 1864); Ibid., Seghers to De Neve, Victoria, 11 April 1864; Ibid., Seghers to "Priest," Victoria, written between 8 August and 19 September 1864; Ibid., Seghers to Rev. Benedict Van Loo, Victoria, 30 September 1864.

41. MacLean, *Catholic Schools in Western Canada*, p. 53.

42. BCARS, CC, F/433.10, Demers to William Young, Colonial Secretary, Victoria, 15 May 1862; *The Colonist*, 25 July 1862. "Letter to Rt. Rev. Dr. Demers."

43. BCARS, CC, B/12307/133, Baudre to Governor Arthur Kennedy, Victoria, 10 May 1865; Ibid., Cary to Baudre, Victoria, 12 May 1865.

44. Adrian G. Morice, Histoire de *l'Église Catholique dans l'Ouest Canadien*, Vol. 3 (Montreal: Granger Freres, 1915), p. 275. Contains the reference to Fouquet's 1865 pamphlet which was published in Victoria; *British Columbian*, 29 April 1865.

45. BCARS, CC, GR/1372/B/1364/F/1585. Seghers and Ten Catholic Laity to W.A.G. Young, Colonial Secretary, Victoria, 19 June 1865; Bid., R/103/1756, Young to Seghers, Victoria, 22 June 1865.

46. Report (1866), pp. 27–28; Ibid. (1867), pp. 92–93; Ibid. (1868), p. 113.

47. *The Colonist*, 2 April 1872; *Daily Standard*, 8 April 1872; C.B. Sissons, *Church and State in Canadian Education* (Toronto: Ryerson, 1959), p. 371. Notes the uniqueness of British Columbia on the issue.

48. With Bishop Demers's death in 1871, Father Charles John Seghers, as administrator of the diocese, was the spokesperson on the issue of separate schools.

49. *Report* (1872), pp. 48–72; Dorothy Blakey Smith, ed., *The Reminiscences of Doctor John Sebastian Helmcken* (Vancouver: University of British Columbia Press, 1975), p. xviii; BCARS, CC, Add. Ms. 505, vol. 1, F/18, Seghers to Helmcken, Victoria, 18 February 1869.

50. Jedin, *History of the Church*, Vol. IX, p. 209; Charles E. Phillips, *The Development of Education in Canada* (Toronto: Gage, 1957), p. 326; *British Columbia Sessional Papers* (Victoria: Queen's Printer, 1876), p. 725.

51. *British Columbia Sessional Papers* (1881), p. 517, 20 March 1881; ACLA, Seghers to De Neve, Victoria, 1 August 1867; PAA, Seghers to F.N. Blanchet, Portland, 10 September 1881; *Catholic Sentinel*, Portland, Oregon, 10 November 1881.

52. *British Columbia Sessional Papers* (1881), p. 517, 20 March 1881; *Dominion Pacific Herald*, 9 March 1881

53. *British Columbia Sessional Papers* (1881), p. 517, 20 March 1881; *Dominion Pacific Herald*, 9 March 1881; *Mainland Guardian*, 4 May 1881; D'Herbomez to Editor of *Herald*, 15 March 1881; AD, P 2255–65, Separate School File, 1881.

54. *British Columbia Sessional Papers* (1883), p. 397, 20 March 1883; Bishops' Petition; VAA, Brondel to D'Herbomez, Victoria, 20 March 1883; Ormsby, *British Columbia: A History*, pp. 290, 295–96; Lawrence B. Palladino, *Indian and White in the Northwest or The History of Catholicism in Montana* (Baltimore: John Murphy & Co. 1894), pp. 361–62; L.W. Downey, "The Aid-to-Independent Schools Movement in British Columbia," in Sheehan, *Schools in the West*, pp. 305–21; *Report* (1882–1883), p. 19.

55. Bonnie S. Anderson and Judith P. Zinsser, *A History of Their Own: Women in Europe from Prehistory to the Present*, Vol. I (New York: Harper & Row, 1988), pp. 250–251. Notes that women were usually canonised in the Catholic Church not for their visions but "for their exemplary lives of compliance, obedience and extreme humility...to the church's [clerical] commands"; Ibid., Vol. I, pp. 354–55; Down, *A Century of Service*, passim; AD, PC 101. V21C.5, "Dix Premiers Annees des Soeurs de Ste. Anne...," n.d.; VDA, Louis Heynen to "Sister Superior," n.d., Nanaimo. Heynan threatens that there will be "no Mass at the Convent" in Nanaimo unless the nuns pay their share of a broken fence. Heynan then challenges the nuns to "go crying to Mama" Provincial as they had in the past; BCARS, H\B\Sa21, Demers's criticisms of St. Ann's Convent, Victoria; ACLA, Seghers to unnamed community of nuns, probably Holy Name, Oregon City, 28 November 1881; AD, P 2242–45, D'Herbomez to Fabre, 1880; AHA, Demers to Bennett, Victoria; ACLA, Seghers to Benedict Van Loo, Victoria, n.d., c. 1870s. Bernard Häring, "Twenty-First Century will have Eucharistic Church," *National Catholic Reporter*, 7 September 1990, p. 13. Speaking of Jansenistic theology, author notes it is dominated by the images of an avenging God who "demands severe acts of penance so as to align oneself with Jesus' sacrifice and to pacify an angry God is...the chief cause of ecclesiastical fears and neurosis and of all kinds of religion-based fear and the moralism that breeds fear."

56. *Catholic Health Association of British Columbia: Anniversary Booklet: Caritas Christi Urget Nos: Living the Mission 1940–1990* (Richmond, B.C.: The Little Printer Ltd., 1990), p. 11. The other hospitals included St. Mary's Hospital (1898), Dawson City, Yukon Territory, Our Lady of Lourdes Hospital (1926), Campbell River, B.C., Bulkley Valley District Hospital (1933), St. Martin's Hospital (1942), Oliver, B.C., Mount St. Mary's (1941), Victoria, B.C., Mount St. Francis (1947), Nelson, B.C; H.H. Murphy, *Royal Jubilee Hospital 1858–1958* (Victoria: Hebden Printing Company, 1958), pp. 1–6; *The Colonist*, 13 February 1859; BCARS, F\49\22, George Cary, Attorney General to Colonial Secretary, Victoria, December 1861; ASSA, "Chronicles of St. Joseph's Hospital Victoria, B.C.," 1875–1883; *The Colonist*, 22 August 1875; Ibid., 26 June 1876; ACLA, Seghers to Benedict Van Loo, Victoria, 25 May 1865; Ibid., Seghers to Van Loo, Victoria, 18 June 1873; Ibid., Seghers to Maurice De Baets, Victoria, 19 June 1875.

57. *Rapport* (1866), pp. 126–34; ASSA, "Chronicles of St. Joseph's Hospital, Victoria, B.C., 1875–1883," pp. 1–11; Laurette Agnew et al., *Presence Francophone a Victoria, C.B., 1843–1987* (Victoria: L'Association Historique Francophone de Victoria, B.C., 1987), pp. 126–28.

58. ASSA, "Chronicles of St. Joseph's Hospital, Victoria, B.C., 1875–1883," ff. 1–11.

59. Capital Regional District, *A Study of Hospital and Related Facilities in the Capital Regional Hospital District, British Columbia, Canada* (Toronto: Agnew Peckham 1964), p. 201.

60. Murphy, *Royal Jubilee Hospital*, passim; *Catholic Health Association of British Columbia: Anniversary Booklet*, pp. 10–11; Ann Pearson, *The Royal Jubilee Hospital School of Nursing, 1891–1982* (Victoria: Alumnae Association of the Royal Jubilee School of Nursing, 1985), pp. 1–17, 24–27; ASSA, "Chronicles of St. Joseph's Hospital School of Nursing, Victoria, B.C., 1900–1940," ff. 3–45.

61. AD, P 2210–39, Report of 1861 to General Chapter by Louis D'Herbomez; Barman, *The West Beyond the West*, p. 363.

62. AD, PC 101.V21C.5, Manuscript remarks from Sisters of St. Ann, n.d., covers years 1858–1868; Ibid., P 1643–46, D'Herbomez to Demers, Esquimalt, 10 December 1862; Ibid., P 1647–48, D'Herbomez to Demers, Esquimalt, 18 November 1863; Ibid., P 1336–37, Demers to D'Herbomez, Victoria, 21 November 1863; Ibid., P 1478–79, D'Herbomez to Demers, Esquimalt, 24 November 1863; Ibid., P 1338–39, Demers to D'Herbomez, 5 December 1863.

63. QAA, Demers to Cazeau, San Francisco, 18 May 1859; PFAR, Udienze, vol. 134, fol. 182, Demers's desires to resign is discussed with Pius IX, but pope rejects, 23 November 1859; Ibid., SOCG, AC, vol. 990, fol. 736, Ignace Bourget to Propaganda, Montreal, 24 August 1860; Ibid., fol. 760, Demers to Propaganda, Victoria, 6 August 1860; Ibid., fol. 760, Demers to Propaganda, Victoria, 6 August 1861; Ibid., Udienze, vol. 146, fol. 604, Morrison appointed to be Demers's coadjutor with right of succession; Ibid., vol. 147, fols. 974, 979.

64. *Rapport* (1863): 76–78, 81–81; ACL, Seghers to De Neve, Victoria, 11 April 1864.

65. *Rapport* (1863): 76–78, 81–82; ACL, Seghers to De Neve, Victoria, 11 April 1864; Higgins, "British Columbia and the Confederation Period," pp. 19–20; *The British Columbian*, 12 May 1864; Ibid., 24 December 1864. Reports on Europeans, especially American attitudes towards the Native People and the American notion of "manifest destiny."

66. Gerald Steckler, *Charles John Seghers: Priest and Bishop in the Pacific Northwest 1839–1886: A Biography* (Fairfield, WA: Ye Galleon Press, 1986), pp. 15–36; ACL, Seghers to "Friends," Louvain, 13 May 1863; Ibid., Seghers to Rector De Neve, Victoria, 16 December 1863; Ibid., Seghers to De Neve, n.d. (probably 1864); PFAR, SOCG, AC, vol. 20, fol. 1394, N.F. Blanchet to Propaganda, Portland, 15 December 1864; *The Colonist*, 12 December 1864.

67. AD, P 1480–85, D'Herbomez to "Chez Abbé," Victoria, 29 July 1864; *Missions* 3 (1864): 131–34.

68. AD, P 1348–50, D'Herbomez to Demers, 28 October 1865; Ibid., Demers to D'Herbomez, 27 November 1865; Ibid., D'Herbomez to Demers, 6 December 1865.

69. AD, P 1353–54, Demers to D'Herbomez, 6 February 1866; Ibid., P 1653, D'Herbomez to Demers, 10 February 1866; Ibid., P 1654–55, D'Herbomez to Demers, 21 February 1866; Ibid., P 1355, Demers to D'Herbomez, 12 February 1866; Ibid., P 1356–60, Demers to D'Herbomez, 5 March 1866; Ibid., P 1658–59, D'Herbomez to Demers, 14 March 1866; Ibid., P 1361–65, Demers to D'Herbomez, 16 April 1866.

70. ROA, Casimir Aubert to D'Herbomez, Rome, 20 April 1858; Ibid., Demers to D'Herbomez, Victoria, 1 September 1860; Carrière, *Dictionnaire Biographique*, Vol. II, pp. 42–43; AD P 1660–1663, D'Herbomez to Demers, 9 April 1866; Ibid., P 1664–65, D'Herbomez to Demers, 25 April 1866.

71. M.M. Ronden, "The Cowichan, Saanich and Kuper Island Missions," *The Historical Number of the British Columbia Orphan's Friend* (1914): 55; AD, P 1366–1367, Mandart to "Reverend Father," 31 May 1866.

72. AD, P 2633–34, Fouquet to Demers, 15 May 1866; Ibid., P 1366–1367, Mandart to "Reverend Father," 31 May 1866; Ibid., HEB 5771.L57c, 5, Ex. 2, pp. 1–2, George Forbes, "Léon Fouquet, OMI," manuscript.

73. VAA, D'Herbomez Register, Circular Letter, 21 November 1887, p. 241.

74. G.P.V. and Helen B. Akrigg, *British Columbia Chronicle 1847–1871* (Vancouver: Discovery Press, 1977), p. 404; Barman, *The West Beyond the West*, pp. 99–102, 363.

75. VAA, D'Herbomez Report to Propaganda Fide, 1870.

76. Ibid., contains a large number of begging letters as well as letters of thanks from D'Herbomez and Durieu from the 1860s through the 1890s; Jedin, *History of the Church*, Vol. VIII, p. 175 ff; Ibid., Vol. IX, p. 557 ff; AD, P 1730–31, Circular letter from D'Herbomez, 28 May 1880.

77. VAA, D'Herbomez Register, f. 128, blessing of new church of St. Peter's, 25 April 1886; ASSA, D'Herbomez to Superior, Sisters of St. Ann in Victoria, 16 August 1864; Ibid., "New Westminster, B.C., St. Ann's Academy," ff. 14–17; Ibid., "M. des Sept-Douleurs, Fondation de N. Westminster," ff. 110–111; Ibid., "Sr. Marie Jean de

Pathmos, *Les Soeurs*," ff. 180–182; ASSA, M. Theodore, "Foundations of the Sisters of St. Ann in the Pacific North-West," f. 72; Ibid., "New Westminster, B.C., St. Ann's Academy," ff. 21–23.

78. "A Reminiscence," *The Month* (August 1892): 163; *Dominion Pacific Herald*, 9 March 1881; VOA, "Memo Re: Christian Brothers," June 1932.

79. AD, PC 101.N56.14, George Forbes, *The History of St. Peter's Parish (Oblate Fathers) New Westminster, B.C., 1860–1960,* printed, pp. 45–46. In 1958, with the essential help of the newly established Provincial Health Service, a new building was finally realised.

80. *The Cariboo Sentinel,* 20 September 1866; Ibid., 11 June 1868; Ibid., 9 July 1868; Ibid., 16 July 1868. Ibid., 22 July 1868; Ibid., 5 August 1868; Ibid., 13 September 1868; VAA, D'Herbomez Register, f. 129; Carrière, *Dictionnaire Biographique*, Vol. II, pp. 342–43; Peake, *The Anglican Church in British Columbia*, pp. 38–45.

81. AD, 4960–61, McGuckin to D'Herbomez, 25 August 1866; Ibid., P 4986–88, McGuckin to D'Herbomez, 24 October 1866.

82. AD, 4960–61, McGuckin to D'Herbomez, 25 August 1866; Ibid., P 4986–88, McGuckin to D'Herbomez, 24 October 1866.

83. AD, P 5017–18, McGuckin to D'Herbomez, 8 July 1867; Ibid., P 5032–54, McGuckin to D'Herbomez, 20 August 1867; Ibid., P 5036–37, McGuckin to Frederick Lima, Esq., Richfield, 22 August1867. Asks for money for the Catholic mission in Portsmouth, England.

✢ *13 The Years After the Railroad*

1. Barman, *The West Beyond the West*, p. 367; VAA, D'Herbomez Register, ff. 59–60, D'Herbomez to Cardinal Simeoni, Prefect of Propaganda Fide, 16 May 1889.

2. Barman, *The West Beyond the West*, pp. 110–16.

3. Ormsby, *British Columbia*, pp. 297, 302–3, 317–18; Janet Cauthers, "A Victorian Tapestry: Impressions of Life in Victoria, B.C., 1880–1914," *Sound Heritage Series* 8, no. 3 (1978): 1–2, 13–16, 21–13, 33–34, 44–45, 54–57; J.R. Miller, "Anti-Catholic Thought in Victorian Canada," *Canadian Historical Review* 64, no. 4 (1985): 474–75, 482, 486, 492–94; Barman, *The West Beyond the West*, p. 367–68; *Census of Canada,* 1890–91, Vol. 2 (Ottawa: Queen's Printer, 1894), pp. 386–87; Bob Stewart, "That's the B.C. Spirit!: Religion and Secularity in Lotus Land," *Canadian Society of Church History Papers* (1983): 22–35.

4. VDA, Letter Book, pp. 67–69, Seghers to Propaganda Paris, Victoria, 24 July 1885; *Victoria Daily Times,* 19 July 1887; *The Colonist,* 19 July 1887; BCARS, BP 4194, "Rectory on Yates Street," history and description; QAA, Demers to Turgeon, Victoria, 26 October 1852; Rapport (1860), pp. 129–30; ASSA, Joseph E. Michaud, "Joseph Michaud, 1822–1902"; Ibid., Mary Theodore Pineault, "Historical Sketches of the Diocese of Victoria," pp. 14–15; *The Colonist,* 23 November 1860; Ibid., 30 October 1892; ACLA, Seghers to De Baets, Victoria, 19 June 1875.

5. ASSA, Lemmens File "Sermons"—"On Eternal Life." Others deal with "On the End of Man," "On Grace," and are dated 1875 or before he had left Belgium. The volume also contains theological notes.

6. PRAR, Acta, col. 2258, fols. 167–168, Appointment of Lemmens, 9 April 1888. Brabant and Althoff were also recommended, ACLA, Seghers to Acting Rector, Sebastian Goens, St. Ann's, Cowichan, 10 January 1876; *The Colonist*, 10 and 13 May 1888; Ibid., 14 August 1888.

7. Johnston, ed., *The Pacific Province*, p. 179.

8. BCDA, *Reports*, pp. 16–17; Ibid., box 2, file 17, "Ritualism in the Anglican Church, 1894.

9. McNally, "A Brief History of the Diocese of Victoria," p. 6; *The Colonist*, 8 April 1885; Ibid., 8 May 1886; BCDA, *Reports*, pp. 16–17; Ibid., box 2, file 17, "Ritualism in the Anglican Church, 1894." Georgetown University Archives, Washington, D.C., Jesuit Alaska Mission File, Report from Bishop Lemmens on financial state of the diocese, c. 1890; BCARS, ms. H/B/sa 2.1, Contract to build Cathedral between Lemmens and architect, J. McDonald, Montreal, 29 January 1890; Martin Segger, "The Structure of St. Andrew's Cathedral" in *St. Andrew's Cathedral, Victoria: A Guide*.

10. *The Colonist*, 25, 27, 28, 30, 31 December 1890.

11. Ibid., 17, 31 January 1891; Ibid., 1 February 1891; *The Colonist* 27 December 1970. An historic section on the issue.

12. *The Colonist*, 27 December 1970.

13. VCA, 1/3/7/8, J.A. Van Nevel to M. Humber, Chairman of the Police Committee, Victoria, 21 August 1892; Ibid., 1/3/7/7, Van Nevel to Mayor Beaven and City Council, Victoria, 7 September 1892; Ibid., 1/3/7/10, Beaven to Van Nevel, Victoria, 13 September 1892.

14. *The Colonist*, 30 October 1892.

15. Ormsby, *British Columbia*, pp. 312–14; Driscoll, *The Untold Story: The Irish in Canada*, Vol. 1, pp. 442–44; Jean R. Burnet, *Coming Canadians: An Introduction to a History of Canada's People* (Toronto: McClelland and Stewart, 1988), pp. 20–22; John Norris, *Strangers Entertained: A History of the Ethnic Groups of British Columbia* (Vancouver: British Columbia Centennial '71 Committee, 1971), pp. 80–85; *The Colonist*, 7 July 1893;

16. *Statutes of the Provincial Legislature* (Victoria: Richard Wolfenden, Printer to the Queen's Most Excellent Majesty, 1892), pp. 361–62; VDA, Estimate of Security by Byrnes Ltd., Victoria, 8 June 1892; Ibid., Indenture between Thomas Dixon Galpin of London, England and John Nicholas Lemmens of the City of Victoria, B.C., 7 April 1893; *The Colonist*, 18 May 1894; Jedin, *History of the Church*, Vol. IX, pp. 133–34; *The Colonist*, 24 March 1896.

17. VDA, Lemmens to Nicolaye, Guatemala, 7 April 1896; Ibid., Lemmens to Nicolaye, San Jose de Guatemala, 23 October 1896; Ibid., Lemmens to Nicolaye, Guatemala, 12 November 1896; Ibid., Lemmens to Nicolaye, Guatemala, Good Friday, 1897; Ibid., Lemmens to Nicolaye, 22 April 1897.

18. VDA, Lemmens to Nicolaye, Peten, Guatemala, Feast of Corpus Christi, 20 June 1897; ASSA, Lemmens File, "Particulars of the Last Moments of Bishop Lemmens and Appreciative Guatemalan References," taken and translated from an article in the Guatemalan newspaper, *La Fe,* 20 August 1897; Georgetown University Archives, Washington, D.C., Jesuit Alaska Mission File, Report from Bishop Lemmens on the financial state of the diocese of Victoria, 1897; VDA, Joseph Nicolaye Report, 3 October 1906. Indicates that funds from Lemmens's work in Guatemala amounted to $38,000. With taxes and improvements, Archbishop B. Orth (1903-08) had raised another $50,000 by 1906, leaving an outstanding sum of just over $10,000.

19. Barman, *The West Beyond the West,* pp. 120-21.

20. Lynne Bowen, *Boss Whistle: The Coal Miners of Vancouver Island Remember* (Victoria: Morriss Press, 1990), pp. 197, 219-21; E. Blanche Norcross, *Nanaimo Retrospective: The First Century* (Victoria: Morriss Press, 1979), pp. 40-46.

21. Peake, *The Anglican Church in British Columbia,* p. 62; ASSA, "Chronicle of Nanaimo Convent, 1877-1910," pp. 4-8; VDA, "St. Peter's Parish 1854-1974," *The Parishioner* 9 (May 1974): 1-2.

22. *Catholic Sentinel,* 5 March 1885; PFA, Acta, vol. 271, fols. 87-89, 12 March 1900; McMillan, *Native Peoples and Cultures of Canada,* p. 171; VDA, Orth File. Contains 18 letters of congratulation from throughout the United States; Whitehead, *Now You Are My Brother,* p. 34.

23. Barman, *The West Beyond the West,* p. 371; QQA, Memos, Cardinal A.E. Taschereau, 8 October 1871; Ibid., 11 November 1871; VDA, Apostolic Delegate Diomede Falconio to Orth, Ottawa, 13 June 1900; Ibid., Orth to Falconio, Victoria, 25 June 1900; Ibid., Orth to Falconio, Victoria, 18 August 1900; Ibid., Falconio to Orth, Ottawa, 11 September 1900; Ibid., Falconio to Orth, Ottawa, 2 November 1900.

24. VDA, Apostolic Delegate Diomede Falconio to Orth, Ottawa, 13 June 1900; Ibid., Orth to Falconio, Victoria, 25 June 1900; Ibid., Orth to Falconio, Victoria, 18 August 1900; Ibid., Falconio to Orth, Ottawa, 11 September 1900; Ibid., Falconio to Orth, Ottawa, 2 November 1900; PFA, Acta, vol. 274, fols. 311-12; Jedin, *History of the Church,* Vol. IX, pp. 148-49.

25. PFAR, Acta, vol. 274, fols. 311-20; 4 May 1903; Ibid., fol. 692, 6 September 1904. It was at this time that the name of the diocese was finally changed by Rome from "Vancouver Island" to "Victoria," though Lemmens had made such a request, Rome had ignored it. For 43 years (1846-1903) Victoria was apparently unique, in that Catholic dioceses have always been named after cities and not regions. See *The Colonist,* 16 September 1903.

26. McNally, "A Brief History of the Diocese of Victoria," p. 6; VDA, Orth File, Propaganda to Orth, Rome, 7, 10 April 1906. Regarding $10,000 debt left on the cathedral, suggests $10,000 assessment from the Sisters of St. Ann would be used for that purpose; *The Colonist,* 6 May 1899. Announces that Fr. Joseph Nicolaye going to Guatemala to bring back funds collected by Lemmens before his death there; Ibid., 3 October 1906. As noted, funds from Lemmens's work amounted to $38,000. With

taxes and improvements, Orth had raised another $50,000 by 1906, leaving an out-standing sum of just over $10,000; Ibid., 5 May 1908. Describes Orth's considerable business and administrative abilities and accomplishments.

27. Jedin, *History of the Church*, Vol. IX, pp. 420–21, 457.
28. Ibid., pp. 420–21, 457; VDA, Apostolic Delegate to Orth, Ottawa, 13 April 1904. Covered number of types of lay societies that were permitted; Ibid., Decree, Rome, 11 May 1904. Covered Mass stipends, Mass times, stipends in general, missals, use of collections; Ibid., Apostolic Delegate to Orth, Ottawa, 18 May 1905. Deals with strict discipline as a way of life for the clergy and seminarians who were all to be under the total control of the bishop, who was to be under the total control of Rome; Ibid., Papal rescript, 4 April 1906. To allow ten boys to attend St. Ann's Academy, Victoria; Ibid., Apostolic Delegate to Orth, Ottawa, 19 March 1906. Demands stricter discipline in clerical life over which bishop is to assert total control; Ibid., *"Motu proprio"* of Pius X, Rome, 16 July 1906. On setting up new lay societies, none were to be estab-lished nor changes made in them without Rome's approval; Ibid., Holy Office of the Inquisition to Orth, Rome, 28 August 1907. Contains copies of *"Lamentabili"* of Pius X that condemns "modernism" in schools and universities throughout the world, as well as certain "Catholic" theologians and the danger of reading their books.
29. VDA, Orth to Propaganda Fide, May 1905; Ibid., Propaganda to Orth, Rome, 30 September 1905; *Report* (Rome: Propaganda Fide, 1906–1907), pp. 8–10; Ibid. (Rome: Holy See, 1908–1909), pp. 10–17.
30. ASSA, Orth file, Orth to Mother Provincial of Sisters of St. Ann, Victoria, 6 March 1903. "We demand" an answer regarding an orphanage by a certain date and ques-tions the delay; Ibid., Orth to Mother Provincial of Sisters of St. Ann, Victoria, 22 June 1903; Ibid., Orth to Mother Provincial of Sisters of St. Ann, Victoria, 20 April 1904. Accuses her of seeking a "shelter for your action behind my letter of March 21st" regarding a site for the new orphanage, and he then stated that "we ordered" obedience to his directives and expected them to be followed without question; Ibid., Orth to Reverend Mother, Victoria, 30 May 1904, deal with funeral of Mother Provincial; Ibid., Orth to Sister Superior, Victoria, 29 March 1905. Donation to Pope.
31. PFAR, Acta, vol. 281, fols. 755–61. Contains review and decision on Orth case.
32. Ibid., VDA, Nicolaye to "My Lord," probably Christie, Beaumont, B.C., Esquimalt Road, 14 March 1907.
33. VDA, Nicolaye to "My Lord," 14 March 1907.
34. PFAR, Acta, vol. 281, fols. 755–761, 10 January 1909; *The Colonist*, 5 January 1908; Ibid., 1 March 1908.
35. Ibid; *The Colonist*, 1 March 1908; Ibid., 5 May 1908.
36. PFAR, Acta, vol. 281, fols. 755–61; VDA, Nicolaye to "My Lord," probably Christie, Beaumont, B.C., Esquimalt Road, 14 March 1907; MAA, Brabant to Maurus, 9 January 1908. Reports that Orth was "in trouble"; *The Colonist*, 5 January 1908; Ibid., 1 March 1908; Ibid., 5 May 1908.
37. Fifth Census of Canada (Ottawa: King's Printer, 1913), Vol. 2, pp. 146, 158–59.

Vancouver was the third (100,401) largest city with 1,727 people of "no religion"; Victoria, with only 31,660 people had 853 of "no religion"; Barman, *The West Beyond the West*, p. 367; V.J. McNally, "Fighting City Hall: The Church Tax Exemption Battle Between the City and the Roman Catholic Diocese of Victoria, 1896–1923," *Journal of the Canadian Church Historical Society* XXXV, no. 1 (April 1993): 60; A.B. Wood, ed., "Souvenir Book: Centenary of the Diocese of Victoria, British Columbia: 1846–1946," *The Torch* 7, no. 9 (1946): 25–26, 48–62.

38. VDA, CWL File, "Fr. Boniface OFM," "Origins in Canada [of the] Catholic Women's League," 1957; Ibid., "First Recorded Victoria Diocesan Minutes, etc, 1933–1952," p. 6; Terrence Murphy, ed,. *Creed and Culture: The Place of English-Speaking Catholics in Canadian Society, 1750–1930* (Montreal and Kingston: McGill-Queen's University Press, 1993), pp. 219–24; Barman, *The West Beyond the West*, pp. 225, 231, 234; *The Bulletin* (14 November 1924): 5; Ibid. (11 June 1926): 6.

39. Barman, *The West Beyond the West*, pp. 248–52.

40. Alexander MacDonald, *A Bit of Autobiography* (Victoria: Willows Press, 1920); not paginated; Books by MacDonald: *The Apostle's Creed* (London: Kegan Paul, Trench, Truber, 1925); 347 pages; *The Primacy of Thought in Poetry* (London: Kegan Paul, Trench, Truber, 1928), 104 pages; *Questions of the Day* (New York: Christian Press, 1905), 117 pages; *A Bit of Autobiography* (Victoria: Willow Press, 1920), 60 pages; *The Holy House of Loreto* (New York: Christian Press, 1913); 386 pages; *The Mass Explained* (Boston: Richard G. Badger, 1930), 75 pages; *The Miracles of the Sacred Heart* (New York: Joseph F. Wagner, 1904), 56 pages; *The Sacraments: A Course of Seven Sermons* (New York: Joseph F. Wagner, 1906), 82 pages; *The Sacrifice of the Mass in the Light of Scripture and Tradition* (London: Kegan, Paul & Co., 1924), 176 pages; *Stray Leaves or Traces of Travel* (New York: Christian Press, 1914), 171 pages; *The Symbol in Sermons* (New York: Christian Association Publishing Co., 1903), 214 pages; *The Symbol of the Apostles* (New York: Christian Press Association Publishing Co., 1903), 377 pages; *Meditations on the Virgin* (Victoria: Willow Press, 1911), 75 pages; *Notes on the Litany of Loreto* (Antigonish: The Casket Press, 1906), 61 pages; *Evolution and the Origin of Species* (Toronto: Extension Print, 1932), 70 pages; *Holy Mass: The Passover* (Toronto: Extension Print, 1932), 81 pages; *How the Mass is a Sacrifice* (Toronto: Extension Print, 1932), 48 pages; *The Prince of this World and If Adam had not Sinned* (Toronto: Catholic Truth Society, 1926), 45 pages; *The Apostles' Creed* (Toronto: Catholic Truth Society, 1925), 27 pages; *Shall and Will* (London: Kegan, Paul and Trench, 1928), 32 pages; *The Temporary Power of the Popes* (Toronto: Catholic Truth Society, 1929), 58 pages; *More about the Mass* (Toronto: Catholic Truth Society, 1934), 59 pages; *The Bee and Evolution* (Victoria: Willow Press, 1920), 43 pages; *Evolution in the Light of Reason and Revelation* (Toronto: Trinity Publishing Co. Ltd., 1932), 49 pages; *Saint Thomas of Aquinas and the Mass* (Toronto: Catholic Truth Society, 1933), 63 pages; *What Think Ye of Christ?* (Toronto: Catholic Truth Society, 1927), 54 pages; MacDonald also published numerous articles, mostly in theological journals; McNally, "A Brief History of the Diocese of Victoria," p. 6.

41. VDA, "Golden Jubilee Celebration of St. Louis College, 1864–1914," p. 41.

42. Ormsby, *British Columbia: A History*, p. 453.; Alexander MacDonald, "Attitude of the Canadian [Catholic] Church towards the War," *Canadian Annual Review* (1917): 411–12; VDA, Alexander MacDonald, "Christianity and Patriotism," 1918, typed ms.; St. Andrew's Cathedral Victoria, World War I Monument: "Victims of the War: 1914 + 1919: Lieut. J. Carey, Lieut. D. Higgins, Corp. H. Lawson, Christina Campbell, Charles Baylis (Lieut.) J.F. McKinnon (Lieut.), H.A. Reardon, Jos. Gorman, J. Cunningham, Fred. Paine, Max. Longpre, Hector Longpre, Michael Neary, James King, Leslie Hill, Norman McDonald, A.V. O'Neill"; St. Andrew's Cathedral Parish Register: 1900–1933, pp. 23–58. Figure represented 5.4% of parish congregation; *Times-Colonist*, "Christian Brothers Left a Mark," 15 January 1989.

43. McNally, "Fighting City Hall": 149–56.

44. Ibid.: 157–61.

45. Ibid.: 160–62.

46. Ibid.: 162.

47. Ibid.: 162–66.

48. VAA, Durieu Register, ff. 2–3; Ibid., Durieu to Propaganda Fide, 24 December 1890; Ibid., D'Herbomez to Propaganda Fide, 16 May 1889; Barman, *The West Beyond the West*, pp. 367–68.

49. Ibid., D'Herbomez Register, f. 130. Ibid., Marchal "Rapport sur la Maison au Kamloops," 10 August 1899; *The Month* (December 1892), p. 258; Ibid. (July 1893), p. 137; Ibid. (November 1894), p. 156; Ibid. (February 1895), p. 30; Down, *A Century of Service*, pp. 91–94, 145–47; *The Cariboo Sentinel*, June-August, 1868. Contains articles on clerical salaries in the region.

50. VAA, D'Herbomez Register, f. 130; *The Month* (December 1892), p. 258; Ibid. (May 1893), p. 97; Ibid. (January 1894), p. 16; Ibid. (July 1893), p. 137; Ibid. (November 1894), p. 156; Ibid. (February 1895), p. 30; Ibid. (June 1893), p. 121. Speaks of Accorsini's arrival; Ibid. (October 1893), p. 191; Ibid. (July-August 1894), p. 113; Ibid. (September 1895), p. 122; Ibid. (July 1893), p. 137; Ibid. (October 1893), p. 191; Ibid. (November 1893), p. 191; Ibid. (March 1894), p. 113; Ibid. (June 1895), p. 92; Ibid. (September 1895), p. 121; Ibid. (February 1896), p. 30; Ibid. (September 1895), p. 122; Ibid. (June 1896), p. 92; VAA, Report, n.d. Anonymous, but appears to be by Le Jeune and in 1899; Ibid., Marchal, Report on Kamloops Mission, 10 August 1899.

51. VAA, Peytavin Report on the parish at Williams Lake Mission, 31 July 1899.

52. Ormsby, *British Columbia: A History*, pp. 314–17.

53. *Catholic Health Association of British Columbia*, pp. 15, 27.

54. VAA, Ouellette, Cranbrook, n.d., but contains Coccola's 1899 Report; Ibid., J. Welch, n.d. Probably 1899 in which he speaks of the region; Ibid., Coccola's hand, n.d., c. 1899.

55. *The Month* (July 1895), p. 108; Ibid. (September 1895), pp. 122–23; Ibid. (January 1896), p. 15; Ibid. (May 1894), p. 79; Ibid. (April 1894), p. 66–67; VAA, Report on St. Charles District, 16 August 1899.

56. *The Month* (September 1892), p. 199; Ibid. (January 1893), p. 15; Ibid. (May 1893), p. 95. Notes choir sang poorly; Ibid. (January 1994), p. 13; Ibid. (April 1894), p. 65; Ibid. (March 1894), p. 50; Ibid. (April 1894), pp. 55–56.

57. Ormsby, *British Columbia: A History*, pp. 312–13; *The Month* (October 1892), p. 219; Ibid. (December 1894), pp. 167–68; ASSA, RG 1, S 27, M. Theodore, "Foundations of the Sisters of St. Ann in the Pacific North-West," ff. 29–30; *The Month* (June 1894), p. 93; Ibid. (October 1896), p. 145.

58. *The Month*, January 1892 to October 1896.

59. Ibid. (December 1894), pp. 161–63.

60. Ibid. (September 1895), p. 122; Ibid. (October 1895), p. 141; Ibid. (November 1895), p. 157; Ibid. (April 1896), p. 58; VOA, St. Peter's Parish, New Westminster, Codex Historicus 1889–1914, fol. 57; Bunoz, "Bishop Durieu System," p. 202.

61. Barman, *The West Beyond the West*, pp. 108–9.

62. Alan Morley, *Vancouver: From Milltown to Metropolis* (Vancouver: Mitchell Press, 1961), pp. 69–71; Jack Richards, "Our Cathedral: A Monument," *British Columbia Catholic*, 4 October 1953; VVA, Durieu to Ledochowski, 31 October 1894.

63. *The Month* (January 1892), p. 17; ASSA, Mary Dorothea, "Sacred Heart Academy, Vancouver, B.C. 1888–1952," ff. 9–10; Down, *A Century of Service*, pp. 74–76, 79, 112.

64. *The Month* (January 1892), p. 17; Ibid. (March 1892), p. 61; Ibid. (August 1892), p. 177; Ibid. (June 1893), p. 118; Ibid. (April 1893), p. 73; "Young Men's Institute," *The Catholic Encyclopaedia* (New York: Robert Appleton Company, 1912), Vol. XV, p. 736; *The Month* (May 1893), p. 93.

65. VAA, Durieu-Fay correspondence, 1886–1892.

66. Ibid., Register of D'Herbomez-Durieu, ff. 163–166, agreements between Eummelen and Durieu, 22 May 1894, 29 March 1895.

67. *The Month* (June 1893), p. 120; Ibid. (October 1894), p. 147; Ibid. (March 1895), p. 45; Ibid. (October 1895), p. 142; Ibid. (December 1893), pp. 230–31; Ibid. (February 1895), pp. 28–29.

68. *The Month* (January 1893), p. 18; Ibid. (October 1893), p. 194; Ibid. (December 1894), p. 169; Ibid. (October 1894), p. 147; Ibid. (November 1894) p. 157; *Catholic Health Association of British Columbia: Anniversary Booklet*, pp. 12–13; *The Month* (December 1895), p. 173; Ibid. (September 1896), pp. 133–34; Ibid. (June 1896), pp. 90–91.

69. Ibid. (March 1894), p. 52.

70. VAA, Durieu to Eummelen, 22 November 1898; Levasseur, *A History*, Vol. 1, p. 264; A.G. Morice, *Histoire de l'Église Catholique dans l'Ouest canadien 1659–1905* (Montreal: Murrow, 1933), Vol. IV, p. 336. *The Monitor*, San Francisco, 2 August 1902, Advertisement; VAA, *Prospectus, Maple Leaf Mining and Development Company*; Ibid., Fr. F.J. Hartman of Maple Park, Illinois to Dontenwill, 28 February 1898 and with

Durieu's reply encouraging Hartman to invest, 12 March 1898; *Rossland Miner*, 14 June 1899. Speaks of Eummelen's illness and departure for California; Ibid., Eummelen to Dontenwill, 15 May 1903.

71. *Los Angeles Daily Times*, 20 April 1898; *The Monitor*, 14 June 1902; Ibid., 2 August 1902; VAA, Eummelen to Dontenwill, 15 May 1903.

72. VAA, Contains a number of letters from angry and frightened investors 1903–04 who blamed Dontenwill especially for allowing the venture to be advertised in the name of the church; TAA, Eummelen to Apostolic Delegate Sbarretti, 8 January 1911; Levasseur, *A History*, Vol. I, p. 264; Morice, *Histoire de l'Église catholique dans l'Ouest 1659–1905*, Vol. IV, p. 336. Morice asserts that Durieu was duped by land speculators into selling the Okanagan Mission, although Durieu freely invested in the mining scheme despite being warned by other Oblates not to do so. As a firm supporter of the "Durieu System," Durieu always favoured Morice, which might explain Morice's defence. See Mulhall, *Will to Power*, p. 62.

73. Carrière, *Dictionnaire Biographique*, Vol. III, pp. 223, 284; VAA, Durieu to Eummelen, 22 November 1898.

74. Jedin, *History of the Church*, Vol. IX, pp. 96–97; Levasseur, *A History*, Vol. I, pp. 199–200.

75. Mulhall, *Will To Power*, passim; AD, P 5975–5978, Martinet to D'Herbomez, 19 January 1873; Carrière *Dictionnaire Biographique*, Vol. II, pp. 42–43

76. Mulhill, *Will to Power*, pp. 178–81

77. Jedin, *History of the Church*, Vol. IX, pp. 507–11.

78. *Missions* 41 (1903): 68–125, 252–354; Ibid., 42 (1904): 188–215; Ibid., 45 (1907): 19–42.

79. Levasseur, *A History*, Vol. 2, pp. 25–34.

80. All of the statistics cited are taken from Carrière, *Dictionnaire Biographique*, passim.

81. Frank Leonard, *A Thousand Blunders: The Grand Trunk Pacific Railroad and Northern British Columbia* (Vancouver: University of British Columbia Press, 1996), pp. 276–77; Barman, *The West Beyond the West*, pp. 189, 196, 371.

82. Carrière, *Dictionnaire Biographique*, Vol. I, pp. 291–92.

83. Ibid., Dontenwill to Oblate Priests and Brothers, 28 September 1898; Ibid., P 2306–2307, Dontenwill to LeJeune, 15 June 1899; *Missions* 43 (1905): 275; Levasseur, *A History*, Vol. I, p. 262.

84. VAA, André Michels, Report on St. Louis's Mission, Kamloops, n.d., c. 1906–8; Carrière, *Dictionnaire Biographique*, passim.

85. *Catholic Health Association of British Columbia: Anniversary Booklet*, p. 27; VAA, Coccola to Dontenwill, 10 June 1904; Ibid., Coccola to Dontenwill, 1906; Ibid., Sbaretti, Apostolic Delegate, Ottawa, to Dontenwill, 25 August 1903; Ibid., Sbaretti to Dontenwill, 11 September 1903; Burnet and Palmer, *"Coming Canadians,"* pp. 125–50.

86. VAA, Peytavin, Report on Williams Lake, n.d., c. 1890s or early 1900s: Ibid., Thomas to Dontenwill, May 1904.

87. Ibid., Chirouse to Dontenwill, 27 June 1904; Ibid., Chirouse to Dontenwill, 9 August 1905.

88. Ibid., Peytavin to Dontenwill, 4 July 1904.

89. Ibid., Peytavin to Dontenwill, 4 July 1904.

90. Jack Richards, "Our Cathedral: A Monument," *British Columbia Catholic*, Souvenir Edition, 4 October 1953, passim; William P. O'Boyle, "Holy Rosary Pro-Cathedral," *The Monthly Bulletin* (February 1917), pp. 5–6.

91. Ibid., pp. 5–6; Robert A.J. McDonald, *Making Vancouver: Class, Status and Social Boundaries, 1863–1913* (Vancouver: University of British Columbia Press, 1966), pp. 143, 196; Patricia E. Roy, *The History of Canadian Cities: Vancouver: An Illustrated History* (Toronto: James Lorimer & Company Publishers, 1980), p. 60.

92. J.W. Duggan, *Knights of Columbus in British Columbia 1906–1986: History in the Making* (Vancouver: Knights of Columbus, 1989), passim; Howay, *British Columbia: From the Earliest Times to the Present,* Vol. IV, pp. 141–42; *The Month* (December, 1892), pp. 256–57; Ibid. (May, 1893), pp. 94–95; "Local History," *The Bulletin,* 6 March 1925, pp. 1–2.

93. *The Month* (February 1896), p. 30; Ibid. (December 1892), p. 256; Ibid. (May 1893), p. 95; "Sacred Heart Church," *The Monthly Bulletin* (March 1917), pp. 1–4.

94. Johnston, *The Pacific Province*, pp. 293–94.

95. Ibid., also see: Maurice Norbert Coté, "The Children's Aid Society of the Catholic Archdiocese of Vancouver: Its Origin and Development, 1905-1953" (M.S.W. thesis: University of British Columbia, 1953), pp. 13–18, 45–78, and passim.

96. Johnston, *The Pacific Province*, pp. 293–94; Coté, "The Children's Aid Society," pp. 45–60; Howay, *British Columbia: From Earliest Times...,* Vol. IV, p. 1136.

97. Coté, "The Children's Aid Society," pp. 23–28 and passim.

98. Johnston, *The Pacific Province*, p. 319

99. ASSA, Mary Dorothea, "History of St. Ann's Academy, Vancouver, August 1888 to August 1946," ff. 7–10.

100. *Catholic Health Association of British Columbia: Anniversary Booklet*, p. 13–14.

✢ 14 The Oblates and the First Secular Archbishops

1. *Le Canada Ecclésiastique* (1908–1917), passim.

2. VAA, *B.C. Western Catholic*, 26 July 1912, vol. 3, no. 41. This is the earliest preserved copy, thus the first would appear to have been initiated late in Welch's term as apostolic administrator.

3. George Boyle, *Pioneer in Purple: The Life and Work of Archbishop Neil McNeil* (Montreal: Palm Publishers, 1951), pp. 24–33.

4. Ibid., pp. 24–33; 152; Murphy and Perin, *A Concise History of Christianity in Canada*, pp. 236–38, 353.

5. VAA, McNeil, Circular Letter, 28 August 1912.

6. Barman, *The West Beyond the West*, pp. 369, 371.

7. VAA, McNeil to Fergus Patrick McEvay, archbishop of Toronto, 10 June 1910.

8. Ibid., Mary Anastasia, Superior General of the Sisters of St. Ann to McNeil, 28 September 1910.

9. Ibid., Mary Anastasia to McNeil, 28 September 1910; "Archbishop McNeil: An Appreciation," *B.C. Western Catholic*, 26 July 1912.

10. TAA, O'Boyle to McNeil, 6 July 1913.

11. Ibid., Brochure for Shannon Place; Ibid., Allan MacDonald, a Nova Scotian Lawyer and investor to McNeil, 17 October 1911; Roy, *Vancouver: An Illustrated History*, pp. 68–78.

12. TAA, Harris, Bull, Hannington and Mason to McNeil, 24 March 1914; Ibid., Contains maps of lots throughout lower mainland, including expenses and valuations; Ibid., John McNeil to McNeil, Comox, B.C., 22 July 1912; Ibid., M. Creighton, Provincial Assessor and Collector to McNeil, New Westminster, 12 November 1912; Ibid., Creighton to McNeil, New Westminster, 20 November 1912; Ibid., R. McDonald to McNeil, 22 October 1913.

13. AD, PB.517.P47R, Minute Book, St. Peter's Province, 1892–1912, no pagination; Roy, *Vancouver: An Illustrated History*, p. 67.

14. AD, PB.517.P47R, Minute Book, St. Peter's Province, 1892–1912, bequest was from Bessetti estate; Ibid., 1913–1931, fols. 7, 14, passim; Levasseur, *A History*, Vol. 2, pp. 150–52; Roy, *Vancouver: An Illustrated History*, pp. 103, 137.

15. TAA, Notices of unpaid taxes from provincial authorities, 1915–1917; Ibid., Donnelly to McNeil, 30 August 1913; Ibid., Donnelly to McNeil, 29 March 1916; Ibid., Donnelly to McNeil, 22 November 1916; Ibid., T.J. McKinnon, Secretary, Canadian Financiers, to McNeil, 24 January 1913; Ibid., Offers by Pitt Meadows Company for a buy-out, 21 October 1913.

16. Ibid., Kientz to McNeil, 7 April 1913; Ibid., Kientz to McNeil, 23 September 1915; Ibid., Canadian Financiers Trust Company to McNeil, 12 July 1916; Ibid., Cahill to McNeil, 28 May 1921.

17. Ibid., Memorandum. Liabilities of Toronto Archdiocese, 24 April 1917. Contains amounts owed by archdiocese of Vancouver.

18. AD, PB.517.P47R, Minute Book, St. Peter's Province, 1913–1931, f. 1.

19. Ibid., 1913–1931, ff. 1–7.

20. TAA, Mostyn to McNeil, 13 August 1913; VAA, A *St. John Globe* article of 28 November 1912 refers to Casey as "unobtrusive," a sign of things to come in Vancouver.

21. Ibid., O'Boyle to McNeil, 6 July 1913; Ibid., Mostyn to McNeil, 13 August 1913; Ibid.; AD, L4321.P47R.3, McNeil to J.D. Byrne, 16 March 1912.

22. TAA, Mother Wenceslaus to McNeil, Providence Hospital, Oakland, California, 17 December 1916.

23. VAA, Althoff to Casey, 16 July 1916.

24. VAA, Casey to Welch, 30 September 1914.

25. Ibid., Casey to Welch, 30 September 1914; Ibid., Bégin to Casey, 13 January 1915.

26. VAA, J. Williamson to Casey, 16 September 1914; Ibid., J. Williamson to Casey, 16 August 1915; Ibid., Kearns to Casey, 16 July 1915; Ibid., Kearns to Casey, 4 August 1915; Ibid., Casey to Kearns, 28 August 1915; Hana Komorous, ed., *Union Catalogue of British Columbia Newspapers* (Vancouver: British Columbia Library Association, 1987). Contains no reference to the *B.C. Western Catholic.*

27. TAA, Patrick Donnelly to McNeil, 29 March 1916.

28. Ibid., Donnelly to McNeil, 29 March 1916; ASSA, Carmelita MacKenzie, "Little Flower Academy, History of the Property"; Ibid., Sister Theodore, "St. Ann's Little Flower Academy," Shaughnessy Heights, Vancouver, British Columbia, fols. 1–17.

29. ASSA, Carmelita MacKenzie, "L [ittle] F [lower] A [cademy], History of the Property"; Ibid., Sister Theodore, "St. Ann's Little Flower Academy," Shaughnessy Heights, Vancouver, British Columbia, 1903, fol. 1–17.

30. TAA, Donnelly to McNeil, 31 July 1916; Ibid., Memorandum of Certain Liabilities of the Archdiocese of Vancouver, 24 April 1917.

31. *The Bulletin* (15 January 1926): 1; "Foreword," *The Monthly Bulletin* 6:11 (November 1922): 4–5.

32. Barman, *The West Beyond the West*, p. 367; Murphy and Perin, *A Concise History of Christianity in Canada*, p. 340.

33. Murphy and Perin, *A Concise History of Christianity in Canada*, p. 340; Barman, *The West Beyond the West*, pp. 233, 367; *The Bulletin* (14 December 1928), p. 13.

34. "What Non-Catholics Say About Catholic Education," *The Monthly Bulletin* 2:8 (August 1918): 25.

35. Ibid., 1:5-8 (May-August 1917): 5–10; Ibid., 4:11 (November 1920): 6–7.

36. Lawrence K. Shook, *Catholic Post-Secondary Education in English-Speaking Canada: A History* (Toronto: University of Toronto Press, 1971), p. 392.

37. *The Bulletin* (13 June 1924): 1; Ibid. (31 October 1924): 1; Ibid. (27 March 1925): 5: Ibid. (6 August 1926): 9; Ibid. (25 February 1927): 4, 6; Shook, *Catholic Post-Secondary Education*, pp. 373–74.

38. Murphy and Perin, *A Concise History of Christianity in Canada*, pp. 250, 331–32; H.P. "Women's Activities," *The Monthly Bulletin* 1:4 (April 1917): 9–14; Ibid., 3:2 (February 1919): 27–28.

39. AD, PB.517.P47R, Minute Book, St. Peter's Province, 1913–1931, passim; Carrière, *Dictionnaire Biographique*, Vol. III, p. 23. Notes that O'Boyle became the vicar general to Casey, though there is no record of this in *Le Canada Ecclésiastique.* However, Carrière mentions his death notice in *The Ensign* for 3 December 1949 and that he had closed a "distinguished career" as a "Reverend." He is buried in the Oblate cemetery at Mission City, B.C.; VOA, Holy Rosary File; Ibid., Copy from General Archives, Rome, Welch to Dontenwill, 21 July 1926; Ibid., Holy Rosary File, O'Boyle left sometime in 1927–28.

1. VOA, A. Dontenwill, Circular Letter 134, 15 March 1926; Levasseur, *A History*, Vol. 2, pp. 152–53.
2. AD, PB.517.P47R, Minute Books of St. Peter's Province, 1892–1912, no pagination; Ibid., 1912–1945, fols. 10, 20, 23, 25.
3. Ibid., 1912–1945, fols. 43, 45, 50–57.
4. Ibid., 1912–1945, fols. 100–13, 140–50; Levasseur, *A History*, Vol. 2, pp. 153–56.
5. Levasseur, *A History*, Vol. 2, pp. 150–52.
6. Ibid.
7. Ibid.; *Le Canada Ecclésiastique*, 1936 to 1998.
8. Jean-Louis Coudert, "Rapport du vicariat de Whitehorse (1938–1947)," *Missions* 74 (1947): 550–51.
9. Émile Bunoz, "Vicariat de Missions du Yukon, Canada," *Missions* 54 (1920): 195–96.
10. Ibid., pp. 195–96; Levasseur, *A History*, Vol. 2, p. 176.
11. Achille Auclair, "Colombie et Yukon," *L'Apostolat* (May 1940), p. 14
12. Ibid., p. 14; "Provinces!...Vicariats!... Prefectures!..." AROMI (1949), p. 107.
13. AD, LCB 4003, W57R.14, Vicariate of the Yukon Minute Book, 1910–1944, fols. 13–15.
14. Ibid., fols. 24–28, 42–43, 50–51.
15. Carrière, *Dictionnaire Biographique*, passim.
16. Joseph Rousseau, *General Act of the Canonical Visitation of the Yukon and Prince Rupert Vicariate* (Rome: General Postulation, 1943), pp. 30–34, 59–60.
17. Jean-Louis Coudert, "Rapport du vicariat de Whitehorse (1938–1947)," *Missions* 74 (1947): 550–55; A. Jordan, "Report of the Vicariate of Prince Rupert (1953)," *Missions* 80 (1953): 169.
18. Barman, *The West Beyond the West*, pp. 233–34, 265–69, 305–14, 321.
19. *The Monthly Bulletin* 1:2 (February 1917), Coast Lumber and Fuel Co., p. 18; Italics added. This ad was consistently carried.
20. Patricia Roy, *A White Man's Province: British Columbia Politicians and Chinese and Japanese Immigrants, 1858–1914* (Vancouver: University Press of British Columbia, 1989), pp. 24, 27–29. *The Bulletin* (13 February 1935), p. 8; Ibid. (22 October 1926), p. 1; Ibid. (5 November 1926), p. 8; *The British Columbia Catholic* (19 September 1931), p. 4.
21. *The Bulletin* (29 August 1924), p. 4; Ibid. (17 October 1924), p. 1; Ibid. (6 February 1925), p. 4; Ibid. (8 May 1925), p. 6. Angela Lee, "From a Humble Beginning, Mt. St. Joseph Blossoms into A First Class Hospital," *Chinatown News* (3 March 1993), pp. 10, 32–33.
22. "Centenary Souvenir Issue of the Diocese of Victoria, British Columbia: 1846–1946," *The Torch* 7, no. 9 (1946): 74–76.
23. A.B. Wood, ed., "Souvenir Book: Centenary of the Diocese of Victoria, British Columbia: 1846–1946," *The Torch* 7, no. 9 (1946): 34–36; McNally, "Fighting City Hall," pp. 150, 163.

24. John Bartle, *125th Anniversary Booklet of Catholic Education in the Diocese of Victoria* (Victoria: privately published, 1988), p. 15; Wood, "Souvenir Book," pp. 54–67

25. McNally, "A Brief History of the Diocese of Victoria," p. 7; Wood, "Souvenir Book," pp. 70–73; *The Times*, 7 July 1946; Ibid., 20 July 1946.

26. AD, HH 7015.C66C.1, "Closed Retreat by Bishop J.C. Cody, Ottawa, September 1–4, 1939."

27. *The Monthly Bulletin* 4:3 (March 1920), pp. 13–19; "Holy Rosary Pays Tribute to Mr McCormick," [head of pro-cathedral finance committee], *The Bulletin* (22 April 1927), p. 6; "Bonded Debt of Pro-Cathedral Paid," Ibid. (27 May 1927), p. 1.

28. *Le Canada Ecclésiastique* (1912–1945).

29. TAA, Rohr to McNeil, 24 June 1913; *Le Canada Ecclésiastique*, 1912–1945.

30. *Le Canada Ecclésiastique*, 1912–1945; Levasseur, *A History*, Vol. 2, p. 150.

31. *Le Canada Ecclésiastique,* 1928–1964; Levasseur, *A History*, Vol. 2, p. 150.

32. AD, HP 5401. P61.5, Indenture between McNeil and Dontenwill, 1911. Safeguarding Oblate interests in the archdiocese of Vancouver; Ibid., PB 351.V22R.95, Report of Interview of Parishioners of St. Peter's Parish, New Westminster with Archbishop Duke, 23 June 1933; Ibid., PA 461. S28A.19, Thomas Labouré, Superior General to Joseph Scannell, Provincial of St. Peter's, 15 July 1936; HEB 1617.J83L.110, Scannell to Joseph Birch, 21 November 1936; Ibid., 112, same to same, 30 November 1936; Ibid., 113, same to same, 4 December 1936; Ibid., PA 461.528A.24, Labouré, 18 December 1936; H.J. Lennon, OMI to Scannell, 20 July 1937; Ibid., PA 461.528A.92, Labouré to Scannell, 28 May 1941; Ibid., PB 351.V22R.105, Draft of Oblate report to Apostolic Delegate complaining of Duke's behaviour, 22 December 1941; Ibid., PA 461.S28A.94, Labouré to Scannell, 14 June 1942; Ibid., PB 517.P47R.16, unnamed to Scannell, 20 July 1948.

33. Barman, *The West Beyond the West*, pp. 253–55.

34. Ibid., pp. 255–58.

35. Ibid., pp. 258–63.

36. Patricia Roy, et al., *Mutual Hostages: Canadians and Japanese during the Second World War* (Toronto: University of Toronto Press, 1990), p. 86; Jacqueline Gresko, "Research Note: Roman Catholic Sisters and Japanese Evacuees in British Columbia," *Journal of the Canadian Church Historical Society* XXXVIII, no. 1 (April 1996): 123–25; Barman, *The West Beyond the West*, pp. 265–69.

37. Gregory Baum, *Catholics and Canadian Socialism: Political Thought in the Thirties and Forties* (New York: Paulist Press, 1980), pp. 87–90, 137–38, 172–74, 212–15.

38. Ibid., pp. 87–90, 137–38, 172–74, 212–15.

39. Barman, *The West Beyond the West*, p. 367; *Catholic Directory for British Columbia and the Yukon 1997/98* (Vancouver: Archdiocese of Vancouver, 1997), passim; Baum, *Catholics and Canadian Socialism*, pp. 87–90, 137–38, 172–76, 212–15; Murphy and Perin, *A Concise History of Christianity in Canada*, pp. 348–54.

1. In examining the history of the Catholic Church in British Columbia after 1945, although the Oblate archives are an exception, there is a major problem in other church archives, since they have an access moratorium that is quite lengthy. For example, at present the Vatican Secret Archives, the major Roman archives in any study of the Catholic Church in Canada after 1908, when Canada ceased to be a missionary church (before then the central archive was that of Propaganda Fide), is not accessible after 1922. When examining local diocesan archives in British Columbia, the cut-off year is even earlier, and one diocese in British Columbia recently extended such a limit and now considers all of its episcopal correspondence as "classified." Thus, outside of public archives and other sources, both primary and secondary, which usually contain little material on the subject, the historian is severely limited in telling the story of the Catholic Church in British Columbia after 1945.

2. Barman, *The West Beyond the West*, pp. 297–305.

3. Ibid., pp. 123–25, 194, 281; *Le Canada Ecclésiastique*, 1887–1998; Maria Santos, *Celebrating the Faith of God's People: Diocese of Nelson 1936–1986* (Nelson: Diocese of Nelson, 1986), passim.

4. Barman, *The West Beyond the West*, pp. 290, 326, 375; Mary Adele St. Cyr, *Jubilee: Celebrating Our Journey in Faith: 1945–1995* (Kamloops: Noran Printing Ltd., 1996), passim; *Le Canada Ecclésiastique*, 1887–1998; Edith Down, *St. Ann's: Mid Twin Rivers and Hills 1880–1980* (Kamloops: Noran Printing Ltd., 1980), passim.

5. Archives of the Catholic Diocese of Whitehorse, Various historical sketches; *Le Canada Ecclésiastique*, 1967–1998.

6. Barman, *The West Beyond the West*, pp. 196, 337, 371, 375; *Le Canada Ecclésiastique*, 1908–1998; *Census of Canada,* 1991, pp. 93–304.

7. AD, LC 4107.P94R. File on Frontier Apostolate and Prince George, 1956–1976; Edith Down, "A Progress Report of the Frontier Apostolate Movement in the Diocese of Prince George, B.C." *Historical Studies* of the Canadian Catholic Historical Association 53 (1986): 71–79.

8. VDA, James Hill correspondence, 1946–1962, Seminarian file, 1950–1956; Ibid., Eucharistic Congress File, 1955; VAA, Eucharist Congress files, 1950–1957.

9. *BC Catholic*, 20 November 1947; *CCF News for British Columbia and the Yukon*, 27 November 1947; *BC Catholic*, 4 December 1947; *CCF News for British Columbia and the Yukon*, 11 December 1947.

10. BCARS, Box 11/File 1, R. Hull to Bennett, 14 December 1954; *CCF News*, 27 November 1947; Ibid., 11 December 1947; J.B. Rowell, *Separate Schools: A Vital Question* (Victoria: Privately published, 1954), pp. 1–32.

11. Barman, *The West Beyond the West*, pp. 335, 312–21; *Census of Canada, 1991*, pp.

93–319; Harro Van Brummelen, "Religiously-based Schooling in British Columbia: An Overview of the Research," *Journal of the Canadian Church Historical Society: British Columbia: Special Issue* XXXVIII, no. 1 (April 1996): 101, 105–6, 117–18.

12. Shook, *Catholic Post-Secondary-Education*, pp. 373–91.

13. Shook, *Catholic Post-Secondary Education*, pp. 395–405; Barman, *The West Beyond the West*, p. 302.

14. Vincent Moore, *Angelo Branco: "Gladiator of the Courts"* (Vancouver: Douglas & McIntyre, 1981), p. 78.

15. Premier Brian Tobin's address following the referendum on education reform in Newfoundland and Labrador, 2 September 1997, www.gov.nf.ca.

16. *British Columbian*, 29 April 1865.

17. Murphy and Perin, *A Concise History of Christianity in Canada*, pp. 252–54, 353; *The Colonist*, 20 November 1959; *The Times*, 24 November 1959; VDA, Charbonneau File, 1892–1959; St. Albert's Diocesan Archives, Laurent Morin papers. According to the diocesan archivist, Pauline Ford, Morin kept "a great many of his sermons," but not the eulogy he preached for Charbonneau in Victoria. Perhaps personal embarrassment over the real causes of his friend's removal from Montreal prompted the decision.

18. Gregory Baum, *Catholicism and Secularization in Quebec* (Ottawa: Novalis, 1991), p. 30.

19. *Census of Canada 1991: Religions in Canada* (Ottawa: Statistics Canada, 1993), p. 1; Reginald Bibby, *Unknown Gods: The Ongoing Story of Religion in Canada* (Toronto: Stoddart 1993), p. 6, 312; Murphy, *A Concise History of Christianity in Canada*, p. 369.

20. Bibby, *Fragmented Gods,* p. 271; Gregory Baum and Duncan Cameron, *Ethics and Economics: Canada's Catholic Bishops on the Economic Crisis* (Toronto: James Lorimer, 1984), pp. 30–31, 60–61.

21. Sharon Doyle Driedger, "Global Parade of Faith," *Maclean's*, 1 June 1998, pp. 66–67.

22. Tim Unsworth, "No Catholic Priests, no Catholic Church?" *National Catholic Reporter*, 20 October 1995, p. 21.

23. Scott Peck, *World Wating to Be Born* (New York: Bantam Books, 1993), p. 353. Peck's *The Road Less Travelled* was on the *New York Times* bestseller list for over ten years.

24. Pope John Paul II, *Tertio Mellennio Adveniente*, pp. 38–41.

Bibliography

THE DOCUMENT SOURCES FOR THIS STUDY are drawn from both public and private archives in Canada and abroad. The most important private source for the Canadian Oblates is the *Archives Deschâtelets* in Ottawa, although for any study of the last 50 years, the Archives of St. Paul's Province housed in Vancouver are also important. In addition, the Archives of Propaganda Fide in Rome and diocesan archives in British Columbia and other parts of Canada as well as abroad, all have material on the Oblates and Catholic Church history. As for public sources, the National Archives of Canada and the British Columbia Archives and Records Service in Victoria contain important collections, especially those dealing with the Department of Indian Affairs. As for other religious orders, especially women's, the Archives of the Sisters of St. Ann in Victoria provide valuable insights into the Oblates as well as the general church in the far west. Time would not permit consulting them all, however, the archival collections of other male and female religious communities who worked in the region would also yield material.

In examining the history of the Catholic Church in British Columbia after 1945, although the Oblate archives are an exception, there is a major problem in other church archives, since they have an access moratorium that is quite lengthy. The Vatican Secret Archives, the major Roman archives in any study of the Catholic Church in Canada after 1908, when Canada ceased to be a missionary church (before then the central archive was that of Propaganda Fide), is not accessible after 1922. When examining local diocesan archives in British Columbia, the cut-off year is even later, and one diocese in British Columbia recently extended such a limit and now considers *all* of its episcopal correspondence as "classified." Thus, outside of public archives and other sources, both primary and secondary, which usually contain little material on the subject, the historian is severely limited in telling the story of the Catholic Church in British Columbia after 1945.

As for published research, most is contained in articles as indicated below, for excluding the numerous historical works of A.G. Morice, which are dated and spotty in dealing with the region, the only general, but short work is Margaret Whitehead's *The Cariboo Mission: A History of the Oblates* (1981). There is no general history of the Catholic Church in Canada, although the place of the Native peoples in Canada is well treated in Olive Dickason's *Canada's First Nations: A History of Founding Peoples from the Earliest Times* as well as John Webster Grant's *The Moon of Wintertime*.

For the Oblates there are several important published sources. Gaston Carrière's four-volumed *Dictionnaire Biographique* is indispensable for chronological and other information as is the series *Missions,* a quarterly which began in 1862 and which was followed in the 1940s by *Oblate Studies* and later *Oblate Life*. Due to its historic extent, *Missions* is the most comprehensive in providing local information on local Missions as well as reports on individual Oblates.

Audruger, Alexandre. *Directoire pour les missions à l'usage de Missionaires Oblats de Marie Immaculée*. Tours: A. Mame et File, 1881.

Carrière, Gaston. *Dictionnaire Biographique des Oblats de Marie Immaculée au Canada*. 4 Vols. Ottawa: Éditions de l'Université d'Ottawa, 1976–1989.

Champagne, Joseph-Étienne. *Manuel d'action missionnaire*. Ottawa: Éditions de l'Université d'Ottawa, 1947.

Constitutiones Et Regulae Congregationis Missionariorum Oblatorum Sanctissimae Et Constitutiones Et Regulae Congregationis Missionariorum Oblatorum Sanctissimae Et Immaculatae Virginis Mariae. Parisiis: E Typis priv. O.M.I., 1887.

Leflon, Jean. *Eugene de Mazenod, Bishop of Marseilles and Founder of the Oblates of Mary Immaculate*. Vol. 4. New York: Fordham University Press, 1961.

de Mazenod, Eugene. *Lettres aux correspondants d'Amérique, 1841–1850. Écrits Oblats I.* Rome: Postulation générale O.M.I., 1977.

——. *Lettres aux correspondants d'Amerique, 1851–1860. Écrits Oblats II.* Rome: Postulation générale O.M.I., 1977.

——. *Lettres à la Sacrée Congrégation et à l'Oeuvre de la Propagation de la Foi, 1832–1861. Écrits Oblats V.* Rome: Postulation générale O.M.I., 1981.

Morice, A.G. *The Déné Syllabary and Its Advantages: A First Collection of Minor Essays, Mostly Anthropological*. Stuart Lake Mission, B.C.: By the Author, 1902.

——. *The History of the Northern Interior of British Columbia Formerly New Caledonia 1660–1880*. Toronto: William Briggs, 1904.

——. *Histoire de l'Église Catholique dans l'Ouest Canadien*. Montreal: Granger Freres, 1915.

——. *History of the Catholic Church in Western Canada: From Lake Superior to the Pacific, 1659–1895*. Vol. 2. Toronto: Musson, 1922.

——. *Histoire de l'Église Catholique dans l'Ouest canadien, du Lac Supérior au Pacifique 1659–1915*. Vol. 4. Winnipeg: chez l'auteur, 1928.

——. *Historie de l'Église Catholique dans l'Ouest canadien, du Lac Supérior au Pacifique 1659–1905*. Vol. 4. Montreal: Murrow, 1933.

——. *Remembrances of a Missionary or Souvenirs d'un Missionaire en Colombie-Britannique*. Winnipeg: Éditions de la Liberté, 1933.

Ortolan, Théodore. *Les Oblats de Marie Immaculée durant le Premier Siècle de leur Existence*. Paris: Librairie Saint-Paul, 1914.

Pielorz, Joseph. *Les Chapitres généraux au temps de Fondateur*. Vol. 2. Ottawa: Éditions de Études Oblates, 1969.

Rambert, Toussaint. *Vie de Monseigneur Charles-Joseph-Eugene de Mazenod, éveque de Marseilles, fondateur de la Congrégation des Oblats de Marie Immaculée*. Vol. 2. Tours: Romber, 1883.

Rey, Achille. *Historie de Monseigneur Charles-Joseph-Eugene de Mazenod, éveque de Marseilles, fondateur de la Congregation des Oblates de Marie Immaculée*. Vol. 2. Rome: General Postulation, 1928.

Selected Oblate Studies and Texts. Vol. 2. Rome: General House: Missionary Oblates of Mary Immaculate, 1986.

BOOKS

Allison, W. *A Study of Hospital and Related Facilities in the Capital Regional Hospital District, British Columbia, Canada*. Toronto: Agnew Peckham, 1964.

Amoss, Pamela. *Coast Salish Spirit Dancing: The Survival of An Ancestral Religion*. Seattle: University of Washington Press, 1978.

Anonymous. *Catholic Health Association of British Columbia, Anniversary Booklet–Living the Mission–1940–1990*. Richmond: The Little Printer Ltd., 1990.

Arima, E.Y. *The West Coast People: The Nootka of Vancouver Island and Cape Flattery: British Columbia Provincial Museum, Special Publication No. 6*. Victoria: British Columbia Provincial Museum, 1983.

Bagley, Clarence B. *Early Catholic Missions in Old Oregon*. Seattle: Lowmann & Hanford Co., 1932.

Bagshaw, Roberta L., ed. *No Better Land: The 1860 Diaries of the Anglican Colonial Bishop, George Hills*. Victoria: Sono Nis Press, 1996.

Baker, Paul E. *The Forgotten Kutenai*. Boise: Mountain State Press, 1955.

Barbeau, Marius. *Totem Poles According to Crests and Topics*. Ottawa: National Museum of Canada, 1950.

Barman, Jean, Yvonne Hèbert, and Don McCaskill, eds. *Indian Education in Canada: Volume 1: The Legacy*. Vancouver: University of British Columbia Press, 1986.

——. *Indian Education in Canada: Volume 2: The Challenge*. Vancouver: University of British Columbia Press, 1987.

Barman, Jean. "Transfer, Imposition or Consensus?: The Emergence of Educational Structure in Nineteenth Century British Columbia," in Nancy M. Sheehan, ed., *Schools in the West: Essays in Canadian Educational History*. Calgary: Detselig Enterprise, 1988.

——. *The West Beyond the West: A History of British Columbia*. Toronto: University of Toronto Press, 1991.

Blanchet, Francis Norbert. *Historical Sketches of the Catholic Church in Oregon During the First Forty Years*. Portland: Catholic Sentinel Press, 1878.

Bibby, Reginald W. *Fragmented Gods: The Poverty and Potential of Religion in Canada*. Toronto: Irwin Publishing, 1987.

——. *Unknown Gods: The Ongoing Story of Religion in Canada*. Toronto: Stoddart, 1993.

Boas, Franz. *Material for the Study of the Inheritance in Man*. New York: Columbia University Press, 1928.

Bowen, Lynne. *Boss Whistle: The Coal Miners of Vancouver Island Remembered*. Victoria: Morriss Press, 1990.

Boyle, George. *Pioneer in Purple: The Life and Work of Archbishop Neil McNeil*. Montreal: Palm Publishers, 1951.

Bryne, John F. *Modern Indian Psychology*. Vermillion, South Dakota: Institute of Indian Studies, 1971.

Buckland, F.M. *Ogopago's Vigil*. Kelowna, B.C.: Okanagan Historical Society, 1979.

Burnet, Jean R. *Coming Canadians: An Introduction to a History of Canada's People*. Toronto: McClelland and Stewart, 1988.

Burridge, Kenelm. *New Heaven, New Earth: A Study of Millenarian Activities*. New York: Schocken Books, 1969.

Cantwell, Margaret. *North To Share: The Sisters of Saint Ann in Alaska and the Yukon Territory*. Victoria: Sisters of St. Ann, 1992.

Carlson, Keith Thor, ed. *You Are Asked to Witness: The Stó:lô in Canada's Pacific Coast History*. Winnipeg: Hignell Printing Limited, 1997.

Cassidy, Thomas M. *Roots and Branches: A Diary of St. Peter's Province*. Ottawa: English Oblates, 1988.

Choquette, Robert. *The Oblate Assault on Canada's Northwest*. Ottawa: University of Ottawa, 1995.

Clutesi, George. *Son of Raven, Son of Deer*. Sidney, B.C.: Gray's Publishing Ltd., 1967.

Cove, John J. and George F. MacDonald, eds. *Tsimshian Narratives I collected by Marius Barbeau and William Beynon*. Ottawa: Canadian Museum of Civilization, 1987.

Cronin, Kay. *Cross in the Wilderness*. Toronto: Mission Press, 1976.

Dickason, Olive P. *Canada's First Nations: A History of Founding Peoples From Earliest Times*. Toronto: McClelland and Stewart, 1992.

Down, Mary Margaret. *A Century of Service: A History of the Sisters of St. Ann and Their Contribution to Education in British Columbia and Alaska*. Victoria: Morriss Press, 1966.

Drake-Terry, Joanne. *The Same as Yesterday: The Lillooet Chronicle: The Theft of Their Lands and Resources*. Lillooet: Lillooet Tribal Council, 1989.

Drouin, Paul, ed. *Les Oblats de Marie Immaculèe en Oregon 1847–1860*. Ottawa: Archives Deschâtelets, 1992.

Drucker, Philip. *Cultures of the North Pacific Coast*. San Francisco: Chandler Publishing Company, 1965.

Duchaussois, Pierre. *Mid Snow and Ice: The Apostles of the North-West*. Ottawa: University of Ottawa, 1937.

Duff, Wilson. *The Upper Stalo Indians of the Fraser Valley, British Columbia, Memoir No. 1*. Victoria: Provincial Museum of British Columbia, 1952.

Englehardt, Zephyrin. *The Missions and Missionaries of California*. Vol. 2. San Francisco: The James Barry Company, 1912.

Fisher, Robin. *Contact and Conflict: Indian-European Relations in British Columbia, 1774–1890*. Vancouver: University of British Columbia Press, 1990.

Furniss, Elizabeth. *Victims of Benevolence: Discipline and Death at the Williams Lake Indian Residential School, 1891–1920*. Williams Lake, B.C.: Cariboo Tribal Council, 1992.

Garraghen, Gilbert J. *The Jesuits of the Middle United States*. 2 vols. New York: American Press, 1939.

Grant, John Webster. *Moon of Wintertime: Missionaries and The Indians of Canada in Encounter since 1534*. Toronto: University of Toronto Press, 1984.

Gregson, Harry. *A History of Victoria, 1842–1970*. Victoria: The Victoria Observer Publishing Co. Ltd., 1970.

Gresko, Jacqueline. "Creating Little Dominions Within the Dominion: Early Catholic Indian Schools in Saskatchewan and British Columbia," in Jean Barman, Yvonne Hèbert, and Don McCaskill, eds., *Indian Education In Canada: Volume 1: The Legacy*. Vancouver: University of British Columbia Press, 1986.

Haegert, Dorothy. *Children of the First People*. Vancouver: Tillicum Library, 1983.

Haig-Brown, Celia. *Resistance and Renewal: Surviving the Indian Residential School*. Vancouver: Tillicum Library, 1988.

Hanley, Philip M. *History of the Catholic Ladder*. Fairfield, WA: Ye Galleon Press, 1993.

Herring, Frances E. *Among the People of British Columbia: Red, White, Yellow and Brown*. London: T. Fisher Unwin, 1903.

Herskovits, Melville. *Acculturation: The Study of Cultural Contact*. Gloucester, MA: Peter Smith, 1958.

Hines, H.K. *Missionary History of the Pacific Northwest*. Chicago: The Lewis Publishing Co., 1899.

Huel, Raymond. *Proclaiming the Gospel to the Indians and the Métis: The Missionary Oblates of Mary Immaculate in Western Canada 1845-1945*. Edmonton: University of Alberta Press/Western Canadian Publishers, 1996.

——. *A Pilgrimage To Our Past: Historical Overview of the Experience of the Oblates in the Canadian North West*. Toronto: Missionary Oblates, 1994.

Jedin, Hubert, ed. *History of the Church*. 10 Vols. New York: Crossroad Press, 1989.

Jessett, Thomas E., ed. *Reports and Letters of Herbert Beaver 1836-1838*. Portland and San Francisco: Champoeg Press, 1959.

Johnson, F. Henry. *A History of Public Education in British Columbia*. Vancouver: University of British Columbia Press, 1964.

Johnson, Robert C. *John McLoughlin: Father of Oregon*. Portland: Smith and Company Publishers, 1935.

Johnston, Basil H. *Indian School Days*. Toronto: Key Porter Books Ltd., 1988.

Johnston, Hugh J.M. *The Pacific Province: A History of British Columbia*. Vancouver: Douglas & McIntyre, 1996.

Keller, Betty C. and Rosella M. Leslie. *Bright Seas, Pioneer Spirits: The Sunshine Coast*. Victoria: Horsdal & Schubart, 1996.

Kowrach, J. Edward, ed. *Rt. Rev. A.M.A. Blanchet, Journal of a Catholic Bishop on the Oregon Trail...from Montreal to Oregon Territory, March 23, 1847 to January 13, 1851*. Fairfield, WA: Ye Galleon Press, 1978.

——. *Historical Sketches of the Catholic Church in Oregon by Most Rev Francis Norbert Blanchet*. Fairfield, WA: Ye Galleon Press, 1983.

——. *Pierre De Smet, New Indian Sketches*. Fairfield, WA: Ye Galleon Press, 1985.

——. *Mie. Charles Pandosy, OMI: A Missionary of the Northwest*. Fairfield, WA: Ye Galleon Press, 1992.

Lamb, W.K., ed. *The Letters and Journals of Simon Fraser*. Toronto: Macmillan, 1960.

Landholm, Carl, ed. *Notices and Voyages of the Famed Quebec Missions to the Pacific Northwest*. Portland: Oregon Historical Society, Champoeg Press, Reed College, 1956.

Lascelles, Thomas A. *Mission on the Inlet: St. Paul's Indian Catholic Church, North Vancouver, B.C. 1863–1984*. Vancouver: Schuman/Harte Ltd., 1984.

——. *Roman Catholic Indian Residential Schools in British Columbia*. Vancouver: Oblates of Mary Immaculate, 1990.

Lee, Daniel and J.M. Frost. *Ten Years in Oregon*. Fairfield, WA: Ye Galleon Press, 1968.

Leonard, Frank. *A Thousand Blunders: The Grand Trunk Pacific Railroad and Northern British Columbia*. Vancouver: University of British Columbia Press, 1996.

Levasseur, Donat. *Les Oblats de Marie Immaculée dans l'Ouest et le Nord du Canada 1845–1967*. Edmonton: University of Alberta Press/Western Canadian Publishers, 1995.

Lillard, Charles. *Mission to Nootka, 1874–1900*. Sidney, B.C.: Gray's Publishing Ltd., 1977.

Lyons, Letitia Mary. *Francis Norbert Blanchet and the Founding of the Oregon Missions, 1848–1948*. Washington, D.C.: Catholic University of America Press, 1940.

McCullum, Hugh and Karmel Taylor McCullum. *Caledonia 100 [A History of the Anglican Church in British Columbia] Years Ahead*. Toronto: The Anglican Book Centre, 1979.

McCarthy, Martha. *From the Great River to the Ends of the Earth: Oblate Missions to the Dene, 1847–1921*. Edmonton: University of Alberta Press and Western Canadian Publishers, 1995.

McDonald, Robert A.J. *Making Vancouver: Class, Status and Social Boundaries, 1863–1913*. Vancouver: University of British Columbia Press, 1966.

McKay, Harvey J. *St. Paul, Oregon 1830–1890*. Portland: Binford & Mort, 1980.

McKendrick, H. Robert. "Amor De Cosmos and Confederation," in W. George Shelton, ed., *British Columbia and Confederation*. Victoria: Morriss Press, 1967.

MacLean, Donald Alexander. *Catholic Schools in Western Canada: Their Legal Status*. Toronto: The Extension Press, 1923.

McMillan, Alan D. *Native Peoples and Cultures of Canada: An Anthropological Overview*. Vancouver: Douglas and McIntyre, 1988.

Marschall, John P. "Diocesan and Religious Clergy: The History of a Relationship," in John Tracy Ellis, ed., *The Catholic Priest in the United States*. Collegeville, MN: Liturgical Press, 1974.

Marty, Martin E. *Pilgrims in Their Own Land: 500 Years of Religion in America*. Boston: Little, Brown and Company, 1984.

Maud, Ralph. *A Guide to B.C. Indian Myth and Legend*. Vancouver: Talonbooks, 1982.

Meyer, Patricia, ed. *Honoré-Timothée Lempfrit, His Oregon Trail Journal and Letters from the Pacific Northwest, 1848–1853*. Fairfield, WA: Ye Galleon Press, 1985.

Miller, J.R. *Skyscrapers Hide the Heavens: A History of Indian-White Relations in Canada*. Toronto: University of Toronto Press, 1989.

——. *Shingwauk's Vision: A History of Native Residential Schools*. Toronto: University of Toronto Press, 1996.

Moir, John S. *The Church in the British Era: From the British Conquest to Confederation*. Toronto: McGraw-Hill/Ryerson, 1972.

Morley, Alan. *Vancouver: From Milltown to Metropolis*. Vancouver: Mitchell Press, 1961.

Mulhall, David. *Will to Power: The Missionary Career of Father Morice*. Vancouver: University of British Columbia Press, 1986.

Murphy, H.H. *Royal Jubilee Hospital 1858–1958*. Victoria: Hebden Printing Company, 1958.

Murphy, Terrence and Roberto Perin. *A Concise History of Christianity in Canada*. Toronto: Oxford University Press, 1996.

Nelson, Denys. *Fort Langley 1827–1927*. Vancouver: Vancouver Art Historical and Scientific Association, 1927.

Norris, John. *Strangers Entertained: A History of the Ethnic Groups of British Columbia*. Vancouver: British Columbia Centennial '71 Committee, 1971.

Norcross, E. Blanche. *Nanaimo Retrospective: The First Century*. Victoria: Morriss Press, 1979.

O'Driscoll, Robert and Lorna Reynolds, eds. *The Untold Story: The Irish In Canada*. Vol. 2. Toronto: Celtic Arts of Canada, 1988.

Ormsby, Margaret A. *British Columbia: A History*. Toronto: Macmillans, 1958.

O'Hara, Edwin V. *Pioneer History of Oregon*. Portland: Glass and Prudhomme, 1911.

Peake, Frank A. *The Anglican Church in British Columbia*. Vancouver: Mitchell Press, 1959.

Pearson, Ann. *The Royal Jubilee Hospital School of Nursing, 1891–1982*. Victoria: Alumnae Association of the Royal Jubilee School of Nursing, 1985.

Pethick, Derek. *Victoria: The Fort*. Vancouver: Mitchell Press, 1968.

Phillips, Charles E. *The Development of Education in Canada*. Toronto: Gage, 1957.

Reid, Jennifer. *Myth, Symbol and Colonial Encounter*. Ottawa: University of Ottawa Press, 1995.

Rich, E.E., ed. *The Letters of John McLoughlin*. Toronto: The Champlain Society 1941–1944.

Roy, Patricia E. *The History of Canadian Cities: Vancouver: An Illustrated History*. Toronto: James Lorimer & Company Publishers, 1980.

——. *A White Man's Province: British Columbia Politicians and Chinese and Japanese Immigrants, 1858–1914*. Vancouver: University of British Columbia Press, 1989.

Roy, Patricia E. et al. *Mutual Hostages: Canadians and Japanese during the Second World War*. Toronto: University of Toronto Press, 1990.

Schoenberg, Wilfred. *A Chronicle of Catholic History of the Pacific Northwest 1743–1960*. Portland: Catholic Sentinel, 1972.

———. *Paths to the Northwest: A Jesuit History of the Oregon Province.* Chicago: Loyola Press, 1982.

———. *A History of the Catholic Church in the Pacific Northwest 1743–1983.* Washington, D.C.: The Pastoral Press, 1987.

Scholefield, E.O.S. and F.W. Howay. *British Columbia from the Earliest Times to the Present.* Vol. 4. Vancouver: S.J. Clarke, 1914.

Shook, Lawrence K. *Catholic Post-Secondary Education in English-Speaking Canada: A History.* Toronto: University of Toronto Press, 1971.

Smith, Dorothy Blakey, ed. *The Reminiscences of Doctor John Sebastian Helmcken.* Vancouver: University of British Columbia Press, 1975.

Spicer, Edward, ed. *Perspectives in American Indian Cultural Change.* Chicago: The University of Chicago Press, 1956.

Steckler, Gerard G. *Charles John Seghers: Priest and Bishop in the Pacific Northwest 1839–1886: A Biography.* Fairfield, WA: Ye Galleon Press, 1986.

Tennant, Paul. *Aboriginal Peoples and Politics: The Indian Land Question in British Columbia.* Vancouver: University of British Columbia Press, 1990.

Titley, E. Brian. *A Narrow Vision: Duncan Campbell Scott and the Administration of Indian Affairs in Canada.* Vancouver: University of British Columbia Press, 1986.

Usher, Jean. *William Duncan of Metlakatla: A Victorian Missionary in British Columbia.* National Museum of Man Publications in History No. 5. Ottawa: National Museum of Canada, 1974.

Whitehead, Margaret. *The Cariboo Mission: A History of the Oblates.* Victoria: Sono Nis Press, 1981.

———. *They Call Me Father: Memoirs of Father Nicolas Coccola.* Vancouver: University of British Columbia Press, 1988.

Yzermans, Vincent A. *Saint Rose of Wrangell: The [Catholic] Church's Beginning in Southeast Alaska.* St. Paul, MN: North Central Publishing Company, 1979.

ARTICLES

Barker, Charles. "Henry George and the California Background of Progress and Poverty," *California Historical Society Quarterly* 24 (1945).

Baskerville, Peter A. "Financial Capital and the Municipal State: The Case of Victoria, British Columbia, 1910–1936," *Studies in Political Economy* 21 (Autumn 1986).

Berkhofer, Robert. "Model Zions for the American Indian," *American Quarterly* 15, no. 2 (1963).

Boas, Franz. "First General Report on the Indians of British Columbia," *Report of the British Association for the Advancement of Science* (London: Murray, 1890).

———. "The Indian Tribes of the Lower Fraser River," *Report of the British Association for the Advancement of Science* (1894).

Carrière, Gaston. "The Yakima War: The Oblates Falsely Accused," *Vie Oblate-Oblate Life* (June 1975).

Cauthers, Janet. "A Victorian Tapestry: Impressions of Life in Victoria, B.C., 1880–1914," *Sound Heritage Series* 8, no. 3 (1978).

Chamberlain, A.F. "Report on the Kootney Indians of South-Eastern British Columbia," *Report of the British Association for the Advancement of Science* (London: Murray, 1893).

"Diary of Jason Lee" *Oregon Historical Quarterly* 17 (June 1916).

Drucker, Philip. "The Northern and Central Nootkan Tribes," *Smithsonian Institution Bureau of American Ethnology: Bulletin* 14 (1951).

Goldring, Philip. "Religion, Missions and Native Culture," *Journal of Canadian Church Historical Society* XXVI (1984).

Gresko, Jacqueline. "Roman Catholic Missions to the Indians of British Columbia: A Reappraisal of the Lemert Thesis," *Journal of the Canadian Church Historical Society* XXIV (1982).

——. "The 'Serfs of the System?' Oblate Brothers and Sisters of St. Ann in British Columbia Schools, 1858–1920," *Western Oblate Studies 4/Études Oblates de l'Ouest 4* (1996).

——. "Research Note: Roman Catholic Sisters and Japanese Evacuees in British Columbia," *Journal of the Canadian Church Historical Society* XXXXVIII, no. 1 (April 1996).

Hill-Tout, Charles. "Ethnological Report on the StsEe'lis and Skau'lits Tribes of the Halkome'lem Division of the Salish of British Columbia," *Journal of the Royal Anthropological Institute* XXXIV (1904).

Holst, Wayne. "Revisiting Our Past: Revisioning Our Future. Reflections on the Next 150 Years of Missionary Activity in Canada," *Western Canadian Oblate Studies 4/Études Oblates de l'Ouest 4* (1996).

Howay, F.W. "The Introduction of Intoxicating Liquors amongst the Indians of the Northwest Coast," *British Columbia Historical Quarterly* 6 (July 1942).

Huel, Raymond. "The Irish-French Conflict in Catholic Episcopal Nominations: The Western Sees and the Struggle for Domination Within the Church." Canadian Catholic Historical Association, *Study Sessions* 42 (1975).

——. "Western Oblate History: The Need for Reinterpretation," *Western Oblate Studies 3/Études Oblates de l'Ouest 3* (1994).

Jenness, Diamond. "The Carrier Indians of the Bulkley River: Their Social and Religious Life." *Anthropological Papers*, no. 25 in *Smithsonian Institution Bureau of American Ethnology Bulletin* 133 (1943).

——. "The Ancient Education of a Carrier Indian," *Bulletin of the Canadian Department of Mines* 62 (1947).

Lamirande, E. "L'Implanation de l'Église catholique en Columbia Brittanique 1838–1848," *Revue de l'Universitè d'Ottawa* XXVIII (1958).

Lamirande, Emilien. "Le Pere Honoré-Timothée Lempfrit et son Ministere aupres des autochtones de l'Ile de Vancouver, 1849–1852," in *Western Oblate Studies 1/l'Études Oblates de l'Ouest 1* (1990)

MacLaurin, D.L. "Education before the [Fraser River] Gold Rush," *British Columbia Historical Quarterly* (October 1958).

McNally, Vincent J. "Challenging the Status Quo: An Examination of the History of Catholic Education in British Columbia," *Historical Studies* of the Canadian Catholic Historical Association 65 (1999).

——. "Fighting for a Foundation: Oblate Beginnings in Far Western Canada 1847–1868," *Western Oblate Studies 4/Études Oblates de l'Ouest 4* (1996).

——. "Fighting City Hall: The Church Tax Exemption Battle Between the City and the Roman Catholic Diocese of Victoria," *Journal of the Canadian Church Historical Society* XXXV, no. 1 (April 1993).

——. "Lost Opportunities?: A Study of Relations between the Native People and the Diocese of Victoria," *Western Oblate Studies 2/Études Oblates de l'Ouest 2* (1992).

——. "Church-State Relations and American Influence in British Columbia before Confederation," *Journal of Church and State* 34 (Winter 1992).

——. "Victoria: An American Diocese in Canada," *Historical Studies* of the Canadian Catholic Historical Association 57 (1990).

Miller, J.R. "Anti-Catholic Thought in Victorian Canada," *Canadian Historical Review* 64, no. 4 (1985).

——. "Denominational Rivalry in Indian Residential Education," *Western Oblate Studies 2/Études Oblates de l'Ouest 2* (1992).

Peake, Frank A. "From the Red River to the Arctic," *Journal of the Canadian Church Historical Association* 31, no. 2 (October 1989).

Pipes, Nellie B. "The Protestant Ladder," *Oregon Historical Review* XXXVII (1936).

Redford, James W. "Attendance at Indian Residential Schools in British Columbia, 1890–1920," *BC Studies* 44 (Winter 1979–80).

Reimer, Derek, ed. "A Victoria Tapestry: Impressions of Life in Victoria, B.C., 1880–1914," *Sound Heritage Series,* VII, no. 3 (1978).

Ridington, Robin. "Swan People: A Study of the Dunne-za Prophet Dance," *National Museum of Man Series, Canadian Ethnology Service Paper,* no. 38 (1978).

Sage, Walter N. "Sir James Douglas and British Columbia." *University of Toronto Studies* 6, no. 1 (1941).

——. "Amor De Cosmos, Journalist and Politician," *British Columbia Historical Quarterly* 8 (1944).

Schaeffer, Claude E. "Early Christian Missions of the Kutenai Indians," *Oregon Historical Quarterly* 71 (1970).

Slater, G. Hollis. "Rev. Robert John Staines: Pioneer Priest, Pedagogue and Political Agitator," *British Columbia Historical Quarterly* 14 (October 1950).

Stewart, Bob. "That's the B.C. Spirit!: Religion and Secularity in Lotus Land," *Canadian Society of Church History Papers* (1983).

Suttles, Wayne. "The Persistence of Intervillage Ties Among the Coast Salish," *Ethnology* (1963).

Turney-High, Harry Holbert. "Ethnography of the Kutenai," *Memoirs of the American Anthropological Association* 56 (1941).

Van Brummelen, Harro. "Religiously-based Schooling in British Columbia: An Overview of the Research," *Journal of the Canadian Church Historical Society: British Columbia, Special Issue* XXXVIII, no. 1 (April 1996).

Walker, Deward E., Jr. "New Light on the Prophet Dance Controversy," *Ethnohistory* 16 (1969).

Whitehead, Margaret. "Now You Are My Brother: Missionaries of British Columbia," in *Sound Heritage Series* 43 (1981).

——. "Christianity, A Matter of Choice: The Historic Role of Indian Catechists in Oregon and British Columbia," *Pacific Northwest Quarterly* 72, no. 3 (July 1981).

Willlis, Grant. "Second Lower Similkameen School," *Okanagan Historical Studies* 37 (1973).

THESES

Coates, Kenneth. "Best Left as Indians: Native-White Relations in the Yukon Territory, 1840–1950," Ph.D. thesis, University of British Columbia, 1984.

Coté, Maurice Norbert. "The Children's Aid Society of the Catholic Archdiocese of Vancouver: Its Origin and Development, 1905–1953," M.S.W. thesis, University of British Columbia, 1953.

Dionne, Gabriel. "Historie de Méthodes Ultilisées par les Oblats de Marie Immaculée dans l'Évangélisation de Indiens du 'Versant Pacifique' au dix-neuvième sièle," M.A. thesis, University of Ottawa, 1947.

Duggar, Anna Clare. "Catholic Institutions of the Walla Walla Valley, 1847–1950," M.A. thesis, Seattle University, 1953.

Fiske, Jo-Anne. "Gender and Politics in a Carrier Indian Community," Ph.D. thesis, University of British Columbia, 1989.

Furniss, Elizabeth Mary. "A Sobriety Movement Among the Shuswap Indians of Alkali Lake," M.A. thesis, University of British Columbia, 1987.

Gresko, Jacqueline. "Qu'Appelle Industrial School: 'White Rites' for Indians of the Old North West," M.A. thesis, Carleton University, 1970.

——. "Roman Catholic Missionary Effort and Indian Acculturation in the Fraser Valley, BC," B.A. essay, University of British Columbia, 1969.

Inglis, Gordan Bahan. "The Canadian Indian Reserve: Community, Population, and Social System," Ph.D. thesis, University of British Columbia, 1970.

Kehoe, James Patrick. "History of the Catholic Missionary Activity Among the Indians of the Oregon Country, 1839–1936," M.A. thesis, University of Oregon, 1936.

Kobrinsky, Vernon. "Ethnohistory and Ceremonial Representation of Carrier Social Structure," M.A. thesis, University of British Columbia, 1968.

Lascelles, Thomas A. "Léon Fouquet and the Kootenay Indians, 1874–1887," M.A. thesis, Simon Fraser University, 1986.

MacLaurin, D.L. "The History of Education in The Crown Colonies of Vancouver Island and British Columbia," Ph.D. thesis, University of Washington, 1936.

Morrow, Mary Claver. "Bishop A.M.A. Blanchet and the Oblates of Mary Immaculate," M.A. thesis, Seattle University, 1956.

O'Donnell, Miriam Margaret. "In Faith and Kindness: The Life of the Most Reverend Alexander Christie," M.A. thesis, University of Portland, 1945.

Pilton, James William. "Negro Settlement in British Columbia, 1858–1871," M.A. thesis, University of British Columbia, 1951.

Prazma, Jerry A. "The North American Indians and the Missionaries: From the Lessons of the Past, A Hope for the Future," Master of Spirituality thesis, Gonzaga University, 1989.

Pritchard, John Charles. "Economic Development and the Disintegration of Traditional Culture among the Haisla," Ph.D. thesis, University of British Columbia, 1977.

Redford, James W. "Attendance at Indian Residential Schools in British Columbia, 1890–1920," M.A. thesis, University of British Columbia, 1978.

Shoop, Greg Brian. "The Participation of the Ohiaht Indians in the Commercial Fisheries of the Bamfield-Barkley Sound Area of British Columbia," M.A. thesis, University of Victoria, 1972.

Sullivan, Nellie. "Eugene Casimir Chirouse O.M.I. and the Indians of Washington," M.A. thesis, University of Washington, 1932.

Tanner, Michael Allan. "'The Wretched Giving Away System Which is the Root of All Iniquity': The Church Missionary Society and Kwakiutl Potlatches, 1878–1912," M.A. thesis, University of Victoria, 1987.

Thomson, Duncan Duane. "A History of the Okanagan: Indians and Whites in the Settlement Era, 1860–1920," Ph.D. thesis, University of British Columbia, 1985.

Thrupp, Sylvia L. "A History of the Cranbrook District in East Kootenay," M.A. thesis, University of British Columbia, 1929.

Verma, B.L. "The Squamish: A Study of Changing Political Organisation," M.A. thesis, University of British Columbia, 1954.

Whitehead, Margaret. "The Early History of St. Joseph's Mission, Williams Lake, British Columbia, 1866–1882," B.A. essay, University of Victoria, 1977.

Index

* Page references to illustrations and photos are given in italic type.

Index